# Ultimate Elastic Kubernetes Service with AWS

*Implement Scalable, Secure Kubernetes Solutions on AWS EKS with Hands-on Architecture Design, Automation, Monitoring, and Performance Tuning*


**Jatinder Singh**

**Manpreet Kour**

**Aneesh Varghese**



AF528205



www.orangeava.com

Copyright © 2025, Orange Education Pvt Ltd, AVA®

All rights reserved. No part of this book may be reproduced, stored in a retrieval system, or transmitted in any form or by any means, without the prior written permission of the publisher, except in the case of brief quotations embedded in critical articles or reviews.

Every effort has been made in the preparation of this book to ensure the accuracy of the information presented. However, the information contained in this book is sold without warranty, either express or implied. Neither the author nor **Orange Education Pvt Ltd** or its dealers and distributors, will be held liable for any damages caused or alleged to have been caused directly or indirectly by this book.

**Orange Education Pvt Ltd** has endeavored to provide trademark information about all of the companies and products mentioned in this book by the appropriate use of capital. However, **Orange Education Pvt Ltd** cannot guarantee the accuracy of this information. The use of general descriptive names, registered names, trademarks, service marks, etc. in this publication does not imply, even in the absence of a specific statement, that such names are exempt from the relevant protective laws and regulations and therefore free for general use.

**First Published:** September 2025

**Published By:** Orange Education Pvt Ltd, AVA®

**Address:** 9, Daryaganj, Delhi, 110002, India

275 New North Road Islington Suite 1314 London,
N1 7AA, United Kingdom

**ISBN (PBK):** 978-93-49888-77-7
**ISBN (E-BOOK):** 978-93-49888-03-6

**Scan the QR code to explore our entire catalogue**

www.orangeava.com

# Dedicated To

*My beloved Parents:*

*Late S. Mohinder Pal Singh*
*Malkinder Kaur*

*And*

*My daughters Avani Kaur and Bhoomika Kaur*

***Jatinder***

*My beloved Parents:*

*Late S. Gurmit Singh Chadha*

*Baljit Kour*

*And*

*My Entire Family*

***Manpreet***

*My family, Whose Love and Support Made Everything Possible, and to All the Mentors, Colleagues, and Learners Who Continue to Shape My Journey in Technology.*

***Aneesh***

# About the Authors

**Jatinder Singh** is a seasoned technology professional with over two decades of experience driving digital transformation and leveraging advanced technologies such as AI and ML. As a Senior Technical Account Manager at Amazon Web Services (AWS), he leads modernization of legacy systems, optimizes performance, and designs innovative cloud-native solutions. His expertise spans solution and enterprise architecture, data security, governance, FinOps, and cloud financial management, with a strong focus on data-driven insights. A sought-after speaker and contributor to industry publications, he is known for leading cross-functional teams to deliver cost-efficient and best-practice-aligned cloud solutions.

**Manpreet Kour**, Senior Technical Account Manager at AWS, brings deep expertise in digital transformation and cloud architecture. Specializing in modernizing legacy systems and architecting cloud-native solutions, she also focuses on FinOps, helping organizations maximize cloud investments, while ensuring operational excellence. Based in Virginia, she is recognized for leading complex AWS migrations and robust data strategies. A regular speaker and contributor to technical publications, Manpreet combines technical depth with strategic business acumen to deliver impactful and cost-effective solutions.

**Aneesh Varghese** is an accomplished AWS Technical Account Manager specializing in enterprise-scale DevOps and MLOps. He has guided customers across industries in designing scalable, resilient, and cost-efficient AWS infrastructures. Author of a book on Amazon EKS, he shares practical insights into building cloud-native applications with Kubernetes. With expertise in automation, observability, and platform engineering, Aneesh simplifies complex systems, and drives innovation through containerization. A passionate advocate for knowledge-sharing, he contributes through reports, blogs, and workshops, while mentoring aspiring technologists.

# About the Technical Reviewer

**Adit Modi** is a Solution Architect at Lauren, with over five years of hands-on experience in Cloud-native architecture, DevOps, and container orchestration on AWS. He specializes in designing scalable, secure, and cost-effective infrastructure using Amazon EKS, Kubernetes, and a range of AWS services, including EC2, Lambda, RDS, and VPC. His technical focus includes building CI/CD pipelines, implementing Infrastructure as Code (IaC) using Terraform and CloudFormation, and enabling containerized workloads in production environments.

Adit holds **12 AWS certifications**, including the **AWS Certified Solutions Architect – Professional**, and has earned the **AWS Golden Jacket** in recognition of his achievements. His deep knowledge of cloud technologies, and commitment to its best practices has helped organizations adopt EKS and DevOps at scale.

Beyond his technical work, Adit is a passionate community advocate and educator. He serves as an **AWS Ambassador**, **AWS Community Builder**, and **HashiCorp Ambassador**, regularly sharing his knowledge through technical blogs, talks, and workshops. As a co-organizer of the **AWS User Group Vadodara**, he helps lead community events, including the highly successful **AWS Community Day Vadodara 2024**, which attracted over 600 attendees. Through these initiatives, Adit promotes hands-on learning and real-world adoption of tools such as Amazon EKS, fostering a stronger and more collaborative cloud community. He is committed to helping developers and organizations succeed with modern infrastructure and container orchestration strategies on AWS.

# Acknowledgments

We would like to express our sincere gratitude to all those who contributed to the completion of this book. First and foremost, we extend our heartfelt appreciation to our families for their unwavering support and encouragement throughout this journey. Their love and understanding have been a constant source of motivation, as we took our valuable time away from our personal lives to bring this book to fruition.

We are immensely grateful to Orange Education Pvt Ltd for their support and assistance in bringing this book to life. Our heartfelt thanks are due to the editors, reviewers, and proofreaders who meticulously guided us at every step. Their attention to detail, and commitment to excellence have significantly improved the quality of this work.

Last but not the least, we want to express our gratitude to the readers who have shown immense interest in our book. We hope this book will inspire and inform you, and may our conversation through these pages spark new understandings, and unfold new avenues in your career.

*Thanks  a lot to everyone who has played a vital role in making this book a reality!*

# Preface

This book covers comprehensive aspects of Amazon Elastic Kubernetes Service (EKS), emphasizing the importance of container orchestration in modern cloud architecture. It introduces readers to the critical role of EKS in today's enterprise environments, and demonstrates how containerized applications are transforming the way organizations deploy and manage their workloads. This book solves the complex challenges of understanding and implementing EKS in production environments, while ensuring readers grasp both theoretical concepts and practical applications.

This book takes a hands-on approach for cloud practitioners, solution architects, and DevOps professionals. It covers numerous real-world scenarios and production-grade implementations. It will demonstrate how EKS is fundamentally used for container orchestration, microservices architecture, and scalable applications. Solution architects will find detailed architectural patterns and best practices for designing resilient systems. The book explains how EKS can be effectively utilized for automated deployments, high availability configurations, and cost-optimized infrastructure. Readers will learn to design resilient architectures across multiple regions, and implement robust security controls for enterprise-grade deployments.

This book is divided into twelve comprehensive chapters. They cover everything from EKS fundamentals to advanced topics such as service mesh implementation, multi-region deployments, and performance optimization. Each chapter builds upon the previous one, creating a logical learning progression. Starting with basic concepts and cluster setup, moving through networking and security, and culminating in advanced operational aspects such as cost optimization and performance tuning. The detailed chapter breakdown follows, providing readers with a clear roadmap for mastering EKS.

By focusing on both theoretical knowledge and practical implementation, this book serves as a complete guide for anyone looking to leverage EKS in their cloud journey. So, whether you are new to containerization or an experienced practitioner, you will find valuable insights and practical solutions throughout these pages.

**Chapter 1:** This provides a comprehensive introduction to Amazon Elastic Kubernetes Service (EKS) and cloud-native principles. Readers will understand the evolution of containerization, the relationship between AWS and Kubernetes, and core cloud-native concepts. The chapter covers fundamental architecture patterns, explaining how EKS fits into the broader AWS ecosystem. Through practical examples, readers will learn the benefits and challenges of running Kubernetes on AWS, setting the foundation for their cloud-native journey. Essential concepts such as control plane management, worker nodes, and basic Kubernetes objects are explained in detail, making complex topics accessible to both the beginners, as well as experienced practitioners.

**Chapter 2:** This dives into the practical aspects of establishing a production-ready EKS environment. It helps the readers to walk through the vital tools and configurations needed for a robust EKS setup. Starting with AWS CLI configuration, it progresses through VPC setup, IAM role configuration, and cluster creation using both eksctl and Infrastructure as Code solutions. Readers will learn the best practices for network planning, security group configuration, and cluster access management. The chapter also includes hands-on exercises for creating and managing clusters, implementing proper security controls, and establishing a solid foundation for production workloads.

**Chapter 3:** It covers the fundamentals of container technology with a focus on Docker, and its integration with EKS. This chapter covers container basics, from writing efficient Dockerfiles to implementing multi-stage builds for optimized images. Readers will learn how to effectively use Amazon Elastic Container Registry (ECR), implement container security scanning, and optimize container performance. The chapter also includes practical examples of container orchestration, image management strategies, and best practices for maintaining a secure container environment. Special attention is given to production considerations such as image tagging strategies, pull policies, and container resource management.

**Chapter 4:** This focuses on the day-to-day operations and management of EKS clusters. Readers will learn advanced node group management techniques, including handling mixed instance types, and implementing effective auto-scaling strategies. The chapter covers essential operational tasks such as cluster upgrades, backup procedures, and maintenance windows. Through real-world examples, readers can understand and learn how to implement proper resource quotas, manage cluster capacity, and handle node lifecycle events. Special attention is given to operational excellence, including monitoring, logging, and troubleshooting methodologies that ensure cluster reliability and performance.

**Chapter 5:** This chapter explores the complex world of Kubernetes networking within AWS. It dives deep into AWS VPC CNI plugin, explaining how pod networking integrates with VPC networking. Readers will learn about service mesh implementation using AWS App Mesh, load balancer integration (ALB/NLB), and advanced network policies. The chapter covers crucial topics such as service discovery, cross-node communication, and network security groups. Practical examples demonstrate how to implement ingress controllers, configure network policies, and optimize network performance for production workloads.

**Chapter 6:** This provides a comprehensive coverage of EKS security best practices. Readers can learn how to implement IAM Roles for Service Accounts (IRSA), configure pod security policies, and manage secrets effectively using AWS Secrets Manager. The chapter also includes detailed examples of network security configurations, encryption at rest and in transit, and security audit procedures. Readers will understand how to implement a defense-in-depth strategy, comply with security standards, and maintain a robust security posture in their EKS clusters.

**Chapter 7:** It covers sophisticated deployment techniques for maintaining high availability, and minimizing risks. This chapter also covers implementation of blue-green deployments, canary releases, and rolling updates in EKS. Readers will learn how to use GitOps with ArgoCD for automated deployments and configuration management. Through practical examples, the chapter demonstrates how to implement deployment strategies that ensure zero-downtime updates, facilitate rollbacks, and maintain application reliability. Special focus is given to automation and monitoring of deployment processes.

**Chapter 8:** This provides comprehensive observability solutions for your EKS clusters. The chapter details the implementation of monitoring and logging solutions using Amazon CloudWatch, Prometheus, and Grafana. Readers will learn how to implement distributed tracing with AWS X-Ray, and set up the ELK stack for log aggregation. The chapter covers creation of custom metrics, alerting strategies, and visualization techniques. Real-world examples demonstrate how to gain deep insights into cluster health, application performance, and user experience.

**Chapter 9:** It addresses the critical aspects of managing stateful applications in EKS. Readers will learn how to implement persistent storage solutions using EBS CSI drivers and EFS integration. The chapter covers StatefulSet configurations, persistent volume management, and backup strategies for stateful workloads. Through practical examples, you can easily understand how to handle data persistence, implement storage classes, and manage storage lifecycle. Special focus has been given to performance optimization, data protection, and disaster recovery considerations for stateful applications in Kubernetes.

**Chapter 10:** This covers the building and maintaining of highly available EKS clusters that can withstand failures at multiple levels. The chapter includes multi-AZ deployment strategies, cross-region failover configurations, and comprehensive backup solutions. Readers can understand and learn how to implement business continuity plans, conduct disaster recovery testing, and ensure data consistency across regions. Through real-world scenarios, the chapter demonstrates how to achieve the desired Recovery Time Objective (RTO) and Recovery Point Objective (RPO), while maintaining operational efficiency.

**Chapter 11:** This chapter helps the readers to master the art and technology of running cost-effective EKS clusters, while maintaining performance. It explores the implementation of Spot instances, capacity planning strategies, and effective resource quota management. Readers will learn how to use AWS Cost Explorer for Kubernetes cost analysis, implement budget alerts, and optimize resource utilization. The chapter includes practical examples of cost allocation strategies, tagging policies, and automated cost optimization techniques. Special focus is given to balancing cost optimization with performance, and reliability requirements.

**Chapter 12:** This chapter teaches you how to optimize your EKS clusters for maximum performance and scalability. It covers implementation of both Horizontal and Vertical Pod Autoscaling, along with Cluster Autoscaler configuration. Readers can easily and quickly understand as well as learn the advanced performance tuning techniques, including resource request/limit optimization, node configuration, and network performance tuning. Through real-world examples, the chapter demonstrates how to conduct performance benchmarking, implement load testing, and optimize application performance at scale.

# Get a Free eBook

We hope you are enjoying your recently purchased book! Your feedback is incredibly valuable to us, and to all other readers looking for great books.

If you found this book helpful or enjoyable, we would truly appreciate it, if you could take a moment to leave a short review with a 5 star rating on Amazon. It helps us grow, and lets other readers discover our books.

As a thank you, we would love to send you a free digital copy of this book, and a **30%** discount code on your next cart value on our official websites:

**www.orangeava.com**

**www.orangeava.in** (For Indian Subcontinent)

☑ **Here's how:**

**Leave a review for the book on Amazon.**

Take a screenshot of your review, and send an email to **info@orangeava.com** (it can be just the confirmation screen).

Once, we receive your screenshot, we will send you the digital file, within 24 hours.

Thank you so much for your support – it means a lot to us!

# Downloading the code bundles and colored images

Please follow the links or scan the QR codes to download the
***Code Bundles and Images*** of the book:

**https://github.com/ava-orange-education/Ultimate-Elastic-Kubernetes-Service-with-AWS**

The code bundles and images of the book are also hosted on
***https://rebrand.ly/9epw5a8***

In case there's an update to the code, it will be updated on the existing GitHub repository.

# Errata

We take immense pride in our work at **Orange Education Pvt Ltd,** and follow best practices to ensure the accuracy of our content to provide an indulging reading experience to our subscribers. Our readers are our mirrors, and we use their inputs to reflect and improve upon human errors, if any, that may have occurred during the publishing processes involved. To let us maintain the quality and help us reach out to any readers who might be having difficulties due to any unforeseen errors, please write to us at :

**errata@orangeava.com**

Your support, suggestions, and feedback are highly appreciated.

## DID YOU KNOW

Did you know that Orange Education Pvt Ltd offers eBook versions of every book published, with PDF and ePub files available? You can upgrade to the eBook version at **www.orangeava.com** and as a print book customer, you are entitled to a discount on the eBook copy. Get in touch with us at: **info@orangeava.com** for more details.

At **www.orangeava.com**, you can also read a collection of free technical articles, sign up for a range of free newsletters, and receive exclusive discounts and offers on Print Books and eBooks.

## PIRACY

If you come across any illegal copies of our works in any form on the internet, we would be grateful if you would provide us with the location address or website name. Please contact us at **info@orangeava.com** with a link to the material.

## ARE YOU INTERESTED IN AUTHORING WITH US?

If there is a topic that you have expertise in, and you are interested in either writing or contributing to a book, please write to us at **business@orangeava.com**. We are on a journey to help developers and tech professionals to gain insights on the present technological advancements and innovations happening across the globe and build a community that believes Knowledge is best acquired by sharing and learning with others. Please reach out to us to learn what our audience demands and how you can be part of this educational reform. We also welcome ideas from tech experts and help them build learning and development content for their domains.

## REVIEWS

Please leave a review. Once you have read and used this book, why not leave a review on the site that you purchased it from? Potential readers can then see and use your unbiased opinion to make purchase decisions. We at Orange Education would love to know what you think about our products, and our authors can learn from your feedback. Thank you!

For more information about Orange Education, please visit **www.orangeava.com**.

# Table of Contents

# CHAPTER 1
# Introduction to EKS

## Introduction

In today's rapidly evolving digital landscape, organizations are increasingly adopting cloud-native technologies to build scalable, resilient, and highly available applications. At the forefront of this transformation is Amazon Elastic Kubernetes Service (EKS) - a managed Kubernetes service that has become instrumental in modernizing application deployment and management.

This chapter lays the foundation for understanding cloud-native architecture and its implementation using AWS EKS. We will further explore the fundamental concepts of Kubernetes orchestration, examining how EKS simplifies the complex task of managing containerized applications at scale. Through a comprehensive overview of cloud-native principles, you will learn why organizations are embracing this architectural approach, and how it enables faster innovation and improved operational efficiency.

As we delve into microservices architecture patterns, you will discover how breaking down monolithic applications into smaller, independently deployable services can enhance development agility and system reliability. This chapter serves as your gateway to understanding the symbiotic relationship between EKS, Kubernetes, and Cloud-native principles, setting the stage for more advanced topics in subsequent chapters.

So, whether you are a developer, architect, or operations professional, this introduction will equip you with the essential knowledge needed to begin your journey into cloud-native application development with AWS EKS.

## Structure

In this chapter, we will discuss the following topics:

- AWS EKS Overview
- Kubernetes Fundamentals
- Cloud-Native Principles in AWS
- Microservices Architecture Patterns

# AWS EKS Overview

Amazon Elastic Kubernetes Service (EKS) stands as AWS's fully managed Kubernetes service, designed to streamline the deployment, management, and scaling of containerized applications. As a certified Kubernetes conformant platform, EKS maintains complete compatibility with the existing Kubernetes tooling and applications, while removing the operational burden of managing the Kubernetes control plane.

In the evolving landscape of container orchestration, Amazon EKS distinguishes itself through a comprehensive set of features that address the complex challenges of running Kubernetes at scale. By combining AWS's infrastructure reliability with Kubernetes' orchestration capabilities, EKS delivers a platform that significantly reduces operational overhead while enhancing application reliability and scalability. The service's key features extend beyond basic container management, offering organizations the tools and capabilities needed to build and maintain production-grade containerized applications efficiently. *Figure* 1.1 provides AWS EKS overview and its core components.

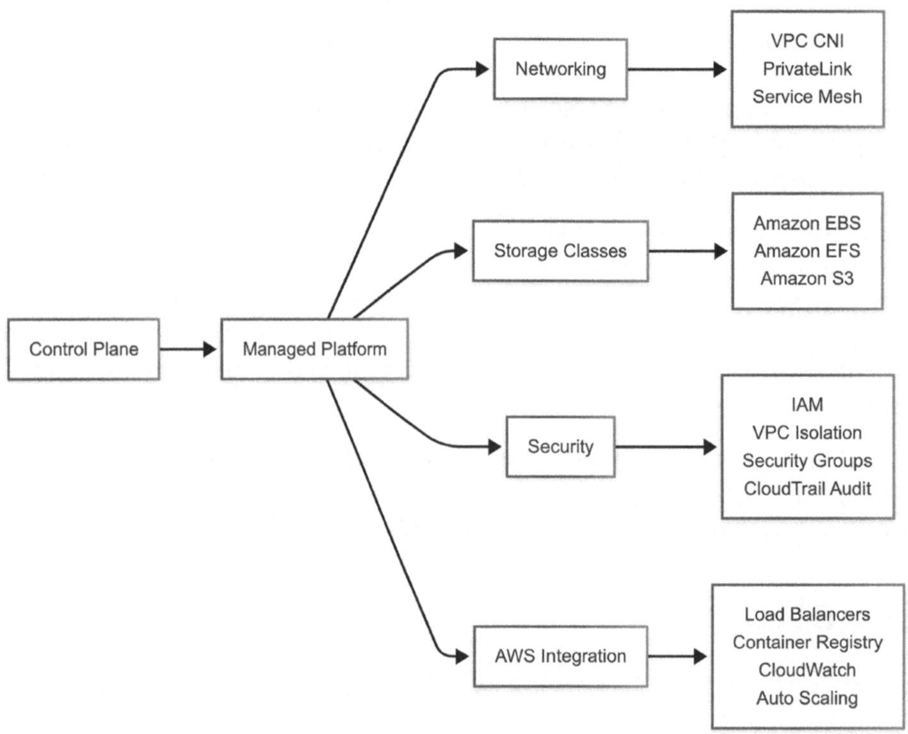


**Figure 1.1:** AWS EKS *Overview*

# Managed Control Plane

At the heart of EKS lies its managed control plane, which automatically handles scaling and ensures high availability by operating across multiple AWS Availability Zones. The service manages version upgrades, security patching, and the complex task of maintaining the Kubernetes master components. This automated management significantly reduces the operational overhead traditionally associated with running Kubernetes clusters.

# EKS Storage Options

Amazon EKS provides comprehensive storage solutions through integration with various AWS storage services and Kubernetes storage primitives. Here is a detailed breakdown of storage options:

- **Persistent Storage with Amazon EBS:** Amazon Elastic Block Store serves as the default storage class for EKS, providing block-level storage volumes with dynamic provisioning through the CSI driver. EBS offers different volume types, including gp3, io2, and st1, each optimized for specific performance requirements. The service enables snapshot and backup capabilities, ensuring data persistence and protection for stateful applications.
- **Shared File Storage with Amazon EFS:** Amazon Elastic File System delivers managed NFS file system capabilities, enabling shared storage across multiple pods with ReadWriteMany access mode support. EFS provides automatic scaling and lifecycle management, making it ideal for shared content repositories and stateful workloads requiring concurrent access from multiple sources.
- **Object Storage with Amazon S3:** Amazon Simple Storage Service integration through CSI driver offers object storage capabilities, suitable for large-scale data storage requirements. S3 provides cost-effective storage for infrequently accessed data, with support for versioning and lifecycle policies, enabling efficient management of long-term data storage needs.
- **Storage Classes and Features:** Dynamic provisioning capabilities enable automated volume creation and attachment, with customizable storage class specifications and parameters. The platform supports volume expansion and provides comprehensive data persistence through PersistentVolumes (PV) and PersistentVolumeClaims (PVC), along with storage quotas and volume snapshot functionality.

Performance optimization requires careful selection of storage classes based on workload requirements, considering IOPS needs, and implementing proper monitoring of storage metrics. Cost management involves choosing appropriate volume types, implementing storage quotas, and enabling auto-scaling where beneficial. Security measures include encryption at rest, IAM roles for service accounts, network policies, and access control through RBAC.

This comprehensive storage framework enables organizations to implement the right storage solution for their specific workload requirements, while maintaining security, performance, and cost efficiency.

## Security and Compliance

Amazon EKS implements enterprise-grade security through a comprehensive, multi-layered architecture seamlessly integrated with AWS's security infrastructure. The service leverages AWS Identity and Access Management (IAM) for fine-grained access control, and deploys encrypted TLS communication channels between all cluster components. Meeting major compliance standards like SOC, PCI DSS, and HIPAA BAA, EKS ensures regulatory adherence across industries while providing robust security across network, data, and container layers. The platform's security framework encompasses VPC isolation, automated security patching, pod security policies, and ECR vulnerability scanning, complemented by CloudTrail audit logging and AWS Config compliance monitoring. These capabilities, along with native IAM integration, Security Group policies, encrypted worker node communications, and systematic security updates, establish a secure and compliant foundation for containerized workloads, while minimizing operational overhead in security maintenance.

## Integration with AWS Services

Amazon EKS provides deep integration with the broader AWS ecosystem, creating a cohesive platform for container orchestration and management. The service seamlessly connects with AWS Application and Network Load Balancers to efficiently distribute traffic across containerized applications, while leveraging Amazon Container Registry (ECR) for secure, scalable container image storage and management. Through native CloudWatch integration, EKS delivers comprehensive monitoring and logging capabilities, enabling detailed insights into cluster performance and application behavior. The platform's compatibility with AWS Auto Scaling enables dynamic resource management, automatically adjusting cluster capacity to meet changing workload demands, ensuring optimal performance and cost efficiency across deployments.

## Networking Options

Amazon EKS offers a flexible and robust networking foundation through the Amazon VPC Container Network Interface (CNI), delivering native AWS networking capabilities that seamlessly integrate with existing infrastructure. The platform supports sophisticated networking architectures, including private cluster deployments and custom networking configurations to meet specific organizational requirements. Enhanced security and controlled access are achieved through AWS PrivateLink integration, enabling private communication between services without traversing the public internet. This comprehensive networking framework extends to support various service mesh solutions, allowing organizations to implement advanced traffic management, security policies, and observability across their microservices architectures.

# EKS Deployment Models

Amazon EKS offers a spectrum of deployment options, each designed to address different organizational needs, technical requirements, and operational preferences. These deployment models range from fully managed, hands-off approaches to highly customizable configurations, enabling organizations to select the perfect balance between control and convenience. Whether prioritizing operational simplicity through Managed Node Groups, embracing serverless architecture with Fargate, or maintaining complete infrastructure control via self-managed nodes, EKS provides the flexibility to align infrastructure management with business objectives and team capabilities. Let us explore these three distinct deployment models that cater to different operational requirements and management preferences:

- **Managed Node Groups:** Amazon EKS Managed Node Groups streamlines cluster administration by automating the provisioning and lifecycle management of worker nodes, significantly reducing operational complexity in Kubernetes deployments. The service offers flexible compute options through support for both on-demand and spot instances, enabling cost-effective resource allocation, while maintaining workload reliability. Through automatic node updates and replacement capabilities, EKS ensures cluster nodes remain current with security patches and version updates without manual intervention. These capabilities are complemented by built-in node scaling features that dynamically adjust cluster capacity based on workload demands, delivering an efficient and automated approach to Kubernetes infrastructure management.

  Managed Node Groups are ideal for organizations seeking a balance between control and automation in their Kubernetes infrastructure. This model serves teams that want to minimize operational overhead, while maintaining flexibility in instance management. It suits environments requiring both spot and on-demand instances, with standard infrastructure requirements and needs for automated scaling and updates. The cost structure includes EC2 instances plus EKS control plane charges, while offering medium-to-low operational effort, moderate learning curve, medium customization capabilities, and low maintenance overhead.

- **AMI Lifecycle Changes:** EKS managed node groups now provide enhanced AMI lifecycle management capabilities. These changes streamline how custom AMIs are handled and maintained within node groups. Administrators can define AMI refresh schedules, enabling automatic updates of node AMIs based on security patches and version updates. The system supports both EKS-optimized AMIs and custom AMIs, with improved controls for AMI validation and rollback procedures. This enhancement reduces operational overhead, while maintaining security compliance through systematic AMI updates and management.
- **EKS Auto Mode:** EKS Auto Mode is an enhanced feature of Managed Node Groups that further simplifies cluster management. It automatically handles the entire lifecycle of nodes, including provisioning, scaling, and updates, based on workload demands. This mode eliminates manual intervention in node management tasks, offering a hands-off approach to cluster operations.

  Auto Mode continuously optimizes capacity by adjusting node count and instance types for optimal resource utilization and cost-efficiency. It provides intelligent scaling based on pod resource requirements and manages node updates automatically, minimizing disruption to workloads. The system can leverage a mix of instance types and manage both Spot and On-Demand instances to balance performance, cost, and reliability.

  This feature is ideal for organizations seeking to minimize operational overhead and focus on application development, rather than infrastructure management.
- **Fargate Profile:** Amazon EKS Fargate represents a serverless computing solution that abstracts away the complexities of node management, allowing organizations to run Kubernetes pods without managing the underlying infrastructure. This profile implements a pay-per-pod pricing model that precisely aligns costs with actual resource consumption, eliminating the need to pay for unused capacity. Through automatic resource provisioning, Fargate dynamically allocates compute resources, based on pod requirements, ensuring optimal performance while maintaining efficiency. Thus, by removing the operational overhead of node management, including patching, scaling, and capacity planning, Fargate enables teams to focus solely on application development and deployment, significantly simplifying Kubernetes operations.

  Fargate Profile is optimized for organizations prioritizing operational simplicity and minimal infrastructure management. This serverless model excels in environments with variable workloads requiring precise scaling, and organizations focused primarily on application development rather than infrastructure management. It particularly benefits teams needing strict workload isolation for compliance requirements. The pricing follows a pay-per-pod model, offering minimal operational effort, low learning curve, and virtually, no maintenance overhead, though with limited customization options.

- **Self-Managed Nodes:** Amazon EKS self-managed nodes provide organizations with complete control over their Kubernetes infrastructure, enabling granular customization of node configurations to meet specific workload requirements. This deployment model supports the use of custom Amazon Machine Images (AMIs), allowing teams to precisely tailor the operating system environment and pre-installed software packages for their applications. Organizations gain full flexibility in selecting instance types, enabling optimal price-performance ratios for diverse workload characteristics. While this approach requires manual node lifecycle management, including updates, scaling, and maintenance, it offers the highest degree of customization and control for teams that require specific infrastructure configurations, or have unique compliance requirements.

  Self-Managed Nodes cater to organizations requiring extensive control and customization of their Kubernetes infrastructure. This model is particularly valuable for teams with specific compliance requirements, needs for specialized instance types, or unique configuration demands. It best serves organizations with the existing infrastructure expertise and resources for hands-on management. While offering maximum customization flexibility, it involves higher operational effort, a steeper learning curve, and significant maintenance overhead, with costs covering EC2 instances and the EKS control plane.

*Figure 1.2* explains various deployment models:

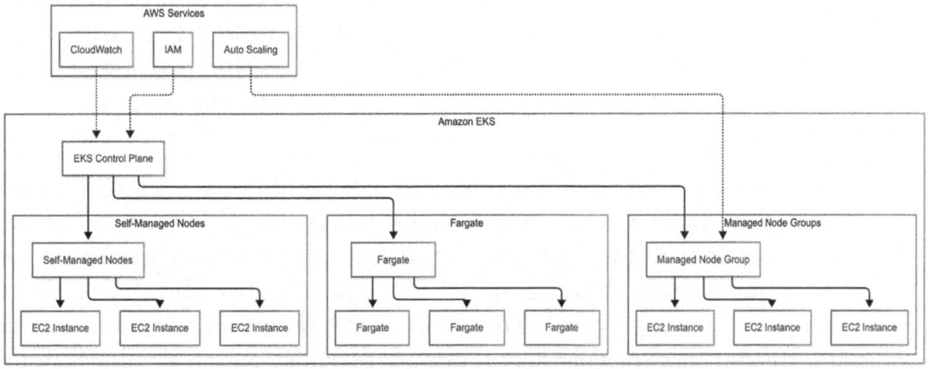


***Figure 1.2:*** *EKS Deployment Models*

The following decision factors matrix helps organizations make informed decisions based on their specific requirements, resources, and operational capabilities. The choice often depends on finding the right balance between control, operational overhead, and customization needs.

| Decision Factor | Managed Node Groups | Fargate Profile | Self-Managed Nodes |
|---|---|---|---|
| **Control** | Medium | Low | High |
| **Operation Overhead** | Low | Minimal | High |
| **Cost Predictability** | Medium | High | Variable |
| **Scaling Complexity** | Low | Minimal | High |
| **Customization** | Medium | Low | High |
| **Maintenance Effort** | Low | Minimal | High |
| **Time to Deploy** | Fast | Fastest | Slow |
| **Learning Curve** | Moderate | Low | Steep |

***Table 1.1:*** *EKS Deployment Models*

# Node Group Update Strategies

Node group update strategies in Amazon EKS are essential mechanisms designed to maintain and upgrade worker nodes, while ensuring cluster stability and application availability. These strategies provide systematic approaches to handle various update scenarios, from routine maintenance to critical security patches, while minimizing disruption to running applications.

- **Rolling Update Strategy:** The most common approach is the Rolling Update strategy, which serves as the default method for updating nodes in EKS. This strategy updates nodes one at a time, ensuring that the cluster maintains its capacity throughout the update process. During a rolling update, new nodes are created with updated configurations, while the existing nodes are cordoned and drained before being terminated. This methodical approach helps maintain service availability, and reduces the risk of application downtime.

  EKS also offers flexibility in update configurations through parameters like maxUnavailable and maxUnavailablePercentage. These settings allow organizations to control the pace of updates by specifying either the number of nodes or the percentage of nodes that can be unavailable during the update process. For instance, setting maxUnavailable to 1 ensures minimal disruption, while using maxUnavailablePercentage provides more flexibility for larger clusters.

- **Force Update Strategy:** For scenarios requiring immediate updates such as critical security patches, the Force Update Strategy can be employed. While this approach does not guarantee workload stability, it ensures quick application of the necessary changes. However, this strategy should be used cautiously as it may cause temporary service disruptions. Organizations typically reserve this option for emergency situations where the security risk outweighs the potential for brief service interruptions.

The best practices for node group updates include proper capacity planning, implementing comprehensive health checks, and configuring Pod Disruption Budgets (PDBs). Organizations should ensure sufficient cluster capacity during updates, account for pod anti-affinity rules, and consider peak workload requirements. Regular monitoring of key metrics such as node health status, pod scheduling success, and resource utilization helps maintain cluster stability during updates.

- **Blue-Green Deployments:** Advanced update patterns include Blue-Green deployments, where a new node group is created alongside the existing one, allowing for careful testing and gradual workload migration. This approach provides additional safety but requires more resources during the transition period. Organizations can also implement scheduled updates during maintenance windows to minimize the impact on business operations.
- **Scheduled Updates Using AWS Systems Manager:** Automation plays a crucial role in managing node group updates effectively. EKS provides various tools and integrations, including AWS CLI commands, the eksctl utility, and AWS Systems Manager, to automate update processes. These tools help reduce operational overhead, and ensure consistency in update procedures across the cluster.

Error handling and rollback procedures are vital components of any update strategy. Organizations should maintain documented procedures for pausing updates, and reverting to previous versions, if necessary. Regular testing of these procedures helps ensure quick recovery in case of update-related issues.

When implementing node group update strategies, organizations should consider their specific requirements regarding application availability, update urgency, and resource constraints. The chosen strategy should align with organizational policies and service level agreements, while maintaining security and performance standards.

Thus, it is important to note that while these strategies provide robust mechanisms for managing node updates, regular testing in non-production environments is crucial. This helps validate update procedures, and identify potential issues before they affect production workloads. Additionally, staying current with AWS best practices and new features helps optimize update strategies over time.

# Cost Considerations

Amazon EKS implements a multi-faceted pricing model that reflects the service's distributed architecture, and integration with various AWS components. The core pricing structure begins with control plane charges calculated per cluster per hour, representing the cost of managing the Kubernetes control plane infrastructure. Worker node costs vary based on the chosen deployment model, with EC2-based nodes incurring standard compute charges and Fargate offering precise per-pod pricing. Additional costs arise from essential supporting services such as load balancers, storage volumes, and data transfer. Organizations can optimize their expenditure through strategic use of spot instances for interruptible workloads, and implementing right-sizing practices to match resource allocation with actual application demands.

# Common Use Cases

Amazon EKS serves as a versatile platform powering diverse enterprise workloads across multiple domains. The platform primarily supports five key use cases:

- **Microservices Applications:** Amazon EKS provides an ideal platform for deploying and managing microservices architectures, enabling organizations to break down complex applications into smaller, independently deployable services. The platform excels in handling the intricate orchestration requirements of microservices, offering native service discovery, load balancing, and automated scaling capabilities. Through EKS, teams can efficiently manage inter-service communication, implement precise resource allocation per service, and maintain isolated deployment environments. The service's integration with AWS's ecosystem further enhances microservices operations through features like Application Load Balancer for intelligent routing, AWS X-Ray for distributed tracing, and Amazon CloudWatch for granular monitoring, ultimately delivering the scalability, reliability, and operational efficiency required for modern microservices deployments.
- **Batch Processing Workloads:** Amazon EKS excels in managing batch processing workloads by combining Kubernetes' native job scheduling capabilities with AWS's scalable infrastructure. The platform efficiently handles resource-intensive batch operations through automated scaling of compute resources, parallel processing capabilities, and intelligent workload distribution. EKS supports both time-sensitive and long-running batch jobs, offering features such as job queuing, prioritization, and automatic retry mechanisms for failed tasks. Organizations can leverage spot instances for cost-effective processing of interruptible workloads, while the platform's integration with AWS services such as CloudWatch enables comprehensive monitoring and logging of batch operations. This makes EKS particularly effective for data processing pipelines, ETL operations, scientific computing, and financial calculations where efficient batch processing is crucial for business operations.

- **Machine Learning Deployments:** Amazon EKS provides robust support for machine learning workloads by seamlessly integrating specialized computing resources with containerized ML frameworks and tools. The platform excels in orchestrating complex ML deployments, from model training to inference, by efficiently managing GPU-enabled instances and optimizing resource allocation for computational demands. Through EKS, organizations can implement end-to-end ML pipelines, leveraging Kubernetes' scheduling capabilities to manage distributed training jobs, while maintaining high resource utilization. The service's integration with AWS's ML ecosystem, including SageMaker and Deep Learning AMIs, enables teams to build scalable ML infrastructure that supports both development and production environments. This makes EKS an ideal platform for organizations deploying deep learning models, running real-time inference services, or managing large-scale ML experimentation workflows.
- **CI/CD Pipelines:** Amazon EKS serves as a powerful foundation for continuous integration and continuous delivery (CI/CD) pipelines, enabling automated and reliable application deployment workflows. The platform seamlessly integrates with popular CI/CD tools like Jenkins, GitLab, and AWS CodePipeline, facilitating automated testing, building, and deployment of containerized applications. Through EKS, organizations can implement sophisticated deployment strategies such as blue-green deployments, canary releases, and rolling updates while maintaining high availability. The service's native integration with AWS Developer Tools, including CodeBuild and CodeDeploy, streamlines the automation of build processes and deployment workflows. This infrastructure supports rapid iteration cycles, ensures consistent deployment environments, and enables teams to maintain reliable, repeatable deployment processes across multiple environments, making it ideal for organizations adopting DevOps practices.
- **Application Modernization Projects:** Amazon EKS stands as a cornerstone platform for application modernization initiatives, providing organizations with a structured path to transform legacy applications into cloud-native architectures. The service facilitates gradual migration from monolithic systems to microservices, enabling teams to modernize applications at their own pace, while maintaining operational stability. Through EKS, organizations can implement modern deployment patterns, containerize existing applications, and adopt cloud-native principles without disrupting current business operations. The platform's support for hybrid architectures allows for phased transitions, while its integration with AWS's comprehensive service portfolio enables teams to leverage modern cloud capabilities such as auto-scaling, service mesh, and serverless computing. This makes EKS particularly valuable for enterprises undertaking digital transformation initiatives, helping them achieve improved scalability, reduced operational

costs, and enhanced application performance through modern containerized architectures.

- **Generative AI Workloads:** Amazon EKS provides a robust platform for deploying and scaling Generative AI applications, offering specialized capabilities for managing complex AI workloads. The platform excels in orchestrating resource-intensive GenAI models through efficient GPU and inference optimization, while supporting popular frameworks like PyTorch, TensorFlow, and Hugging Face. Through EKS, organizations can implement scalable inference endpoints, manage Large Language Models (LLMs), and handle dynamic workload requirements with automated scaling. The service's integration with AWS's AI infrastructure, including Amazon SageMaker, GPU-enabled instances, and AWS Inferentia chips, enables cost-effective deployment of GenAI applications. Teams can leverage EKS to build and operate AI-powered applications such as chatbots, content generation systems, and image synthesis services, while maintaining optimal performance, cost efficiency, and resource utilization. This makes EKS particularly valuable for organizations implementing enterprise-scale GenAI solutions that require high availability, scalability, and reliable performance.

# Operational Excellence and Best Practices

Successful Amazon EKS implementations require a comprehensive approach to operational excellence, focusing on key pillars of scalability, availability, security, observability, and service connectivity. Horizontal Pod Autoscaling (HPA) enables automatic scaling of applications based on CPU, memory, or custom metrics, while Karpenter provides just-in-time node provisioning for optimized cluster scaling. Cluster sizing begins with analyzing workload requirements, considering factors such as CPU, memory, network throughput, and storage needs, along with overhead for system components and future growth.

Service mesh implementations using AWS App Mesh or Istio provide advanced traffic management, security, and observability features, while handling service-to-service communication. Service discovery is facilitated through AWS Cloud Map and Kubernetes' native DNS service, enabling dynamic endpoint discovery and load balancing. Resource management follows a structured approach with proper resource requests and limits, employing Quality of Service (QoS) classes and Priority Classes for workload prioritization.

Integration with CNCF projects enhances cluster capabilities: Prometheus and Thanos for scalable metrics, Flux and ArgoCD for GitOps workflows, Harbor for container registry, Crossplane for infrastructure provisioning, OpenTelemetry for observability standardization, and Cilium for eBPF-based networking and security. External-DNS manages external DNS records, Cert-Manager handles certificate automation, and Velero provides backup and disaster recovery.

The observability strategy incorporates comprehensive monitoring through CloudWatch and Prometheus for metrics, Fluent Bit or Fluentd for logging, and AWS X-Ray or Jaeger for distributed tracing. This three-pillar approach ensures complete visibility into application and cluster health. Following the twelve-factor app methodology, applications should maintain configuration in the environment, treat logs as event streams, and ensure strict separation of build and run stages.

High availability is achieved through multi-AZ deployments, utilizing managed node groups across availability zones, and implementing proper Pod Disruption Budgets (PDBs) for controlled maintenance. Role-Based Access Control (RBAC) provides granular access management, enabling organizations to implement the principle of least privilege across teams and services. These practices, combined with proper capacity planning, automated scaling configurations, and regular security audits, establish a foundation for reliable, observable, and cost-efficient Kubernetes operations that align with cloud-native best practices as well as the twelve-factor application principles.

# Kubernetes Fundamentals

Kubernetes has emerged as the de facto standard for container orchestration, providing a robust platform for automating the deployment, scaling, and management of containerized applications. This section explores the fundamental concepts and components that form the foundation of Kubernetes architecture and operations. Refer to *Figure* 1.3 for Kubernetes fundamental components, and how various components fit together.

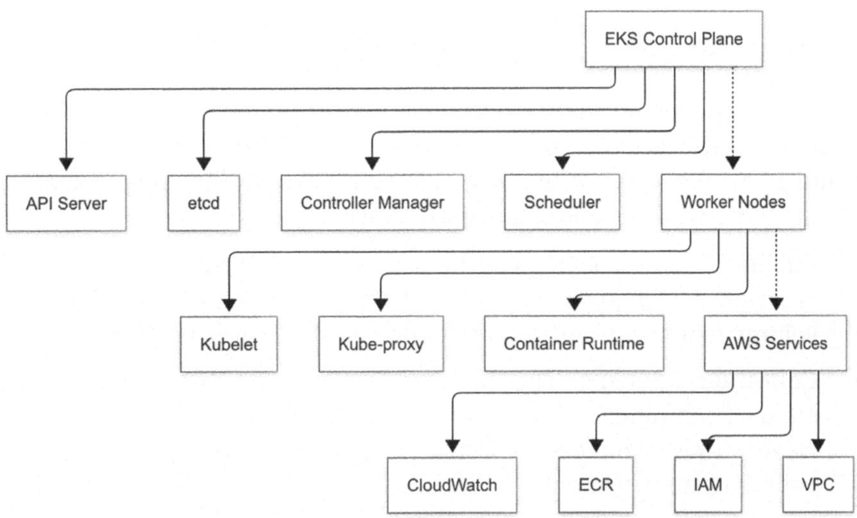


**Figure 1.3:** *Kubernetes Fundamental Components*

# Control Plane Architecture

The Kubernetes control plane represents the brain of the cluster, consisting of several critical components working together to maintain the desired state. This critical system component acts as the cluster's central nervous system, making decisions about scheduling, detecting and responding to events, and maintaining the desired state of all workloads.

- **API Server:** The API server serves as the primary entry point for all administrative operations and cluster communication. It processes REST operations, validates them, and updates the corresponding objects in etcd. All communication between components flows through the API server, making it central to cluster operations.
- **Etcd:** As the cluster's distributed key-value store, etcd maintains the state of all Kubernetes objects. It ensures consistency, and provides reliable data storage for the entire cluster configuration, making it crucial for cluster stability and recovery.
- **Scheduler:** The scheduler assigns pods to nodes based on resource availability, constraints, and policies. It implements complex algorithms to ensure optimal pod placement, considering factors like resource requirements, node selection criteria, and affinity/anti-affinity rules.
- **Controller Manager:** Multiple controllers work together to maintain the desired state of the cluster. Key controllers include the Node Controller, Replication Controller, and Endpoints Controller, each responsible for specific aspects of cluster state management.

# Worker Node Components

While the control plane makes decisions, worker nodes perform the actual work of running containerized applications. These components form the execution environment where applications live, managing everything from container runtime operations to networking and storage integration.

- **Kubelet:** The Kubelet acts as the primary node agent, ensuring that containers are running in pods as specified. It manages container lifecycle, handles volume mounting, and reports node and pod status to the control plane.
- **Container Runtime:** The container runtime (such as containerd or CRI-O) handles container operations including image pulling, container startup, and cleanup. It implements the Container Runtime Interface (CRI) for standardized container management.

- **Kube-proxy:** Maintaining network rules and enabling service abstraction, kube-proxy handles pod-to-pod and external-to-pod networking. It implements load balancing for service endpoints and manages network policies.

# Kubernetes Objects and Workloads

Kubernetes objects represent the building blocks for deploying and managing applications within the cluster. These fundamental abstractions provide the vocabulary for expressing application requirements, from basic pod definitions to complex deployment strategies.

- **Pod Management:** Pods represent the smallest deployable units in Kubernetes, encapsulating one or more containers. The key concepts include:
- **Deployments and ReplicaSets:** These resources manage stateless applications, handling replica scaling, rolling updates, and rollbacks. They ensure that the specified number of pod replicas are running smoothly, and are healthy.
- **StatefulSets:** Designed for stateful applications, StatefulSets maintain pod identity and state, ensuring ordered deployment and scaling. They provide stable network identities and persistent storage for applications requiring state management.
- **DaemonSets:** DaemonSets ensure specific pods run on all (or selected) nodes, typically used for cluster-wide operations like monitoring or logging agents.

# Networking Architecture

Networking in Kubernetes implements a sophisticated model that enables seamless communication between application components. This architecture provides the foundation for service discovery, load balancing, and external access, essential elements for building distributed applications.

**Service Types**

Services provide stable endpoints for pod access:

- ClusterIP for internal cluster communication
- NodePort for external access through node ports
- LoadBalancer for cloud provider load balancer integration
- ExternalName for external service mapping

**Ingress Resources:** Ingress controllers manage external access to services, providing HTTP/HTTPS routing, SSL termination, and name-based virtual hosting.

# Storage Management

Persistent storage management represents a critical aspect of running stateful applications in Kubernetes. The platform's storage architecture provides flexible abstractions that accommodate various storage requirements, while maintaining portability across different environments.

**Volume Management**

Kubernetes supports various volume types and persistent storage options through:

- PersistentVolumes (PV) for storage resources
- PersistentVolumeClaims (PVC) for storage requests
- StorageClasses for dynamic provisioning
- Volume snapshots and cloning capabilities

# Security and Access Control

Security stands as a paramount concern in Kubernetes deployments, requiring a comprehensive approach to access control and resource protection. The platform's security framework provides multiple layers of defense, from authentication and authorization to network policies and container security.

**RBAC (Role-Based Access Control)**

RBAC implements authorization through:

- Roles and ClusterRoles defining permissions
- RoleBindings and ClusterRoleBindings assigning permissions
- Service Accounts for pod identity management

**Security Contexts**

Security contexts define privilege and access control settings for pods and containers, including:

- User and group contexts
- Linux capabilities
- SELinux options
- Seccomp profiles

# Resource Management

Efficient resource utilization and allocation form the backbone of successful Kubernetes operations. Through sophisticated resource management capabilities,

Kubernetes ensures applications receive necessary resources, while maintaining the overall cluster efficiency.

**Resource Allocation**

Effective resource management through:

- Resource requests and limits
- Quality of Service (QoS) classes
- Namespace resource quotas
- LimitRanges for default values

**Autoscaling**

Automatic scaling capabilities include the following:

- Horizontal Pod Autoscaling (HPA)
- Vertical Pod Autoscaling (VPA)
- Cluster Autoscaling

# Best Practices

Success with Kubernetes requires more than just technical knowledge; it demands adherence to proven practices and patterns. These best practices, derived from real-world implementations, help organizations avoid common pitfalls and achieve operational excellence.

**Operational Excellence**

- Implement proper monitoring and logging.
- Maintain backup and disaster recovery procedures.
- Follow security best practices.
- Plan for cluster scaling and upgrades.
- Leverage AMI lifecycle management features for consistent and secure node images.
    - Schedule regular AMI updates.
    - Implement AMI validation procedures.
    - Maintain AMI version control.
    - Monitor AMI deployment status.
    - Configure rollback procedures.
- Implement proper resource management.

**Application Design**

- Design for container-native operations.
- Implement proper health checks.
- Handle configuration through ConfigMaps and Secrets.
- Design for horizontal scaling.
- Implement proper security controls.

This comprehensive overview of Kubernetes fundamentals provides the essential knowledge required for understanding and implementing containerized applications in a Kubernetes environment. The subsequent sections will build upon these concepts to explore specific implementations in Amazon EKS.

# Cloud-Native Principles in AWS

Cloud-native principles in AWS establish the foundation for building modern, scalable, and resilient applications. Amazon's extensive service portfolio enables organizations to implement these principles effectively, creating architectures that leverage the full potential of cloud computing, while maintaining operational excellence and cost efficiency.

## AWS Integration

- **Containerization and Orchestration:** Amazon Elastic Container Registry (ECR) provides secure container image storage and management, integrating seamlessly with Amazon EKS for container orchestration. The combination enables streamlined image lifecycle management, vulnerability scanning, and efficient deployment processes. AWS Fargate extends containerization benefits by offering serverless container execution, eliminating infrastructure management overhead, while maintaining containerization advantages.
- **Microservices Implementation:** AWS App Mesh provides service mesh capabilities for microservices architectures, offering traffic management, service discovery, and monitoring. Amazon API Gateway enables API management and request routing, while AWS Cloud Map provides service discovery across the AWS infrastructure. These services create a robust foundation for building and managing microservices architectures at scale.
- **Infrastructure as Code:** AWS CloudFormation and AWS CDK enable declarative infrastructure definition, supporting version-controlled and repeatable deployments. These tools integrate with AWS Organizations and AWS Control Tower for multi-account management, ensuring consistent infrastructure deployment across environments, while maintaining security and compliance requirements.

## Resilience and Availability

- **High Availability Design:** Amazon EKS implements multi-AZ deployments for both control plane and worker nodes, ensuring application availability during zone failures. Integration with AWS Auto Scaling enables automated capacity management, while Elastic Load Balancing provides intelligent request distribution across multiple availability zones.
- **Fault Tolerance:** AWS Route 53 enables DNS-based routing and failover capabilities, complementing EKS cluster resilience. AWS Systems Manager provides automated remediation capabilities, while AWS Health Dashboard offers insights into AWS service health and planned maintenance activities affecting your applications.

## Observability and Monitoring

- **Metrics and Logging:** Amazon CloudWatch integrates with EKS for comprehensive monitoring, collecting metrics from clusters, nodes, and applications. AWS CloudWatch Logs centralizes log management, while CloudWatch Container Insights provides specialized container monitoring capabilities. AWS X-Ray enables distributed tracing across AWS services and applications.
- **Performance Management:** AWS CloudWatch Synthetics enables proactive monitoring through canary testing, while CloudWatch Alarms provide automated response to performance issues. Integration with AWS Lambda enables automated remediation actions based on monitoring data.

## Security Implementation

- **Identity and Access Management:** AWS IAM provides fine-grained access control through roles and policies, integrating with EKS through IAM roles for service accounts. AWS KMS enables encryption key management, while AWS Certificate Manager handles SSL/TLS certificate provisioning and renewal.
- **Network Security:** AWS VPC offers isolated network environments with security groups and network ACLs. AWS PrivateLink enables private service access, while AWS WAF provides web application firewall capabilities for ingress protection.

## Operational Excellence

- **Automation and CI/CD:** AWS CodePipeline orchestrates continuous integration and delivery workflows, integrating with AWS CodeBuild for build processes and AWS CodeDeploy for deployment automation. AWS Systems

Manager provides configuration management and automation capabilities across the infrastructure.

- **Cost Optimization:** AWS Cost Explorer and AWS Budgets enable financial monitoring and optimization of container workloads. Integration with AWS Savings Plans and Spot Instances provides cost-effective compute options for containerized applications.

## Best Practices

- **Resource Management:** Effective use of EKS node groups and Fargate profiles optimizes resource utilization. Implementation of appropriate instance types and scaling policies ensures cost-effective operations while maintaining performance requirements.
- **Security and Compliance:** Regular security assessments using AWS Security Hub and AWS Config ensure compliance with security standards. Integration with AWS Organizations enables centralized security policy management across multiple accounts and clusters.
- **Disaster Recovery:** Implementation of cross-region backup strategies using AWS Backup ensures data protection. Regular testing of disaster recovery procedures maintains business continuity capabilities.

# Application Architecture

- **Service Communication:** Implementation of asynchronous communication patterns using Amazon SQS and Amazon SNS for reliable message handling. Use of Amazon EventBridge for event-driven architectures enables loose coupling between services.
- **Data Management:** Integration with Amazon RDS for relational databases, Amazon DynamoDB for NoSQL requirements, and Amazon ElastiCache for caching layers provides comprehensive data management capabilities.

# Development Workflow

- **Local Development:** AWS Cloud9 and AWS CLI facilitate local development and testing of containerized applications. AWS SAM enables local testing of serverless components integrated with containerized services.
- **Testing and Validation:** Implementation of testing strategies across multiple environments using AWS CodeBuild and AWS Device Farm. Integration testing across AWS services ensures reliable application behavior.

This comprehensive approach to implementing cloud-native principles on AWS provides organizations with a robust foundation for building modern applications. The integration of AWS services with EKS creates a powerful platform for deploying and managing containerized applications, while maintaining security, scalability, and operational efficiency.

# Microservices Architecture Patterns

Microservices architecture represents a modern approach to building distributed applications where complex systems are decomposed into smaller, independently deployable services. In the context of Amazon EKS, these patterns provide proven solutions for common architectural challenges, while leveraging AWS's extensive service portfolio for implementation.

# Core Architecture Patterns

- **Service Decomposition Pattern:** Service decomposition involves breaking down applications into discrete services based on business capabilities. Each service owns its data model and business logic, communicating through well-defined APIs. In AWS, this pattern leverages services like Amazon API Gateway for interface management, while EKS provides the runtime environment for these decomposed services.
- **Database Per Service Pattern:** Each microservice maintains its own database, ensuring loose coupling and independent scalability. This pattern utilizes various AWS database services, including Amazon RDS for relational data, DynamoDB for NoSQL requirements, and Amazon ElastiCache for caching layers. Data consistency is maintained through event-driven updates and eventual consistency models.
- **API Gateway Pattern:** Amazon API Gateway serves as the entry point for external clients, providing routing, authentication, and rate limiting. The pattern implements API versioning, request/response transformation, and security policies, while integrating with AWS WAF for protection against common web exploits.

# Communication Patterns

- **Synchronous Communication:** REST and gRPC protocols enable direct service-to-service communication. AWS App Mesh provides service mesh capabilities for managing this communication, implementing features such as circuit breaking, retry logic, and timeout management. Load balancing is handled through EKS Services and AWS Load Balancers.
- **Asynchronous Communication:** Event-driven patterns utilize Amazon SQS for queue-based processing and Amazon SNS for pub/sub messaging. Amazon EventBridge enables complex event routing and processing, while maintaining

loose coupling between services. This pattern ensures reliability through message persistence and retry mechanisms.

- **Saga Pattern:** Distributed transactions are managed through choreography or orchestration-based sagas. AWS Step Functions coordinates complex workflows across multiple services, maintaining data consistency while handling compensation transactions for failure scenarios.

# Data Management Patterns

- **CQRS Pattern:** Command Query Responsibility Segregation separates read and write operations. Amazon Aurora's read replicas support read scaling, while write operations are directed to the primary instance. DynamoDB streams enable event sourcing for maintaining read models.
- **Event Sourcing Pattern:** State changes are captured as a sequence of events. Amazon Kinesis handles real-time event streaming, while Amazon S3 provides event storage. This pattern enables complete audit trails and system state reconstruction from historical events.

# Resilience Patterns

- **Circuit Breaker Pattern:** Prevents cascading failures across service boundaries. AWS App Mesh implements circuit breaking logic, while Amazon CloudWatch monitors service health, and triggers circuit state changes based on defined thresholds.
- **Bulkhead Pattern:** Resource isolation prevents failures from spreading. EKS namespaces and resource quotas implement logical separation, while AWS Auto Scaling groups provide physical resource isolation between service groups.

# Deployment Patterns

- **Blue-Green Deployment:** Zero-downtime deployments through parallel environments. AWS Route 53 manages traffic switching, while EKS deployments handle container version management. This pattern enables rapid rollback capabilities when needed.
- **Canary Releases:** Gradual traffic shifting to new service versions. AWS App Mesh provides fine-grained traffic control, while CloudWatch monitors service health metrics to automate rollout decisions.

# Security Patterns

- **Identity and Access Management:** Fine-grained access control through AWS IAM roles for service accounts. Integration with Amazon Cognito provides user authentication and authorization, while AWS Secrets Manager handles sensitive configuration data.

- **Service Mesh Security:** AWS App Mesh implements mutual TLS between services, while AWS Certificate Manager handles certificate lifecycle management. Network policies in EKS provide additional security through traffic control between services.

# Operational Patterns

- **Observability Pattern:** Comprehensive monitoring through CloudWatch Container Insights, while AWS X-Ray provides distributed tracing. Centralized logging uses CloudWatch Logs with structured logging formats for efficient analysis.
- **Service Discovery Pattern:** AWS Cloud Map provides service discovery across the infrastructure. EKS ServiceAccounts integrate with IAM for secure service identity, while DNS-based service discovery handles internal service resolution.

# Performance Patterns

- **Caching Pattern:** Multi-level caching using Amazon ElastiCache for application caching and CloudFront for content delivery. Cache aside and write-through strategies optimize data access patterns.
- **Scaling Pattern:** Automatic scaling based on demand through Horizontal Pod Autoscaling in EKS and AWS Auto Scaling. Custom metrics enable business-aware scaling decisions.

# Best Practices

### Design Principles

- Service independence through clear boundaries
- Data ownership and encapsulation
- Resilient communication patterns
- Automated deployment and operations
- Security at every layer

### Implementation Guidelines

- API design and versioning strategies
- Data consistency models
- Error handling and retry strategies

- Monitoring and alerting approaches
- Security implementation patterns

This comprehensive overview of microservices patterns provides architects and developers with proven solutions for building robust and scalable applications on Amazon EKS. These patterns, when properly implemented, enable organizations to create maintainable and resilient microservices architectures, while leveraging AWS services for optimal performance and reliability.

# Conclusion

Thus, Amazon EKS represents a powerful foundation for modern application deployment, combining the robustness of Kubernetes with AWS's comprehensive service portfolio. Throughout this chapter, we have explored how EKS enables organizations to build and manage containerized applications efficiently, from basic deployment models to sophisticated microservices architectures. We have also explored the core components and architecture of Amazon EKS, various deployment models and their use cases, storage options and implementation strategies, as well as crucial security and compliance considerations. Additionally, we have examined EKS's integration capabilities with other AWS services, cloud-native principles, microservices patterns, and fundamental Kubernetes concepts as they apply to EKS.

With this foundational knowledge in place, readers are now well-equipped to delve into more advanced implementation patterns and operational practices in the chapters that follow. This comprehensive understanding of EKS enables organizations to construct scalable and resilient applications, while optimizing operational costs and maintaining security compliance. The exploration of operational excellence and best practices further enhances the ability to leverage EKS effectively, setting the stage for more sophisticated containerized application management and deployment strategies.

# Points to Remember

- EKS is AWS's managed Kubernetes service that automates control plane operations, providing a highly available and secure container orchestration platform.
- Three EKS deployment models (Managed Node Groups, Fargate, and Self-Managed Nodes) offer different levels of control and automation.
- Storage options in EKS include EBS for block storage, EFS for shared file systems, and S3 for object storage.
- Security implementation integrates with AWS IAM, VPC networking, and encryption services.

- Cloud-native principles emphasize containerization, microservices architecture, and declarative configuration.
- Kubernetes architecture consists of control plane components (API server, etcd, scheduler) and worker nodes.
- Microservices patterns include service decomposition, API gateway, and communication patterns.
- Operational excellence requires monitoring, logging, and proper resource management.
- Cost optimization involves proper instance selection, spot usage, and resource right-sizing.
- High availability is achieved through multi-AZ deployments and proper service design.

# Multiple Choice Questions

1. Which EKS deployment model provides serverless container execution?
    a. Managed Node Groups
    b. Fargate Profile
    c. Self-Managed Nodes
    d. Worker Nodes
2. Which component serves as the primary entry point for Kubernetes API operations?
    a. etcd
    b. Controller Manager
    c. API Server
    d. Scheduler
3. Which AWS service provides service mesh capabilities for EKS?
    a. AWS Cloud Map
    b. AWS App Mesh
    c. AWS CloudWatch
    d. AWS Route 53

4. Which storage option is the best for shared file systems in EKS?
   a. Amazon EBS
   b. Amazon EFS
   c. Amazon S3
   d. Instance Store
5. Which pattern helps prevent cascading failures in microservices?
   a. Saga Pattern
   b. CQRS Pattern
   c. Circuit Breaker Pattern
   d. Bulkhead Pattern
6. Which AWS service is used for container image storage with EKS?
   a. Amazon S3
   b. Amazon EBS
   c. Amazon ECR
   d. Amazon EFS
7. Which feature enables automatic scaling of pods based on metrics?
   a. Cluster Autoscaler
   b. Vertical Pod Autoscaler
   c. Horizontal Pod Autoscaler
   d. Node Auto Scaling
8. What provides DNS-based service discovery in AWS?
   a. Route 53
   b. Cloud Map
   c. App Mesh
   d. API Gateway
9. Which deployment strategy enables gradual traffic shifting?
   a. Blue-Green Deployment
   b. Canary Release

   c. Rolling Update
   d. Recreate
10. Which AWS service integrates with EKS for distributed tracing?
   a. CloudWatch
   b. X-Ray
   c. CloudTrail
   d. Systems Manager

# Answers

1. b
2. c
3. b
4. b
5. c
6. c
7. c
8. b
9. b
10. b

# Key Terms

- **Amazon EKS** (Elastic Kubernetes Service)**:** AWS's managed Elastic Kubernetes Service
- **Control Plane:** Kubernetes management layer that controls the cluster
- **Fargate:** Serverless compute engine for containers
- **Microservices:** Architectural style breaking applications into small, independent services
- **Container Orchestration:** Automated management of containerized applications
- **Service Mesh:** Infrastructure layer managing service-to-service communication

- **Pod:** Smallest deployable unit in Kubernetes
- **Node Group:** Collection of EC2 instances managing containerized applications
- **IAM Roles for Service Accounts** (IRSA): AWS IAM integration with Kubernetes service accounts
- **Container Network Interface** (CNI): Networking framework for containers
- **Persistent Volume:** Storage resource in Kubernetes
- **Horizontal Pod Autoscaling:** Automatic scaling of pod replicas
- **CloudWatch Container Insights:** Monitoring solution for containers
- **AWS App Mesh:** Service mesh implementation for AWS
- **Cluster Autoscaler:** Automatic scaling of worker nodes

# CHAPTER 2
# Setting Up Your EKS Environment

## Introduction

Setting up a production-grade Amazon Elastic Kubernetes Service (EKS) environment requires a thorough understanding of cloud infrastructure components, Kubernetes orchestration tools, and AWS-native services. This chapter guides readers through every foundational element needed to establish a secure, scalable, and operationally efficient EKS environment. Beginning with environment planning and prerequisite tools, it covers key areas such as IAM configuration, networking architecture, security practices, and the deployment of essential Kubernetes utilities. Whether creating clusters via eksctl, the AWS Management Console, or Infrastructure as Code tools like Terraform and CloudFormation, this chapter emphasizes automation, governance, and adherence to the best practices.

Through detailed examples, command-line instructions, and architectural diagrams, readers will gain hands-on experience with setting up the AWS CLI, configuring IAM roles, provisioning VPCs and subnets, as well as managing cluster add-ons. The chapter is especially valuable for platform engineers, DevOps professionals, and cloud architects who aim to build reliable Kubernetes platforms on AWS. By the end of this chapter, learners will have a fully configured, secure EKS cluster foundation that supports enterprise-grade workloads, and is ready for advanced topics such as autoscaling, observability, and continuous delivery covered in later chapters.

## Structure

In this chapter, we will discuss the following topics:

- Prerequisites and Planning
- AWS CLI and Essential Tools Configuration
- Network Foundation
- Identity and Access Management

- EKS Cluster Creation and Configuration
- Infrastructure as Code Implementation

# Prerequisites and Planning

Before diving into the technical setup, it is important to emphasize the value of thoughtful planning when preparing to deploy an EKS environment. Identifying key requirements—such as region selection, availability zones, IAM boundaries, and network topology—helps ensure that the cluster is aligned with organizational policies, security standards, and scalability goals. This planning phase lays the groundwork for a reliable and maintainable Kubernetes architecture by enabling teams to make informed decisions on tools, resource allocation, and integration strategies. A well-planned environment reduces rework, simplifies automation, and accelerates the overall delivery timelines.

A production-grade Amazon EKS deployment follows a carefully structured architecture as shown in *Figure* 2.1, designed for security, high availability, and scalability. The setup begins with a VPC (10.0.0.0/16) distributed across multiple Availability Zones, each containing both public subnets (10.0.0.0/24, 10.0.1.0/24) for NAT Gateways and private subnets (10.0.16.0/20, 10.0.32.0/20) for worker nodes. The AWS-managed EKS control plane, comprising the API server, etcd, and controller manager, operates across these AZs for resilience. Worker nodes are organized into managed node groups using different instance types (m5.large, m5.xlarge) to accommodate varying workload requirements. Essential add-ons, including VPC CNI, CoreDNS, and Kube Proxy provide core functionality. The architecture implements security best practices through private VPC endpoints for AWS services (S3, ECR), OIDC integration for pod-level IAM authentication, and an Application Load Balancer for secure external access. Network traffic flows through NAT Gateways in public subnets, enabling private worker nodes to access external resources while maintaining security. This infrastructure layout, combined with proper IAM roles and security groups, creates a secure, scalable, and maintainable Kubernetes environment suitable for enterprise workloads.

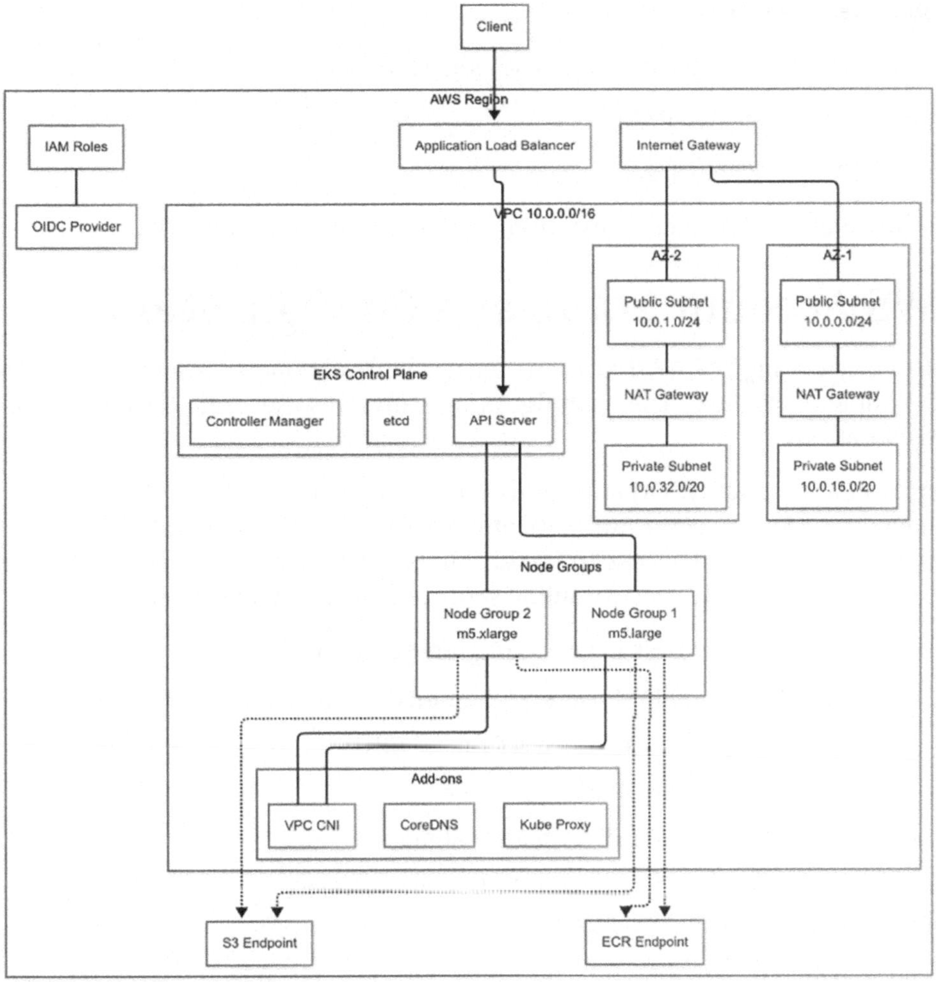


***Figure 2.1:*** *Reference Architecture for a Production Read Single-region EKS Cluster Setups*

# Required Tools and Dependencies

Before proceeding with an Amazon EKS deployment, organizations must ensure that their environment meets specific prerequisites. The following components are necessary for a successful EKS implementation:

- AWS CLI version 2.11.0 or later
- kubectl version compatible with the target EKS cluster version
- eksctl version 0.164.0 or later
- A code editor (such as Visual Studio Code)
- Git client for version control

**System Requirements:**

Operating System: Linux, macOS, or Windows 10/11

Memory: Minimum 4GB RAM

Storage: 10GB available space

Network: Reliable internet connection with access to AWS endpoints

# AWS Account Setup and Configuration

A properly configured AWS account forms the backbone of a secure and efficient EKS implementation. This configuration involves several critical steps and considerations.

**Root Account Security:** Organizations must first secure their AWS root account by implementing Multi-Factor Authentication (MFA). This fundamental security measure prevents unauthorized access to the account's most privileged credentials. The root account should only be used for initial setup and critical account changes.

**Administrative Access Best Practice Implementation:**

- Create dedicated IAM users for administrative tasks.
- Implement Role-Based Access Control (RBAC).
- Apply the principle of least privilege.
- Enable AWS CloudTrail for audit logging.

**Service Quotas and Limits:** Amazon EKS operates under specific service quotas that organizations must consider during planning:

- Clusters per region: 100 (soft limit)
- Nodes per cluster: 1000 (hard limit)

Organizations should monitor these limits, and request increases, when necessary, through the AWS Support Center.

Reference - https://docs.aws.amazon.com/eks/latest/userguide/service-quotas.html

# Environment Planning Considerations

Effective environment planning requires careful consideration of various architectural aspects to ensure scalability, security, and operational efficiency.

**High Availability Design:** EKS clusters should be designed with high availability in mind from the start. This involves:

- Distributing worker nodes across multiple availability zones
- Implementing proper load balancing strategies
- Planning for disaster recovery scenarios

**Network Architecture Planning:**

- CIDR Allocation Strategy:

```
VPC: 10.0.0.0/16 (65,536 IP addresses)
│
├── Public Subnets:
│   ├── AZ-1: 10.0.0.0/24 (256 IPs)
│   ├── AZ-2: 10.0.1.0/24 (256 IPs)
│   └── AZ-3: 10.0.2.0/24 (256 IPs)
│
└── Private Subnets:
    ├── AZ-1: 10.0.16.0/20 (4,096 IPs)
    ├── AZ-2: 10.0.32.0/20 (4,096 IPs)
    └── AZ-3: 10.0.48.0/20 (4,096 IPs)
```

## Security Requirements

Security forms a fundamental pillar of EKS deployment, requiring careful consideration across multiple dimensions. While comprehensive security details are covered in *Chapter 6, Security Best Practices*, here are the essential security requirements to consider during initial environment planning such as:

- **Network Isolation:** Network isolation implements the principle of least privilege at the network level, establishing clear boundaries between different components of the EKS infrastructure:

  **Control Plane Isolation**:

  - Private API endpoint configuration
  - Custom endpoint access controls
  - VPC endpoint policies

  **Workload Isolation**:

  - Separate subnets for different workload types
  - Network policy enforcement
  - Service mesh implementation

  **Access Controls**:

  - Security group segmentation

  - Network ACL implementation
  - VPC flow logs monitoring
- **Data Encryption Standards:** Data encryption must be implemented comprehensively across all data states:

  **Encryption Requirements**:

  **Data at Rest**:

  - EBS volume encryption
  - Secrets encryption
  - EFS encryption

  **Data in Transit**:

  - TLS 1.3 enforcement
  - mTLS between services
  - VPC traffic encryption

  **Key Management**:

  - AWS KMS integration
  - Automatic key rotation
  - Access auditing

# AWS CLI and Essential Tools Configuration

The AWS Command Line Interface (CLI) is a foundational tool for managing and automating AWS services, including the provisioning and configuration of EKS clusters. Installing and configuring the AWS CLI enables users to interact with AWS APIs directly from the terminal, allowing for efficient scripting, repeatability, and integration with infrastructure-as-code pipelines. Proper configuration includes setting up credentials, specifying the default region, and verifying access permissions—all of which are vital for seamless cluster deployment and management. Ensuring that the AWS CLI is installed and tested early in the setup process minimizes connectivity issues, and streamlines subsequent steps.

# Installing and Configuring AWS CLI

The AWS CLI installation process varies by operating system, but the configuration process remains consistent. Here's a detailed walkthrough of the installation and configuration process:

**For Linux Systems:**

```
curl "https://awscli.amazonaws.com/awscli-exe-linux-x86_64.zip"
-o "awscliv2.zip"
unzip awscliv2.zip
sudo./aws/install
```

This installation method ensures that you have the latest version of the AWS CLI. After installation, verify the installation:

```
aws --version
```

**Installation Process for macOS:**

```
brew install awscli
```

**Windows**

**Configuration Process:**

The AWS CLI requires configuration with your credentials and default settings. The best practice is to use IAM user credentials, rather than root credentials:

```
aws configure
AWS Access Key ID [None]: AKIAXXXXXXXXXXXXXXXX
AWS Secret Access Key [None]: XXXXXXXXXXXXXXXXXXXXXXXXXXXXXXXXXXX
XXXXX
Default region name [None]: us-west-2
Default output format [None]: json
```

# Setting Up eksctl

**eksctl** serves as the official CLI tool for Amazon EKS, significantly simplifying cluster management operations. This tool, developed by Weaveworks in collaboration with AWS, automates many common tasks in the EKS lifecycle.

**Installation Process:** For Linux systems, the installation involves downloading the latest release, and placing it in the system path:

**Linux/macOS:**

```
curl --silent --location "https://github.com/weaveworks/eksctl/
releases/latest/download/eksctl_$(uname -s)_amd64.tar.gz" | tar
xz -C /tmp
sudo mv /tmp/eksctl /usr/local/bin
eksctl version
```

After installation, create a basic configuration file to define your cluster specifications. This file serves as a blueprint for cluster creation:

```
# cluster-config.yaml
apiVersion: eksctl.io/v1alpha5
```

```
kind: ClusterConfig
metadata:
  name: production-eks
  region: us-west-2
  version: "1.28"
nodeGroups:
  - name: ng-1
    instanceType: m5.large
    desiredCapacity: 3
    ssh:
      allow: false
```

# Configuring `kubectl`

**`kubectl`** is the command-line interface for interacting with Kubernetes clusters. Proper configuration ensures seamless communication between your local environment and the EKS cluster.

**Installation and Setup: For Linux systems:**

```
# Download the latest stable release
curl -LO "https://dl.k8s.io/release/$(curl -L -s https://dl.k8s.
io/release/stable.txt)/bin/linux/amd64/kubectl"

# Make the binary executable
chmod +x kubectl

# Move to system PATH
sudo mv kubectl /usr/local/bin/
```

**Configuration with EKS:**

After installing kubectl, configure it to work with your EKS cluster:

```
Update kubeconfig for EKS cluster access
aws eks update-kubeconfig \
    --region us-west-2 \
    --name production-eks \
    --alias prod-cluster

# Verify the configuration
kubectl cluster-info
```

The resulting kubeconfig file contains sensitive cluster access information and should be protected accordingly:

```
# Example kubeconfig structure
apiVersion: v1
kind: Config
```

```
clusters:
- cluster:
    certificate-authority-data: DATA+OMITTED
    server: https://XXXXX.gr7.us-west-2.eks.amazonaws.com
  name: prod-cluster
contexts:
- context:
    cluster: prod-cluster
    user: prod-cluster-admin
  name: prod-cluster
current-context: prod-cluster
```

# Authentication and Credentials Management

Proper authentication management is crucial for maintaining cluster security. EKS uses AWS IAM Authenticator to integrate with AWS IAM for cluster access control.

**IAM Authentication Setup**

```
# Download the authenticator
curl -o aws-iam-authenticator \
    https://amazon-eks.s3.us-west-2.amazonaws.com/1.21.2/2021-07-
05/bin/linux/amd64/aws-iam-authenticator

# Apply execute permissions
chmod +x ./aws-iam-authenticator

# Move to system PATH
sudo mv aws-iam-authenticator /usr/local/bin
```

**Credential Configuration:** Organizations should implement a robust credential management strategy:

- **Short-term Credentials:**

```
    # Use AWS STS for temporary credentials
aws sts get-session-token \
    --duration-seconds 3600 \
    --serial-number arn:aws:iam::123456789012:mfa/user
```

- **Role-based Access:**

```
  # Example AWS IAM role configuration
apiVersion: v1
kind: ConfigMap
metadata:
  name: aws-auth
  namespace: kube-system
data:
  mapRoles: |
```

```
- rolearn: arn:aws:iam::123456789012:role/EKSAdminRole
  username: admin
  groups:
    - system:masters
```

# Network Foundation

Establishing a strong network foundation is necessary for ensuring the performance, availability, and security of your EKS cluster. Network design decisions–such as IP address planning, subnet layout, and access control–directly influence how workloads communicate internally and with external systems. Before configuring the VPC and related components, it is important to understand how EKS leverages AWS networking services, and how these choices align with organizational standards, compliance requirements, as well as future scalability needs.

# VPC Architecture for EKS

A well-designed VPC architecture is fundamental to a secure and scalable EKS deployment. The network design must accommodate both current requirements and future growth.

**VPC Design Principles:**

- **IP Address Space Planning:**

  ```
  VPC CIDR: 192.168.0.0/16 (65,536 IP addresses)

  Subnet Distribution:
  AZ-1:
    Public:  192.168.0.0/18 (16,384 IPs)
    Private: 192.168.128.0/18 (16,384 IPs)
  AZ-2:
   Public: 192.168.64.0/18 (16,384 IPs)
  Private: 192.168.192.0/18 (16,384 IPs)
  Example VPC CloudFormation Template:
  https://s3.us-west-2.amazonaws.com/amazon-eks/cloudformation
  /2020-10-29/amazon-eks-vpc-private-subnets.yaml
  ```

# Subnet Planning and Configuration

Proper subnet configuration is critical for EKS workload distribution and network isolation. The implementation requires careful consideration of both public and private subnet arrangements.

Public subnets host NAT gateways and load balancers, requiring specific configurations:

- **Public Subnets:**

```
Subnet-1:
  CIDR: 192.168.0.0/18
  IPs: 16,384
  AZ: us-west-2a
  Route: Internet Gateway
  Range: 192.168.0.0 - 192.168.63.255


Subnet-2:
  CIDR: 192.168.64.0/18
  IPs: 16,384
  AZ: us-west-2b
  Route: Internet Gateway
  Range: 192.168.64.0 - 192.168.127.255
```

Private subnets host EKS worker nodes, and require specific configurations for optimal cluster operation:

- **Private Subnets:**

```
Subnet-1:
  CIDR: 192.168.128.0/18
  IPs: 16,384
  AZ: us-west-2a
  Route: NAT Gateway
  Range: 192.168.128.0 - 192.168.191.255

Subnet-2:
  CIDR: 192.168.192.0/18
  IPs: 16,384
  AZ: us-west-2b
  Route: NAT Gateway
  Range: 192.168.192.0 - 192.168.255.255
```

# Security Group Design

Security groups form the foundation of network security in EKS. A comprehensive security group strategy includes multiple layers of protection.

# Cluster Security Group

The cluster security group controls communication between the control plane and worker nodes:

```
EKS Cluster Security Group:
  Inbound Rules:
    - Type: HTTPS (443)
```

```
    Source: Worker Node Security Group
    Description: Allow worker nodes to communicate with control plane

  - Type: Custom TCP (10250)
    Source: Worker Node Security Group
    Description: Allow kubelet communication

Outbound Rules:
  - Type: All Traffic
    Destination: 0.0.0.0/0
    Description: Allow all outbound traffic
```

- **Worker Node Security Group:** Worker nodes require specific security group rules for pod-to-pod and pod-to-service:

```
Worker Node Security Group:
Inbound Rules:
  - Type: All TCP
    Source: Self
    Description: Allow inter-node communication

  - Type: Custom TCP (1025-65535)
    Source: Cluster Security Group
    Description: Allow control plane communication

Outbound Rules:
  - Type: All Traffic
    Destination: 0.0.0.0/0
    Description: Allow all outbound traffic
```

# VPC Endpoints for EKS

VPC endpoints enable private communication with AWS services, enhancing security and reducing data transfer costs:

**Required Endpoints Configuration:**

```
Interface Endpoints:
 - com.amazonaws.region.eks:
   Security Group: endpoint-sg
   Subnets: private-subnet-1, private-subnet-2
   Private DNS: Enabled

 - com.amazonaws.region.ecr.api:
   Security Group: endpoint-sg
   Subnets: private-subnet-1, private-subnet-2
   Private DNS: Enabled

 - com.amazonaws.region.ecr.dkr:
```

```
        Security Group: endpoint-sg
        Subnets: private-subnet-1, private-subnet-2
        Private DNS: Enabled

    Gateway Endpoints:
      - com.amazonaws.region.s3:
        Route Tables: private-rt-1, private-rt-2
```

- **Implementation Example:**

```
# Create VPC Endpoint for EKS API
aws ec2 create-vpc-endpoint \
    --vpc-id vpc-0123456789abcdef0 \
    --vpc-endpoint-type Interface \
    --service-name com.amazonaws.us-west-2.eks \
    --subnet-ids subnet-0123456789abcdef0 subnet-0123456789abcdef1
\
    --security-group-ids sg-0123456789abcdef0 \
    --private-dns-enabled

# Create VPC Endpoint for ECR API
aws ec2 create-vpc-endpoint \
    --vpc-id vpc-0123456789abcdef0 \
    --vpc-endpoint-type Interface \
    --service-name com.amazonaws.us-west-2.ecr.api \
  --subnet-ids subnet-0123456789abcdef0 subnet-0123456789abcdef1 \
    --security-group-ids sg-0123456789abcdef0 \
    --private-dns-enabled
```

# Identity and Access Management

Identity and Access Management (IAM) plays a critical role in securing and operating an Amazon EKS environment. Defining clear IAM boundaries ensures that only authorized users and services can interact with cluster resources, reducing the risk of unauthorized access or misconfigurations. EKS leverages IAM for authenticating API requests, controlling access to node resources, and enabling integrations with AWS services. Before defining the specific IAM roles, it is important to understand the types of identities involved—such as users, roles, and service accounts—and how they map to Kubernetes RBAC within the cluster.

# IAM Role Requirements

EKS requires specific IAM roles for both the cluster and worker nodes. These roles must be properly configured to ensure secure cluster operations.

- **Cluster Service Role:** This role allows EKS to manage AWS resources on behalf of the cluster:

1. **Cluster Service Role:**

```
{
"Version": "2012-10-17",
"Statement": [
    {
        "Effect": "Allow",
        "Action": [
            "eks:*",
            "ec2:CreateTags",
            "ec2:DescribeInstances",
            "ec2:DescribeRouteTables",
            "ec2:DescribeSecurityGroups",
            "ec2:DescribeSubnets",
            "ec2:DescribeVpcs",
            "iam:GetRole",
            "iam:ListRoles"
        ],
        "Resource": "*"
    }
]
}
```

2. **Node Instance Role:**

```
{
  "Version": "2012-10-17",
  "Statement": [
    {
        "Effect": "Allow",
        "Action": [
            "ec2:DescribeInstances",
            "ec2:AttachVolume",
            "ec2:DetachVolume",
            "ecr:GetAuthorizationToken",
            "ecr:BatchCheckLayerAvailability",
            "ecr:GetDownloadUrlForLayer",
            "ecr:GetRepositoryPolicy",
            "ecr:DescribeRepositories",
            "ecr:ListImages",
            "ecr:BatchGetImage"
        ],
        "Resource": "*"
    }
  ]
}
```

# Service Account Configuration

Service accounts in EKS provide identity for pods, and enable fine-grained access control through IAM Roles for Service Accounts (IRSA).

OIDC Provider Setup: Before implementing service accounts, an OIDC provider must be configured for the cluster:

- **OIDC Provider Setup:**

```
# Extract OIDC provider URL
OIDC_URL=$(aws eks describe-cluster \
    --name production-eks \
    --query "cluster.identity.oidc.issuer" \
    --output text)

# Create OIDC provider
aws iam create-open-id-connect-provider \
    --url $OIDC_URL \
    --client-id-list sts.amazonaws.com \
    --thumbprint-list $(openssl s_client -servername oidc.eks.
us-west-2.amazonaws.com -showcerts -connect oidc.eks.us-west-2.
amazonaws.com:443 </dev/null 2>/dev/null | openssl x509 -finger-
print -sha1 -noout | cut -d= -f2)
```

- **Service Account Creation:**

```
# service-account.yaml
apiVersion: v1
kind: ServiceAccount
metadata:
  name: app-service-account
  namespace: production
  annotations:
    eks.amazonaws.com/role-arn: arn:aws:iam::111122223333:role/
app-role
    eks.amazonaws.com/audience: sts.amazonaws.com
    eks.amazonaws.com/token-expiration: "86400"

---
# corresponding IAM role trust policy
{
  "Version": "2012-10-17",
  "Statement": [
    {
      "Effect": "Allow",
      "Principal": {
        "Federated": "arn:aws:iam::111122223333:oidc-provider/
```

```
oidc.eks.us-west-2.amazonaws.com/id/EXAMPLED539D4633E53DE1B71EX-
AMPLE"
      },
      "Action": "sts:AssumeRoleWithWebIdentity",
      "Condition": {
        "StringEquals": {
          "oidc.eks.us-west-2.amazonaws.com/id/EXAMPLED-
539D4633E53DE1B71EXAMPLE:sub": "system:serviceaccount:produc-
tion:app-service-account"
        }
      }
    }
  ]
}
```

# RBAC Setup

Role-Based Access Control (RBAC) is essential for managing access to Kubernetes resources. A comprehensive RBAC strategy includes roles, cluster roles, and their bindings.

**Role Definition Examples:**

```
# Developer Role
apiVersion: rbac.authorization.k8s.io/v1
kind: Role
metadata:
  namespace: production
  name: developer-role
rules:
- apiGroups: ["", "apps"]
  resources: ["pods", "deployments"]
  verbs: ["get", "list", "watch", "create", "update", "patch"]
- apiGroups: [""]
  resources: ["configmaps", "secrets"]
  verbs: ["get", "list"]

---
# Operations Role
apiVersion: rbac.authorization.k8s.io/v1
kind: ClusterRole
metadata:
  name: ops-role
rules:
- apiGroups: [""]
  resources: ["nodes", "namespaces"]
  verbs: ["get", "list", "watch"]
```

```
- apiGroups: ["metrics.k8s.io"]
  resources: ["pods", "nodes"]
  verbs: ["get", "list", "watch"]
```

**Role Binding Implementation:**

```
# Developer RoleBinding
apiVersion: rbac.authorization.k8s.io/v1
kind: RoleBinding
metadata:
  name: dev-binding
  namespace: production
subjects:
- kind: Group
  name: development-team
  apiGroup: rbac.authorization.k8s.io
roleRef:
  kind: Role
  name: developer-role
  apiGroup: rbac.authorization.k8s.io

---
# Operations ClusterRoleBinding
apiVersion: rbac.authorization.k8s.io/v1
kind: ClusterRoleBinding
metadata:
  name: ops-binding
subjects:
- kind: Group
  name: operations-team
  apiGroup: rbac.authorization.k8s.io
roleRef:
  kind: ClusterRole
  name: ops-role
  apiGroup: rbac.authorization.k8s.io
```

**Common IAM and Networking Troubleshooting Scenarios:**

| Type | Problem Scenario | Symptom or Error Message | Troubleshooting Tip |
|---|---|---|---|
| IAM | Cluster role missing EKS permissions | AccessDeniedException, failed cluster or node creation. | Ensure that Amazon EKS Cluster Policy is attached to the EKS control plane IAM role. |

| IAM | IRSA not functioning | Pods cannot access AWS services ( for example, S3, STS, and so on). | Verify that OIDC provider is associated, and trust relationship references correct SA ARN. |
|---|---|---|---|
| IAM | Karpenter provisioning fails | Logs show IAM access denied errors. | Attach Karpenter-specific IAM policy with EC2 and pricing permissions. |
| Networking | Node group fails to join EKS | Nodes appear in EC2, but not in kubectl get nodes. | Check VPC subnet tagging, and ensure that nodes have access to cluster endpoint. |
| Networking | Pods cannot reach external services | Timeout errors or DNS resolution failures. | Confirm that NAT gateway is configured for private subnets, and security groups allow egress. |
| Networking | Load balancer not created for service | ELB not provisioned, Events show failure reason | Ensure that correct service type (LoadBalancer) and subnet/SG are used. |

***Table 2.1:*** *IAM and Networking Troubleshooting Matrix*

# EKS Cluster Creation and Configuration

With the network, IAM, and tooling foundations in place, the next step is to create and configure the Amazon EKS cluster itself. This involves provisioning the control plane, integrating required add-ons, and defining node group specifications. Amazon EKS supports multiple provisioning methods–ranging from CLI tools like eksctl to infrastructure-as-code solutions–allowing teams to choose the most suitable approach, based on their automation strategy and operational preferences. Selecting the right configuration method ensures that the cluster is provisioned consistently, and aligns with organizational security and scalability standards.

# Using `eksctl` for Cluster Creation

eksctl provides a streamlined approach to creating and managing EKS clusters. The following section details the complete cluster creation process. Amazon EKS typically supports Kubernetes versions up to three minor releases behind the latest upstream version. As of this writing, EKS supports Kubernetes 1.33 on standard support, and 1.26 on extended support. Developers should verify the current version support in the EKS documentation when planning production upgrades.

Comprehensive Cluster Configuration:

```
# production-cluster.yaml
apiVersion: eksctl.io/v1alpha5
kind: ClusterConfig
```

```yaml
metadata:
  name: production-eks
  region: us-west-2
  version: "1.28"
  tags:
    environment: production
    department: platform

vpc:
  id: vpc-0123456789abcdef0
  subnets:
    private:
      us-west-2a:
        id: subnet-0123456789abcdef0
        cidr: "10.0.16.0/20"
      us-west-2b:
        id: subnet-0123456789abcdef1
        cidr: "10.0.32.0/20"
    public:
      us-west-2a:
        id: subnet-0123456789abcdef2
        cidr: "10.0.0.0/24"
      us-west-2b:
        id: subnet-0123456789abcdef3
        cidr: "10.0.1.0/24"

nodeGroups:
  - name: managed-ng-1
    instanceType: m5.large
    desiredCapacity: 3
    minSize: 2
    maxSize: 6
    privateNetworking: true
    labels:
      role: application
    tags:
      k8s.io/cluster-autoscaler/enabled: "true"
    iam:
      withAddonPolicies:
        autoScaler: true
        albIngress: true
        cloudWatch: true

managedNodeGroups:
  - name: managed-ng-2
    instanceType: m5.xlarge
    desiredCapacity: 2
```

```
      minSize: 1
      maxSize: 4
      privateNetworking: true
      labels:
        role: monitoring
      taints:
        - key: dedicated
          value: monitoring
          effect: NoSchedule

addons:
  - name: vpc-cni
    version: latest
  - name: coredns
    version: latest
  - name: kube-proxy
    version: latest
```

# Manual Cluster Setup through Console

While eksctl provides automation, understanding the manual cluster creation process through the AWS Management Console is vital for comprehensive cluster management knowledge.

**Control Plane Configuration:** The following settings are crucial for production-grade EKS clusters:

**Cluster Configuration Details:**

Basic Settings:

```
    Cluster name: production-eks
    Kubernetes version: 1.28
    Cluster service role: eks-cluster-role

  Networking:
    VPC: Custom VPC (vpc-0123456789abcdef0)
    Subnets:
      - private-subnet-1 (us-west-2a)
      - private-subnet-2 (us-west-2b)
      - public-subnet-1 (us-west-2a)
      - public-subnet-2 (us-west-2b)
    Security groups: Auto-create new

  Security:
    Secrets encryption: Enabled with KMS
    Control plane logging:
      - API server
```

```
        - Audit
        - Authenticator
        - Controller manager
        - Scheduler
```

**Implementation Steps:**

1. VPC and Network Configuration

```
# Create security group for cluster
aws ec2 create-security-group \
    --group-name EKS-Cluster-SG \
    --description "EKS cluster security group" \
    --vpc-id vpc-0123456789abcdef0

# Configure security group rules
aws ec2 authorize-security-group-ingress \
    --group-id sg-0123456789abcdef0 \
    --protocol tcp \
    --port 443 \
    --cidr 10.0.0.0/16
```

# Node Group Configuration

Node groups require careful planning for optimal performance and resource utilization.

Here is a comprehensive node group configuration strategy:

**Managed Node Group Implementation:**

```
# Production node group configuration
apiVersion: eks.amazonaws.com/v1alpha1
kind: NodeGroup
metadata:
  name: prod-ng-1
spec:
  clusterName: production-eks
  nodeRole: arn:aws:iam::111122223333:role/EKS-NodeGroup-Role
  subnets:
    - subnet-0123456789abcdef0
    - subnet-0123456789abcdef1
  instanceTypes:
    - m5.large
  scaling:
    minSize: 2
    maxSize: 6
    desiredSize: 3
```

```
    labels:
      Environment: production
      Application: core
    taints:
      - key: dedicated
        value: production
        effect: NoSchedule
    launchTemplate:
      id: lt-0123456789abcdef0
      version: "1"
```

**Custom Launch Template:**

```
# Create launch template
aws ec2 create-launch-template \
--launch-template-name EKS-Production-LT \
--version-description Production \
--launch-template-data '{
    "ImageId": "ami-0123456789abcdef0",
    "InstanceType": "m5.large",
    "UserData": "BASE64_ENCODED_USER_DATA",
    "BlockDeviceMappings": [
        {
            "DeviceName": "/dev/xvda",
            "Ebs": {
                "VolumeSize": 100,
                "VolumeType": "gp3",
                "DeleteOnTermination": true,
                "Encrypted": true
            }
        }
    ],
    "MetadataOptions": {
        "HttpEndpoint": "enabled",
        "HttpTokens": "required",
        "HttpPutResponseHopLimit": 1
    }
}'
```

# Add-ons and Extensions

Essential add-ons enhance cluster functionality. Here is a detailed implementation guide:

1. **Core Add-ons Configuration:**

   Core Add-ons Installation:

```
  # VPC CNI Configuration
apiVersion: eks.amazonaws.com/v1alpha1
kind: Addon
metadata:
  name: vpc-cni
  namespace: kube-system
spec:
  addonVersion: v1.12.1-eksbuild.1
  configurationValues: |
    {
      "enableNetworkPolicy": "true",
      "warmIPTarget": "5",
      "minimumIPTarget": "10"
    }

# CoreDNS Configuration
apiVersion: eks.amazonaws.com/v1alpha1
kind: Addon
metadata:
  name: coredns
  namespace: kube-system
spec:
  addonVersion: v1.8.7-eksbuild.3
  configurationValues: |
    {
      "computeType": "Fargate",
      "replicaCount": 2
    }
```

2. **Additional Add-ons Configuration:**

```
  Recommended Add-ons:
- AWS Load Balancer Controller
- Cluster Autoscaler
- Metrics Server
- Container Insights
```

# Infrastructure as Code Implementation

Infrastructure as Code (IaC) enables the declarative, repeatable, and version-controlled provisioning of Amazon EKS environments. By defining infrastructure in code, teams can automate cluster creation, reduce manual errors, and enforce consistency across development, staging, and production environments. IaC also facilitates easier auditing, rollback, and collaboration among team members. Among the available IaC tools, Terraform is widely adopted for its cloud-agnostic design and robust AWS provider support, making it a reliable choice for provisioning and managing EKS clusters at scale.

# Terraform Configuration for EKS

Terraform provides a robust approach to EKS infrastructure management. When using Terraform to provision EKS resources, it is necessary to store the Terraform state file in a remote backend such as Amazon S3, rather than keeping it locally. The state file contains the current infrastructure configuration, and is used to track resource changes across runs.

Remote state enables collaboration and consistency, especially in team environments. Combined with DynamoDB-based state locking, it prevents concurrent terraform apply operations that could lead to resource conflicts or corruption.

Here is a comprehensive implementation:

```
# main.tf
provider "aws" {
  region = "us-west-2"
}

module "eks" {
  source          = "terraform-aws-modules/eks/aws"
  version         = "~> 19.0"
  cluster_name    = "production-eks"
  cluster_version = "1.28"

  vpc_id     = module.vpc.vpc_id
  subnet_ids = module.vpc.private_subnets

  cluster_endpoint_private_access = true
  cluster_endpoint_public_access  = true

  # Node group configuration
  eks_managed_node_groups = {
    general = {
      desired_size = 3
      min_size     = 2
      max_size     = 6

      instance_types = ["m5.large"]
      capacity_type  = "ON_DEMAND"

      labels = {
        Environment = "production"
        GithubRepo = "terraform-aws-eks"
```

```
          }

          taints = {
            dedicated = {
              key    = "dedicated"
              value  = "production"
              effect = "NO_SCHEDULE"
            }
          }

          update_config = {
            max_unavailable_percentage = 50
          }
        }
      }

      # Add-on configuration
      cluster_addons = {
        coredns = {
          resolve_conflicts = "OVERWRITE"
        }
        kube-proxy = {}
        vpc-cni = {
          resolve_conflicts = "OVERWRITE"
        }
      }

      # Authentication and RBAC
      manage_aws_auth_configmap = true
      aws_auth_roles = [
        {
          rolearn  = "arn:aws:iam::111122223333:role/Admin"
          username = "admin"
          groups   = ["system:masters"]
        }
      ]
    }
```

# CloudFormation Templates

### EKS Cluster CloudFormation Template:

```
AWSTemplateFormatVersion: '2010-09-09'
Description: 'Production EKS Cluster with associated resources'

Parameters:
  ClusterName:
```

```
    Type: String
    Default: production-eks
    Description: Name of the EKS cluster

  KubernetesVersion:
    Type: String
    Default: '1.28'
    Description: Kubernetes version for the cluster

Resources:
  EKSCluster:
    Type: AWS::EKS::Cluster
    Properties:
      Name: !Ref ClusterName
      Version: !Ref KubernetesVersion
      RoleArn: !GetAtt EKSClusterRole.Arn
      ResourcesVpcConfig:
        SecurityGroupIds:
          - !Ref ClusterSecurityGroup
        SubnetIds:
          - !Ref PrivateSubnet1
          - !Ref PrivateSubnet2
      EncryptionConfig:
        - Resources: ['secrets']
          Provider:
            KeyArn: !GetAtt KMSKey.Arn

  ManagedNodeGroup:
    Type: AWS::EKS::Nodegroup
    Properties:
      ClusterName: !Ref ClusterName
      NodegroupName: managed-ng-1
      ScalingConfig:
        MinSize: 2
        DesiredSize: 3
        MaxSize: 6
      InstanceTypes:
        - m5.large
      Subnets:
        - !Ref PrivateSubnet1
        - !Ref PrivateSubnet2
      Labels:
        Environment: production
      Tags:
        Owner: platform-team
        Cost-Center: platform-infrastructure
```

```
  KMSKey:
    Type: AWS::KMS::Key
    Properties:
      Description: KMS key for EKS cluster encryption
      EnableKeyRotation: true
      KeyPolicy:
        Version: '2012-10-17'
        Statement:
          - Sid: Enable IAM User Permissions
            Effect: Allow
            Principal:
              AWS: !Sub 'arn:aws:iam::${AWS::AccountId}:root'
            Action: 'kms:*'
            Resource: '*'
```

# State Management

**Managing Infrastructure State:**

1. Remote State Configuration:

```
# terraform/backend.tf
terraform {
  backend "s3" {
    bucket         = "terraform-state-eks-prod"
    key            = "production/terraform.tfstate"
    region         = "us-west-2"
    dynamodb_table = "terraform-locks"
    encrypt        - true
    kms_key_id     = "arn:aws:kms:us-west-
2:111122223333:key/1234abcd-12ab-34cd-56ef-1234567890ab"
  }
}
```

2. **State Lock Management:**

```
 # DynamoDB Lock Table
resource "aws_dynamodb_table" "terraform_locks" {
  name           = "terraform-locks"
  billing_mode   = "PAY_PER_REQUEST"
  hash_key       = "LockID"

  attribute {
    name = "LockID"
    type = "S"
  }

  point_in_time_recovery {
```

```
    enabled = true
  }

  server_side_encryption {
    enabled = true
  }

 tags = {
    Environment = "production"
    Purpose     = "terraform-state-locking"
  }
}
```

# Conclusion

This chapter provided a comprehensive walkthrough of setting up an Amazon EKS environment, covering every foundational aspect required for a production-ready Kubernetes deployment. The topics included prerequisite planning, installing essential tools such as the AWS CLI and eksctl, designing secure VPC architectures, configuring IAM roles and policies, and provisioning clusters, using both eksctl and Infrastructure as Code tools such as Terraform. Emphasis was placed on aligning with AWS best practices to ensure security, scalability, and automation from the outset. These building blocks are critical for establishing a stable platform on which run containerized applications.

In the next chapter, we shift our focus to Container Management and Docker Essentials, where readers will learn the fundamentals of container technology, how Docker works, and how to build, tag, push, and manage container images.

# Points to Remember

- Planning Before Provisioning: Thoughtful planning is essential to ensure region selection, subnet design, IAM boundaries, and resource scaling align with enterprise requirements.
- EKS Reference Architecture: Includes a VPC with private and public subnets, managed node groups across multiple AZs, NAT Gateways, OIDC integration, and VPC endpoints for secure AWS access.
- IAM and Authentication: IAM roles are required for the cluster (control plane) and worker nodes. IAM service roles and trust relationships are central to EKS operations.
- OIDC and IRSA: OIDC enables pod-level authentication to AWS services through IAM Roles for Service Accounts (IRSA).

- Networking Design: EKS requires a VPC with carefully planned CIDR blocks, subnet allocation across AZs, and properly configured NAT Gateways and route tables.
- Security Groups: Define cluster and worker node communication rules. Cluster SG permits kubelet and HTTPS; node SG permits inter-node communication and access to control plane.
- VPC Endpoints: Use Interface endpoints for eks, ecr.api, and ecr.dkr; use Gateway endpoint for s3 to keep traffic within AWS network boundaries.
- Cluster Provisioning: EKS can be created using eksctl, AWS Console, Terraform, or CloudFormation. Configuration should align with tagging, encryption, IAM, and node group sizing.
- Infrastructure as Code: Terraform with remote state in S3 and lock management via DynamoDB is a recommended practice for managing infrastructure collaboratively and safely.
- Add-ons: Core add-ons include vpc-cni, coredns, and kube-proxy. Recommended ones include AWS Load Balancer Controller and Cluster Autoscaler.
- Troubleshooting Common Issues: Includes IRSA misconfiguration, VPC subnet tagging errors, and load balancer provisioning failures due to service or security group misalignment.

# Multiple Choice Questions

1. In a production-grade EKS setup, worker nodes are typically placed in:
   a. Public subnets
   b. Edge locations
   c. Private subnets
   d. Transit Gateway
2. Which add-on is used for DNS resolution within an EKS cluster?
   a. kube-proxy
   b. Metrics Server
   c. CoreDNS
   d. vpc-cni

3. Which AWS service is used to encrypt EKS secrets?
    a. ACM
    b. AWS Vault
    c. AWS IAM
    d. AWS KMS

# Answers

1. c
2. c
3. d

# Key Terms

- **EKS (Elastic Kubernetes Service)**: AWS managed Elastic Kubernetes Service to run containerized applications
- **Eksctl:** Official CLI tool for creating and managing EKS clusters
- **Kubectl:** Command-line tool for interacting with Kubernetes clusters
- **VPC (Virtual Private Cloud):** Isolated network environment within AWS
- **CIDR (Classless Inter-Domain Routing):** IP addressing scheme for subnets
- **NAT Gateway:** AWS-managed service to allow outbound internet access from private subnets
- **CoreDNS:** DNS service within Kubernetes used for name resolution
- **vpc-cni**: EKS add-on for managing network interfaces and IPs for pods
- **AWS KMS (Key Management Service)**: AWS service for encrypting secrets and storage volumes
- **Terraform**: Infrastructure as Code tool used for declarative resource provisioning
- **CloudFormation**: AWS-native tool for infrastructure provisioning via templates
- **RBAC (Role-Based Access Control):** Kubernetes method for controlling user and group access to resources

# CHAPTER 3
# Container Management and Docker Essentials

## Introduction

Container technology represents a fundamental advancement in modern software deployment, revolutionizing how organizations build and deliver applications. This chapter presents a comprehensive examination of container management systems, focusing on Docker and its integration with Amazon Elastic Kubernetes Service (EKS).

This chapter systematically explores container management fundamentals, progressing from basic architectural principles to advanced deployment strategies. The key areas of focus include container optimization, security protocols, and integration with enterprise-grade registries. Through practical examples and technical insights, readers will develop the expertise necessary to implement and maintain robust container-based solutions in production environments.

This chapter serves as both an educational foundation and a technical reference, addressing the needs of practitioners responsible for container infrastructure and application deployment strategies. The content encompasses necessary aspects of modern containerization, from multi-stage builds to security best practices, providing readers with actionable knowledge for immediate implementation.

## Structure

In this chapter, we will discuss the following topics:

- Introduction to Containers and Docker
- Docker Fundamentals
- Writing Efficient Dockerfiles

- Multi-stage Builds
- Container Optimization Techniques
- Amazon Elastic Container Registry
- Container Security Scanning
- Container Orchestration Basics
- Image Management Strategies
- Production Considerations

# Introduction to Containers and Docker

Containers are lightweight, standalone, and executable packages that include everything needed to run a piece of software, including the code, runtime, system tools, libraries, and settings. They provide consistency across different development and release cycles, ensuring that applications work seamlessly, regardless of the environment.

Traditional virtualization approaches pale in comparison to containers' inherent advantages. Containers share the host system's OS kernel, making them remarkably efficient and lightweight. Their portability ensures that they can run on any system supporting the container runtime, while providing consistent environments from development to production. Each container operates in its own isolated environment, significantly enhancing security without compromising performance.

The evolution of containerization traces back to Unix-like operating systems, with concepts like chroot emerging in 1979. The 2000s saw the introduction of FreeBSD Jails and Solaris Zones, bringing more advanced isolation capabilities. Google's internal systems introduced Process Containers in 2006, later renamed to Control Groups. The landscape evolved further with LXC (Linux Containers) in 2008, providing a userspace interface for Linux Kernel containment features. Docker's release in 2013 marked a turning point, democratizing containerization, and making it accessible to a wider audience. From 2014 onwards, the rapid adoption of Docker catalyzed the emergence of container orchestration platforms such as Kubernetes.

Docker has established itself as the industry standard for containerization through its user-friendly approach and robust ecosystem. Its intuitive Command-Line Interface (CLI) and streamlined the workflow for building, sharing, and running containers have transformed the development landscape. Docker Hub serves as a centralized repository for sharing and distributing container images, while extensive documentation and community support ensure widespread adoption. The platform's seamless integration with popular DevOps tools and cloud platforms, coupled with its standardized container format, has secured its position as the preferred choice among major cloud providers and technology companies. This standardization has created a unified approach to containerization, enabling consistent deployment practices across diverse technological environments.

# Docker Fundamentals

Docker architecture follows a client-server model built around three core components. The Docker Client serves as the primary interface through which users interact with Docker via the CLI. The Docker Host represents the machine running the Docker daemon (dockerd), which handles the essential tasks of building, running, and distributing Docker containers. The Docker Registry functions as a repository for storing Docker images, with options ranging from the public Docker Hub to private registries such as Amazon ECR.

The typical workflow in this architecture begins with the client sending commands to the Docker daemon. When needed, the daemon pulls images from a registry if they are not available in the local cache. Following this, the daemon proceeds to create and run containers based on these images. This streamlined process ensures efficient container management and deployment, with each component playing a distinct role in the overall system architecture. The interaction between these components creates a robust and reliable platform for container operations, enabling seamless application deployment and management across various environments. The architectural layout and components of Docker are shown in *Figure* 3.1.

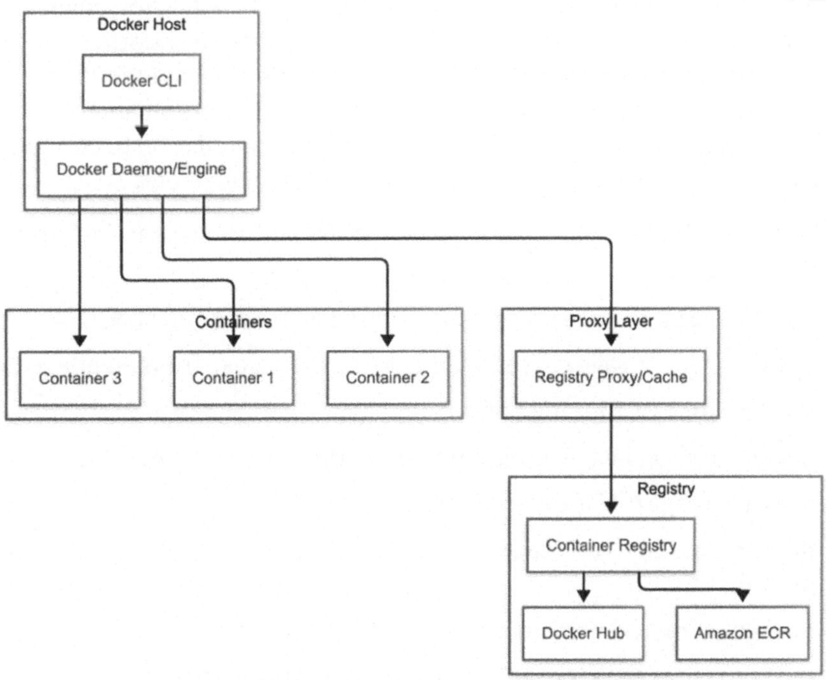


**Figure 3.1:** *Docker Architecture and Components*

## Installing Docker

To install Docker, follow these general steps (specific commands may vary by OS):

1. **For Ubuntu**:

   ```
   sudo apt-get update
   sudo apt-get install docker-ce docker-ce-cli containerd.io
   ```

2. **For macOS and Windows**: Download and install Docker Desktop from the official Docker website.

3. **Verify the installation**:

   ```
   docker --version
   docker run hello-world
   ```

## Basic Docker Commands

Getting started with Docker requires familiarity with several fundamental commands that form the foundation of container operations. The command line interface provides comprehensive control over container lifecycle management, from image creation to runtime operations. Users can execute these commands through any terminal interface connected to a Docker installation, enabling both local development and remote container management.

Through these commands, users can pull images from registries, manage container states, list available resources, and perform basic troubleshooting. Understanding these core commands is crucial for effective container management, and serves as a stepping stone to more advanced Docker operations. The command set encompasses all essential container operations, from basic image manipulation to container runtime control, providing a complete toolkit for container management.

Let us examine these salient Docker commands, and their practical applications in container management.

- **docker pull <image>**: Download an image from a registry.
- **docker run <image>**: Create and start a container from an image.
- **docker ps**: List running containers.
- **docker ps -a**: List all containers (including stopped ones).
- **docker images**: List the available images.
- **docker build -t <tag>**: Build an image from a Dockerfile in the current directory.
- **docker stop <container>**: Stop a running container.
- **docker rm <container>**: Remove a stopped container.
- **docker rmi <image>**: Remove an image.

## Docker Images and Containers

Docker images are read-only templates used to create containers. They contain:

- A base operating system
- Application code
- Dependencies
- Environment variables
- Other configuration files

Containers are runnable instances of images. The key points are:

- Multiple containers can be created from a single image.
- Containers add a writable layer on top of the image layers.
- Changes made in a running container are not reflected in the underlying image.
- Containers can be committed to create new images, and preserving changes.

## Writing Efficient Dockerfiles

A Dockerfile serves as the blueprint for building Docker images, using a structured syntax to define each step of the image creation process. A Dockerfile follows a straightforward syntax pattern, where each instruction defines a specific build step as shown below:

```
# Comment
INSTRUCTION arguments
```

The following instructions represent the most frequently used commands in Dockerfile construction.

- **`FROM`**: Specifies the base image.
- **`RUN`**: Executes commands in a new layer.
- **`COPY`** and **`ADD`**: Copy files from host to the container.
- **`WORKDIR`**: Sets the working directory for subsequent instructions.
- **`ENV`**: Sets environment variables.
- **`EXPOSE`**: Informs Docker that the container listens on specified network ports.
- **`CMD`**: Provides defaults for an executing container.

Some of the following best practices ensure efficient Docker image builds and optimal container performance:

- Use specific tags for base images, not the latest.

- Combine related commands in a single RUN instruction, using && to reduce layers.
- Use COPY instead of ADD, unless you need TAR extraction or remote URL support.
- Set the WORKDIR, instead of using cd commands.
- Use environment variables for version numbers and paths to make updates easier.

Selecting an appropriate base image is crucial for building efficient Docker images, as this foundational choice determines the overall security, size, and performance of your container.

Several key considerations guide the selection of appropriate base images for your containerized applications:

- **Official images:** Prefer official images from Docker Hub for security and regular updates.
- **Minimal images:** Use Alpine-based images or distroless images for smaller footprints.
- **Language-specific images:** Choose images tailored for your application's programming language.
- **Consider security:** Use images with minimal attack surface and regular security updates.

Here are practical examples of base image selections for common application types:

- For a Node.js application: **`node:14-alpine`**
- For a Python application: **`python:3.9-slim`**
- For a Java application: **`openjdk:11-jre-slim`**

Layer optimization in Docker images is necessary for achieving faster builds and smaller image sizes, accomplished through several key techniques:

1. **Combine multiple RUN commands:** To minimize image layers and improve build efficiency, multiple RUN commands should be consolidated into a single instruction as shown in the following example:

```
# Bad
RUN apt-get update
RUN apt-get install -y package1
RUN apt-get install -y package2

# Good
RUN apt-get update && \
    apt-get install -y \
```

```
        package1 \
        package2 \
    && rm -rf /var/lib/apt/lists/*
```

2. **Use multi-stage builds** (covered in detail in the upcoming section).

3. **Clean up unnecessary files in the same layer they are created:**

```
RUN wget https://example.com/big-file.tar.gz \
&& tar -xzf big-file.tar.gz \
&& make -C big-file \
&& rm -rf big-file big-file.tar.gz
```

4. To optimize Docker builds, use a **dockerignore** file to exclude the unnecessary files from the build context. Here is a typical configuration:

```
# Exclude version control files
.git
.gitignore
# Exclude node modules (for Node.js projects)
node_modules

# Exclude development and test files
*.test.js
*.spec.js
__tests__

# Exclude documentation
README.md
docs

# Exclude logs and temporary files
*.log
.tmp
```

Using .dockerignore files provides several key advantages in Docker build optimization and security management. By reducing the amount of data sent to the Docker daemon, builds complete more quickly and efficiently. The file prevents sensitive information from being inadvertently included in the image, enhancing security controls. Additionally, it ensures consistency by explicitly defining what should be included in the build context, maintaining predictable and reproducible builds across different environments. When combined with multi-stage builds, these optimizations become even more powerful, allowing developers to create minimal production images, while maintaining full development capabilities. The integration of dockerignore and multi-stage builds establishes a robust foundation for efficient and secure container development workflows.

# Understanding Multi-Stage Builds

Multi-stage builds represent a significant advancement in Docker image optimization, and have become an industry best practice for several compelling reasons. By separating the build environment from the runtime environment, they substantially reduce final image sizes, often by orders of magnitude. This approach effectively solves the traditional dilemma of balancing development dependencies with production efficiency. A typical Node.js application, for instance, might require build tools, development dependencies, and source code during compilation, but only needs the runtime and compiled assets in production. Through multi-stage builds, developers can include all the necessary build tools in an initial stage, and then copy only the essential artifacts to a clean, minimal production image. This technique not only results in significantly smaller images without unnecessary development dependencies but also enhances security by reducing the attack surface of production containers. Since build tools and development dependencies are excluded from the final image, potential vulnerabilities in these components do not affect the production environment.

Moreover, multi-stage builds simplify CI/CD pipelines by encapsulating the entire build process within the Dockerfile, ensuring consistency across different environments and reducing build script complexity. Using multiple FROM statements, each beginning a new stage of the build, developers can selectively copy artifacts between stages, while leaving behind unnecessary components. Although this approach requires careful planning and understanding of application dependencies, the resulting benefits in terms of image size, build performance, security, and maintainability make multi-stage builds a necessary tool in modern container development.

Multi stage build process is shown in *Figure* 3.2. The arrows between stages represent the copying of necessary artifacts, while discarding unnecessary build tools and dependencies.

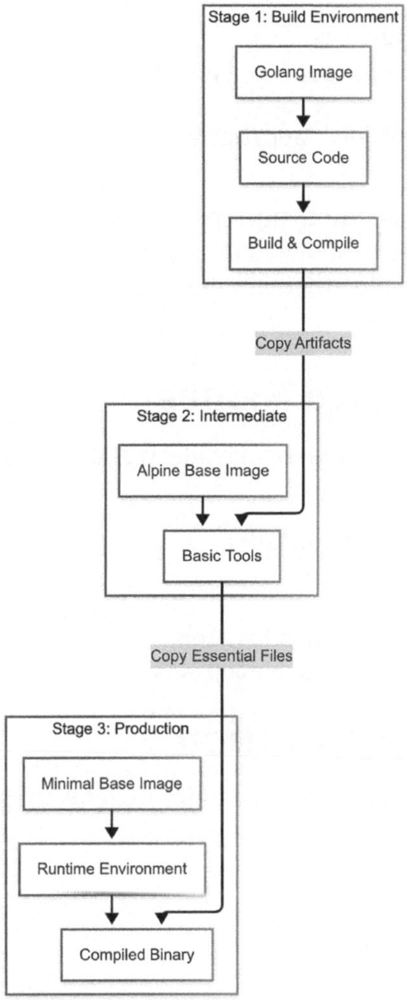


**Figure 3.2:** *Multi-stage Build*

The following example illustrates how to implement multi-stage builds for creating optimized Docker images. The build process demonstrates progressive optimization across three stages: First, utilizing the full Golang image for compilation, and then transitioning to a minimal Alpine base image, and finally copying only the essential compiled binary to create an efficient production container.

```
# Build stage
FROM golang:1.16 AS builder
WORKDIR /app
COPY . .
RUN CGO_ENABLED=0 GOOS=linux go build -a -installsuffix cgo -o main
.
```

```
# Final stage
FROM alpine:3.14
RUN apk --no-cache add ca-certificates
WORKDIR /root/
COPY --from=builder /app/main .
CMD ["./main"]
```

Thus, Multi-stage builds become more powerful when following the established best practices and patterns. The following examples demonstrate the key implementation strategies that enhance build efficiency, testing integration, and environment-specific optimization.

## Using Explicit Stage Names

Explicit stage naming improves Dockerfile readability and maintenance by clearly identifying each build phase:

```
FROM golang:1.16 AS builder
# ... build steps ...

FROM alpine:3.14 AS production
# ... production image setup ...
```

## Efficient Cache Utilization

Strategic ordering of build steps maximizes cache usage, reducing build times in iterative development:

```
FROM node:14 AS builder
WORKDIR /app
COPY package*.json ./
RUN npm install
COPY . .
RUN npm run build

FROM nginx:alpine AS production
COPY --from=builder /app/build /usr/share/nginx/html
```

## Integrated Testing Stages

Including testing stages ensures quality control within the build process:

```
FROM node:14 AS builder
# ... build steps ...

FROM builder AS tester
RUN npm run test
```

```
FROM nginx:alpine AS production
# ... production setup ...
```

## Environment-Specific Optimization

Creating distinct configurations for development and production environments enhances workflow efficiency:

```
FROM node:14 AS base
WORKDIR /app
COPY package*.json ./
RUN npm install
COPY . .

FROM base AS development
CMD ["npm", "run", "dev"]

FROM base AS builder
RUN npm run build

FROM nginx:alpine AS production
COPY --from=builder /app/build /usr/share/nginx/html
```

These patterns demonstrate how multi-stage builds can be structured to achieve optimal results across different development scenarios, while maintaining clean and efficient production images.

# Container Optimization Techniques

Container optimization techniques form the cornerstone of efficient Docker deployments, significantly impacting performance, resource utilization, and scalability. Through systematic refinement, these strategies enhance Docker container performance and efficiency, while maximizing resource usage, reducing consumption, and improving overall application performance in production environments.

## Reducing Image Size

Minimizing Docker image size requires a systematic approach across several key areas. Start by selecting minimal base images, such as Alpine Linux variants or distroless images for compiled languages. The vital dependencies should be managed efficiently, as demonstrated in this example:

```
RUN apt-get update && apt-get install -y \
    package1 \
    package2 \
 && rm -rf /var/lib/apt/lists/*
```

Layer optimization plays a crucial role through multi-stage builds, strategic use of .dockerignore files, and combining related commands. Clean-up operations should occur within the same layer as their corresponding installation or build steps:

```
RUN wget https://example.com/large-package.tar.gz \
 && tar -xzf large-package.tar.gz \
 && make -C large-package \
 && make clean \
 && rm large-package.tar.gz
```

These techniques work together to create compact, efficient images, while maintaining full functionality. By implementing these strategies consistently, organizations can significantly reduce storage requirements, and improve deployment performance across their container ecosystem.

# Improving Build Time

Docker build optimization relies on several key acceleration techniques. Effective cache utilization begins with strategically ordering Dockerfile instructions, placing less frequently changed components first and handling dependency files before source code. Build context optimization through .dockerignore and parallel processing via multi-stage builds significantly reduce build times.

BuildKit integration provides additional performance improvements through concurrent build capability:

```
DOCKER_BUILDKIT=1 docker build -t myimage .
```

For enhanced caching mechanisms, BuildKit's inline cache offers persistent build acceleration:

```
docker build --build-arg BUILDKIT_INLINE_CACHE=1 -t myimage .
```

These techniques, when implemented together, create a streamlined build process that significantly reduces development cycle times, while maintaining build consistency and reliability.

# Optimizing Runtime Performance

Container runtime performance optimization encompasses several critical strategies. Base image selection and focusing on Alpine or distroless options, establishes a minimal runtime footprint. Logging strategies should be tailored to infrastructure requirements, while avoiding excessive production logging. Application optimization includes removing unused libraries, and implementing production-specific builds.

Storage performance benefits from strategic volume management and tmpfs utilization for temporary data:

```
docker run --tmpfs /tmp:rw,noexec,nosuid,size=65536k myimage
```

Container reliability monitoring is enhanced through health check implementation:

```
HEALTHCHECK CMD curl --fail http://localhost:8080/health || exit 1
```

These optimizations collectively ensure efficient resource utilization, improved performance, and reliable container operations in production environments.

# Resource Management and Constraints

Resource management plays a vital role in container performance and stability. Memory constraints can be implemented through explicit limits:

```
docker run -m 512m myimage
```

CPU utilization control ensures fair resource distribution:

```
docker run --cpus=.5 myimage
```

Storage allocation maintains system stability through defined boundaries:

```
docker run --storage-opt size=10G myimage
```

Effective resource management extends beyond individual containers through cgroups utilization and orchestration strategies in multi-container environments. These controls, when properly implemented, ensure consistent performance and reliability across containerized applications.

# Introduction to Elastic Container Registry (ECR)

Amazon Elastic Container Registry (ECR) offers a comprehensive, fully-managed Docker container registry solution that simplifies the storage, management, and deployment of container images. The service integrates seamlessly with AWS IAM for granular access control, while ensuring data security through AWS KMS encryption for images at rest. ECR's automated lifecycle policies streamline image management, enabling efficient repository maintenance and cost optimization. Its native compatibility with Docker CLI, and various Docker-based tools ensure smooth integration into the existing development workflows, making it an ideal choice for organizations leveraging AWS infrastructure for container deployments.

Setting up Amazon ECR requires following initial configuration steps to establish secure repository access and authentication:

1. Install and configure the AWS CLI.

2. Create an ECR repository:

```
aws ecr create-repository --repository-name my-repo --region
us-west-2
```

3. Authenticate Docker to ECR:

```
aws ecr get-login-password --region us-west-2 | docker login
--username AWS --password-stdin 123456789
```

Working with ECR images requires proper tagging, pushing, and pulling commands to manage your container artifacts described as follows:

1. Tag your local image with the ECR repository URI:

```
docker tag myapp:latest 123456789.dkr.ecr.us-west-2.amazonaws.
com/my-repo:latest
```

2. Push the image to ECR:

```
docker push 123456789.dkr.ecr.us-west-2.amazonaws.com/my-
repo:latest
```

3. Pull images from ECR:

```
docker pull 123456789.dkr.ecr.us-west-2.amazonaws.com/my-
repo:latest
```

ECR lifecycle policies provide automated image management through JSON-based rules that define image retention criteria. These policies enable systematic cleanup of container images, based on parameters such as age, tag status, and count limits. For instance, a policy can be configured to expire untagged images after 30 days, while preserving tagged production images, thereby optimizing storage utilization, and maintaining repository organization through automated governance.

The following lifecycle policy example demonstrates automated image management in ECR, defining retention rules for optimizing repository storage:

```
{
  "rules": [
      {
          "rulePriority": 1,
          "description": "Keep last 30 days of images",
          "selection": {
              "tagStatus": "untagged",
              "countType": "sinceImagePushed",
              "countUnit": "days",
              "countNumber": 30
          },
          "action": {
              "type": "expire"
          }
```

```
            }
        ]
    }
```

## Container Security Scanning

Container security represents a critical consideration in modern application deployment environments. The shared nature of host OS kernels among containers introduces potential security implications that require careful management. Container images often incorporate various dependencies which may harbor vulnerabilities that can compromise application security. Additionally, misconfigurations in container settings or access controls can create security breaches that affect the entire systems. The rising prevalence of supply chain attacks further emphasizes the need for robust security measures, as compromised base images or dependencies can introduce vulnerabilities across multiple applications and environments. These factors collectively underscore the importance of implementing comprehensive security practices throughout the container lifecycle.

Container security scanning should be integrated at three critical stages: During pre-build analysis of source code and dependencies, after image creation but before deployment, and within CI/CD pipelines for automated security validation. Each stage provides unique security insights, and helps to prevent vulnerabilities from reaching production environments.

The following examples demonstrate the key integration points for security scanning throughout your container development pipeline, from pre-build checks to CI/CD automation:

1. **Pre-build scanning**:

   ```
   # Example using Trivy
   trivy fs --security-checks vuln,config ./
   ```

2. **Image scanning**:

   ```
   # Scan a Docker image
   trivy image myapp:latest
   ```

3. **CI/CD pipeline integration**: The following CI/CD configuration implements automated security gates through GitHub Actions. The workflow utilizes Trivy's official action to perform container vulnerability scanning, with specific parameters controlling scan behavior: '`format: table`' for readable output, '`exit-code: 1`' to fail unsafe builds, and severity filtering for **`HIGH`** and **`CRITICAL`** vulnerabilities. By ignoring unfixed vulnerabilities, the pipeline maintains efficiency, while ensuring detection of patchable security issues.

   ```
   # GitHub Actions example
   name: Security Scan
   ```

```
on: [push]
jobs:
  scan:
    runs-on: ubuntu-latest
    steps:
      - uses: actions/checkout@v2
      - name: Run Trivy vulnerability scanner
        uses: aquasecurity/trivy-action@master
        with:
          image-ref: 'myapp:latest'
          format: 'table'
          exit-code: '1'
          ignore-unfixed: true
          severity: 'CRITICAL,HIGH'
```

The following comparison outlines the key features and use cases for three leading container scanning solutions, helping teams make informed security tooling decisions:

| **Feature/Tool** | **Trivy** | **Clair** | **Amazon ECR Scanning** |
|---|---|---|---|
| Type | • Open-source vulnerability scanner | • Open-source project by CoreOS | Native AWS service |
| Key Strengths | • Easy integration<br>• Comprehensive vulnerability database<br>• Fast scanning speed | • Static analysis capabilities<br>• API-driven architecture<br>• Community-backed | • Native AWS integration<br>• SecurityHub integration<br>• Automatic scan triggers |
| Best For | • CI/CD pipelines<br>• Developer workflows<br>• Quick vulnerability checks | • Enterprise deployments<br>• Custom security workflows<br>• Large-scale scanning | • AWS-based deployments<br>• Automated security<br>• Integrated compliance |
| Integration | Command-line and CI tools | RESTful API | AWS services ecosystem |
| Automation | Built-in CI/CD support | API-based automation | Automatic on image push |

***Table 3.1:*** *Comparison of Container Scanning Tools*

Container security maintenance demands a comprehensive strategy encompassing scheduled scans, consistent updates, and a well-defined vulnerability management workflow. Following are some of the best practices that are employed for vulnerability management:

- **Regular scanning schedule:** By implementing automated, periodic scans, organizations can proactively identify and address security issues before they impact production systems. This practice typically involves configuring automated scanning tools like Trivy to run at scheduled intervals, as demonstrated in this cron job configuration:

  ```
  # Cron job for regular scanning
  0 0 * * * trivy image --light myapp:latest > /var/log/security
  -scan.log
  ```

  This automated approach ensures consistent security monitoring without manual intervention, enabling teams to detect newly discovered vulnerabilities in the existing images quickly. The scanning results can be logged and analyzed systematically, creating an audit trail of security checks, and facilitating prompt remediation of identified issues. Regular scanning becomes particularly crucial as new vulnerabilities are discovered and published, helping organizations maintain a strong security posture in their container environments.

- **Update base images regularly:** Regular base image updates serve as a critical security practice in container vulnerability management. By maintaining current base images and system packages, organizations significantly reduce their exposure to known vulnerabilities. This practice involves using specific version tags, rather than the **'latest'** and implementing systematic update procedures in Dockerfiles:

  ```
  # Use specific versions and update regularly
  FROM ubuntu:22.04
  RUN apt-get update && apt-get upgrade -y
  ```

  This approach ensures that containers are built with the most recent security patches while maintaining version control for consistency. Regular updates are particularly important for base images as they form the foundation of all derived containers. Establishing a routine update schedule, combined with proper testing procedures, helps prevent security gaps while ensuring application stability. Organizations should also monitor security advisories from base image providers and maintain a process for rapidly deploying critical security updates when necessary.

- **Implement a vulnerability management workflow:** A structured vulnerability management workflow creates a systematic approach to container security through a continuous cycle of detection, analysis, and remediation. This cyclical process follows five key stages:
  - **Scan**: Conduct comprehensive vulnerability scans of container images and dependencies.
  - **Assess**: Evaluate detected vulnerabilities for impact and exposure risks.

- `Prioritize`: Rank issues based on severity, exploitability, and business impact.
- `Fix`: Implement necessary patches, updates, or configuration changes.
- `Verify`: Confirm remediation effectiveness through follow-up scans.

```
graph LR
    A[Scan] --> B[Assess]
    B --> C[Prioritize]
    C --> D[Fix]
    D --> E[Verify]
    E --> A
```

This iterative workflow ensures continuous security improvement, while maintaining operational efficiency, enabling teams to address vulnerabilities systematically, and prevent security debt accumulation. Each stage informs the next, creating a comprehensive security maintenance process that adapts to the emerging threats and organizational needs.

# Container Orchestration Basics

Container orchestration represents a comprehensive approach to managing containerized applications at scale. It automates critical operational tasks across the application lifecycle, handling deployment strategies, dynamic scaling based on demand, and complex networking configurations. The orchestration layer manages load balancing to ensure optimal resource utilization, and implements service discovery mechanisms for seamless component communication. Additionally, it provides continuous health monitoring capabilities to maintain system reliability and performance.

In the current landscape, Kubernetes has emerged as the industry standard platform for container orchestration, particularly relevant when working with Amazon EKS which provides managed Kubernetes services. As this chapter focuses on Kubernetes, we will explore its architecture and capabilities in managing critical operational aspects, including automated deployments, dynamic scaling, and networking configurations. We will examine how Kubernetes handles service discovery and health monitoring, while emphasizing its integration with AWS services and EKS-specific features. This focused approach will help readers understand how Kubernetes orchestrates containers in production environments, especially within the AWS ecosystem.

This integration creates a robust, self-healing infrastructure that can efficiently manage containerized applications across distributed environments, while maintaining operational stability and scalability.

Kubernetes provides a powerful container orchestration platform built around several core concepts. At its foundation, Pods serve as the smallest deployable units, while

Services enable network connectivity between application components. Deployments manage application scaling and updates, with **ConfigMaps** and **Secrets** handling configuration and sensitive data management. Storage persistence is managed through Volumes, ensuring data availability across container lifecycles.

A typical Kubernetes deployment demonstrates these concepts in action:

```
apiVersion: apps/v1
kind: Deployment
metadata:
  name: myapp
spec:
  replicas: 3
  selector:
    matchLabels:
      app: myapp
  template:
    metadata:
      labels:
        app: myapp
    spec:
      containers:
      - name: myapp
        image: myapp:latest
        ports:
        - containerPort: 80
```

Amazon Elastic Kubernetes Service (EKS) elevates Kubernetes orchestration by providing a fully managed service with deep AWS integration. The managed control plane eliminates operational complexity by automatically handling the deployment, maintenance, and scaling of Kubernetes master nodes. This includes automated version updates, patch management, and high availability across multiple availability zones.

Auto-scaling in EKS operates at multiple levels. Through integration with AWS Auto Scaling Groups, EKS automatically adjusts worker node count based on demand, while the Kubernetes Cluster Autoscaler optimizes pod scheduling and resource utilization. The auto-scaling capabilities ensure efficient resource usage and cost optimization, while maintaining application performance.

Load balancing integrates natively with AWS Application Load Balancer (ALB) and Network Load Balancer (NLB), automatically provisioning and configuring load balancers for Kubernetes services. The AWS Load Balancer Controller manages this integration, simplifying the exposure of applications to external traffic, while maintaining high availability.

Security is enhanced through seamless IAM integration, allowing fine-grained access control using AWS IAM roles and policies. This extends to pod-level security through IAM roles for service accounts, enabling secure access to AWS services from within containers, while maintaining compliance with organizational security policies.

VPC networking in EKS provides advanced networking capabilities, including custom networking configurations, security groups, and VPC endpoints. This enables secure communication between pods and AWS services, while maintaining network isolation. The integration with AWS networking services ensures consistent security policies and network management across the entire infrastructure.

These features collectively create a robust, enterprise-grade Kubernetes platform that leverages AWS's infrastructure, while maintaining native Kubernetes compatibility, making it an ideal choice for organizations requiring scalable, secure, and managed container orchestration.

These EKS concepts and features will be thoroughly explored in the following chapters, where we will provide detailed architectural guidance, implementation strategies, and operational best practices for enterprise deployments.

# Image Management Strategies

Effective container image management forms the backbone of reliable container deployments, requiring well-defined strategies for versioning, tracking, and distribution. A systematic approach to image management ensures reproducibility, security, and efficient container lifecycle management across development as well as production environments.

The following are some of the components that form the foundation of a robust image management strategy, each playing a crucial role in maintaining secure and efficient container operations:

## Tagging Strategies

Image tagging strategies are essential for maintaining order and traceability in container deployments. Without a proper tagging system, organizations face challenges in version control, rollback capabilities, and deployment management. Effective tagging enables teams to track image history, identify specific builds, and maintain consistent deployments across different environments. For example, semantic versioning helps track major and minor releases, git-based tags provide direct correlation to source code, and environment-specific tags ensure proper image deployment across different stages of the development lifecycle:

```
# Semantic version tagging
docker tag myapp:latest myapp:1.0.0

# Git-based tagging
```

```
docker tag myapp:latest myapp:$(git rev-parse --short HEAD)

# Environment-based tagging
docker tag myapp:latest myapp:prod-v1.0.0
```

## Implementing CI/CD for Container Images

Continuous Integration and Continuous Delivery (CI/CD) pipelines automate the container image lifecycle, from building to deployment, ensuring consistency and reliability across environments. By automating these processes, organizations reduce manual errors, maintain quality standards, and accelerate deployment cycles, while enforcing security practices.

A typical CI/CD workflow for container images includes several critical stages:

- Source code checkout and validation
- Image building with proper tagging
- Security scanning and quality checks
- Registry authentication and image pushing
- Deployment trigger and verification

For example, this GitHub Actions workflow demonstrates these concepts:

```
name: Build and Push
on:
  push:
    branches: [ main ]
jobs:
  build:
    runs-on: ubuntu-latest
    steps:
    - uses: actions/checkout@v2
    - name: Build and push
      env:
        AWS_ACCESS_KEY_ID: ${{ secrets.AWS_ACCESS_KEY_ID }}
        AWS_SECRET_ACCESS_KEY: ${{ secrets.AWS_SECRET_ACCESS_KEY
}}
      run: |
  aws ecr get-login-password | docker login --username AWS
--password-stdin ${{
 secrets.ECR_REGISTRY }}
        docker build -t myapp .
        docker tag myapp:latest ${{ secrets.ECR_REGISTRY }}/
myapp:${{ github.sha }}
        docker push ${{ secrets.ECR_REGISTRY }}/myapp:
${{ github.sha }}
```

This automation ensures that container images are consistently built, properly tagged, and securely deployed to the appropriate registry, maintaining a reliable and efficient deployment pipeline.

# Production Considerations

Deploying containerized applications in production environments demands careful attention to operational stability, performance optimization, and resource management. Unlike development environments, production deployments must address critical concerns such as image availability, resource constraints, monitoring capabilities, and scaling requirements. This chapter explores the vital considerations that ensure reliable and efficient container operations in production settings.

Production environments require systematic approaches to image pull policies which affect deployment reliability and performance. Resource management becomes crucial for maintaining application stability and cost efficiency. Comprehensive monitoring and logging strategies provide necessary visibility into application health and performance. Additionally, implementing appropriate scaling mechanisms ensures applications remain responsive under varying workloads, while optimizing resource utilization.

The following sections examine these critical aspects of production container deployments, providing practical configurations and best practices for maintaining robust containerized applications in production environments. We will explore specific implementations that address common challenges, and ensure operational excellence in production deployments.

# Pull Policies and Their Impact

Image pull policies significantly affect container deployment behavior and system performance. Different policies serve various operational needs, while considering rate limiting and resource utilization:

The Always pull policy ensures containers consistently fetch the latest image version, regardless of local cache:

```
spec:
  containers:
  - name: myapp
    image: myapp:1.0.0
    imagePullPolicy: Always
```

The **`IfNotPresent`** policy optimizes deployment performance by using cached images when available:

```
spec:
  containers:
```

```
    - name: myapp
      image: myapp:1.0.0
      imagePullPolicy: IfNotPresent
```

Rate limiting must be monitored to prevent deployment disruptions, particularly in high-traffic environments:

```
aws ecr get-repository-policy --repository-name myapp \
    --query 'policyText' --output text
```

These policies work together with rate limiting considerations to ensure reliable and efficient image management in production environments.

# Container Resource Management in Production

Effective resource management is crucial for maintaining stable container performance and optimal resource utilization. Container resource management requires careful configuration of memory, CPU, and storage allocations to ensure optimal performance and stability. Each resource type demands specific consideration:

**Memory Configuration:** Memory limits and requests define the minimum and maximum memory available to containers:

```
spec:
  containers:
  - name: myapp
    resources:
      requests:
        memory: "64Mi"
      limits:
        memory: "128Mi"
```

**CPU Allocation:** CPU resources can be precisely controlled to balance performance and resource sharing:

```
spec:
  containers:
  - name: myapp
    resources:
      requests:
        cpu: "250m"
      limits:
        cpu: "500m"
```

**Storage Configuration:** Persistent storage ensures data durability through volume claims:

```
volumes:
- name: data-store
```

```
        persistentVolumeClaim:
          claimName: myapp-pvc
```

These configurations work together to create a balanced resource profile that maintains application performance, while ensuring efficient resource utilization.

## Monitoring and Logging for Containerized Applications

Modern containerized environments demand robust observability practices due to their inherently complex and distributed nature. Unlike traditional monolithic applications, containers introduce multiple layers of complexity through ephemeral instances, dynamic scaling, and intricate service dependencies, making traditional monitoring approaches insufficient. A comprehensive observability strategy, combining AWS native services (CloudWatch, X-Ray) with industry-standard tools (Prometheus, Grafana, ELK stack), becomes crucial for maintaining system health, troubleshooting issues, and ensuring optimal performance. This approach provides essential insights into system behavior, enables proactive problem detection, supports root cause analysis, and ensures compliance requirements are met. Furthermore, proper observability practices facilitate data-driven decision-making for scaling, optimization, and continuous improvement, directly impacting business operations and user experience. In production environments, where system reliability is paramount, this multi-faceted approach to observability becomes not just beneficial but vital for maintaining robust and reliable containerized applications.

## Scaling Strategies for Containerized Workloads

Effective scaling capabilities are fundamental to modern containerized applications, particularly in dynamic cloud environments like EKS. As application workloads fluctuate with varying user demands, proper scaling ensures optimal resource utilization, while maintaining performance and cost efficiency. EKS supports multiple scaling strategies: Horizontal Pod Autoscaling (HPA) adjusts the number of pod replicas based on metrics such as CPU and memory utilization, while Cluster Autoscaling automatically manages the underlying EC2 node capacity. Vertical Pod Autoscaling (VPA) optimizes resource requests, and limits by analyzing historical usage patterns.

The ecosystem has evolved with sophisticated tools like Karpenter, AWS's next-generation node provisioning solution, which provides faster and more efficient node scaling compared to traditional Cluster Autoscaler. Additionally, tools like Kubernetes Event-Driven Autoscaling (KEDA), enable scaling based on custom metrics and event sources, while Knative offers serverless-style autoscaling for containerized applications. These can be complemented with AWS Application Auto Scaling for comprehensive resource management. Some organizations also leverage Prometheus

Adapter with custom metrics for more granular scaling decisions, or Goldilocks for VPA recommendations.

In production environments, implementing the right combination of these scaling strategies and tools ensure that applications remain responsive under varying loads, while optimizing infrastructure costs through efficient resource allocation. The choice of scaling solution often depends on specific use cases, with many organizations adopting a hybrid approach that combines multiple tools to meet their unique requirements.

# Conclusion

This chapter has provided a comprehensive foundation in container management and Docker essentials, equipping readers with crucial knowledge for modern application deployment. We began with fundamental container concepts, understanding Docker's architecture and basic operations, before progressing to advanced topics like multi-stage builds and optimization techniques. The chapter emphasized practical implementations, from writing efficient Dockerfiles to implementing robust security practices, including image optimization, vulnerability management, and integration with Amazon ECR.

We explored container orchestration principles, production considerations, monitoring strategies, and resource management, establishing the building blocks for enterprise container deployments. As organizations continue to adopt containerized architectures, these fundamentals become increasingly critical for successful implementations. The integration of Docker with AWS services, particularly through Amazon ECR and EKS, demonstrates the powerful capabilities available for enterprise container deployments.

In the next chapter, we will dive deep into Amazon EKS cluster operations and management, exploring advanced topics such as cluster architecture, node group management, networking configurations, and operational procedures. This progression will build upon the container fundamentals covered here, moving into the practical aspects of managing production-grade Kubernetes clusters on AWS, ensuring that readers are well-prepared for real-world container orchestration challenges.

# Points to Remember

- Docker containers provide lightweight, portable application environments that include all necessary dependencies, making applications consistent across different environments, and easier to deploy.
- Multi-stage builds are crucial for optimizing Docker images, significantly reducing final image size by separating build-time dependencies from runtime requirements, and enhancing security through reduced attack surface.

- Container security requires a multi-layered approach, including regular vulnerability scanning, proper image management, and implementation of least privilege principles. Integration of security scanning in CI/CD pipelines ensures continuous security validation.
- Image management strategies, including proper tagging conventions and lifecycle policies, are necessary for maintaining organized and efficient container repositories. This becomes particularly important when working with Amazon ECR.
- Resource management in production environments requires careful consideration of memory, CPU, and storage allocations, along with appropriate scaling strategies to maintain application performance and cost efficiency.
- Container orchestration through Kubernetes and EKS provides automated deployment, scaling, and management of containerized applications, with EKS offering additional AWS-integrated capabilities for enhanced operational efficiency.
- Monitoring and observability in containerized environments require a comprehensive approach, combining AWS native services (CloudWatch, X-Ray, and so on) with industry-standard tools (Prometheus and Grafana) for complete operational visibility.
- Container optimization techniques, including proper base image selection, layer management, and build cache utilization, are fundamental for creating efficient and maintainable container images.

# Multiple Choice Questions

1. Which of the following best describes a container?
    a. A complete virtual machine with its own operating system.
    b. A lightweight, standalone package containing application code and dependencies.
    c. A backup system for application data.
    d. A virtual network interface for applications.
2. In a multi-stage Docker build, what is the primary benefit?
    a. Increased build speed
    b. Better network connectivity
    c. Reduced final image size by excluding build dependencies
    d. Improved application performance

3. What is the purpose of a .dockerignore file?
    a. To specify which containers to run
    b. To exclude files and directories from the build context
    c. To define container networking
    d. To configure Docker daemon settings
4. Which ECR feature helps manage image lifecycle and storage costs?
    a. Image scanning
    b. Lifecycle policies
    c. Tag mutability
    d. Cross-region replication
5. What is the recommended approach for container security scanning?
    a. Scan only in production
    b. Scan only before deployment
    c. Integrate scanning throughout the development pipeline
    d. Scan only third-party images
6. In Kubernetes, what is the smallest deployable unit?
    a. Container
    b. Pod
    c. Service
    d. Deployment
7. Which pull policy should be used when you want to ensure that the latest image is always used?
    a. `IfNotPresent`
    b. `Never`
    c. `Always`
    d. `Latest`

8. Which tool provides next-generation node provisioning for EKS clusters?
    a. Auto Scaling Groups
    b. Karpenter
    c. Kubernetes Scheduler
    d. Docker Swarm
9. When implementing container monitoring, which combination of tools is recommended?
    a. Only AWS CloudWatch
    b. Only Prometheus
    c. A combination of AWS native and open-source tools
    d. Only custom monitoring solutions
10. What is the primary purpose of container resource limits?
    a. To increase application performance
    b. To prevent containers from consuming excessive resources
    c. To reduce cloud costs
    d. To improve network connectivity

# Answers

1. b
2. c
3. b
4. b
5. c
6. b
7. c
8. b
9. c
10. b

# Key Terms

- **Container:** A lightweight, standalone package that includes everything needed to run an application, including code, runtime, system tools, libraries, and settings.
- **Docker Image:** A read-only template containing an application's code, runtime, libraries, dependencies, and configuration files used to create containers.
- **Dockerfile:** A text file containing a series of instructions and commands used to automatically build a Docker image.
- **Multi-stage Build:** A Docker build pattern that uses multiple stages to optimize the final container image by separating build-time dependencies from runtime requirements.
- **Elastic Container Registry (ECR):** A repository service for storing, managing, and deploying Docker container images, such as Amazon Elastic Container Registry.
- **Kubernetes (K8s):** An open-source platform designed to automate deploying, scaling, and managing containerized applications.
- **Pod:** The smallest and most basic deployable unit in Kubernetes that encapsulates one or more containers sharing storage and network resources.
- **Resource Management:** The practice of allocating and controlling compute resources (CPU, memory and storage) for containers to ensure optimal performance and stability.
- **Container Security:** The practice of protecting containers and their infrastructure through vulnerability scanning, access controls, and security policies.
- **Container Orchestration:** The automated configuration, coordination, and management of containerized applications and their lifecycle.

# CHAPTER 4
# Cluster Operations and Management

## Introduction

Throughout this chapter, we emphasize actionable best practices, advanced techniques, and proven strategies that can be implemented in both small-scale and enterprise-grade environments. Whether you are handling multi-tenant clusters, optimizing cost with Spot Instances, or configuring secure maintenance windows, the knowledge gained here will help ensure your clusters remain resilient, secure, and cost-efficient.

In today's fast-evolving IT landscape, Kubernetes has emerged as the gold standard for orchestrating containerized applications. Amazon EKS takes this a step further by providing a fully managed Kubernetes service that integrates seamlessly with AWS's rich ecosystem. However, operational excellence requires more than just spinning up clusters—it demands meticulous planning, real-time monitoring, and robust scaling mechanisms. This chapter is designed to address these critical needs by offering a step-by-step approach to the everyday challenges faced by EKS administrators.

Managing an Amazon EKS cluster involves continuous operational tasks that ensure the reliability, scalability, and security of workloads. This chapter delves into the practical aspects of running production-ready clusters, covering advanced node group management, autoscaling strategies, resource governance, monitoring, logging, and maintenance workflows. The goal is to equip you with the best practices, actionable steps, and troubleshooting techniques that align with operational excellence.

## Structure

In this chapter, we will explore the following key areas to build a holistic understanding of EKS cluster operations:

- Node Groups Management
- Cluster Autoscaling Strategies

- Resource Management Techniques
- Monitoring and Logging Basics
- Cluster Maintenance and Updates

# Node Groups Management

Node groups management constitutes a fundamental component of Amazon EKS cluster operations, ensuring the systematic provisioning, scaling, and maintenance of worker nodes that support Kubernetes workloads. Effective management encompasses selecting suitable EC2 instance types, configuring appropriate scaling parameters, and implementing robust health monitoring to maintain cluster stability. While managed node groups automate many lifecycle activities such as updates and fault recovery, self-managed node groups provide administrators with greater control over custom configurations, security policies, and deployment scripts.

Advanced node group management strategies often involve the integration of mixed instance types, leveraging both On-Demand and Spot Instances to balance cost efficiency and availability. Administrators are advised to employ multi-AZ deployment for enhanced fault tolerance, and to establish clear procedures for graceful node draining during scale-in events. Regular audits of IAM roles and proactive monitoring through CloudWatch metrics further contribute to a resilient and optimized environment. Mastery of node group management ensures that clusters are scalable, reliable, and capable of sustaining high-performance workloads under dynamic conditions.

# Understanding Node Groups

A thorough understanding of node group management extends beyond basic creation and configuration tasks; it requires insight into how node groups interact with Kubernetes scheduling, autoscaling mechanisms, and resource governance. This knowledge enables administrators to align node group configurations with workload characteristics, ensuring balanced resource utilization, and minimizing operational risks. Informed management decisions facilitate the continuous delivery of performant and cost-effective services within the Amazon EKS environment.

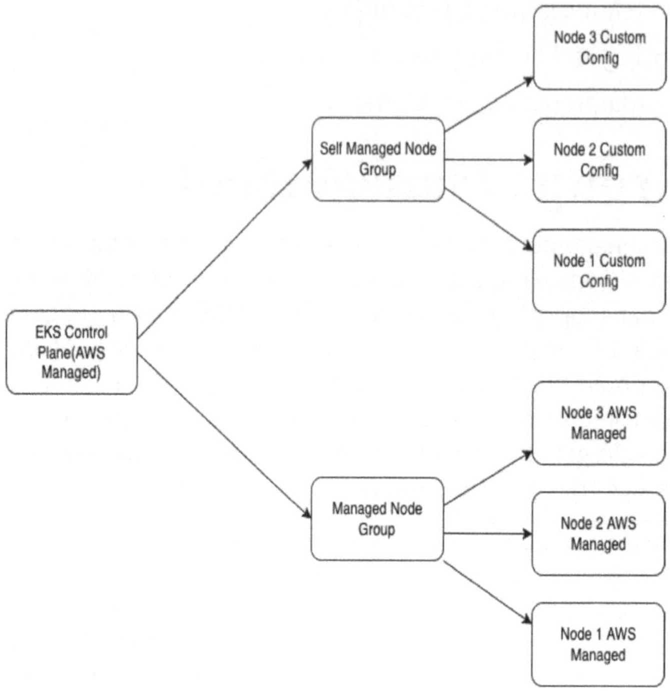


***Figure 4.1:*** *Reference Flowchart Comparison for Managed and Self-Managed Node Groups*

The following comparison outlines the key features of Managed and Self-Managed Node Groups:

| **Feature** | **Managed Node Groups** | **Self-Managed Node Groups** |
|---|---|---|
| Provisioning and Lifecycle | Fully managed by Amazon EKS; automates provisioning, updates, health checks, and node replacement. | User is responsible for provisioning, configuring, and maintaining node lifecycle manually. |
| Control and Customization | Limited customization ( For example, AMI selection, labels, taints via EKS-provided settings). | Full control over AMIs, bootstrap scripts, security groups, and other configurations. |
| Updates and Upgrades | Supports automated rolling updates and node draining during version upgrades. | Updates must be manually coordinated; requires scripting and careful rollout management. |
| Monitoring and Health Checks | Native integration with EKS for automated node health monitoring and auto-replacement. | Monitoring and health checks must be implemented and managed by the user. |

| Scaling | Integrated with Cluster Autoscaler; supports dynamic scaling policies out of the box. | Compatible with Cluster Autoscaler, but requires manual ASG and scaling policy setup. |
|---|---|---|
| IAM and Permissions | IAM roles are automatically created and managed with predefined policies for worker nodes. | IAM roles and associated policies must be manually created, attached, and maintained. |
| Availability Zones (AZ) Support | Automatically distributes nodes across multiple AZs in the cluster's region. | Distribution across AZs must be manually configured within the Auto Scaling Group. |
| Use Case Suitability | Recommended for most workloads seeking ease of management and operational simplicity. | Suitable for workloads requiring deep customization, specific AMIs, or legacy constraints. |
| Operational Overhead | Low operational burden due to AWS automation of most routine tasks. | Higher operational burden due to manual lifecycle and configuration management. |
| Cost Considerations | No additional EKS-specific charges beyond EC2 and other resource costs. | Same cost structure; however, manual management may incur additional operational effort. |

**Table 4.1:** *Comparison of Key Features between Managed and Self-Managed Node Groups in Amazon EKS*

# Creating Managed Node Groups

Managed Node Groups streamline the deployment and management of nodes. The following example shows how to create a managed node group using **`eksctl`**:

Command Example:

```
eksctl create nodegroup \
  --cluster my-cluster \
  --name managed-workers \
  --node-type t3.medium \
  --nodes 3 \
  --nodes-min 1 \
  --nodes-max 5 \
  --managed
```

# Mixed Instance Types

Using mixed instance types improves resiliency, and optimizes cost. By combining On-Demand and Spot Instances, clusters can maintain high availability even during

Spot interruptions. The following snippet demonstrates a YAML configuration for a mixed-instance node group.

**YAML Example:**

```
yaml
apiVersion: eksctl.io/v1alpha5
kind: ClusterConfig
metadata:
  name: my-cluster
  region: us-east-1
nodeGroups:
  - name: mixed-instances
    instanceTypes: ["t3.medium", "t3.large", "m5.large"]
    desiredCapacity: 4
    spot: true
```

# Scaling Node Groups

Scaling node groups is a critical operational task that ensures an Amazon EKS cluster can dynamically meet varying workload demands. By scaling nodes appropriately, the cluster maintains application availability and performance during traffic spikes and optimizes resource usage during periods of low demand. Scaling strategies can be broadly categorized into manual and automatic approaches.

**Manual Scaling** involves directly adjusting the number of nodes in a group using the AWS Management Console, the AWS CLI, or infrastructure-as-code tools like eksctl. This method is straightforward and useful for predictable workloads or temporary changes, such as scaling up for a planned batch job. However, manual scaling lacks responsiveness to real-time workload fluctuations, and can lead to inefficiencies or service disruptions, if not closely monitored.

**Manual Scaling Example**

```
eksctl scale nodegroup \
  --cluster my-cluster \
  --name managed-workers \
  --nodes 5
```

**Automatic Scaling** enables the cluster to respond dynamically to resource needs without manual intervention. The Kubernetes Cluster Autoscaler monitors unschedulable pods, and scales the node group by adding new instances when needed. It also downsizes the cluster by removing underutilized nodes to optimize costs. Karpenter, an alternative to the Cluster Autoscaler, provides advanced capabilities such as faster scaling decisions and the ability to provision nodes that precisely match pod requirements, further enhancing efficiency. Both tools integrate with Amazon EC2 Auto Scaling Groups to manage the underlying infrastructure seamlessly.

**Key Points:**

- Set reasonable min and max node counts to avoid over-provisioning.
- Regularly review CloudWatch metrics to fine-tune scaling parameters.

# Updating Node Groups

Node groups require updates to patch vulnerabilities, update Kubernetes versions, or upgrade instance types. Managed Node Groups support rolling updates, ensuring minimal disruption. To upgrade a node group, use:

```
eksctl upgrade nodegroup \
  --cluster my-cluster \
  --name managed-workers
```

To ensure smooth and reliable updates, node groups should be kept aligned with the Kubernetes control plane version to avoid compatibility issues. For managed node groups, rolling updates are recommended to minimize workload disruption, with adherence to Pod Disruption Budgets. Administrators should monitor each phase of the update lifecycle–setup, scaling, upgrading, and scale-down–to promptly detect and resolve issues. The eksctl tool offers a consistent and automated method for performing updates across both managed and self-managed node groups. In self-managed environments, adopting a blue/green deployment strategy enhances rollback capabilities and limits downtime. When using custom launch templates, updates must be applied cautiously to maintain configuration consistency. All updates should be tested in a staging environment prior to production rollout to validate stability and performance.

# Troubleshooting Node Group Issues

Efficient troubleshooting of node group issues is vital for maintaining the reliability and performance of Amazon EKS clusters. Node-related problems can arise due to misconfigurations, permissions errors, resource constraints, or underlying infrastructure failures. A systematic approach to diagnosing and resolving these issues minimizes service disruption, and ensures cluster stability.

Common node group issues include nodes failing to join the cluster, nodes becoming unresponsive, and pods remaining in a pending or failed state. In cases where nodes fail to register, administrators should verify that the worker node IAM role includes the required permissions, such as the **`AmazonEKSWorkerNodePolicy`**, AmazonEC2ContainerRegistryReadOnly, and **`AmazonEKS_CNI_Policy`**. Additionally, it is essential to confirm that the node's security groups allow necessary communication with the control plane endpoints.

For nodes that are registered but fail health checks, logs from the Kubelet and container runtime provide critical diagnostic insights. Tools such as kubectl describe node and kubectl get events can reveal issues related to resource pressure, taints, or networking problems. When pods are unschedulable, reviewing resource requests, taints, tolerations, and affinity settings can help identify conflicts preventing successful deployment. Furthermore, Auto Scaling Group (ASG) health status and Amazon CloudWatch metrics offer visibility into the underlying EC2 instances' performance and health.

To support proactive troubleshooting, it is advisable to establish monitoring and alerting mechanisms that track node health, capacity utilization, and scaling activity. Periodic audits of node group configurations, IAM roles, and security settings help prevent recurring issues, and maintain optimal cluster operation.

# Best Practices for Node Group Management

Effective node group management is necessary for optimizing performance, ensuring cost-efficiency, and maintaining high availability in Amazon EKS clusters. The following best practices provide actionable guidance for configuring, scaling, and monitoring node groups to support dynamic workloads reliably.

- **Distribute Nodes across Multiple Availability Zones (AZs):** Deploying worker nodes across multiple AZs enhances fault tolerance, and minimizes the impact of zonal failures. This distribution ensures that workloads remain available, even if an entire AZ experiences issue.
- **Utilize Mixed Instance Types:** Incorporating a variety of instance types within node groups can improve resiliency and cost-effectiveness. By combining On-Demand and Spot Instances, clusters can maintain high availability, while optimizing costs.
- **Implement Auto Scaling:** Leverage tools like the Kubernetes Cluster Autoscaler to automatically adjust the number of nodes in response to workload demands. This dynamic scaling ensures efficient resource utilization and application performance.
- **Regularly Update Node AMIs:** Keeping the Amazon Machine Images (AMIs) up to date is crucial for security and performance. Regular updates ensure that nodes have the latest patches and features.
- **Monitor Node Health:** Continuously monitor the health of nodes using tools like Amazon CloudWatch. Implementing health checks and automated remediation strategies can proactively address issues, and maintain cluster stability.
- **Adhere to the Principle of Least Privilege:** Assign minimal necessary permissions to IAM roles associated with node groups. This practice reduces the attack surface, and enhances the security posture of the cluster.
- **Plan for Node Group Upgrades:** Establish a strategy for upgrading node groups

to newer Kubernetes versions. This includes testing upgrades in staging environments, and ensuring compatibility with existing workloads.

- **Use Launch Templates for Customization:** Employ launch templates to define custom configurations for node groups, such as specifying AMIs, instance types, and user data scripts. This approach provides consistency, and simplifies management.
- **Implement Pod Disruption Budgets (PDBs):** Define PDBs to control the number of pods that can be disrupted during maintenance or scaling events. This ensures application availability during node group changes.
- **Optimize for Workload Characteristics:** Tailor node group configurations based on workload requirements. For instance, separate high-churn batch jobs from long-running services by assigning them to different node groups optimized for their specific needs.

# Cluster Autoscaling Strategies

Autoscaling is a cornerstone of cloud-native operations, allowing Amazon EKS clusters to elastically adapt to workload fluctuations without manual intervention. A robust autoscaling strategy typically integrates node-level scaling (infrastructure) and pod-level scaling (application layer), ensuring both resource availability and application responsiveness. By combining multiple autoscaling mechanisms– Cluster Autoscaler, Karpenter, HPA, and VPA–administrators can achieve a highly responsive and cost-efficient architecture.

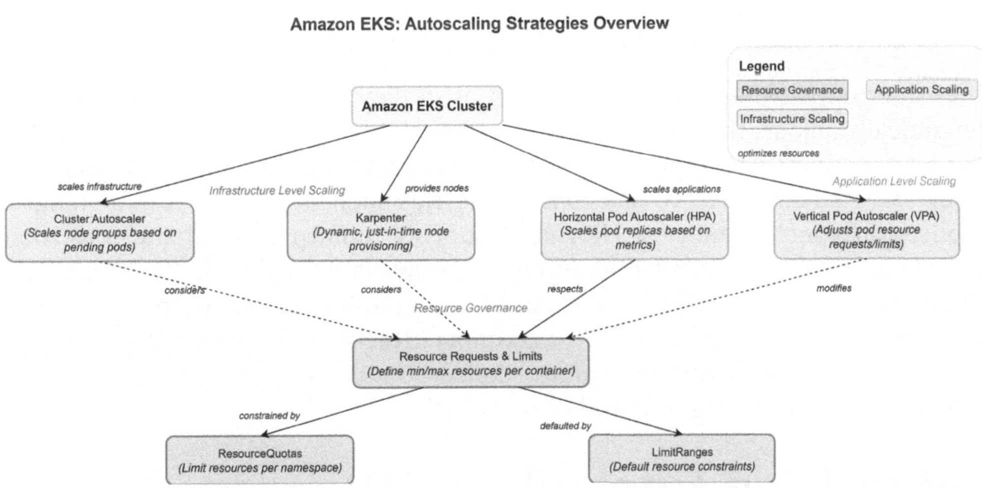


**Figure 4.2:** *Reference Flowchart for Autoscaling Strategies*

# Comparing Cluster Autoscaler and Karpenter

Although both Cluster Autoscaler and Karpenter address the same core objective of infrastructure autoscaling, they differ in operational design and flexibility. Cluster Autoscaler operates by interacting with the existing Auto Scaling Groups, making it well-suited for environments with predefined node groups. In contrast, Karpenter provisions nodes dynamically based on pending pod specifications, offering faster scaling and broader support for diverse instance types. Administrators should assess their workload patterns, cost optimization goals, and infrastructure constraints when selecting between these autoscaling tools–or consider running both in specialized scenarios.

## EKS Auto Mode

EKS Auto Mode is a simplified cluster provisioning experience designed to reduce operational burden by automating infrastructure setup, scaling, and management. It abstracts away traditional node group configurations, and uses Karpenter for dynamic resource provisioning, enabling compute to scale precisely with workload demand. Auto Mode clusters are optimized for multi-tenant workloads, and adhere to AWS best practices by default, including secure IAM configurations, minimal permissions, and integrated monitoring. Auto Mode also supports enhanced features such as Amazon VPC Lattice for service connectivity and Cloud Map for service discovery. This mode is best suited for teams looking to minimize infrastructure management effort, while maintaining flexibility and scalability. Developers can launch a fully functional EKS cluster with a single command

```
eksctl create cluster --auto-mode
```

# Horizontal Pod Autoscaler (HPA)

The Horizontal Pod Autoscaler (HPA) is a key Kubernetes component that dynamically adjusts the number of pod replicas in a deployment or replica set based on observed metrics. Commonly, it scales workloads based on CPU utilization, but it can also be configured to use custom metrics such as memory, queue length, or application-specific metrics. HPA continuously monitors workload performance and ensures that sufficient pod replicas are available to handle incoming traffic efficiently. It is particularly well-suited for stateless applications and services with fluctuating load patterns. To maximize effectiveness, administrators should set realistic minimum and maximum replica bounds, and ensure that the metrics server is properly configured and operational.

# Vertical Pod Autoscaler (VPA)

The Vertical Pod Autoscaler (VPA) complements HPA by focusing on optimizing resource allocations–specifically, CPU and memory requests and limits–for individual pods. VPA observes the historical and current resource usage of pods and makes recommendations or automatically adjusts these settings to align with actual workload demands. This dynamic adjustment helps prevent over-provisioning or under-provisioning, leading to better resource efficiency and cost savings. VPA is best suited for workloads with unpredictable or evolving resource requirements, such as data processing jobs or machine learning applications. It is important to note that automatic application of VPA updates can trigger pod restarts, which may affect availability; therefore, careful configuration of update policies is recommended.

# Setting Up Cluster Autoscaler

The Cluster Autoscaler automatically adjusts the size of the cluster by adding or removing nodes based on pending pods. To install it on your EKS cluster, follow these steps:

**Apply Cluster Autoscaler Deployment**

```
kubectl apply -f https://github.com/kubernetes/autoscaler/releas-
es/download/cluster-autoscaler.yaml
```

**Annotate the Cluster Autoscaler for Safe Eviction**

```
kubectl annotate deployment cluster-autoscaler \
  -n kube-system \
  cluster-autoscaler.kubernetes.io/safe-to-evict=false
```

# Configuring Karpenter

Karpenter is an advanced autoscaler designed for rapid provisioning, and efficient resource usage. Unlike the Cluster Autoscaler, Karpenter directly interacts with the Kubernetes scheduler to make real-time decisions.

**Key Advantages of Karpenter**

- Supports a wider range of instance types dynamically.
- Faster response to scaling events.
- Simplifies node provisioning with minimal configuration.

**Installation Example**

```
helm repo add karpenter https://charts.karpenter.sh
helm install karpenter karpenter/karpenter \
  --namespace karpenter \
  --set serviceAccount.annotations.'eks\.amazonaws\.com/
role-arn'=arn:aws:iam::<ACCOUNT_ID>:role/KarpenterRole
```

# Horizontal Pod Autoscaler (HPA)

The HPA adjusts the number of pod replicas based on observed CPU utilization or custom metrics. It is essential for managing application load dynamically.

### YAML Example for HPA

```
yaml
apiVersion: autoscaling/v2
kind: HorizontalPodAutoscaler
metadata:
  name: webapp-hpa
spec:
  scaleTargetRef:
    apiVersion: apps/v1
    kind: Deployment
    name: webapp
  minReplicas: 2
  maxReplicas: 10
  metrics:
  - type: Resource
    resource:
      name: cpu
      target:
        type: Utilization
        averageUtilization: 60
```

# Vertical Pod Autoscaler (VPA)

The Vertical Pod Autoscaler (VPA) adjusts resource requests, and limits for pods automatically. Unlike the HPA, which scales the number of pods, VPA focuses on optimizing the CPU and memory allocations for individual pods.

### Installation Example

```
kubectl apply -f https://github.com/kubernetes/autoscaler/releas-
es/latest/download/vertical-pod-autoscaler.yaml
```

### Sample VPA Configuration

```
yaml
apiVersion: autoscaling.k8s.io/v1
kind: VerticalPodAutoscaler
metadata:
  name: backend-vpa
spec:
  targetRef:
    apiVersion: apps/v1
    kind: Deployment
    name: backend
  updatePolicy:
    updateMode: Auto
```

# Best Practices for Autoscaling

- **Implement Horizontal Pod Autoscaler (HPA):** Utilize HPA to automatically adjust the number of pod replicas, based on observed CPU utilization or other select metrics. This enables applications to scale out during increased demand, and scale in when demand decreases, maintaining efficient resource usage.
- **Leverage Cluster Autoscaler:** Deploy the Kubernetes Cluster Autoscaler to automatically adjust the number of nodes in a cluster. It adds nodes when pods fail to schedule due to insufficient resources, and removes underutilized nodes, thereby optimizing infrastructure costs.
- **Adopt Karpenter for Node Provisioning:** Consider using Karpenter, an open-source autoscaling solution that provisions nodes, based on pending pod requirements. It offers rapid scaling, and supports a wide range of instance types, enhancing flexibility and efficiency.
- **Define Resource Requests and Limits**: Clearly specify resource requests, and limits for each container to inform the scheduler of the minimum and maximum resources required. This practice ensures appropriate scaling decisions, and prevents resource contention.
- **Distribute Workloads across Availability Zones**: Spread applications across multiple Availability Zones to enhance fault tolerance and availability. This distribution ensures that the failure of a single zone does not impact the entire application.
- **Monitor and Adjust Scaling Parameters**: Continuously monitor application performance, and adjust scaling parameters as necessary. Utilize Amazon CloudWatch and other monitoring tools to gain insights into resource utilization and scaling activities.
- **Avoid Scaling Churn**: Implement cool down periods and appropriate thresholds to prevent rapid scaling in and out, which can lead to instability and increased costs. This approach ensures that scaling actions are deliberate, and based on sustained demand.
- **Utilize Predictive Scaling**: Employ predictive scaling to forecast future traffic patterns and scale resources proactively. This technique helps maintain application performance during anticipated demand spikes.
- **Integrate with Application Load Balancers**: Ensure that autoscaling groups are integrated with load balancers to distribute traffic evenly across instances, enhancing application responsiveness and reliability.
- **Regularly Review and Test Scaling Policies**: Periodically assess scaling policies, and test their effectiveness under various load conditions. This practice ensures that the autoscaling configuration aligns with the current application requirements and performance goals.

# Resource Management Techniques

Resource management is a foundational pillar of Kubernetes operations, enabling clusters to maintain stability, fairness, and efficiency in multi-tenant environments. By defining explicit resource requests and limits, administrators ensure that workloads are allocated appropriate CPU and memory resources, preventing resource starvation and promoting optimal scheduling. Kubernetes provides a suite of native tools–such as ResourceQuotas and LimitRanges–that allow fine-grained control over resource consumption at the namespace level, helping to enforce governance and operational discipline.

# How Kubernetes Uses Resource Requests and Limits

The Kubernetes scheduler relies on resource requests to make scheduling decisions, ensuring that a pod is only placed on a node with sufficient available capacity to meet its minimum requirements. Limits, on the other hand, define the upper boundary of resource consumption; if a pod exceeds its defined limit, the system may throttle its CPU or terminate it in case of memory overuse. Defining these parameters carefully ensures that no single workload can monopolize resources to the detriment of others, and it provides predictable performance across the cluster.

# Resource Requests and Limits

Resource requests and limits define how much CPU and memory a pod can consume:

**Requests:** Guaranteed minimum resources a pod will have.

**Limits:** The maximum resources a pod can use.

**Example Configuration:**

```
 yaml
apiVersion: v1
kind: Pod
metadata:
  name: app-pod
spec:
  containers:
  - name: app-container
    image: my-app:latest
    resources:
      requests:
        memory: "256Mi"
        cpu: "250m"
```

```
      limits:
        memory: "512Mi"
        cpu: "500m"
```

# Importance of Setting Resource Requests and Limits

Defining resource requests and limits is essential for maintaining cluster stability, fairness, and efficiency. Resource requests inform the Kubernetes scheduler of the minimum CPU and memory required for a pod to function properly, ensuring that the pod is only scheduled on nodes with sufficient available resources. Limits establish the maximum amount of resources a pod can consume, preventing individual workloads from monopolizing cluster capacity. This mechanism helps avoid common issues such as resource contention, Out-Of-Memory (OOM) errors, and unpredictable performance degradation. By enforcing these parameters consistently across workloads, administrators can achieve balanced resource utilization, improve scheduling accuracy, and enhance the overall reliability of the Kubernetes environment.

# Resource Quotas

Resource quotas allow administrators to limit resource consumption across namespaces. They help enforce fair usage policies, and prevent any single tenant from monopolizing resources in a shared cluster environment.

**Sample `ResourceQuota` Definition**

```
 yaml
apiVersion: v1
kind: ResourceQuota
metadata:
  name: namespace-quota
spec:
  hard:
    pods: "20"
    requests.cpu: "10"
    requests.memory: 32Gi
    limits.cpu: "20"
    limits.memory: 64Gi
```

# Limit Ranges

Limit Ranges are used to define default resource requests and limits for pods and containers within a namespace. They help ensure that new pods have sensible defaults, even if developers do not specify resource constraints.

**Example `LimitRange`**

```
 yaml
apiVersion: v1
kind: LimitRange
metadata:
  name: default-limits
spec:
  limits:
  - default:
      cpu: 500m
      memory: 512Mi
    defaultRequest:
      cpu: 200m
      memory: 256Mi
    type: Container
```

# Best Practices for Resource Management

Effective resource management in Kubernetes is crucial for ensuring fair distribution, and maintaining workload stability. The following best practices outline how to configure limits, quotas, and autoscaling to optimize resource usage in Amazon EKS environments:

- **Define Resource Requests and Limits:** Specify resource requests and limits for each container to inform the Kubernetes scheduler of the minimum and maximum resources required. This practice ensures appropriate scheduling decisions, and prevents resource contention.
- **Implement Namespace-Level Resource Quotas:** Utilize Kubernetes **`ResourceQuota`** objects to limit the aggregate resource consumption within a namespace. This approach helps prevent any single team or application from monopolizing cluster resources.
- **Use LimitRanges for Default Constraints:** Apply LimitRange objects to set default resource requests, and limits for containers in a namespace. This ensures that all workloads have defined resource constraints, promoting fair resource distribution.
- **Leverage Vertical Pod Autoscaler (VPA):** Employ VPA to automatically adjust resource requests and limits for pods, based on historical usage patterns. This dynamic adjustment helps maintain optimal resource allocation over time.
- **Monitor Resource Utilization:** Continuously monitor resource usage using tools like Amazon CloudWatch Container Insights. Regular monitoring aids in identifying underutilized or overutilized resources, enabling timely adjustments.
- **Optimize Node Selection:** Choose appropriate EC2 instance types for worker

nodes, based on workload requirements. Consider using a mix of On-Demand and Spot Instances to balance cost and availability.

- **Distribute Workloads across Availability Zones:** Deploy worker nodes and schedule pods across multiple Availability Zones to enhance fault tolerance and availability. This distribution mitigates the impact of zonal failures.
- **Implement Topology Spread Constraints:** Use topology spread constraints to evenly distribute pods across different nodes and zones, preventing resource hotspots, and ensuring balanced utilization.
- **Regularly Review and Adjust Resource Allocations:** Periodically, assess resource allocations, and adjust them based on changing workload demands. This proactive approach ensures that resources are neither over-provisioned nor under-provisioned.
- **Employ Infrastructure as Code (IaC):** Manage resource configurations using IaC tools such as AWS CloudFormation or Terraform. This practice promotes consistency, repeatability, and easier auditing of resource changes.
- **Define Resource Requests and Limits:** Specify resource requests and limits for each container to inform the Kubernetes scheduler of the minimum and maximum resources required. This practice ensures appropriate scheduling decisions, and prevents resource contention.
- **Implement Namespace-Level Resource Quotas:** Utilize Kubernetes `ResourceQuota` objects to limit the aggregate resource consumption within a namespace. This approach helps prevent any single team or application from monopolizing cluster resources.
- **Use LimitRanges for Default Constraints:** Apply LimitRange objects to set default resource requests and limits for containers in a namespace. This ensures that all workloads have defined resource constraints, promoting fair resource distribution.
- **Leverage Vertical Pod Autoscaler (VPA):** Employ VPA to automatically adjust resource requests and limits for pods, based on historical usage patterns. This dynamic adjustment helps maintain optimal resource allocation over time.
- **Monitor Resource Utilization:** Continuously monitor resource usage, using tools like Amazon CloudWatch Container Insights. Regular monitoring aids in identifying underutilized or overutilized resources, enabling timely adjustments.
- **Optimize Node Selection:** Choose appropriate EC2 instance types for worker nodes, based on workload requirements. Consider using a mix of On-Demand and Spot Instances to balance cost and availability.
- **Distribute Workloads across Availability Zones:** Deploy worker nodes and schedule pods across multiple Availability Zones to enhance fault tolerance and availability. This distribution mitigates the impact of zonal failures.

- **Implement Topology Spread Constraints:** Use topology spread constraints to evenly distribute pods across different nodes and zones, preventing resource hotspots, and ensuring balanced utilization.
- **Regularly Review and Adjust Resource Allocations:** Periodically, assess resource allocations, and adjust them based on changing workload demands. This proactive approach ensures that resources are neither over-provisioned nor under-provisioned.
- **Employ Infrastructure as Code (IaC):** Manage resource configurations using IaC tools like AWS CloudFormation or Terraform. This practice promotes consistency, repeatability, and easier auditing of resource changes.

# Monitoring and Logging Basics

Observability is a critical component of Kubernetes operations, offering visibility into the performance and health of both the cluster infrastructure and application workloads. Effective monitoring and logging empower administrators to detect anomalies early, troubleshoot failures efficiently, and optimize resource usage proactively. In Amazon EKS, combining native AWS tools with open-source solutions provides a robust and flexible observability framework that supports both operational needs and compliance requirements.

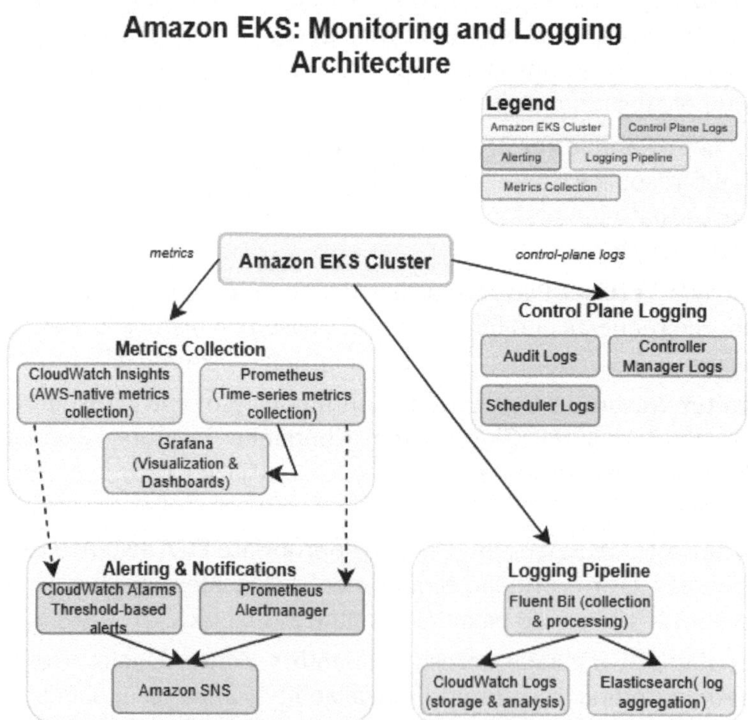


**Figure 4.3:** *Reference Flowchart for Monitoring and Logging Architecture*

# Understanding Metrics vs. Logs

Metrics and logs serve complementary roles in observability. Metrics are numerical data points that represent the state of a system over time—for example, CPU utilization or memory usage—enabling trend analysis and threshold-based alerting. Logs, on the other hand, capture detailed event data, including error messages, application outputs, and system diagnostics. While metrics provide a high-level overview of system health, logs deliver granular insights needed for root cause analysis. A well-architected monitoring system leverages both data types to achieve full operational visibility.

# CloudWatch Metrics and Logs

Amazon CloudWatch provides seamless integration with Amazon EKS, enabling administrators to collect, store, and analyze both infrastructure and application-level metrics and logs. By activating Container Insights, CloudWatch automatically gathers performance data such as CPU, memory, disk I/O, and network usage from nodes, pods, and containers within the cluster. This centralized observability facilitates proactive monitoring, capacity planning, and troubleshooting. To enable Container Insights for EKS, use the following command:

```
curl https://raw.githubusercontent.com/aws-samples/amazon-cloud-
watch-container-insights/latest/k8s-deployment.yaml | kubectl
apply -f -
```

# Prometheus and Grafana

Prometheus is an open-source monitoring and alerting toolkit that is widely adopted for Kubernetes environments due to its robust support for time-series data collection. In an Amazon EKS cluster, Prometheus scrapes metrics from Kubernetes components, nodes, and application workloads, storing them in an efficient time-series database. Grafana serves as a visualization layer, enabling the creation of detailed dashboards, and facilitating real-time monitoring of cluster health and application performance.

**Installation Example**

```
kubectl create namespace monitoring
helm install prometheus prometheus-community/prometheus -n
monitoring
helm install grafana grafana/grafana -n monitoring
```

# Fluent Bit Logging Pipeline

Fluent Bit is a lightweight, high-performance log processor and forwarder designed for cloud-native environments. In Amazon EKS, Fluent Bit operates as a DaemonSet, running an instance on each node to collect logs from Kubernetes pods, system components, and the underlying infrastructure. These logs are then parsed, filtered, and forwarded to external destinations such as Amazon CloudWatch Logs, Elasticsearch, or third-party logging systems, providing centralized visibility and long-term retention.

**Installation Example**

```
kubectl apply -f https://raw.githubusercontent.com/fluent/
bit-kubernetes-logging/master/fluent-bit-service-account.yaml
kubectl apply -f https://raw.githubusercontent.com/fluent/
bit-kubernetes-logging/master/fluent-bit-configmap.yaml
kubectl apply -f https://raw.githubusercontent.com/fluent/
bit-kubernetes-logging/master/fluent-bit-daemonset.yaml
```

# Setting Up Alerts and Dashboards

To maintain proactive monitoring, setting up alerts and visual dashboards is essential. Grafana enables the configuration of alert rules on top of Prometheus metrics, offering flexibility in defining custom alerting logic. Additionally, Grafana supports direct integration with Amazon CloudWatch, allowing users to visualize CloudWatch metrics, and configure alerts within a single monitoring platform. CloudWatch Alarms continues to provide native AWS integration for infrastructure-level alerting.

**CloudWatch Alarm Example**

```
aws cloudwatch put-metric-alarm \
  --alarm-name HighCPUUsage \
  --metric-name CPUUtilization \
  --namespace AWS/EKS \
  --statistic Average \
  --period 300 \
  --threshold 80 \
  --comparison-operator GreaterThanThreshold \
  --evaluation-periods 2 \
  --alarm-actions <SNS_TOPIC_ARN>
```

# Best Practices for Monitoring and Logging Basics

- **Centralize Observability Data:** Aggregate metrics, logs, and traces in a unified platform to facilitate comprehensive analysis.
- **Automate Alerting and Responses:** Implement automated alerts and remediation actions to promptly address issues.

- **Regularly Review and Tune Configurations:** Continuously assess and adjust monitoring configurations to align with the evolving system architectures and requirements.

# Cluster Maintenance and Updates

Regular maintenance is essential to sustain the performance, security, and reliability of Amazon EKS clusters over time. Kubernetes environments are dynamic by nature, with frequent updates to address vulnerabilities, improve features, and optimize performance. Effective maintenance includes applying Kubernetes version upgrades, patching operating system vulnerabilities, rotating secrets, and continuously monitoring system health. A well-planned maintenance strategy minimizes downtime, reduces operational risks, and ensures compliance with organizational and regulatory requirements.

# Upgrading Kubernetes Versions

Amazon EKS regularly releases new Kubernetes versions that include enhanced features, security patches, and bug fixes. Keeping clusters updated is necessary to maintain compatibility, security, and performance. A systematic upgrade strategy reduces the risk of downtime, or service disruption.

To upgrade safely:

- Review the EKS release notes for the target Kubernetes version to understand changes, deprecations, and compatibility considerations.
- Test the upgrade process in a staging or non production environment to validate workloads and third-party integrations.
- Plan upgrades during predefined maintenance windows to minimize impact on end users.

**Upgrade Command Example**

```
eksctl upgrade cluster \
  --name my-cluster \
  --region us-east-1 \
  --version 1.27
```

This command upgrades the control plane to Kubernetes version 1.27. Managed Node Groups must be upgraded separately after the control plane upgrade is complete.

- **Understand the Kubernetes Version Lifecycle:** Amazon EKS supports each Kubernetes minor version for 14 months of standard support, followed by 12 months of extended support. It is crucial to plan and execute upgrades within this timeframe to avoid unexpected auto-upgrades, and ensure continued support.

- **Leverage Cluster Insights before Upgrades:** Before initiating a Kubernetes version upgrade, utilize Amazon EKS Cluster Insights to identify and address potential issues that could impact the upgrade process. This proactive approach ensures smoother transitions, and minimizes disruptions.
- **Review Kubernetes Change Logs and Deprecation Notices:** Thoroughly review the Kubernetes change logs and deprecation notices to understand any possible impacts on your cluster, such as breaking changes that may affect your workloads.
- **Assess Cluster Add-Ons Compatibility:** Amazon EKS does not automatically update add-ons when new versions are released or after you update your cluster to a new Kubernetes minor version. Review the compatibility of the existing cluster add-ons with the target cluster version, and update them accordingly.
- **Enable Control Plane Logging:** Enable control plane logging to capture logs, errors, or issues that can arise during the upgrade process. Review these logs for any anomalies to ensure a smooth upgrade.
- **Test Upgrades in Non-Production Environments:** Before applying upgrades to production clusters, test them in staging or development environments. This helps to identify potential issues, and ensures that your applications remain compatible with the new Kubernetes version.
- **Use eksctl for Managing Upgrades:** Consider using eksctl to manage your EKS cluster. It provides the ability to update the control plane, manage add-ons, and handle worker node updates efficiently.
- **Utilize kubectl Convert Plugin:** Leverage the kubectl convert plugin to facilitate the conversion of Kubernetes manifest files between different API versions. This ensures that your configurations remain compatible with the new Kubernetes version.
- **Regularly Review and Update Cluster Add-Ons:** Ensure that cluster add-ons such as the Amazon VPC CNI plugin, CoreDNS, and kube-proxy are kept up to date. Regular updates help maintain compatibility, and leverage performance improvements.
- **Implement Health Checks and Monitoring:** Continuously monitor the health of your cluster components and workloads. Utilize tools such as Amazon CloudWatch and AWS CloudTrail to detect anomalies, and respond promptly to issues.
- **Document and Automate Maintenance Procedures:** Maintain clear documentation of maintenance procedures, and consider automating routine

tasks using Infrastructure as Code (IaC) tools. Automation reduces the risk of human errors, and enhances consistency across environments.

# Backup and Disaster Recovery

Ensuring data resilience and business continuity in Amazon Elastic Kubernetes Service (EKS) necessitates robust backup and Disaster Recovery (DR) strategies. This section outlines methodologies for safeguarding both cluster state and application data, leveraging tools such as Velero and Amazon Elastic File System (EFS) replication.

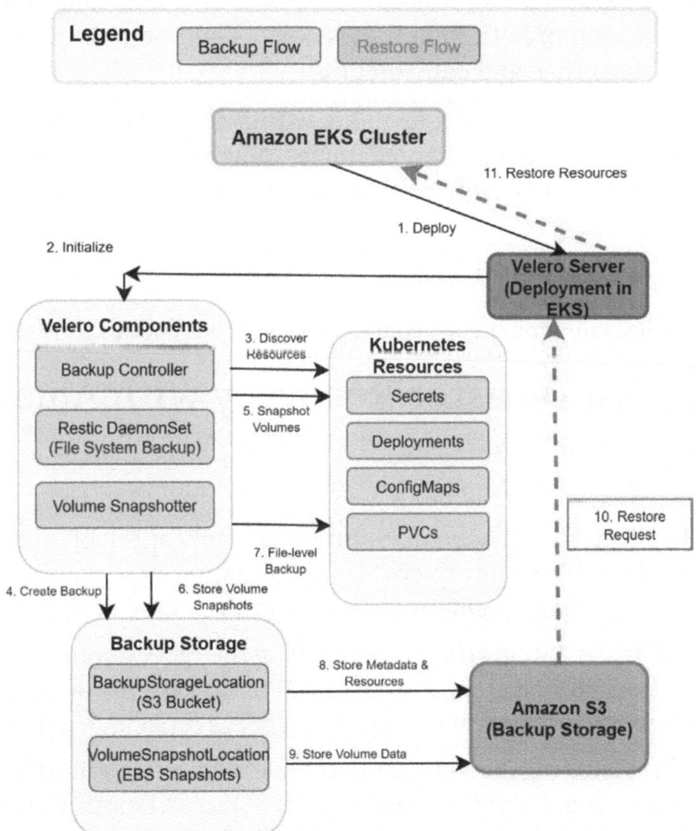


**Figure 4.4:** *Reference Flowchart for Velero and EKS Backup Workflow*

# Cluster State and Persistent Volume Backups with Velero

Velero is an open-source tool designed for backing up and restoring Kubernetes cluster resources and persistent volumes. It integrates seamlessly with Amazon EKS, enabling users to:

- **Backup Kubernetes Objects:** Velero captures the state of Kubernetes resources (for example, Deployments, Services, ConfigMaps and so on) by interfacing with the Kubernetes API server. This approach allows for selective backups based on namespaces, labels, or resource types.
- **Backup Persistent Volumes:** For data stored in persistent volumes, Velero supports snapshotting of Amazon Elastic Block Store (EBS) volumes. Additionally, it utilizes Restic to perform file-level backups, accommodating scenarios where volume snapshotting is not feasible.
- **Restore Operations:** In the event of data loss or cluster failure, Velero facilitates the restoration of both Kubernetes objects and persistent volumes, ensuring minimal downtime and data integrity.

Implementing Velero involves deploying it within the EKS cluster, and configuring appropriate storage backends (for example, Amazon S3 for backups). Regularly, scheduled backups and periodic restoration tests are recommended to validate the DR strategy.

**Example Backup Command (Velero):**

```
velero backup create my-backup --include-namespaces app-namespace
```

# Multi-Region Disaster Recovery with Amazon EFS

For stateful applications requiring high availability across regions, Amazon EFS offers a solution through its native replication capabilities:

- **EFS Replication:** Amazon EFS supports replication of file systems across AWS Regions. This feature enables the creation of a standby environment in a secondary region, facilitating rapid failover in case of regional disruptions.
- **EFS CSI Driver Integration:** By employing the EFS Container Storage Interface (CSI) driver, EKS clusters can mount EFS file systems as persistent volumes. This integration allows applications to access replicated data seamlessly.
- **Static Provisioning Considerations:** While EFS replication effectively duplicates file system data, it does not replicate EFS Access Points. Consequently, in the DR region, access points must be manually configured, and persistent volumes statically provisioned to match the primary region's setup.

This multi-region approach aligns with AWS's "Pilot Light" and "Warm Standby" DR strategies, offering a balance between cost and recovery time objectives.

# Security Operations

Security operations are fundamental to maintaining the integrity, confidentiality, and availability of workloads running in Amazon EKS. Kubernetes clusters are dynamic environments where misconfigurations or stale credentials can expose vulnerabilities. A disciplined approach to security operations ensures that access controls remain tight, sensitive data is protected, and compliance requirements are met.

**Key Security Tasks:**

- **Secret Rotation:** Regular rotation of Kubernetes Secrets and AWS IAM credentials reduces the risk of unauthorized access due to credential leakage or compromise. Best practice involves automating secret rotation, using tools such as AWS Secrets Manager, in conjunction with Kubernetes External Secrets or other secret syncing mechanisms.
- **Audit Logging:** Enabling Kubernetes audit logs provides a detailed record of all API requests, including the identity of the requester, the action taken, and the resource targeted. This is critical for forensic analysis, compliance audits, and detecting suspicious activity.
- **RBAC Review:** Periodic review of Role-Based Access Control (RBAC) policies ensures that permissions are tightly scoped, and adhere to the principle of least privilege. Overly broad permissions are a common source of security risks in Kubernetes environments.

**Enabling Audit Logs Example:** Audit logs can be enabled via the EKS Console or using eksctl after cluster creation. The following command enables audit logging for an existing cluster:

````
```
eksctl utils update-cluster-logging \
  --cluster my-cluster \
  --enable-types audit \
  --region us-east-1
```
````

# Conclusion

This chapter has provided a deep dive into the operational aspects of managing Amazon EKS clusters, covering everything from node group management and autoscaling to resource governance, observability, maintenance, and security operations. Through example and guidance, readers have gained insight into building scalable, resilient, and secure Kubernetes environments on AWS. Mastering these operational tasks is critical for maintaining performance, controlling costs, and ensuring business continuity in dynamic production settings. By adopting the best practices–such as balancing Spot and On-Demand Instances, implementing layered autoscaling strategies, and enforcing strict security policies–administrators can achieve operational excellence. Additionally, the integration of robust monitoring, logging, and disaster recovery mechanisms ensure that clusters remain healthy and responsive to evolving workload demands. As Kubernetes and EKS continue to evolve, maintaining a proactive, well-architected operational approach will remain pivotal for long-term success. This chapter equips you with the foundational skills and strategic mindset required to confidently manage EKS clusters in modern cloud-native environments. In the next chapter, you will have a comprehensive understanding of EKS networking concepts and the practical knowledge to implement production-grade networking configurations for your Kubernetes workloads on AWS.

# Points to Remember

- Use a combination of On-Demand and Spot Instances across multiple Availability Zones to optimize cost, and enhance node group resiliency, leveraging Managed Node Groups for simplicity or Self-Managed Node Groups for advanced customization.
- Implement robust autoscaling by combining Cluster Autoscaler, Karpenter, HPA, and VPA, ensuring that parameters are fine-tuned to balance responsiveness with resource efficiency.
- Maintain cluster stability by defining resource requests and limits for all workloads, enforcing governance with `ResourceQuotas` and LimitRanges, and utilizing the Vertical Pod Autoscaler for dynamic resource adjustments.
- Establish full-stack observability by integrating CloudWatch, Prometheus, Grafana, and Fluent Bit, and routinely review alerting rules as well as dashboards to maintain effective monitoring.
- Execute Kubernetes upgrades and maintenance tasks in staging environments before production, using rolling updates, blue/green deployments, and validated Velero backups to minimize disruption, and ensure recovery readiness.
- Enforce strong security operations by rotating Kubernetes Secrets and AWS IAM credentials regularly, enabling audit logs for compliance, and reviewing RBAC policies to uphold the least privilege principles.

# Multiple Choice Questions

1. Which of the following is NOT a valid autoscaling method in EKS?

   a. Cluster Autoscaler

   b. Horizontal Pod Autoscaler

   c. Vertical Pod Autoscaler
   d. Static Pod Scheduler
2. What is the primary purpose of a `ResourceQuota`?
   a. To assign IAM roles
   b. To limit resource consumption in a namespace
   c. To upgrade Kubernetes versions
   d. To monitor application logs
3. In an Amazon EKS observability setup, which tool is typically used for log forwarding?
   a. Karpenter
   b. Prometheus
   c. Fluent Bit
   d. CloudTrail

## Answers

1. d
2. b
3. b

# Key Terms

- **Node Group:** A collection of EC2 instances (nodes) within an EKS cluster that provide compute resources for running pods.
- **Managed Node Group:** An AWS-managed group of nodes where EKS automates provisioning, updates, and lifecycle management.
- **Self-Managed Node Group:** A user-managed group of nodes that offers more control, but requires manual handling of updates and scaling.
- **Mixed Instance Types:** A strategy where different EC2 instance types (for example, Spot and On-Demand) are combined within a node group for cost optimization and resilience.
- **Cluster Autoscaler:** A Kubernetes component that automatically adjusts the number of nodes in a cluster based on pending pod demands.

- **Karpenter:** An advanced autoscaler that provisions nodes dynamically in real-time, offering faster scaling, and more efficient resource utilization.
- **Horizontal Pod Autoscaler (HPA):** Automatically, scales the number of pod replicas in response to observed CPU, memory, or custom metrics.
- **Vertical Pod Autoscaler (VPA):** Automatically adjusts CPU and memory resource requests, and limits for running pods to optimize performance.
- **Resource Requests and Limits:** Kubernetes settings that define the minimum (requests) and maximum (limits) CPU as well as memory a container can use.
- **`ResourceQuota`:** A Kubernetes resource that restricts the total amount of resources (CPU, memory, pods, and so on), a namespace can consume.
- **LimitRange:** A Kubernetes object that sets default, and the maximum resource requests/limits for pods and containers within a namespace.
- **Fluent Bit:** A lightweight log processor and forwarder that collects, processes, and routes Kubernetes logs to destinations like CloudWatch or Elasticsearch.
- **CloudWatch:** AWS's native observability service that collects metrics, logs, and events from EKS clusters, and other AWS resources.
- **Maintenance Window**: A scheduled period during which maintenance tasks (for example, upgrades, patches, and so on) are performed to minimize service disruption.

This completes *Chapter 4, Cluster Operations and Management*, providing a comprehensive guide to day-to-day EKS cluster operations and management. By mastering these concepts and techniques, you are well-equipped to maintain highly available, secure, and scalable Kubernetes clusters in production environments.

# CHAPTER 5
# Networking in EKS

## Introduction

Networking is the cornerstone of any Kubernetes deployment, and Amazon Elastic Kubernetes Service (EKS) brings its own unique approach to container networking by seamlessly integrating with AWS's robust networking infrastructure. This chapter explores the intricate world of EKS networking, where container orchestration meets cloud-native networking capabilities.

In modern microservices architectures, understanding how pods communicate, how services are discovered, and how traffic is routed is crucial for building resilient and scalable applications. EKS leverages AWS's Virtual Private Cloud (VPC) infrastructure through its VPC CNI plugin, providing native integration with AWS networking services, while maintaining Kubernetes networking principles.

**Consider a typical scenario:** Your team has successfully deployed a microservices application on EKS, but now faces challenges with cross-pod communication, service discovery, and external access patterns. How do you ensure secure communication between services? How do you optimize network performance for production workloads? How do you implement proper ingress controls and load balancing? This chapter answers these questions and much more.

We will dive deep into the AWS VPC CNI plugin, exploring how it enables pod networking by integrating directly with Amazon VPC networking. You will learn about implementing service mesh patterns, using AWS App Mesh for advanced traffic management, and observability. We will cover load balancing strategies, using both Application Load Balancers (ALB) and Network Load Balancers (NLB) as well as discuss network security through policies and security groups. Additionally, we shall explore service discovery mechanisms for robust microservices communication.

Thus, by the end of this chapter, you will have a comprehensive understanding of EKS networking concepts and practical knowledge to implement production-grade networking configurations for your Kubernetes workloads on AWS. You will be well-equipped to tackle complex networking challenges, optimize performance, and ensure secure and efficient communication within your EKS clusters.

So, let us begin our journey into the networking foundations that power EKS clusters and the applications they host, unraveling the complexities, and empowering you to architect robust, scalable, and secure Kubernetes networks on AWS.

# Structure

In this chapter, we will discuss the following topics:

- Introduction to EKS Networking
- AWS VPC CNI Implementation
- Service Mesh with AWS App Mesh
- Load Balancing in EKS
- Network Policies and Security
- Service Discovery
- Advanced Networking Topics

# Introduction to EKS Networking

Kubernetes networking follows several fundamental principles that form the basis for container communication. At its core, every Pod in a Kubernetes cluster must be able to communicate with every other Pod without Network Address Translation (NAT). This requirement establishes a flat networking space, where Pods can communicate directly, regardless of their physical location within the cluster.

**The key networking principles include:**

- **Pod-to-Pod Communication:** Every Pod receives a unique IP address within the cluster network space. This enables direct communication between Pods, whether they reside on the same node or different nodes.
- **Node-to-Pod Communication:** Nodes must be able to communicate with all Pods running on them, facilitating vital cluster operations such as health checks and metrics collection.
- **Pod-to-Service Communication:** Services abstract Pod endpoints, providing stable networking endpoints regardless of Pod lifecycle changes.
- **External-to-Service Communication:** External traffic must be able to reach services within the cluster through defined ingress points.

Amazon EKS implements these Kubernetes networking principles through a sophisticated integration with AWS networking services. The EKS architecture shown in *Figure* 5.1 consists of several interconnected layers and components, with networking playing a crucial role throughout the system:

- **External Access Layer:** The External Access Layer serves as the entry point from the Internet, protected by WAF (Web Application Firewall), with traffic managed through Application and Network Load Balancers (ALB/NLB) for distribution to backend services. These load balancers distribute incoming requests to the EKS cluster services, and are protected by AWS WAF for additional security. This layer handles all external traffic routing and initial security controls.
- **VPC:** The VPC Structure implements a traditional multi-tier network design where Public Subnets contain the NAT Gateway for outbound internet access and Bastion Host for secure administrative access. The Private Subnets host the EKS cluster components, providing network isolation for the worker nodes and pods, ensuring secure workload execution. This network segregation is crucial for maintaining security, and controlling traffic flow within the infrastructure.
- **EKS Components:** Within the EKS Components, network connectivity is managed between the control plane handling cluster management communications, managed Node Groups running the workloads, and application workloads distributed across nodes for high availability and scalability. The control plane manages all Kubernetes orchestration, while the worker nodes execute the actual workloads.
- **Security Layer:** The Security Layer integrates network security through Security Groups for network access control, along with IAM Roles for permission management, KMS Keys for encryption, and Secrets Manager for sensitive data protection, forming a comprehensive security stack. These components work together to ensure secure communication, and access controls across the entire infrastructure.
- **AWS Services Integration:** AWS Services Integration incorporates essential networking services, including Route 53 for DNS management and service discovery, ECR for container images, S3 for storage, CloudWatch for monitoring, and Systems Manager for operational tasks. These services provide critical infrastructure support for the EKS environment, with Route 53 playing a key role in service discovery and DNS resolution.
- **Database Tier:** The Database Tier encompasses RDS for relational databases, ElastiCache for caching solutions, and DynamoDB for NoSQL storage requirements. Network connectivity to these database services is managed through VPC endpoints and security groups, ensuring secure and efficient data access for applications running in the EKS cluster.

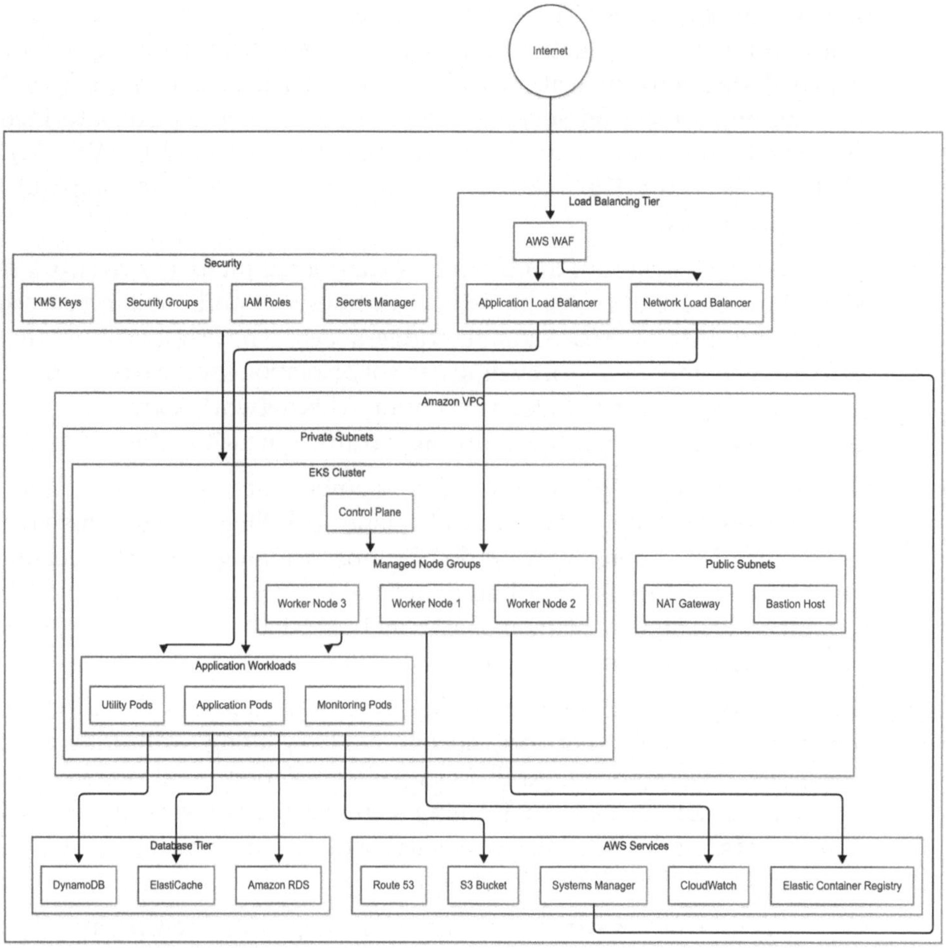


***Figure 5.1:*** *AWS EKS Architecture with Multi-Layer Network and Security Components*

This integrated architecture ensures high availability, security, and scalability for containerized applications running on AWS EKS, with networking components, providing the crucial connectivity and communication paths between all elements of the system.

After understanding the overall EKS architecture and its networking components, let us delve into the AWS VPC CNI (Container Network Interface), which is a crucial component not explicitly shown in our architecture diagram but fundamental to EKS networking.

# AWS VPC CNI Implementation

The AWS VPC CNI (Container Network Interface) serves as the foundational networking component in Amazon EKS, enabling seamless integration between Kubernetes pod networking and Amazon VPC networking capabilities. This section explores the core components, IP address management strategies, and implementation differences between EC2 and Fargate environments.

# Core Components

The VPC CNI architecture consists of three primary components that work together to enable pod networking in EKS:

- The CNI Plugin handles the core network interface configuration for pods. When a pod is created or deleted, this component configures the necessary network interfaces, sets up routing tables, and manages network policies. It interacts directly with the container runtime and the Linux Kernel to establish network connectivity.
- The IPAMD (IP Address Management Daemon), also known as L-IPAM, runs as a DaemonSet on each node, and manages IP address allocation as well as ENI configuration. It maintains a warm pool of IP addresses, and handles address assignment requests from the CNI plugin. This component is crucial for ensuring efficient IP address utilization, and rapid pod startup times.
- The CNI Agent monitors the health of the networking components, collects metrics, and provides debugging information. It ensures the overall health and performance of the CNI implementation, and facilitates troubleshooting when issues arise.

# IP Address Management

IP address management strategies differ significantly between **EC2 Managed Node Groups** and **Fargate implementations**.

# EC2 Managed Node Groups

In EC2 environments, the VPC CNI manages IP addresses through a sophisticated pooling mechanism. Each EC2 instance can have multiple Elastic Network Interfaces (ENIs), with each ENI supporting multiple secondary IP addresses. The primary ENI's primary IP address is reserved for node-level networking, while secondary ENIs, and their associated IP addresses are available for pod assignment.

The IPAMD maintains a "*warm pool*" of available IP addresses, pre-allocating them to ensure rapid pod startup times. The size of this pool is configurable through parameters such as **`WARM_IP_TARGET`** and **`MINIMUM_IP_TARGET`**. When a pod requests an IP address, it can be assigned immediately from this pre-allocated pool instead of waiting for a new IP address to be assigned through the EC2 API.

Instance types determine the maximum number of ENIs and IP addresses per ENI, directly affecting the maximum number of pods that can run on a node. For example, a `t3.large` instance supports 2 ENIs with 12 IP addresses per ENI, allowing for approximately 24 pods (minus system overhead).

## AWS Fargate

AWS Fargate implements a fundamentally different approach to IP address management. Each Fargate pod receives its own dedicated ENI with a single IP address, establishing a 1:1 relationship between pods and ENIs. This architecture eliminates the need for IP address pooling but introduces different scaling considerations.

When a pod is scheduled on Fargate, the control plane automatically provisions a new ENI, and assigns it directly to the pod. This process is fully managed by AWS, and integrates directly with VPC networking, providing isolated network interfaces for each pod.

# Implementation Considerations: EC2 Versus Fargate Nodes in EKS

The networking architecture in Amazon EKS presents distinct implementation patterns between EC2 Managed Node Groups and Fargate, each offering unique advantages and considerations for container networking. EC2 nodes utilize a multi-ENI architecture where the AWS VPC CNI manages a pool of IP addresses across multiple network interfaces, enabling high-density pod deployment with efficient local node communication. Each EC2 instance can support multiple pods sharing network interfaces, with IP addresses pre-allocated in a warm pool for rapid pod initialization. The number of available pods per node is determined by the instance type's ENI and IP address limits, requiring careful capacity planning.

In contrast, Fargate implements a simplified yet more isolated networking model where each pod receives its dedicated ENI with a single IP address directly from the VPC. This 1:1 mapping between pods and ENIs in Fargate provides stronger network isolation but introduces additional ENI provisioning overhead during pod startup. While EC2 nodes offer greater flexibility in network configuration, including custom CNI settings and prefix delegation, Fargate provides a more managed experience with AWS handling the networking complexity.

Network performance characteristics also differ significantly between the two options. EC2 nodes share the instance's network bandwidth among pods, potentially offering higher throughput for co-located pods, while Fargate pods receive dedicated network bandwidth that scales with the pod's compute resources. This distinction becomes particularly important when designing applications with specific network performance requirements or when planning for high-throughput workloads.

Security group implementation varies substantially between EC2 and Fargate deployments. EC2 supports both node and pod-level security groups, providing flexible network security options, whereas Fargate exclusively uses pod-level security groups. This architectural difference influences how network policies are implemented and managed across the cluster, affecting both security posture and operational procedures.

These architectural differences influence not only the operational aspects of container networking but also impact application design decisions, particularly regarding service communication patterns and network policy implementation in EKS clusters. Organizations must carefully consider these networking characteristics when choosing between EC2 and Fargate for their workloads, often leading to hybrid implementations that leverage the strengths of both platforms.

For example, a typical production implementation might look like:

```
# EC2 Node Group Network Configuration
apiVersion: v1
kind: ConfigMap
metadata:
  name: aws-vpc-cni
  namespace: kube-system
data:
  WARM_IP_TARGET: "5"
  MINIMUM_IP_TARGET: "10"
  ENABLE_PREFIX_DELEGATION: "true"
  AWS_VPC_CNI_CUSTOM_NETWORK_CFG: "true"
  ENI_CONFIG_LABEL_DEF: "topology.kubernetes.io/zone"

# Fargate Profile Network Configuration
apiVersion: eks.amazonaws.com/v1
kind: FargateProfile
metadata:
  name: prod-workload
spec:
  selectors:
    - namespace: production
      labels:
        type: fargate-workload
  subnets:
    - subnet-private1
    - subnet-private2
  securityGroupIds:
    - sg-prod-pods
```

This configuration demonstrates how networking setup differs between the two compute types, highlighting the balance between operational complexity and network isolation that must be considered when designing EKS cluster networking architecture.

Understanding these differences enables architects and operators to make informed decisions about their EKS networking strategy, and implement solutions that best meet their application requirements.

# Configuration Management in EKS Networking

The configuration management of networking components in Amazon EKS requires a systematic approach that varies significantly between EC2 and Fargate implementations. At its core, the AWS VPC CNI plugin serves as the primary networking component, manageable through Kubernetes `ConfigMaps` and annotations, enabling fine-grained control over network behavior and performance characteristics.

The primary configuration for EC2 managed nodes centers around the aws-vpc-cni **`ConfigMap`** in the **`kube-system`** namespace. This configuration object manages critical networking parameters such as IP address allocation strategies, prefix delegation, custom networking rules, and security group policies. Administrators can tune these settings to optimize pod density, network performance, and resource utilization based on their specific requirements.

For example:

```
apiVersion: v1
kind: ConfigMap
metadata:
  name: aws-vpc-cni
  namespace: kube-system
data:
  WARM_IP_TARGET: "5"
  MINIMUM_IP_TARGET: "10"
  ENABLE_PREFIX_DELEGATION: "true"
  AWS_VPC_K8S_CNI_CUSTOM_NETWORK_CFG: "true"
  ENABLE_POD_ENI: "true"
  AWS_VPC_ENI_MTU: "9001"
```

Fargate pods, by contrast, follow a more streamlined configuration model where networking settings are primarily defined through the Fargate Profile specification. This approach abstracts much of the underlying network complexity, focusing instead on subnet selection, security group assignment, and basic network policy enforcement. The configuration is typically handled at the cluster or namespace level through Fargate profiles:

```
apiVersion: eks.amazonaws.com/v1
kind: FargateProfile
metadata:
  name: application-profile
spec:
```

```
  podExecutionRoleArn: arn:aws:iam::111122223333:role/pod-
execution-role
  selectors:
    - namespace: default
      labels:
        runtime: fargate
  subnets:
    - subnet-1234567890abcdef0
  securityGroupIds:
    - sg-123456789
```

# Service Mesh with AWS App Mesh

A service mesh is an infrastructure layer that facilitates service-to-service communication in a microservices architecture. It provides features such as traffic management, security, and observability, without requiring changes to application code.

AWS App Mesh is a service mesh that provides application-level networking to make it easy for your services to communicate with each other across multiple types of compute infrastructure. It standardizes how your services communicate, giving you end-to-end visibility and ensuring high availability for your applications.

AWS App Mesh brings service mesh capabilities to your Amazon EKS clusters, providing a framework for service-to-service communication with enhanced control, visibility, and security. This service mesh implementation helps you standardize how your services communicate, offering fine-grained control over traffic flow and robust observability features. Here are the core capabilities that make App Mesh a powerful addition to your EKS environment:

- **Traffic Control:** Route and shape traffic between services.
- **Security:** Implement mutual TLS encryption and fine-grained access controls.
- **Observability:** Gain insights into service behavior through metrics, logs, and traces.
- **Health Monitoring:** Configure health checks and circuit breakers for improved resilience.
- **Compatibility:** Works with AWS services such as EKS, ECS, EC2, and Fargate.

# Integrating AWS App Mesh with EKS

To use AWS App Mesh with EKS, follow these steps:

1. **Install the App Mesh Controller:** Use Helm or YAML manifests to install the App Mesh Controller for Kubernetes in your EKS cluster.

```
helm repo add eks https://aws.github.io/eks-charts
helm install appmesh-controller eks/appmesh-controller \
  --namespace appmesh-system \
  --set region=${AWS_REGION} \
  --set serviceAccount.create=false \
  --set serviceAccount.name=appmesh-controller
```

2. **Define Mesh Resources:** Create Kubernetes custom resources to define your mesh, virtual nodes, and virtual services.

```
apiVersion: appmesh.k8s.aws/v1beta2
kind: Mesh
metadata:
  name: my-mesh
spec:
  namespaceSelector:
    matchLabels:
      mesh: my-mesh
```

3. **Inject Envoy Sidecar:** Enable automatic Envoy sidecar injection by adding annotations to your pod specifications.

```
annotations:
  appmesh.k8s.aws/sidecarInjectorWebhook: enabled
```

4. **Configure Traffic Routing:** Use virtual routers and routes to define traffic rules between your services.

```
apiVersion: appmesh.k8s.aws/v1beta2
kind: VirtualRouter
metadata:
  name: my-router
  namespace: my-namespace
spec:
  listeners:
    - portMapping:
        port: 8080
        protocol: http
  routes:
    - name: my-route
      httpRoute:
        match:
          prefix: /
        action:
          weightedTargets:
            - virtualNodeRef:
                name: my-service-v1
              weight: 90
```

```
          - virtualNodeRef:
              name: my-service-v2
            weight: 10
```

While implementing AWS App Mesh in EKS clusters introduces additional complexity through sidecar proxies and infrastructure layers, its benefits significantly outweigh these considerations for organizations running microservices at scale. The key to successful implementation lies in following established best practices: starting with a gradual adoption strategy, leveraging AWS X-Ray and CloudWatch for comprehensive observability, implementing mTLS for secure service-to-service communication, and carefully tuning Envoy proxy resources for optimal performance.

Organizations must carefully consider the operational impacts, including the performance overhead from sidecar proxies and the additional CPU and memory resources required. However, App Mesh's powerful capabilities in traffic management, security, and observability provide the necessary control and insight for managing complex microservices architectures. The ability to implement canary deployments through weighted routing enables safer, more controlled application updates, while the deep integration with AWS services streamlines operations and monitoring.

Ultimately, AWS App Mesh serves as a strategic tool for organizations looking to standardize service communication, enhance security, and gain deeper operational insights into their EKS environments. When implemented thoughtfully and gradually, it becomes an invaluable component of a robust, scalable, and manageable Kubernetes infrastructure on AWS.

# Load Balancing in EKS

Load balancing is crucial for distributing traffic across multiple pods and nodes in your EKS cluster. AWS offers two primary load balancer types for EKS: Application Load Balancer (ALB) and Network Load Balancer (NLB).

# Application Load Balancer (ALB)

The AWS ALB operates at Layer 7 (application layer) and is ideal for HTTP/HTTPS traffic. It provides advanced routing capabilities, including path-based routing and host-based routing. In EKS, ALBs are primarily provisioned through **Ingress resources** which define rules for HTTP routing and SSL termination. While Kubernetes natively supports various ingress controllers, the AWS Load Balancer Controller (formerly known as ALB Ingress Controller) is the recommended choice for EKS clusters. It leverages AWS Application Load Balancers to provide advanced routing capabilities, SSL/TLS termination, and WebSocket support.

# Network Load Balancer (NLB)

The Network Load Balancer (NLB) operates at Layer 4 (transport layer) and is ideal for TCP/UDP traffic, offering ultra-high performance and low latency. In EKS, NLBs are typically provisioned through **Service Resources** of type **LoadBalancer**. They are particularly useful for exposing services that require static IP addresses or need to handle non-HTTP/HTTPS protocols. The AWS Load Balancer Controller automatically provisions and manages NLBs when it detects appropriate Service resources in your cluster.

When setting up a NLB with Amazon EKS, you will need to choose between IP and Instance target modes, each offering distinct advantages. **`IP mode`** directly routes traffic to pod IPs, providing better source IP preservation and eliminating extra network hops, making it ideal for latency-sensitive applications and Fargate workloads. However, **`Instance mode`**, which routes traffic to worker nodes, offers simpler management and higher scaling limits of up to 1000 targets per target group, making it more suitable for large-scale deployments where cost optimization is a priority. While Instance Mode introduces an additional network hop through kube-proxy, its operational simplicity and lower cost often make it the preferred choice for clusters that do not require source IP preservation or direct pod routing.

# AWS Load Balancer Controller

The AWS Load Balancer Controller serves as a crucial bridge between Kubernetes and AWS load balancing services, providing a unified solution for managing both ALBs and NLBs in Amazon EKS. This controller handles Layer 7 (HTTP/HTTPS) traffic through Ingress resources using ALBs, and Layer 4 (TCP/UDP) traffic typically through Service type LoadBalancer using NLBs.

The controller follows a systematic process to manage load balancing resources. Upon detecting either Ingress or Service resources from the API server, it automatically provisions the necessary AWS infrastructure:

## For Ingress Resources

- Creates an ALB (internet-facing or internal)
- Places in specific subnets (controlled via annotations)
- Establishes target groups for each Kubernetes service
- Configures listeners (defaults: ports 80/443)
- Sets up routing rules for traffic distribution

## For Service Resources

- Provisions NLBs for TCP/UDP traffic
- Provides static IP addresses
- Preserves source IP addresses

**Here are its core functionalities:**

1. **Ingress Management:** The controller automatically provisions ALBs when Kubernetes ingress resources are created in the cluster.
2. **Service Integration:** It can also create NLBs for Kubernetes services of type LoadBalancer.
3. **AWS Resource Orchestration:** Manages the creation, modification, and deletion of AWS resources such as target groups and listeners.
4. **Annotation-based Configuration:** Allows fine-grained control over load balancer behavior through Kubernetes annotations.
5. **IP and Instance Mode Support:** Can register pods (IP mode) or nodes (instance mode) as targets for the load balancers.
6. **Multi-architecture Support:** Works with both EC2-based nodes and Fargate profiles.

The AWS Load Balancer Controller delivers significant advantages for organizations running workloads on Amazon EKS. Through its seamless AWS integration, it brings native AWS load balancing capabilities directly to Kubernetes workloads, eliminating the complexity of managing separate load balancing solutions. Operations teams benefit from automated load balancer provisioning and management, dramatically reducing the manual effort typically required for service exposure and traffic management. The controller's support for ingress groups enables cost optimization by allowing multiple services to share a single ALB, potentially reducing infrastructure costs. Furthermore, its deep integration with AWS security services, including AWS WAF and Shield, provides robust protection against web-based attacks and DDoS threats, ensuring applications remain secure and available. These benefits combine to create a powerful, efficient, and secure solution for managing external access to Kubernetes services in AWS environments.

Before we can start creating ingress resources, we need to set up the AWS Load Balancer Controller in our EKS cluster. This process involves several key steps:

**Prerequisites**

- Existing EKS cluster
- AWS CLI configured with appropriate permissions

- kubectl installed and configured
- Helm (recommended for installation)

1. **Creating the necessary IAM Resources**
    a. Create IAM policy for the controller
    b. Set up service account with necessary permissions
    c. Configure OIDC provider for EKS cluster

2. **Installing the controller using Helm:** Using Helm is the recommended method for deploying the AWS Load Balancer Controller as it simplifies the installation process and manages dependencies effectively. This command sequence adds the official AWS EKS Helm repository, and installs the controller with the necessary configurations:

    ```
    helm repo add eks https://aws.github.io/eks-charts
    helm repo update
    ```

    For basic configuration of the AWS Load Balancer Controller, execute the following command:

    ```
    helm install aws-load-balancer-controller eks/aws-load-balancer
    -controller \
      -n kube-system \
      --set clusterName=<your-cluster-name>
      --set region=<your-aws-region>
    ```

    After installation, it is crucial to verify that the controller is running correctly in your cluster. The following commands help confirm successful deployment and proper operation of the controller components:

    ```
    kubectl get deployment -n kube-system aws-load-balancer-controller
    ```

3. **Configuring the controller with your cluster-specific settings**: The AWS Load Balancer Controller requires specific configurations to operate effectively in your EKS environment. These settings determine how the controller interacts with your cluster and AWS resources.

    *Table* 5.1 provides a quick reference for the most important settings and their purposes. These configuration parameters can be applied during the initial installation or subsequent upgrades of the AWS Load Balancer Controller. The settings may be specified either as command-line arguments to Helm or incorporated into a values file for more comprehensive configuration management. It is recommended to review and adjust these parameters to align with your specific cluster requirements and operational best practices. *Tables* 5.2 *and* 5.3 provide a quick reference for ALB and NLB specific settings respectively.

**Common Controller Settings**

| Category | Setting | Description |
|---|---|---|
| Essential | clusterName | Name of your EKS cluster |
| Essential | region | AWS region of your cluster |
| Essential | vpcId | ID of the VPC where cluster resides |
| Essential | serviceAccount.create | Whether to create a service account |
| Essential | serviceAccount.name | Name of the service account |
| Resources | replicaCount | Number of controller replicas |
| Resources | resources.requests.cpu | CPU request for each replica |
| Resources | resources.requests.memory | Memory request for each replica |
| Resources | resources.limits.cpu | CPU limit for each replica |
| Resources | resources.limits.memory | Memory limit for each replica |
| Monitoring | metrics.enabled | Enable Prometheus metrics |
| Monitoring | logLevel | Logging level |

***Table 5.1:*** *AWS Load Balancer Controller Common Settings*

**ALB Specific Settings**

| Category | Setting | Description |
|---|---|---|
| Ingress | ingressClass | Default ingress class |
| ALB | scheme | Load balancer scheme |
| ALB | enableIPTargetType | Enable IP target type for Fargate/IP mode |
| ALB | group.name | ALB group name for sharing |
| ALB | ssl-policy | SSL policy for HTTPS listeners |
| ALB | wafv2-acl-arn | WAF web ACL ARN |

***Table 5.2:*** *AWS Load Balancer Controller ALB Specific Settings*

**NLB Specific Settings**

| Category | Setting | Description |
|---|---|---|
| Service | targetType | Target type for NLB |
| NLB | cross-zone | Enable cross-zone load balancing |
| NLB | target-group-attributes | Target group settings |
| NLB | healthcheck-interval | Health check interval in seconds |
| NLB | healthcheck-timeout | Health check timeout in seconds |

| NLB | proxy-protocol | Enable proxy protocol v2 |
|---|---|---|
| NLB | preserve-client-ip | Preserve client source IP |

**Table 5.3:** *AWS Load Balancer Controller NLB Specific Settings*

Once you configure the custom settings in **your-custom-values.yaml**, execute the following command in order to apply the custom settings:

```
helm upgrade aws-load-balancer-controller eks/aws-load-balancer
-controller \
  -n kube-system \
  -f <your-custom-values.yaml>
```

# Network Policies and Security Groups Policies

Network security is a crucial aspect of running containerized applications in Kubernetes, particularly in Amazon EKS environments. The dynamic nature of these deployments, where microservices communicate constantly and pods are ephemeral, creates a complex security landscape that requires sophisticated network controls. Traditional perimeter-based security approaches are insufficient in this context, necessitating multiple layers of protection from network policies at the pod level to security groups at the infrastructure level.

Network Policies function as pod-level firewalls, enabling fine-grained control over pod-to-pod communication within a cluster, while Security Groups provide an additional layer of defense by controlling traffic at the compute instance and network interface level. Understanding and implementing both these mechanisms is necessary for creating a robust security posture in Kubernetes environments.

In practice, these security mechanisms frequently encounter challenging scenarios. Newly deployed microservices often face communication issues with existing components, particularly when accessing databases or backend services, requiring careful verification of both network policies and security group configurations. External API access problems are common, where pods struggle to reach external endpoints despite seemingly correct configurations, necessitating thorough examination of egress rules and security group outbound permissions. Ingress controller deployments frequently experience routing difficulties to backend services, especially in environments with complex networking requirements.

Multi-tenant clusters present particular challenges in maintaining proper workload isolation, where inadvertent communication between different tenants' applications can occur without properly configured namespace isolation. Service mesh implementations often face connectivity issues between sidecar proxies, requiring careful consideration of both network policies and security group configurations to ensure proper mesh communication, while maintaining security boundaries.

Without proper network security measures, organizations risk exposing sensitive workloads to both internal and external threats, potentially compromising data integrity, service availability, and regulatory compliance. Therefore, a comprehensive understanding of these security mechanisms and their interplay is crucial for maintaining the flexibility and scalability that makes Kubernetes powerful, while ensuring robust protection for containerized applications.

# Network Policy Implementation

Network Policies in Kubernetes act as a firewall, allowing you to control the traffic flow between pods. They are crucial for implementing the principle of least privilege, and securing communication within your cluster.

Network Policies in Kubernetes follow a declarative model that defines allowed connections to and from pods. Hence, let us break down each component of a basic Network Policy:

```
apiVersion: networking.k8s.io/v1
kind: NetworkPolicy
metadata:
  name: access-nginx
spec:
  podSelector:
    matchLabels:
      app: nginx
  ingress:
  - from:
    - podSelector:
        matchLabels:
          access: allowed
```

**Key Components:**

1. **Policy Selection**
   - **`podSelector`**: Determines which pods the policy applies to.

     In this example, the policy targets all pods with label **`app: nginx`**.
   - An empty podSelector (**`{}`**) would select all pods in the namespace.
2. **Traffic Direction**
   - **`ingress`**: Rules for incoming traffic.
   - **`egress`**: Rules for outgoing traffic (not shown in example).

- `Policies` can specify either or both.

3. **Rule Specification**
   - `from`: Defines the source of allowed traffic.
   - `to`: Defines the destination for allowed traffic (used in egress rules).
   - Can include multiple rules and combinations.

**Common Selectors:**

```
# Namespace selector
- namespaceSelector:
    matchLabels:
      environment: production

# IP Block selector
- ipBlock:
    cidr: 172.17.0.0/16
    except:
    - 172.17.1.0/24

# Combined selectors
- from:
  - namespaceSelector:
      matchLabels:
        environment: production
    podSelector:
      matchLabels:
        role: frontend
```

**Default Behavior:**

- If no Network Policies select a pod, all traffic is allowed.
- Once a pod is selected by a policy, only traffic explicitly allowed by the policy is permitted.
- Multiple policies affecting the same pod are additive.

**Example Use Cases:**

1. **Frontend-Backend Isolation**:

```
apiVersion: networking.k8s.io/v1
kind: NetworkPolicy
metadata:
  name: frontend-to-backend
spec:
  podSelector:
    matchLabels:
      app: backend
```

```
  ingress:
  - from:
    - podSelector:
        matchLabels:
          app: frontend
    ports:
    - protocol: TCP
      port: 8080
```

2. **Database Access Control**:

```
apiVersion: networking.k8s.io/v1
kind: NetworkPolicy
metadata:
  name: db-access
spec:
  podSelector:
    matchLabels:
      app: database
  ingress:
  - from:
    - namespaceSelector:
        matchLabels:
          type: application
    - podSelector:
        matchLabels:
          role: backend
    ports:
    - protocol: TCP
      port: 5432
```

This structure provides the foundation for implementing more complex network security patterns, while maintaining clarity and manageability. Understanding these basic components is crucial for building effective network security policies in your Kubernetes environment.

# Security Group Policies

Security groups provide an additional layer of network security at the infrastructure level, particularly important in cloud environments like AWS EKS. When using Amazon EKS, you can assign security groups directly to pods, using the `SecurityGroupPolicy` custom resource:

```
apiVersion: vpcresources.k8s.aws/v1beta1
kind: SecurityGroupPolicy
metadata:
  name: allow-specific-ports
spec:
```

```
      podSelector:
        matchLabels:
          role: web
      securityGroups:
        groupIds:
          - sg-123456789
```

**Best practices for security group management:**

1. **Principle of Least Privilege**
   - Only open necessary ports
   - Limit source CIDR ranges
   - Regular audit of security group rules
2. **Security Group Organization**
   - Use meaningful naming conventions
   - Tag security groups appropriately
   - Document security group purposes

# Troubleshooting

Effective troubleshooting of network policies and security groups requires a systematic approach combining various tools and methodologies. Begin with policy verification using kubectl commands to list and analyze existing network policies, followed by detailed inspection of policy specifications. Traffic flow analysis should utilize tools like tcpdump for packet-level inspection and temporary logging policies to track connection attempts. Regular security group auditing through AWS Config rules and VPC Flow Logs helps identify potential security gaps and blocked connections. When investigating complex issues, implement temporary policy relaxation strategies to isolate the root cause, but always maintain proper change documentation and revert changes promptly. Utilize visualization tools like kube-netc, and monitoring solutions such as Prometheus and Grafana to gain insights into network behavior and policy effectiveness. Implement incremental policy changes, starting with broader permissions, and gradually restricting them based on actual requirements. Maintain comprehensive documentation of policy intentions and changes as well as establish regular health checks including connectivity tests between critical services. This methodical approach, combined with proper tools and monitoring, enables effective resolution of network policy and security group issues, while maintaining security standards.

# Best Practices for Security Groups

- Maintain separate security groups for different tiers (web, app, and database).

- Regularly review and remove unused rules.
- Use security group references, instead of CIDR ranges where possible.
- Implement automated compliance checking.

# Service Discovery

Service discovery is a critical component in containerized environments, enabling applications to locate and communicate with each other dynamically. In Amazon EKS, service discovery is implemented through multiple mechanisms, combining Kubernetes native capabilities with AWS-specific integrations. Service Discovery in EKS enables applications to find and communicate with each other dynamically. It primarily works through:

# Kubernetes Services

Kubernetes Services provide stable networking endpoints for pods, with three main types:

- **ClusterIP (internal)**: The default service type in Kubernetes, providing a stable internal IP address accessible only within the cluster. ClusterIP is ideal for internal communication between applications and microservices where external access isn't required, making it the most common choice for internal service-to-service communication.
- **LoadBalancer (external)**: Creates an external load balancer in cloud providers like AWS, exposing the service to the internet with a public IP or DNS name. This type automatically handles traffic distribution and is the standard choice for production applications that need to be accessible from outside the cluster.
- **NodePort (node-level)**: Exposes the service on each cluster node's IP address at a static port. While useful for development and testing scenarios, NodePort is generally not recommended for production use due to security considerations and limited port availability. It provides a simpler alternative when external access is needed without cloud provider integration.

# DNS Resolution

Amazon EKS uses CoreDNS for internal DNS resolution, providing automatic service discovery within the cluster. When a service is created, it automatically gets a DNS entry following the pattern `<service-name>.<namespace>.svc.cluster.local`, enabling pods to communicate using human-readable names instead of IP addresses.

CoreDNS runs as a cluster service, intercepting DNS queries from pods. When a pod looks up a service name, CoreDNS resolves it to the appropriate cluster IP or pod IP addresses. For example, a frontend service can connect to a backend service simply by using `backend-service` or `backend-service.default` as the hostname.

DNS Patterns:

- Service DNS: `service-name.namespace.svc.cluster.local`
- Pod DNS: `pod-ip.namespace.pod.cluster.local`
- Headless Service: Returns individual pod IPs instead of service IP

This DNS-based service discovery is transparent to applications, and works seamlessly with both internal services and external endpoints, making it a fundamental building block for containerized applications in EKS.

# AWS Cloud Map Integration

AWS Cloud Map is a cloud resource discovery service that enables applications to find services and resources in AWS through API calls, DNS queries, or cloud-native service discovery patterns.

**Key Features:**

- Registers application resources (IP addresses, URLs, AWS resources, and so on).
- Automatically updates service health status.
- Integrates with EKS for cross-cluster discovery.
- Supports custom attributes for service metadata.

**EKS Integration:** When used with EKS, Cloud Map can register services running in Kubernetes clusters and make them discoverable across your AWS infrastructure. Services can be registered automatically through annotations, enabling seamless service discovery between EKS clusters, and other AWS services.

**Common Use Cases:**

- Microservices discovery across multiple EKS clusters.
- Hybrid cloud service discovery.
- Integration with AWS services such as ECS, EC2, and Lambda.
- Health-aware service routing.

Cloud Map simplifies the complex task of service discovery in modern distributed applications by providing a single registry for all your application resources, regardless of where they run.

# Advanced Networking Topics

Amazon EKS advanced networking extends beyond basic container connectivity, focusing on critical aspects that enable modern, scalable applications. This section explores three fundamental areas: IP Address Management, which covers prefix delegation, secondary IP addressing, and IPAM strategies for optimal resource utilization; Cross-Region Networking, addressing multi-cluster connectivity, global load balancing, and disaster recovery patterns across AWS regions; and IPv6 Support, including dual-stack networking, IPv6-only pod configurations, and migration strategies. Understanding these concepts is crucial for building resilient, globally distributed applications, while ensuring efficient resource utilization and future-proofing your infrastructure. These topics form the cornerstone of sophisticated EKS deployments, enabling organizations to architect solutions that are both scalable and maintainable across global infrastructure.

## IP Address Management

The AWS VPC CNI plugin is fundamental to EKS networking, responsible for allocating IP addresses to pods. When a node starts, it's assigned one or more Elastic Network Interfaces (ENIs), each capable of supporting multiple secondary IP addresses. These IPs are then assigned to pods as they're scheduled on the node. The number of available IPs per ENI varies by instance type, directly impacting the pod density possible on each node. For example, a t3.large instance supports up to three ENIs with ten secondary IPs each, allowing for approximately 30 pods.

The optimal configuration of VPC CNI requires careful consideration of several key parameters and settings. For production environments, we recommend enabling prefix delegation (**`ENABLE_PREFIX_DELEGATION: "true"`**) to improve IP allocation efficiency and reduce API calls. Set **`WARM_IP_TARGET`** to maintain approximately 10-20% of the node's maximum pod capacity as a buffer (e.g., for a node supporting 100 pods, set it to 10-20), while **`MINIMUM_IP_TARGET`** should be configured at 5-10% to ensure a baseline availability of IPs. Enable **`WARM_PREFIX_TARGET: "1"`** when using prefix delegation to maintain one /28 CIDR block ready for immediate use. For security isolation, activate **`ENABLE_POD_ENI: "true"`** to support security groups for pods.

Instance selection is crucial - Nitro-based instances are recommended for optimal networking performance. For example, an m5.large instance supports 3 ENIs with multiple IPs each, providing capacity for approximately 28 usable pods after accounting for reserved IPs. In multi-AZ deployments, distribute nodes across a minimum of three availability zones using subnets sized at /20 or larger to accommodate growth. Monitor IP utilization and maintain a 20% buffer capacity for unexpected spikes in pod creation.

Pod IP assignment in EKS is a critical networking component that determines how IP addresses are allocated and managed for pods across your cluster. In the default configuration, the AWS VPC CNI plugin handles IP assignment using a combination of ENIs and secondary IP addresses. When a pod is scheduled, it receives an IP address from the available pool managed by the CNI plugin, either through individual IP assignment or prefix delegation (/28 CIDR blocks). The CNI maintains a "warm pool" of available IPs (configured via **`WARM_IP_TARGET`** and **`MINIMUM_IP_TARGET`**) to reduce pod startup latency. For efficient pod density planning, each node's capacity is calculated based on its instance type, where **`maximum pods = (Number of ENIs × IPs per ENI) - Reserved IPs`**. To prevent IP exhaustion, implement proactive monitoring with alerts at 80% utilization and configure the cluster autoscaler appropriately. Custom IP assignment is supported through security group policies and ENIConfig resources, allowing for specific network configurations based on workload requirements. For example, an m5.large instance with 3 ENIs and 10 IPs per ENI can support up to 28 pods after accounting for reserved IPs, making instance type selection crucial for optimal pod density.

**Example Configuration:**

```
apiVersion: v1
kind: ConfigMap
metadata:
  name: amazon-vpc-cni
  namespace: kube-system
data:
  ENABLE_PREFIX_DELEGATION: "true"
  WARM_IP_TARGET: "15"          # Assuming ~100 pods per node
  MINIMUM_IP_TARGET: "7"        # Baseline IP availability
  WARM_PREFIX_TARGET: "1"       # Pre-allocated prefix block
  ENABLE_POD_ENI: "true"        # For security group support
  MAXIMUM_PODS: "110"           # Adjusted based on instance type
  AWS_VPC_K8S_CNI_CUSTOM_NETWORK_CFG: "true"
  ENI_CONFIG_LABEL_DEF: "topology.kubernetes.io/zone"
```

# Cross-Region Networking

Cross-region networking in Amazon EKS forms the backbone of globally distributed Kubernetes applications, enabling seamless communication between clusters across different AWS regions. At its core, this architecture is built upon three fundamental components. First, multi-cluster communication establishes reliable connectivity between EKS clusters in different regions through mechanisms like VPC peering or Transit Gateway, enabling applications to span multiple geographical locations, while maintaining consistent networking policies and security postures. Second, Transit Gateway serves as a central hub, simplifying the network topology by providing a single point of control for cross-region traffic, route management, and security policy enforcement. This integration enables efficient routing between VPCs and on-premises networks while maintaining high availability and security. Finally, AWS Global Accelerator optimizes the application's global footprint by leveraging AWS's global network infrastructure to route users to the nearest regional endpoint, significantly reducing latency and improving overall application performance.

For example, an organization might deploy their EKS clusters across us-east-1 and us-west-1 regions, connected via Transit Gateway, with Global Accelerator directing users to the nearest available endpoint. This setup ensures high availability, disaster recovery capabilities, and compliance with regional data sovereignty requirements. The architecture supports sophisticated traffic management patterns, including regional failover, load balancing, and progressive rollouts, while maintaining consistent security policies and monitoring across regions. When implementing cross-region networking, careful consideration must be given to CIDR planning, security group consistency, IAM roles, and cost implications of cross-region data transfer. *Figure* 5.2 demonstrates active-active multi region EKS architecture.

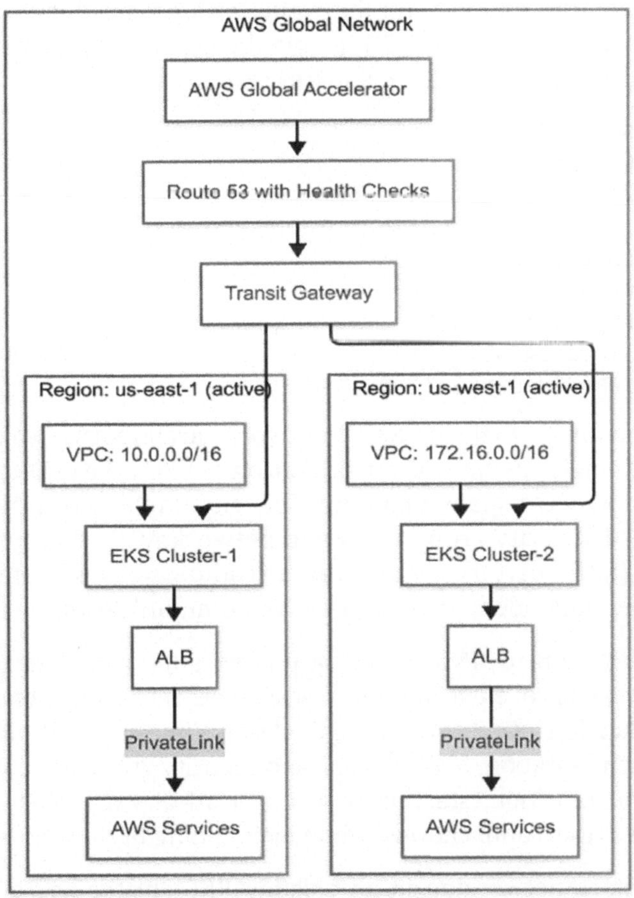


**Figure 5.2:** *Example Active-Active Multi-Region EKS Architecture*

# IPv6 Support

Amazon EKS provides comprehensive IPv6 support through dual-stack networking, enabling organizations to modernize their container networking infrastructure, while maintaining compatibility with existing IPv4 workloads. A dual-stack VPC configuration allows pods to communicate over both IPv4 and IPv6 protocols simultaneously, making it ideal for gradual transitions. When implementing IPv6, organizations must consider address allocation strategies, as each pod receives both an IPv4 and IPv6 address, impacting networking policies, security groups, and routing configurations. Migration strategies typically follow a phased approach: first enabling dual-stack networking, then gradually transitioning workloads to IPv6-preferred communication, and finally optimizing for IPv6-first operations. This approach ensures minimal disruption, while leveraging IPv6's benefits such as larger address space, improved security through simplified network addressing, and enhanced support for modern cloud-native applications.

The foundation of IPv6 support in EKS begins with proper dual-stack configuration. This involves configuring the VPC CNI plugin through a ConfigMap that enables IPv6, and sets appropriate parameters for address management:

```
apiVersion: v1
kind: ConfigMap
metadata:
  name: amazon-vpc-cni
  namespace: kube-system
data:
  ENABLE_IPV6: "true"
  WARM_IPV6_TARGET: "1"
  IPV6_PREFIX_DELEGATION: "true"
```

When implementing IPv6 in EKS, network architecture planning becomes paramount. This includes careful consideration of VPC IPv6 CIDR allocation, subnet sizing, and pod address space planning. Security implications must be addressed through updated security group rules and network ACLs that accommodate both IPv4 and IPv6 traffic patterns. Application readiness assessment ensures that all components and dependencies support IPv6 communication.

A successful migration to IPv6 follows a phased approach. The preparation phase involves comprehensive environment assessment, including network architecture review and application inventory. During dual-stack implementation, careful attention is paid to VPC configuration, CNI settings, and security group updates. The final phase involves gradual transition, starting with non-critical workloads and progressively moving to more critical applications, while maintaining performance baselines.

Enabling dual-stack networking in an existing EKS cluster has minimal immediate impact on running workloads. Existing IPv4 connectivity remains unchanged, and running pods maintain their current networking configuration. Changes take effect only for new pods, during pod recreation, or through rolling updates. This gradual approach allows for careful monitoring and validation of dual-stack behavior.

Effective IPv6 implementation requires comprehensive monitoring of both protocols. Key metrics include connectivity status, protocol distribution, latency measurements, and network policy effectiveness. Testing in non-production environments precedes any production implementation. A phased rollout helps manage risks, while maintaining IPv4 fallback capabilities that ensures operational stability. Regular performance monitoring and security assessments ensure the health of dual-stack networking.

As IPv6 adoption increases, organizations should prepare for IPv6-only workloads, enhanced cross-region connectivity requirements, and evolution of service mesh architectures. Through careful planning, phased implementation, and proper monitoring, organizations can successfully embrace IPv6, while maintaining operational stability and preparing for future networking requirements in EKS environments.

This implementation represents a significant step toward modern container networking, ensuring readiness for the IPv6-centric future, while maintaining compatibility with existing IPv4 workloads. The key to success lies in careful planning, thorough testing, and methodical implementation, ultimately leading to a robust and future-proof networking infrastructure.

# Conclusion

Networking in Amazon EKS represents a sophisticated integration of Kubernetes networking principles with AWS's robust infrastructure. Through this chapter, we've explored how EKS implements container networking using the AWS VPC CNI, enables advanced traffic management with AWS App Mesh, and provides flexible load balancing options. The transition to modern networking paradigms, including IPv6 support and cross-region connectivity, demonstrates EKS's ability to meet evolving infrastructure needs. Understanding these networking concepts is crucial for building scalable, secure, and resilient containerized applications on AWS. In the next chapter, we will explore comprehensive Security Best Practices for Amazon EKS, focusing on critical aspects such as identity and access management, network security, data protection, and compliance frameworks. Thus, understanding and implementing these security best practices is vital for maintaining a robust security posture in your EKS clusters, protecting sensitive workloads, and ensuring compliance with organizational and regulatory requirements.

# Points to Remember

- VPC CNI Architecture serves as the primary networking component in EKS, managing IP address allocation and ENI configuration. It supports both IPv4 and IPv6 addressing, while efficiently handling pod-to-pod communication within the cluster. The CNI plugin's implementation is crucial for maintaining network performance and scalability in EKS environments.
- Load Balancing Options provide flexibility through ALB for Layer 7 (HTTP/HTTPS) traffic and NLB for Layer 4 (TCP/UDP) traffic. The AWS Load Balancer Controller automates the provisioning and management of these resources, supporting both internal and external load balancing scenarios, ensuring efficient traffic distribution across pods.
- Service Discovery Mechanisms combine Kubernetes Services (ClusterIP, LoadBalancer, NodePort) with CoreDNS for internal DNS resolution. AWS Cloud Map integration enables comprehensive service discovery capabilities, including cross-cluster discovery, making it easier for applications to locate and communicate with required services.
- Network Security implements multiple layers of protection through Network Policies for pod-level security and Security Groups for VPC-level security. IAM roles for service accounts provide identity-based security, while SSL/TLS termination at load balancers ensures secure communication endpoints.
- Cross-Region Networking enables global application deployment through Transit Gateway for inter-region connectivity and Global Accelerator for traffic optimization. This architecture supports multi-cluster management and robust disaster recovery configurations, ensuring high availability across geographical regions.
- IPv6 Support through dual-stack networking capabilities enables gradual migration strategies, while maintaining the existing IPv4 connectivity. Proper pod IP address management and security considerations for IPv6 ensure smooth transition and operation in modern networking environments.
- Service Mesh Implementation with AWS App Mesh provides advanced traffic management capabilities and enhanced observability. This integration facilitates sophisticated service-to-service communication patterns and enables detailed monitoring of application behavior.
- IP Address Management encompasses secondary IP addressing, prefix delegation, and warm pool management strategies. ENI configuration optimization ensures efficient use of available network resources and supports high-density pod deployments.
- Monitoring and Troubleshooting capabilities integrate with CloudWatch and utilize VPC Flow Logs for comprehensive visibility. Network performance

metrics and connectivity diagnostics tools enable proactive management and rapid problem resolution.

- Best Practices guide the implementation of security group management, network policy configuration, and load balancer setup. Service discovery optimization ensures efficient resource utilization and reliable application communication patterns, leading to robust and maintainable EKS deployments.

# Multiple Choice Questions

1. What is the primary function of AWS VPC CNI in EKS?
    a. Load balancing
    b. IP address management
    c. DNS resolution
    d. Security group management
2. Which AWS service provides global traffic management for EKS clusters?
    a. Route 53
    b. Global Accelerator
    c. CloudFront
    d. ALB
3. How does EKS handle pod-to-pod communication within a cluster?
    a. Through Internet Gateway
    b. Using NAT Gateway
    c. Via ENIs
    d. Through VPN
4. What is the purpose of prefix delegation in EKS networking?
    a. Security enhancement
    b. Load balancing
    c. Efficient IP address allocation
    d. DNS resolution

5. Which component provides service discovery in EKS?
    a. Route 53
    b. CloudMap
    c. CoreDNS
    d. All of the above
6. What is the recommended load balancer for HTTP/HTTPS traffic in EKS?
    a. Classic Load Balancer
    b. Network Load Balancer
    c. Application Load Balancer
    d. Internal Load Balancer
7. Which feature enables IPv6 support in EKS clusters?
    a. VPC peering
    b. Dual-stack networking
    c. Transit Gateway
    d. Direct Connect
8. What is the primary purpose of AWS App Mesh in EKS?
    a. Container storage
    b. Service mesh implementation
    c. Load balancing
    d. Security management
9. How does EKS handle cross-region connectivity?
    a. Internet Gateway
    b. Transit Gateway
    c. VPC peering
    d. All of the above
10. Which security feature operates at the pod level in EKS?
    a. Security Groups
    b. Network Policies

c. NACL

d. IAM Roles

# Answers

1. b
2. b
3. c
4. c
5. d
6. c
7. b
8. b
9. b
10. b

# Key Terms

- **VPC CNI (Container Network Interface):** Extended networking plugin that enables native VPC networking for EKS pods.
- **ENI (Elastic Network Interface):** Virtual network interface that can be attached to EC2 instances in a VPC.
- **App Mesh:** AWS service mesh offering that provides application-level networking.
- **ALB (Application Load Balancer):** Layer 7 load balancer optimized for HTTP/HTTPS traffic.
- **NLB (Network Load Balancer):** Layer 4 load balancer for TCP/UDP traffic.
- **CoreDNS:** DNS server that provides Kubernetes cluster DNS services.
- **Cloud Map:** AWS service discovery service for cloud resources.
- **Transit Gateway:** Network transit hub that interconnects VPCs and on-premises networks.
- **Global Accelerator:** Service that improves availability and performance, using the AWS global network.

- **Network Policy:** Kubernetes resource that defines pod-to-pod communication rules.
- **Security Group:** Virtual firewall for controlling inbound and outbound traffic.
- **Prefix Delegation:** Feature that enables efficient IP address allocation in EKS.
- **Dual-stack Networking:** Configuration that supports both IPv4 and IPv6 protocols.
- **Service Mesh:** Infrastructure layer for managing service-to-service communication.
- **Load Balancer Controller:** Kubernetes controller that manages AWS load balancer resources.

# CHAPTER 6
# Security Best Practices

## Introduction

As we delve deeper into the intricacies of Amazon Elastic Kubernetes Service (EKS), we arrive at a crucial juncture: Security. In this chapter, we turn our attention to the critical security best practices that every EKS user and administrator must understand and implement.

The importance of robust security measures in EKS environments cannot be overstated. As organizations increasingly rely on EKS to manage their containerized workloads, they also face an ever-evolving landscape of cyber threats. This chapter aims to equip you with the knowledge and tools necessary to fortify your EKS clusters against potential vulnerabilities and attacks.

While EKS provides a powerful platform for container orchestration, its complexity can lead to security gaps, if not properly managed. The shared responsibility model of AWS means that while the cloud provider secures the underlying infrastructure, the security of your applications and data within EKS falls squarely on your shoulders. This chapter will guide you through fulfilling your part of this crucial responsibility.

Many industries operate under strict regulatory requirements, making security not just a technical consideration but a legal necessity. Understanding how to secure your EKS environment is essential for maintaining compliance, and avoiding potential legal and financial repercussions. Moreover, the cost implications of security breaches extend far beyond immediate financial losses, potentially causing long-term reputational damage.

In this chapter, we will explore the key aspects of EKS security, including IAM roles for service accounts, pod security policies, network security configurations, secret management with AWS Secrets Manager, and security auditing and compliance. Each section provides detailed insights and practical implementations to help you build and maintain secure and robust EKS environments.

Security is not a one-time setup, but an ongoing process that requires constant attention and refinement. As we progress through this chapter, you will gain the knowledge to implement critical security measures, and develop a mindset for continuous security improvement in your EKS infrastructure.

Hence, whether you are running mission-critical applications or developing new services, the security practices outlined here will help ensure your EKS environment remains resilient against current and emerging threats. So, let us embark on this crucial exploration of EKS security, arming ourselves with the expertise to protect our applications and data in today's challenging security landscape.

# Structure

In this chapter, we will discuss the following topics:

- EKS Security: A Holistic Approach
- IAM Roles for Service Accounts (IRSA)
- Pod Security Policies
- Network Security Configurations
- Secret Management with AWS Secrets Manager
- Security Auditing and Compliance
- Security Best Practices Checklist

# EKS Security: A Holistic Approach

EKS security is multi-faceted, encompassing various layers of protection from the infrastructure level to the application level. At its core, EKS security aims to protect your containerized applications, data, and the underlying infrastructure from unauthorized access, data breaches, and other security threats.

The key aspects of EKS security include:

- **Access Control:** Managing who can access your cluster, and what actions they can perform.
- **Network Security:** Protecting communication within the cluster, and with external resources.
- **Data Protection:** Safeguarding sensitive information, both at rest and in transit.
- **Workload Security:** Ensuring the security of pods and containers running in your cluster.
- **Compliance and Auditing:** Maintaining regulatory compliance, and monitoring for security events.

The following table shows how each security topic contributes to the different aspects of EKS security:

| Topic | Access Control | Network Security | Data Protection | Workload Security | Compliance and Auditing |
|---|---|---|---|---|---|
| IRSA | ✓ | | ○ | | ○ |
| Pod Security Policies | ○ | | | ○ | |
| Network Security Configurations | ○ | ✓ | ○ | | |
| Secret Management | | | ○ | | |

✓ = Primary focus, ○ = Secondary focus

***Table 6.1:*** *EKS Security Coverage Matrix*

EKS operates on AWS's shared responsibility model. While AWS manages the security of the EKS control plane, customers are responsible for securing their worker nodes, applications, and data. This shared model emphasizes the significance of implementing robust security measures at your end.

As we explore each security feature in this chapter, keep in mind that effective EKS security is not about implementing individual measures in isolation. Rather, it is about creating a comprehensive security strategy that combines these various elements to provide defense in depth.

# IAM Roles for Service Accounts (IRSA)

IAM Roles for Service Accounts (IRSA) is a feature in Amazon Elastic Kubernetes Service (EKS) that enhances security and simplifies access management for Kubernetes applications. Introduced by Amazon Web Services (AWS), IRSA allows Kubernetes service accounts to assume IAM roles directly, eliminating the need for storing long-term AWS credentials in pods, and replacing the traditional method of assigning broad permissions at the node level. This feature provides fine-grained access control, enabling administrators to grant specific AWS permissions to individual Kubernetes pods or namespaces. By leveraging IRSA, organizations can adhere to the principle of least privilege, reduce the risk of credential exposure, and streamline the process of managing permissions for applications running on EKS clusters that need to interact with other AWS services. The implementation of IRSA has become a best practice for securing Kubernetes workloads in AWS environments, representing a significant advancement in EKS security through its granular approach to authentication and authorization.

IRSA operates through OpenID Connect (OIDC) federation, establishing a trust relationship between AWS and the EKS cluster's OIDC provider. The OIDC provider issues JSON Web Tokens (JWTs) to Kubernetes service accounts, creating a secure authentication chain. When a pod initiates an AWS API call, the AWS SDK retrieves the pod's service account token, which is then exchanged for temporary AWS credentials through AWS Security Token Service (STS). These temporary credentials enable the pod to access AWS resources within the boundaries defined by the IAM role's permissions.

The architecture consists of several vital components working in harmony such as:

- EKS OIDC Provider handles identity federation.
- Service Account Annotations link Kubernetes resources to AWS IAM roles.
- IAM Role Trust Policy defines the permissions boundary.
- The Token Projector, a crucial component in this architecture, automatically mounts the service account token into the pod's filesystem at a predefined path (**`/var/run/secrets/kubernetes.io/serviceaccount/token`**), making it accessible to applications running in the pod.
- The AWS STS **`AssumeRoleWithWebIdentity`** functionality facilitates the secure credential exchange process.

IRSA provides significant advantages compared to traditional instance-level IAM roles. It enables granular access control at the pod level, rather than broad node-level permissions, substantially improving security posture. The architecture eliminates the need to store AWS credentials within pods and reduces the potential impact of security breaches. From an operational perspective, IRSA simplifies permission management with automated credential rotation and easier maintenance of access policies. The system provides enhanced auditability through clear tracking of pod-level AWS service access, supporting compliance requirements and security monitoring.

The implementation follows a logical sequence where pods reference Kubernetes Service Accounts, which are annotated with IAM Role ARNs. These IAM roles maintain trust relationships with the OIDC provider, while the AWS SDK handles credential exchange automatically. This streamlined flow creates a secure, efficient, and maintainable system for managing AWS permissions within Kubernetes workloads, embodying security best practices, and operational excellence.

In the next section we will cover the comprehensive architecture that demonstrates how IRSA bridges the gap between Kubernetes and AWS security models, providing a robust solution for managing cross-service authentication and authorization.

# Authentication vs Authorization

Authentication in EKS determines who you are. At the Kubernetes level, it uses AWS IAM credentials, OIDC tokens, X.509 certificates, and service account tokens. The IRSA primarily leverages the EKS OIDC provider for authentication. In this context, authentication determines the identity of pods running in the EKS cluster.

As shown in *Figure* 6.1, the authentication flow for a pod using IRSA typically looks like:

1. The pod starts and receives a service account token.
2. It uses this token to request an OIDC token from the Kubernetes API server.
3. The OIDC token, signed by the EKS OIDC provider, is then used to authenticate with AWS STS (Security Token Service).
4. If successful, STS returns the temporary AWS credentials that the pod can use to access AWS services.

It is important to note that IRSA does not use the AWS IAM authenticator or the aws-auth ConfigMap, which are more relevant for user and node authentication to the EKS cluster itself. IRSA is specifically designed for pod-to-AWS service authentication.

The kubectl command and IAM user authentication are not directly relevant to IRSA, as IRSA operates at the pod level within the cluster, not at the user, or external access level.

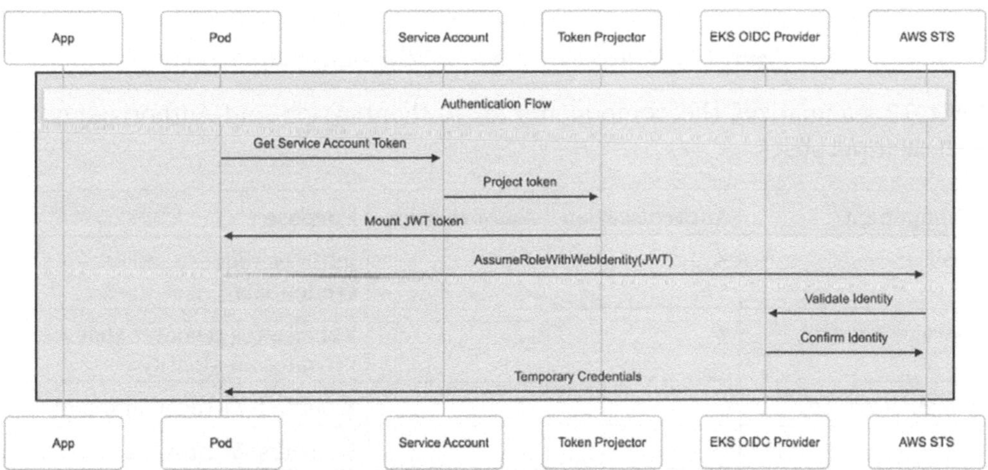


**Figure 6.1:** *Sequence Diagram for IRSA Authentication Flow*

Authorization in EKS determines what you can do. At the Kubernetes level, it primarily uses Role-Based Access Control (RBAC). This includes **Roles** and **ClusterRoles**, as well as **RoleBindings** and **ClusterRoleBindings**. Service Accounts also play a role in authorization. At the AWS level, authorization is managed through IAM Policies, IAM Roles, and resource-based policies. As shown in *Figure* 6.2, once authenticated, the pod receives temporary AWS credentials. These credentials' permissions are defined by the IAM role's policies. The role determines which AWS services and resources the pod can access, such as reading from specific S3 buckets, or writing to particular DynamoDB tables. The scope of these permissions is controlled through standard IAM policy documents.

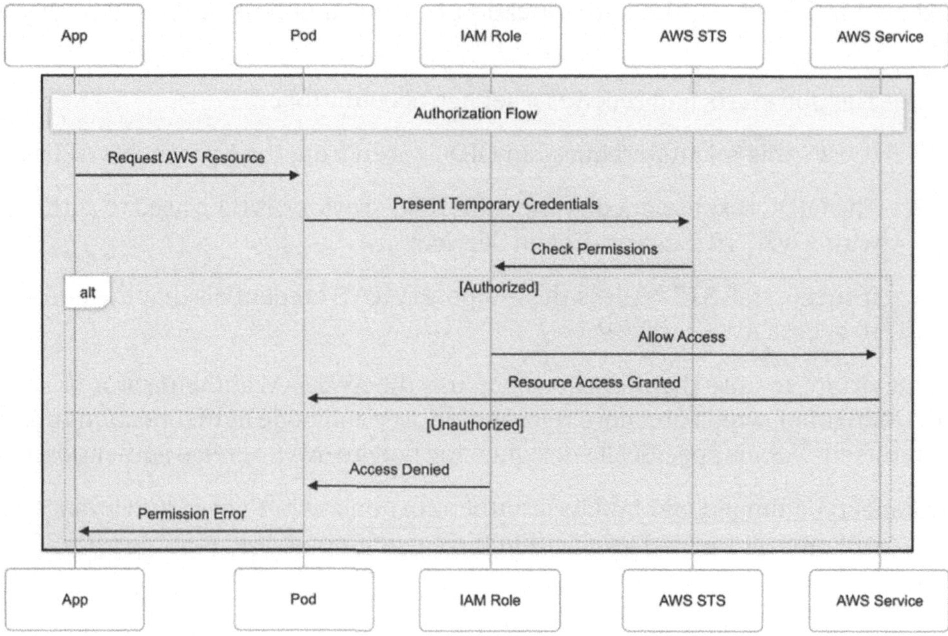


***Figure 6.2:*** *Sequence Diagram for IRSA Authorization Flow*

*Table* 6.2 summarizes the components for Authentication and Authorization, along with their purposes.

| **Component** | **Authentication** | **Authorization** | **Purpose** |
|---|---|---|---|
| Pod | ✓ | ✓ | Initiates request and uses credentials |
| Service Account | ✓ | | Kubernetes resource that provides an identity |
| Token Projector | ✓ | | Mounts JWT token into pod |
| OIDC Provider | ✓ | | Validates JWT tokens |
| AWS STS | ✓ | | Exchanges JWT for temporary AWS credentials |
| IAM Role | | ✓ | Defines permissions for the pod |
| IAM Policies | | ✓ | Specifies allowed actions and resources |
| AWS Services | | ✓ | Target of access requests |
| Policy Evaluation Engine | | ✓ | Evaluates whether a request is allowed |

***Table 6.2:*** *Components Involved in Authentication and Authorization*

# Implementing IRSA

IRSA implementation bridges the gap between Kubernetes and AWS IAM, eliminating the need for storing long-term AWS credentials, or managing sensitive access keys within your cluster. IRSA works by establishing a trust chain through an OpenID Connect (OIDC) provider, allowing pods to automatically receive temporary AWS credentials, based on their service account configuration. Implementing IRSA involves three key steps: Setting up an IAM OIDC provider for your cluster, creating IAM roles with appropriate trust relationships, followed by configuring Kubernetes service accounts with the corresponding role annotations. This solution enhances security by following the principle of least privilege, and provides a robust, manageable way to handle AWS authentication for your EKS workloads. *Figure* 6.3 details the IRSA implementation.

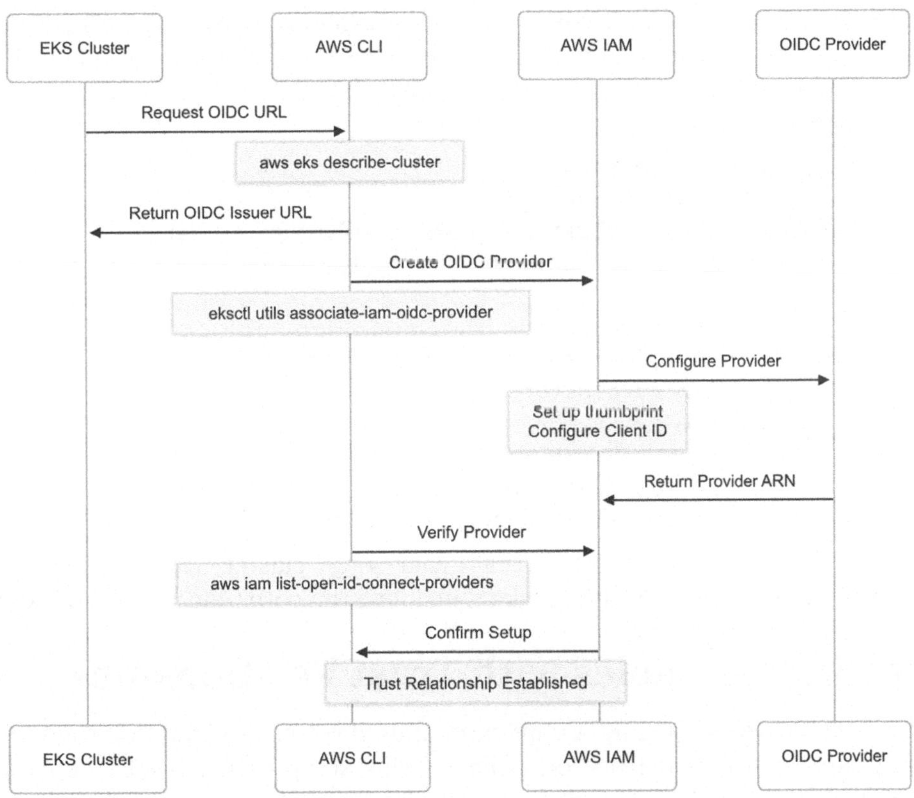


***Figure 6.3:*** *Sequence Diagram for Implementing IRSA*

Let us now explore each component of IRSA implementation in detail.

## Creating an IAM OIDC Provider for Your Cluster

The first critical step in implementing IRSA is establishing an IAM OIDC (OpenID Connect) provider for your EKS cluster. This provider creates a trust bridge between AWS IAM and your Kubernetes cluster's service accounts.

Begin by retrieving your cluster's OIDC issuer URL using the AWS CLI command '**aws eks describe-cluster**'. You can create the provider using either **eksctl**, or manual configuration through the AWS Console. With eksctl, the process is streamlined using the command '**eksctl utils associate-iam-oidc-provider --cluster <cluster-name> --approve**'.

For manual setup through the AWS Console, navigate to **IAM** > **Identity Providers** > **Add Provider**, select **OpenID Connect**, and input your cluster's OIDC issuer URL. The provider's thumbprint and client ID must be properly configured to establish the trust relationship. Once created, you will receive a provider ARN that will be necessary for subsequent role configurations. Verify the provider's successful creation by checking its status in the IAM console, or using the AWS CLI command '**aws iam list-open-id-connect-providers**'.

```
# Example CLI command
# Get OIDC issuer URL
aws eks describe-cluster --name my-cluster --query
"cluster.identity.oidc.issuer" --output text

# Create OIDC provider
eksctl utils associate-iam-oidc-provider \
    --cluster my-cluster \
    --approve

# Verify provider creation
aws iam list-open-id-connect-providers
```

This foundational step ensures that your EKS cluster can establish secure communications with AWS IAM services, enabling the core functionality of IRSA.

## Creating IAM Roles with Trust Relationships

The second crucial step in IRSA implementation involves creating IAM roles with the appropriate trust and permission policies. This setup enables Kubernetes service accounts to assume AWS IAM roles securely. Here is a systematic breakdown:

1. **Create Trust Policy**

```
{
  "Version": "2012-10-17",
  "Statement": [
    {
```

```
        "Effect": "Allow",
        "Principal": {
          "Federated": "arn:aws:iam::ACCOUNT_ID:oidc-provider/oidc.
eks.REGION.amazonaws.com/id/EXAMPLE"
        },
        "Action": "sts:AssumeRoleWithWebIdentity",
        "Condition": {
          "StringEquals": {
            "oidc.eks.REGION.amazonaws.com/id/EXAMPLE:sub":
"system:serviceaccount:NAMESPACE:SERVICE_ACCOUNT_NAME"
          }
        }
      }
    ]
  }
```

2. **Create IAM Role**

```
aws iam create-role \
    --role-name my-eks-role \
    --assume-role-policy-document file://trust-policy.json
```

3. **Attach Required Permissions**

```
aws iam put-role-policy \
    --role-name my-eks-role \
    --policy-name my-policy \
    --policy-document file://permission-policy.json

# Or attach AWS managed policy
aws iam attach-role-policy \
    --role-name my-eks-role \
    --policy-arn arn:aws:iam::aws:policy/needed-policy
```

The trust relationship ensures that only specified service accounts from your EKS cluster can assume the role, while the permissions policy defines what AWS resources, they can access.

# Annotating Service Accounts

The final step in IRSA implementation involves configuring Kubernetes service accounts with the appropriate IAM role annotations. This configuration enables pods to automatically receive AWS credentials through the service account. Here is a structured approach:

1. **Create Service Account with IAM Role Annotation**:

```
apiVersion: v1
kind: ServiceAccount
metadata:
```

```
  name: my-service-account
  namespace: my-namespace
  annotations:
    eks.amazonaws.com/role-arn: arn:aws:iam::ACCOUNT_ID:role/my-
eks-role
```

2. **Apply the Service Account**:

```
kubectl apply -f service-account.yaml
```

3. **Reference in Pod/Deployment**:

```
apiVersion: apps/v1
kind: Deployment
metadata:
  name: my-application
spec:
  template:
    spec:
      serviceAccountName: my-service-account
      containers:
      - name: my-app
        image: my-image:tag
```

# Best Practices

Implementing IAM Roles for Service Accounts (IRSA) in Amazon EKS requires careful consideration of security, scalability, and operational efficiency. These best practices establish a robust foundation for managing AWS credentials within your Kubernetes workloads, while maintaining security standards and operational excellence. By following these guidelines, organizations can effectively implement IRSA, while minimizing security risks, and maintaining operational control. The key areas of focus include implementing the principle of least privilege, establishing clear role boundaries, and following proven patterns for common use cases. Let us explore these in detail.

# Principle of Least Privilege

The principle of least privilege stands as a cornerstone of security best practices in IRSA implementation for EKS clusters. This fundamental approach ensures that applications and services are granted only the minimum permissions necessary to perform their intended functions, significantly reducing the potential attack surface and limiting the impact of any security breaches.

When implementing least privilege in IRSA, begin by defining granular permissions that specify exact actions and resources. Instead of using broad permissions like "**`s3:*`**", configure specific actions such as "**`s3:GetObject`**" and "**`s3:ListBucket`**" for precisely defined resource ARNs.

Resource-level restrictions should be implemented using explicit ARNs and conditional statements. Utilize AWS tags to further refine access control, and establish clear resource naming conventions. Consider implementing separate roles for read and write operations, and group related permissions by function to maintain clarity and control. Regular auditing of these permissions through AWS IAM Access Analyzer helps identify and remove unused or excessive permissions.

Monitoring and compliance form crucial components of the least privilege strategy. Implement CloudTrail logging for IAM activities, set up alerts for denied access attempts, and establish automated policy compliance checks. Regular validation of role configurations and service account settings ensures the maintenance of security standards.

To maintain this security posture effectively, establish a systematic approach to permission management. Start with zero permissions and add them incrementally based on validated requirements. Document all permission changes with clear justification, implement change control procedures for role modifications, and conduct regular security assessments. Set up automated compliance checking and maintain a comprehensive inventory of roles and permissions.

## Role Scope and Boundaries

Role scope and boundaries in IRSA represent a critical framework for maintaining security and operational control within your EKS environment. By establishing clear delineations between different environments, teams, and applications, organizations can effectively manage access permissions, while minimizing security risks. This structured approach ensures that roles remain properly segregated and maintain appropriate access levels across your Kubernetes infrastructure.

The foundation of effective role boundaries begins with namespace-based isolation. Each namespace should have distinct roles that reflect its purpose and security requirements. For example, production environments should utilize more restrictive roles compared to development environments, as demonstrated in this configuration:

```
# Production configuration
apiVersion: v1
kind: ServiceAccount
metadata:
  name: app-service-account
  namespace: production
  annotations:
    eks.amazonaws.com/role-arn: arn:aws:iam::ACCOUNT_ID:role/
prod-app-role
```

Permission boundaries serve as guardrails that define the maximum permissions any role can have, regardless of the policies attached to it. These boundaries should implement strict controls through conditions that limit access based on tags, regions, or other relevant attributes. Consider this example of a boundary policy:

```
{
    "Version": "2012-10-17",
    "Statement": [
        {
            "Effect": "Allow",
            "Action": [
                "s3:*",
                "dynamodb:*"
            ],
            "Resource": "*",
            "Condition": {
                "StringEquals": {
                    "aws:ResourceTag/Environment":
"${aws:PrincipalTag/Environment}",
                    "aws:RequestedRegion": ["us-west-2",
"us-east-1"]
                }
            }
        }
    ]
}
```

A comprehensive IRSA boundary strategy combines structured environmental separation with robust monitoring mechanisms. Environmental isolation encompasses naming conventions, tagging strategies, and environment-specific roles, ensuring proper workload separation across development, staging, and production. This is supported by monitoring through CloudWatch metrics, boundary violation detection, and regular audits. Success depends on clear documentation, consistent governance, and regular reviews to maintain security as the infrastructure scales.

# Common Use Cases and Patterns

In the landscape of IRSA implementation within EKS, several common use cases and patterns have emerged, providing tried-and-tested approaches for securing and managing AWS service access from Kubernetes workloads. These patterns typically align with specific operational requirements and common AWS service integrations, offering a blueprint for organizations to follow.

One of the most prevalent patterns involves infrastructure management components such as External DNS, ALB Ingress Controller, and Cluster Autoscaler. These components often require specific AWS permissions to function effectively within an

EKS environment. For instance, an External DNS service account might be configured with an IAM role that allows it to manage Route53 records, while an ALB Ingress Controller would need permissions to create and manage Application Load Balancers.

Data service integration patterns are another crucial category, encompassing access to services like S3, DynamoDB, and SQS. These patterns often involve creating service accounts with tailored permissions for specific data operations. For example, an S3 accessor service account might be granted read and write permissions to specific buckets, while a DynamoDB accessor could be limited to specific tables or operations.

Operational patterns focus on cross-cutting concerns such as logging, monitoring, backup, and secret management. These often involve integrations with services such as CloudWatch for logging and monitoring, AWS Backup for disaster recovery, and AWS Secrets Manager for secure credential management. Each of these patterns requires careful consideration of the principle of least privilege, ensuring that the associated IAM roles have only the necessary permissions to perform their intended functions.

When implementing these patterns, it is crucial to follow the best practices such as using separate service accounts for different functions, implementing clear error handling mechanisms, and regularly monitoring service account usage. Organizations should also conduct regular security assessments, maintain version control for configurations, and thoroughly document integration points.

By leveraging these established patterns and adhering to the best practices, organizations can implement IRSA effectively, ensuring a balance between security and operational efficiency in their EKS environments. Regular testing and refinement of these access patterns help maintain a robust and secure infrastructure as the application ecosystem evolves.

# Pod Security Policies

Pod Security Policies (PSPs) form a critical security foundation in EKS clusters by enforcing security standards and maintaining a robust security posture. Despite their pending deprecation in favor of Pod Security Admission (PSA), understanding PSP principles remains essential for implementing effective security controls in Kubernetes environments. PSPs provide cluster-level mechanisms to control sensitive aspects of pod specifications, ensuring that workloads consistently adhere to security best practices and organizational requirements.

Security contexts represent a fundamental component of pod security, operating at both pod and container levels. Pod-level security contexts manage settings that affect all containers within the pod, including user/group IDs, SELinux contexts, and file system permissions. These settings establish a baseline security posture for the entire pod. Container-level security contexts provide more granular control, allowing specific security configurations for individual containers such as capability management, privilege escalation prevention, and root access restrictions. This dual-layer approach ensures comprehensive security control, while maintaining flexibility for container-specific requirements.

The introduction of Pod Security Standards brings a structured approach to security enforcement through three distinct profiles: Privileged, Baseline, and Restricted. The Privileged Profile allows unrestricted access, typically reserved for system components and administrative tasks. The Baseline Profile implements moderate controls that prevent known privilege escalation vectors, while maintaining operational flexibility. The Restricted Profile enforces the most stringent security controls, suitable for high-security environments and sensitive workloads. These standardized profiles simplify security policy management, while ensuring consistent security practices across the cluster.

As Kubernetes evolves, the transition from PSPs to Pod Security Admission represents a significant advancement in container security management. PSA, integrated into Kubernetes versions 1.23 and newer, offers a more streamlined and maintainable approach to pod security enforcement. Organizations should approach this migration strategically, beginning with an assessment of existing PSP configurations and mapping them to equivalent PSA policies. This transition should be executed gradually, ensuring continuous security coverage, while adapting to the new framework. The migration process provides an opportunity to reassess and strengthen security controls, leveraging the improved features and simplified configuration model of PSA.

# Understanding Pod Security Context

Pod Security Context serves as a fundamental security mechanism in EKS environments, defining crucial privilege and access control settings for pods and their containers. This feature is necessary in EKS deployments as it ensures consistent security practices across workloads, and helps prevent common security vulnerabilities such as privilege escalation, unauthorized access, and container breakouts. In the context of EKS, where multiple workloads often share cluster resources, properly configured security contexts become vital for maintaining strong security boundaries between applications, and protecting sensitive workloads.

At the pod level, security context establishes cluster-wide security parameters that apply uniformly to all containers within the pod. These settings encompass critical security aspects such as file system group IDs (**`fsGroup`**), user and group IDs (**`runAsUser`**/**`runAsGroup`**), and SELinux contexts. Pod-level security contexts provide a baseline security posture that ensures consistent security practices across all containers within the pod. This uniformity is particularly important in EKS environments where standardized security configurations help maintain compliance requirements, and simplify security auditing processes. The following is an example implementation:

```
# Example - Pod level security implementation
apiVersion: v1
kind: Pod
metadata:
  name: secure-pod
spec:
  securityContext:
    fsGroup: 2000
    runAsNonRoot: true
    runAsUser: 1000
    runAsGroup: 3000
    seccompProfile:
      type: RuntimeDefault
  containers:
  - name: app
    image: app:latest
```

Container-level security context offers more granular control, allowing specific security configurations for individual containers within a pod. These settings can override pod-level configurations, and include detailed controls such as Linux capabilities, privilege escalation restrictions, and root file system access limitations. This granularity is crucial in EKS deployments where different containers within the same pod might require varying levels of access or privileges. For instance, while one container might need specific Linux capabilities for network operations, another might require read-only file system access for enhanced security. The following is the example implementation:

```
# Example - Container level security implementation
apiVersion: v1
kind: Pod
metadata:
  name: secure-pod
spec:
  containers:
  - name: app
    image: app:latest
    securityContext:
      capabilities:
        drop: ["ALL"]
        add: ["NET_BIND_SERVICE"]
      allowPrivilegeEscalation: false
      readOnlyRootFilesystem: true
      runAsNonRoot: true
      runAsUser: 1000
```

*Figure* 6.4 provides a clear overview of Pod Security at pod level and container level.

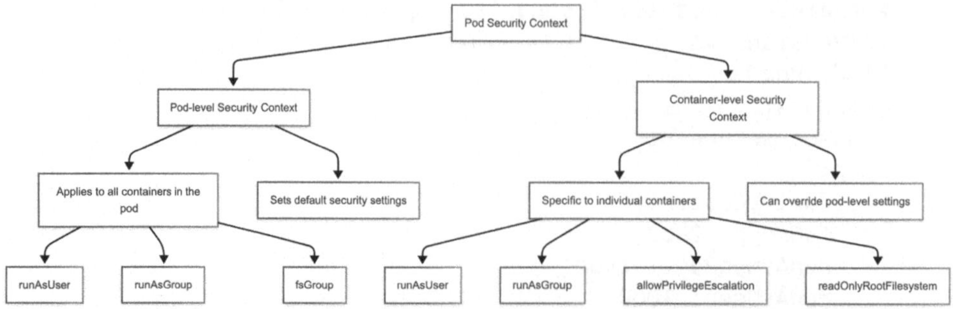


***Figure 6.4:*** *Pod Security Overview*

Implementing security contexts in EKS environments requires careful consideration of the best practices such as running containers as non-root users, dropping unnecessary Linux capabilities, and enabling read-only root file systems where possible. Regular audits of security context configurations ensure continued alignment with security requirements, while consistent documentation helps maintain transparency, and facilitates troubleshooting. This comprehensive approach to security context configuration helps organizations maintain a robust security posture, while ensuring their applications have the necessary permissions to function effectively within the EKS environment.

# Implementing Pod Security Policies

Pod Security Policies (PSPs) serve as a critical security enforcement mechanism in EKS, providing cluster-level controls to ensure consistent security standards across all workloads. Although PSPs are transitioning to Pod Security Admission, their fundamental principles remain essential for maintaining robust container security in Kubernetes environments. These policies function as security gatekeepers, enforcing controls over privileged operations, host resource access, volume management, and container runtime behaviors. In EKS applications, PSPs become particularly crucial due to the multi-tenant nature of clusters, where multiple applications and teams share cluster resources, requiring strict security boundaries and access controls.

The implementation of PSPs involves configuring comprehensive security rules that govern pod deployment and execution. These policies control various security aspects, including container privilege settings and capability management, host namespace access and resource sharing, volume mount restrictions and file system permissions, user and group ID controls, SELinux, AppArmor, and Seccomp profiles, as well as runtime class specifications. By meticulously defining these parameters, organizations can ensure that all pods adhere to prescribed security standards, mitigating risks associated with misconfigured or overly permissive container environments.

Baseline policies establish the minimum security standards that all pods must meet before being scheduled in the cluster. These standards ensure consistent security compliance across workloads, while maintaining operational flexibility. By implementing baseline policies, organizations create a security foundation that applies uniformly across the entire EKS cluster, reducing the likelihood of security gaps or inconsistencies. The distinction between privileged and non-privileged pods creates clear security boundaries, with privileged access strictly limited to essential system components. This separation is crucial in maintaining the principle of least privilege, and preventing potential security breaches or unauthorized escalations. Runtime class restrictions add another security layer by controlling container execution environments, enabling granular control over pod execution contexts and isolation requirements. This fine-grained control allows organizations to align security configurations with specific workload needs, while maintaining overall cluster security integrity.

# Defining Baseline Policies

Defining baseline policies serve as the cornerstone of pod security in EKS clusters. These policies establish minimum security standards that all pods must meet to be scheduled, creating a consistent security foundation across the entire cluster. A typical baseline policy might include restrictions on privileged operations, enforcing non-root user execution, limiting Linux capabilities, and controlling volume types. By implementing these baseline policies, organizations ensure that all pods maintain a minimum acceptable security posture, even in the absence of more specific policies. This approach is particularly beneficial in EKS environments where diverse teams may deploy various applications, each with different security requirements. A typical baseline policy might include:

```
# Example of Baseline Policy
apiVersion: policy/v1beta1
kind: PodSecurityPolicy
metadata:
  name: baseline-psp
spec:
  privileged: false
  allowPrivilegeEscalation: false
  requiredDropCapabilities:
    - ALL
  runAsUser:
    rule: 'MustRunAsNonRoot'
  seLinux:
    rule: 'RunAsAny'
  fsGroup:
    rule: 'RunAsAny'
  supplementalGroups:
    rule: 'RunAsAny'
  volumes:
    - 'configMap'
```

```
    - 'emptyDir'
    - 'projected'
    - 'secret'
    - 'downwardAPI'
    - 'persistentVolumeClaim'
```

## Privileged vs Non-privileged Pods

The distinction between privileged and non-privileged pods is a critical aspect of maintaining robust security in EKS environments. Privileged pods, which have elevated access to host resources, should be strictly limited, carefully monitored, and typically reserved for system-level operations within specific, tightly controlled namespaces. Non-privileged pods, on the other hand, operate with restricted capabilities, providing better isolation and security. This separation is crucial in EKS, where maintaining clear boundaries between different workloads, and preventing potential security breaches is paramount. Implementing distinct policies for privileged and non-privileged pods allows organizations to maintain a clear separation of concerns, and enforce the principle of least privilege across their EKS cluster. Here is an example configuration showing both types:

```
# Privileged PSP (restricted to system namespaces)
apiVersion: policy/v1beta1
kind: PodSecurityPolicy
metadata:
  name: privileged-psp
spec:
  privileged: true
  allowPrivilegeEscalation: true
  hostNetwork: true
  hostPID: true

# Non-privileged PSP (default for application workloads)
apiVersion: policy/v1beta1
kind: PodSecurityPolicy
metadata:
  name: restricted-psp
spec:
  privileged: false
  allowPrivilegeEscalation: false
  hostNetwork: false
  hostPID: false
```

## Runtime Class Restrictions

Runtime class restrictions add another layer of security by controlling which container runtimes pods can use. In EKS environments, where different workloads might require varying levels of isolation or specific security features, this becomes particularly important. By defining allowed runtime classes, setting default runtime configurations, and enforcing runtime restrictions per namespace, organizations can ensure that pods use appropriate container runtimes based on their security requirements. This granular control over runtime environments allows for optimized security configurations that align with specific workload needs, while maintaining overall cluster security. Regular monitoring and auditing of runtime usage further enhance the security posture by ensuring ongoing compliance with defined policies, and quickly identifying any deviations or potential security risks.

# Pod Security Standards

Pod Security Standards provide a standardized approach to securing workloads in EKS clusters, offering well-defined security profiles that cater to different operational requirements. These standards are crucial in EKS environments where maintaining consistent security postures across diverse workloads is essential for overall cluster security. The standards define three distinct profiles – Privileged, Baseline, and Restricted – each offering progressively stricter security controls, enabling organizations to implement appropriate security measures based on workload requirements, and sensitivity levels.

The Privileged Profile represents the most permissive security configuration, providing unrestricted access to pod and container capabilities. This profile is typically reserved for system-critical components and administrative tasks that require elevated privileges such as infrastructure management tools, logging agents, or monitoring systems. While offering maximum flexibility, the Privileged Profile should be used sparingly, and only for workloads that absolutely require elevated access. Strict controls should be in place to monitor and audit pods running with this profile, as they represent potential security risks, if compromised. Therefore, let us dive deeper into these.

- **Privileged Profile:** The Privileged Profile represents the most permissive security configuration, providing unrestricted access to pod and container capabilities. This profile is typically reserved for system-critical components and administrative tasks that require elevated privileges such as infrastructure management tools, logging agents, or monitoring systems. While offering maximum flexibility, the privileged profile should be used sparingly and only for workloads that absolutely require elevated access. Strict controls should be in place to monitor and audit pods running with this profile, as they represent potential security risks, if compromised.
- **Baseline Profile:** The Baseline Profile implements moderate security controls that prevents known privilege escalation paths, while maintaining compatibility with most standard workloads. This profile serves as a middle

ground, suitable for general application deployments that require standard Kubernetes functionality without elevated privileges. The Baseline Profile enforces common security best practices such as preventing privilege escalation, requiring non-root users, and implementing basic container security contexts. This profile is often used as the default security stance for most applications running in an EKS cluster, providing a good balance between security and functionality.

- **Restricted Profile:** The Restricted Profile enforces the most stringent security controls, providing the highest level of pod security within the standard profiles. This profile is ideal for security-critical applications and environments with strict compliance requirements. It implements comprehensive security measures, including mandatory non-root execution, strict capability controls, read-only root file systems, and Seccomp Profile enforcement. While this profile offers the strongest security posture, it requires careful consideration of application requirements, as it may impact certain functionalities that depend on elevated privileges, or specific system access.

# Migration from PSP to PSA

The transition from Pod Security Policies (PSPs) to Pod Security Admission (PSA) represents a significant shift in Kubernetes security architecture, driven by the deprecation of PSPs in version 1.21, and their planned removal in version 1.25. This migration is particularly crucial for EKS clusters, where maintaining robust security controls during and after the transition is  crucial. Pod Security Admission offers a more streamlined and standardized approach to implementing pod security controls, aligning with the built-in Pod Security Standards.

The migration process involves several key steps and considerations. First, organizations need to audit their existing PSPs to understand the current security requirements, and map them to equivalent PSA configurations. Here is an example of transitioning from a PSP to PSA:

```
# Original PSP
apiVersion: policy/v1beta1
kind: PodSecurityPolicy
metadata:
  name: restricted-psp
spec:
  privileged: false
  allowPrivilegeEscalation: false
  requiredDropCapabilities:
    - ALL
```

```
# Equivalent PSA Configuration
apiVersion: v1
kind: Namespace
metadata:
  name: secure-workload
  labels:
    pod-security.kubernetes.io/enforce: restricted
    pod-security.kubernetes.io/audit: restricted
    pod-security.kubernetes.io/warn: restricted
```

# Network Security Configurations

Network security configurations play a pivotal role in ensuring the security and integrity of applications deployed in Amazon EKS. As containerized applications often handle sensitive data and critical operations, implementing robust network security measures is essential to protect against unauthorized access, data breaches, and potential attacks. In EKS environments, where multiple applications and microservices coexist within the same cluster, proper network segmentation and access control become paramount to maintain isolation between workloads and limit the potential blast radius in case of a security incident.

Effective network security encompasses three key areas: VPC and subnet design, pod networking, and external access control. A well-architected Virtual Private Cloud (VPC) provides the foundation for network isolation, with carefully planned subnets enabling granular control over network traffic. Best practices include separating public and private subnets, with EKS nodes typically placed in private subnets to reduce exposure. Implementing NAT gateways allows outbound internet access for nodes in private subnets, while maintaining protection from inbound traffic. Additionally, utilizing multiple Availability Zones for subnet distribution enhances resilience, and ensures high availability of EKS workloads. The following *Figure* 6.5 illustrates VPC and subnet design with pod networking:

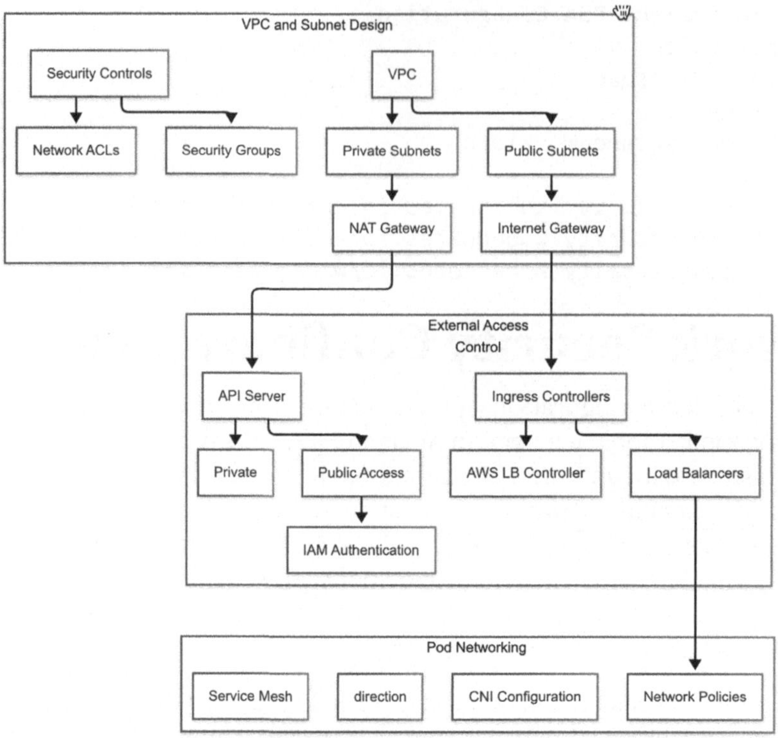


***Figure 6.5:*** *VPC and Subnet Design with Pod Networking*

# VPC and Subnet Design

In Amazon EKS, the design of Virtual Private Cloud (VPC) and subnets is crucial for establishing a secure and efficient network architecture. This design forms the foundation of network isolation and traffic control for EKS clusters. A well-structured VPC typically incorporates both public and private subnets, each serving distinct purposes in the EKS environment. Public subnets are primarily used for resources that require direct internet connectivity such as load balancers or NAT gateways. These subnets have routes to an Internet Gateway, allowing inbound and outbound internet traffic. In contrast, private subnets host the EKS worker nodes and pods, providing an additional layer of security by isolating them from direct internet access. Private subnets typically route their outbound internet traffic through NAT gateways placed in public subnets, enabling controlled internet access while protecting nodes from inbound connections.

Network Access Control Lists (NACLs) and security groups work in tandem to provide multi-layered security within the VPC. NACLs act as a stateless firewall at the subnet level, controlling inbound and outbound traffic, based on predefined rules. They offer a broad, subnet-wide control over network traffic. Security groups, on the other hand, operate at the instance or ENI (Elastic Network Interface) level, providing stateful firewalling capabilities. In EKS, security groups are particularly important for controlling traffic to and from worker nodes and pods. Best practices involve configuring NACLs with broad allow rules and using security groups for fine-grained access control. For example, a security group for EKS nodes might allow incoming traffic only on specific ports from the Kubernetes control plane and other nodes within the cluster. This layered approach of using both NACLs and security groups provides defense-in-depth, enhancing the overall security posture of the EKS environment.

# Pod Networking

Pod networking in Amazon EKS establishes the foundation for container-to-container communication and external connectivity. The Amazon VPC CNI plugin, the default networking solution for EKS, provides native integration with VPC networking capabilities by allocating VPC IP addresses directly to pods. This integration enables pods to communicate with other AWS services, and the existing VPC resources, while maintaining consistent network policies and security controls. Network policies in EKS define how pods communicate with each other and other network endpoints, acting as a pod-level firewall to control ingress and egress traffic. Using network policy providers like Calico or Cilium, administrators can implement fine-grained rules that restrict pod communication, based on labels, namespaces, and IP ranges, effectively creating micro-segmentation within the cluster.

CNI configurations in EKS require careful planning to optimize networking performance and security. The VPC CNI can be configured to support different IP address management modes, including prefix delegation for improved IP address utilization and custom networking for specialized requirements. These configurations affect important aspects such as the maximum number of pods per node, IP address allocation efficiency, and network performance. For example, enabling prefix delegation can significantly increase the available IP addresses per node, while custom networking allows pods to be assigned IP addresses from specific CIDR ranges. Service mesh integration, typically implemented through AWS App Mesh or Istio, adds another layer of networking capabilities by providing advanced traffic management, security, and observability features. The service mesh facilitates sophisticated routing patterns, implements mutual TLS between services, and enables detailed monitoring of service-to-service communication. This integration is particularly valuable in microservices architectures where complex networking patterns and security requirements necessitate fine-grained control over service communication.

# External Access Control

External access control in Amazon EKS requires careful orchestration of multiple components to ensure secure and efficient traffic management into the cluster. Load balancer configurations play a crucial role, with AWS Application Load Balancers (ALBs) and Network Load Balancers (NLBs) serving as the primary entry points for external traffic. These load balancers can be automatically provisioned and configured through the AWS Load Balancer Controller, which integrates seamlessly with Kubernetes service resources. Best practices include implementing SSL/TLS termination at the load balancer level, configuring appropriate health checks, and utilizing security groups to restrict the access to specific IP ranges or VPCs.

Ingress controllers in EKS provide a sophisticated layer of traffic routing and management for HTTP/HTTPS traffic. The AWS Load Balancer Controller, when configured as an ingress controller, automatically provisions and manages ALBs based on Kubernetes Ingress resources. This enables features such as path-based routing, SSL/TLS termination, and integration with AWS Certificate Manager for automated certificate management. Example configurations include setting up host-based routing for multiple applications, implementing rate limiting, and configuring cross-zone load balancing for improved availability. The controller also supports important security features such as authentication through Amazon Cognito, and granular access control through annotations.

API server endpoint access requires particular attention, as it controls how the Kubernetes control plane can be accessed. EKS offers both public and private endpoint access configurations, allowing organizations to align with their security requirements. Private endpoint access restricts API server communication to within the VPC, enhancing security by eliminating exposure to the public internet. When public access is required, it should be limited to specific IP ranges through endpoint policies. Additionally, implementing AWS IAM authentication for Kubernetes (**`aws-iam-authenticator`**) provides integrated access control, ensuring only authorized users and roles can interact with the cluster. Regular audit logging of API server access through AWS CloudTrail helps maintain security compliance, and enables threat detection.

# Secret Management with AWS Secrets Manager

Effective secret management is crucial for maintaining security in containerized applications running on Amazon EKS. As organizations deploy increasingly complex applications, the need to securely handle sensitive information such as database credentials, API keys, and certificates becomes paramount. AWS Secrets Manager, when integrated with EKS, provides a robust solution that addresses these challenges while ensuring scalability and maintaining security best practices. This integration supports automated secret rotation, version control, and fine-grained access management, essential features for modern cloud-native applications.

# Integration Architecture

The integration architecture for AWS Secrets Manager in EKS environments combines several key components to create a seamless and secure secret management system. At its core, AWS Secrets Manager serves as the centralized repository for storing and managing sensitive information such as database credentials, API keys, and certificates. The setup process involves creating secrets within Secrets Manager, configuring encryption settings, using AWS Key Management Service (KMS), and establishing appropriate IAM policies to control access. This foundational layer ensures that secrets are securely stored and encrypted at rest.

The External Secrets Operator (ESO) plays a pivotal role in bridging the gap between AWS Secrets Manager and Kubernetes. ESO is deployed as a controller within the EKS cluster, and is responsible for synchronizing secrets from AWS Secrets Manager to Kubernetes secrets. It operates by watching for custom resources called Secret Store and External Secret, which define the mapping between AWS secrets and their Kubernetes counterparts. ESO handles the periodic refresh of secrets, ensuring that any updates in Secrets Manager are promptly reflected in the cluster. This automation significantly reduces the operational overhead of managing secrets across environments.

IRSA (IAM Roles for Service Accounts) configuration is crucial for enabling secure access to AWS Secrets Manager from within EKS pods. IRSA allows Kubernetes service accounts to assume IAM roles, providing fine-grained access control to AWS resources, including Secrets Manager. The setup involves creating an IAM role with appropriate permissions to access specific secrets, configuring the EKS cluster's OIDC provider, and annotating Kubernetes service accounts with the IAM role, ARN. This configuration enables pods to authenticate with AWS services, using short-lived credentials, eliminating the need for long-term access keys, and enhancing overall security. By leveraging IRSA, organizations can implement the principle of least privilege, ensuring that each application only has access to the secrets, it requires.

# Implementation Patterns

Static secrets management in EKS follows straightforward pattern where predefined, long-lived credentials are stored in AWS Secrets Manager and synchronized to Kubernetes, using External Secrets Operator. These secrets, such as API keys or service account credentials, typically remain constant over extended periods. The implementation involves creating Secret Store resources that map AWS secrets to Kubernetes secrets, allowing applications to consume them through standard Kubernetes mechanisms. This pattern is particularly useful for managing configuration data that changes infrequently such as third-party API credentials or encryption keys, where automated rotation is not readily available, or necessary.

Dynamic secrets present a more sophisticated pattern, where credentials are generated on-demand and have limited lifespans. In EKS environments, this often involves integration with services such as AWS RDS or external systems that support dynamic credential generation. The implementation leverages AWS Secrets Manager's dynamic secrets capability, where temporary credentials are generated when requested and automatically revoked after their designated lifetime expires. This pattern is particularly valuable for database access credentials or temporary API tokens, as it significantly reduces the risk window associated with credential exposure, and eliminates the need for manual credential rotation.

Rotation policies form a critical pattern in secret management, automating the process of updating credentials at regular intervals. AWS Secrets Manager supports both automated and manual rotation strategies, which can be integrated with EKS workloads through External Secrets Operator. The implementation includes defining rotation schedules, configuring rotation lambda functions for custom rotation logic, and ensuring that applications can handle credential updates gracefully. This pattern is especially important for compliance requirements that mandate regular credential rotation. The rotation process is managed transparently to applications, with Secrets Manager maintaining, both the current and previous versions of secrets to prevent disruption during rotation events. This approach ensures continuous application availability, while maintaining strong security practices through regular credential updates.

# Best Practices

Effective secret management in Amazon EKS environments requires careful attention to security, monitoring, and lifecycle management when utilizing AWS Secrets Manager. These practices ensure that sensitive information remains protected while maintaining operational efficiency across containerized workloads.

Encryption at rest serves as the foundational security measure, leveraging AWS KMS to protect secrets stored in Secrets Manager. In EKS environments, this typically involves creating custom KMS keys for different environments or application tiers, enabling granular control over encryption and decryption processes. Organizations should configure their EKS pods to use IAM Roles for Service Accounts (IRSA) to securely access these encrypted secrets, ensuring that sensitive data remains protected throughout its lifecycle while maintaining the principle of least privilege.

Access logging and monitoring form the second critical component, with AWS CloudTrail automatically capturing all interactions with Secrets Manager. EKS administrators should integrate these logs with Amazon CloudWatch or third-party SIEM solutions to monitor for unusual access patterns or potential security breaches. Implementing alerts for specific events, such as failed access attempts from EKS pods or changes to critical secrets, helps maintain a proactive security posture. Regular audit reviews of these logs ensure compliance with security policies and help identify potential areas for improvement in secret access patterns.

Version management capabilities enable controlled updates and rollbacks of secrets while maintaining operational stability. In EKS deployments, this feature is particularly valuable for implementing secret rotation without disrupting running applications. Organizations should establish clear policies for version retention and implement regular secret rotation schedules, leveraging Secrets Manager's automatic rotation feature where possible. Applications deployed in EKS should be designed to handle credential updates gracefully, ensuring continuous operation during rotation events. This comprehensive approach to version management supports both security objectives and operational requirements, ensuring that changes to sensitive information remain controlled and documented throughout their lifecycle.

# Security Auditing and Compliance

In the dynamic landscape of containerized applications, maintaining robust security and ensuring compliance within Amazon EKS environments is paramount. As organizations deploy increasingly complex workloads on Kubernetes, the need for comprehensive security auditing and compliance measures becomes critical. This multifaceted approach encompasses audit logging through AWS CloudTrail for detailed API activity tracking, compliance tools like AWS Config and Security Hub for continuous assessment, robust monitoring and alerting mechanisms using GuardDuty and CloudWatch, and adherence to industry standards such as PCI DSS, HIPAA, and GDPR. By implementing these strategies, organizations can not only protect their containerized applications from potential threats but also demonstrate their commitment to regulatory compliance and best practices in cloud-native security. So, let us dive deeper into logging and compliance.

# Audit Logging

Comprehensive audit logging in Amazon EKS environments forms a critical component of security and compliance strategies, providing visibility into cluster operations across multiple layers.

- **Control Plane Logging:** Control plane logging enabled through EKS-managed Kubernetes API server flags, captures detailed information about API requests, authentication events, and controller activities. These logs, stored in Amazon CloudWatch Logs, offer insights into cluster-level operations, user actions, and potential security incidents. Organizations should configure control plane logging for all available log types, including audit, API server, authenticator, controller manager, and scheduler logs, to ensure complete visibility into cluster management activities.

- **Worker Node Logging:** Worker node logging extends the audit trail to individual nodes within the EKS cluster. This involves configuring the Amazon CloudWatch agent on each worker node to collect system logs, application logs, and kubelet logs. By leveraging CloudWatch Logs, administrators can centralize node-level logs, facilitating easier troubleshooting and security analysis. Best practices include setting up log retention policies, implementing log stream naming conventions for easy identification, and using CloudWatch Logs Insights for advanced log analysis. Additionally, organizations should consider integrating worker node logs with Security Information and Event Management (SIEM) systems for comprehensive security monitoring.
- **Application Logging:** Application logging within EKS requires a thoughtful approach to capture container-specific logs while maintaining scalability and performance. Implementing a logging sidecar pattern, where a dedicated container handles log collection and forwarding, can be an effective strategy for containerized applications. This approach allows for consistent log handling across different applications and simplifies log management at scale. Organizations should leverage Kubernetes-native logging solutions like Fluentd or Fluent Bit, deployed as DaemonSets, to collect logs from all pods and forward them to centralized logging systems such as Amazon CloudWatch Logs or Amazon OpenSearch Service. Implementing structured logging practices and including relevant metadata (such as pod name, namespace, and container ID) in log entries enhances the ability to correlate logs across the cluster and perform effective troubleshooting and security analysis.

# Compliance Tools

In the complex landscape of container orchestration, maintaining security compliance in Amazon EKS requires sophisticated tooling that adapts to the dynamic nature of Kubernetes workloads. AWS offers a comprehensive suite of compliance tools - AWS Config rules, Security Hub, and GuardDuty - that work together to ensure EKS clusters meet security standards and regulatory requirements through continuous assessment, centralized monitoring, and advanced threat detection.

These tools prove invaluable in real-world compliance scenarios across various industries. Financial services companies undergoing PCI DSS audits use AWS Config rules to verify encryption, logging, and network policy implementation for cardholder data isolation. Healthcare providers conducting HIPAA compliance checks leverage GuardDuty to detect potential PHI data exfiltration while ensuring proper encryption and access restrictions. SaaS companies facing SOC 2 Type II audits employ Security Hub to review security controls over extended periods, focusing on data availability and confidentiality. For GDPR compliance, multinational corporations verify data residency requirements and ensure least privilege access through IAM Access Analyzer. Organizations seeking ISO 27001 certification utilize a combination of these tools to demonstrate comprehensive security posture and incident response capabilities.

The seamless integration between these services creates a unified compliance and security framework that addresses both infrastructure and application-level requirements. This enables organizations to maintain strong security postures while effectively managing the complexities of containerized applications, highlighting the critical role of AWS compliance tools in meeting diverse regulatory requirements across industries. Let us examine each component of this compliance toolkit and how they work together to enhance EKS security.

- **AWS Config Rules:** AWS Config Rules play a crucial role in EKS compliance by continuously evaluating cluster configurations against predefined security and compliance standards. Organizations can leverage both AWS-managed rules specific to EKS, and create custom rules to address unique requirements. These rules can monitor critical aspects such as control plane logging, encryption settings, and network policies. When non-compliant configurations are detected, AWS Config can trigger automated remediation actions, ensuring rapid response to potential security vulnerabilities. The ability to track configuration changes over time also provides valuable audit trails for compliance reporting.
- **Security Hub Integration:** Security Hub integration brings a unified view of security alerts and compliance status across EKS clusters and other AWS services. By aggregating findings from multiple sources, including AWS Config and third-party tools, Security Hub provides a comprehensive overview of an organization's security posture. For EKS environments, Security Hub offers specific insights into Kubernetes security best practices, evaluating clusters against industry standards and generating actionable recommendations. The service's dashboards and reports facilitate easy tracking of compliance scores and trends, enabling teams to prioritize and address the most critical security issues efficiently.
- **GuardDuty for EKS:** GuardDuty for EKS extends AWS's threat detection capabilities to Kubernetes workloads, offering real-time monitoring and alerting for potential security threats. By analyzing various data sources, including control plane audit logs and VPC flow logs, GuardDuty can detect sophisticated threats such as container escape attempts, suspicious API calls, or potential data exfiltration activities. The service's machine learning models continuously evolve to identify new attack patterns, providing organizations with up-to-date protection against emerging threats. GuardDuty findings can be integrated with automated response workflows through Amazon EventBridge, enabling rapid mitigation of security incidents in EKS environments.

# Monitoring and Alerting

Effective monitoring and alerting form the cornerstone of operational excellence in Amazon EKS environments, providing essential visibility into cluster health, security events, and application performance. By leveraging AWS's native monitoring capabilities alongside Kubernetes-specific metrics, organizations can build a comprehensive observability framework that supports both proactive issue detection and rapid incident response. Through the seamless integration of CloudWatch, custom security metrics, and intelligent alert configurations, teams can maintain continuous awareness of their EKS infrastructure, while ensuring timely responses to potential security threats and operational challenges. This integrated approach enables organizations to correlate events across different layers of their infrastructure, from container-level metrics to cluster-wide security incidents, providing context-rich insights for better decision-making. The ability to customize monitoring parameters and alert thresholds allows teams to adapt their observability strategy to specific application requirements and compliance standards, creating a flexible yet robust monitoring framework.

- **CloudWatch Integration:** CloudWatch integration with EKS provides deep visibility into cluster operations through Container Insights and custom metric collection, serving as the foundation of a comprehensive monitoring strategy. The integration collects metrics from multiple layers of the EKS infrastructure, including control plane metrics for API server performance and etcd health, node-level metrics for CPU, memory, and network utilization, and pod and container-level performance metrics. Through CloudWatch Container Insights, organizations can automatically gather performance data, track resource utilization, and monitor the health of their Kubernetes workloads. This comprehensive data collection, combined with customized dashboards, enables teams to gain real-time insights into both the overall cluster health and individual workload performance, facilitating efficient troubleshooting and capacity planning.
- **Security Metrics:** Security metrics form a critical component of EKS monitoring, encompassing both platform and application-level security indicators crucial for maintaining a robust security posture. Key metrics include authentication and authorization failures, pod security policy violations, unusual network traffic patterns, container runtime security events, and API server audit logs analysis. Organizations should configure CloudWatch to collect and analyze security-relevant logs from various sources, including AWS WAF, Security Groups, and Kubernetes audit logs. Custom metrics can be created to track specific security events such as privilege escalation attempts, unauthorized API calls, and resource access patterns and anomalies. By continuously monitoring these security-specific metrics, organizations can quickly identify potential threats or misconfigurations, enabling rapid response to

security incidents and maintaining compliance with security standards. This comprehensive approach to security monitoring provides valuable insights into the security posture of EKS clusters, and helps identify potential threats before they escalate.

- **Alert Configuration:** Alert configuration in EKS environments requires a balanced approach that ensures timely awareness of critical issues while preventing alert fatigue. This strategy involves implementing a multi-tiered alerting system using CloudWatch Alarms, with severity-based thresholds tailored for different environments. Notifications are delivered through various channels like SNS, Slack, or PagerDuty, focusing on critical security events and providing context-rich information for quick response. Key aspects include alert correlation and aggregation, integration with incident management systems, and automated responses through EventBridge for critical issues. Organizations should carefully manage thresholds, implement alert aggregation, establish clear escalation paths, and utilize custom notification channels. Regular reviews and adjustments of these configurations help maintain an effective balance between comprehensive monitoring and operational efficiency, ensuring that EKS clusters remain secure and performant, while teams can respond efficiently to both security and operational incidents.

# Compliance Standards

In today's highly regulated cloud environments, maintaining compliance standards in Amazon EKS deployments is crucial for organizations handling sensitive data and critical workloads. EKS provides a robust foundation for implementing various compliance frameworks, from industry-standard security benchmarks to strict regulatory requirements. Through a combination of native Kubernetes security features, AWS services, and third-party tools, organizations can achieve and maintain compliance with CIS benchmarks, SOC 2 standards, and regulated industry requirements like HIPAA and PCI DSS. This comprehensive approach ensures that containerized applications meet security and compliance obligations, while maintaining operational efficiency.

- **CIS Benchmarks:** CIS benchmarks provide a foundational security framework for EKS configurations, offering specific guidelines for securing Kubernetes clusters. These benchmarks cover critical aspects such as control plane security, worker node configurations, network policies, and access controls. Organizations can leverage tools like kube-bench and AWS Security Hub to automatically assess their EKS clusters against these benchmarks, ensuring continuous compliance with security best practices.

- **SOC 2 Compliance:** SOC 2 compliance in EKS environments focuses on ensuring the security, availability, and confidentiality of customer data processed by containerized applications. This involves implementing robust access controls through IAM roles and RBAC, enabling comprehensive audit logging through CloudTrail and CloudWatch, and maintaining proper network segmentation using security groups and network policies. Organizations must demonstrate effective change management processes, regular security assessments, and incident response procedures. EKS features such as encrypted etcd storage, private endpoints, and pod security policies help meet SOC 2 trust service criteria.
- **HIPAA/PCI Requirements:** HIPAA and PCI requirements in EKS demand stringent controls for protecting sensitive healthcare and payment card data. For HIPAA compliance, organizations must ensure end-to-end encryption of Protected Health Information (PHI), implement strict access controls, and maintain detailed audit trails of all data access. PCI DSS compliance requires secure network architecture, regular vulnerability scanning of container images, and strict access control to cardholder data. EKS supports these requirements through features such as AWS KMS integration for encryption, Network Policies for network segmentation, and Pod Security Policies for workload isolation. Regular compliance audits, vulnerability assessments, and security monitoring help maintain ongoing adherence to these standards.

# Security Best Practices Checklist

Securing Amazon EKS deployments requires a methodical and comprehensive approach that addresses security concerns across all aspects of container orchestration. As containerized applications become increasingly critical to business operations, organizations must implement robust security measures that protect their workloads, while maintaining operational efficiency. This security checklist encompasses three fundamental levels – infrastructure, application, and operational – creating a defense-in-depth strategy that addresses both current security requirements and emerging threats in container environments. By following these guidelines, organizations can build and maintain secure EKS environments that support both innovation and compliance requirements.

## Infrastructure Level

At the infrastructure level, securing Amazon EKS environments requires a comprehensive approach to protecting foundational elements through robust cluster configuration, node hardening, and effective network isolation. This includes implementing proper network segmentation through VPC design and security groups, enabling encryption at rest for etcd and in transit for all API communications, and utilizing AWS Key Management Service (KMS) for managing encryption keys. Regular patching and updates of EKS clusters and worker nodes, coupled with strict access controls through IAM roles and RBAC, form the backbone of infrastructure security. Organizations should also enable control plane logging and utilize AWS CloudTrail for comprehensive audit trails, ensuring visibility into all cluster operations. Hence, let us examine each of these critical infrastructure security components in detail.

- **Cluster Configuration:** Cluster configuration forms the foundation of EKS security, involving careful setup of control plane components and API server access. Organizations should enable control plane logging to capture all API requests for auditing purposes and implement encryption for etcd data at rest. Utilizing AWS Key Management Service (KMS) for managing encryption keys adds an extra layer of security. It is crucial to regularly update and patch the EKS cluster to the latest supported version, addressing known vulnerabilities and leveraging new security features.
- **Node Hardening:** Node hardening is essential for protecting the worker nodes that run containerized workloads. This process includes implementing strict access controls through IAM roles and instance profiles, ensuring nodes run minimal, container-optimized operating systems such as Amazon Linux 2, and regularly applying security patches. Organizations should utilize Amazon Inspector for automated vulnerability assessments and implement systems manager for centralized patch management. Configuring nodes with read-only root file systems, and implementing runtime defenses such as Seccomp and AppArmor profiles further enhance security posture.
- **Network Isolation:** Network isolation plays a critical role in containing potential security breaches, and enforcing the principle of least privilege. Implementing a well-designed VPC architecture with private subnets for worker nodes and utilizing security groups for fine-grained access control is fundamental. Organizations should leverage Calico or AWS VPC CNI plugin for implementing network policies, controlling pod-to-pod and pod-to-service communication. Implementing AWS PrivateLink for private API server access, and utilizing VPC endpoints for AWS services minimizes exposure to the public internet. Additionally, considering the implementation of service mesh technologies like AWS App Mesh can provide advanced network security features such as mTLS encryption for service-to-service communication within the cluster.

## Application Level

Securing applications in Amazon EKS requires a defense-in-depth strategy that addresses security concerns across container lifecycle, runtime environments, and access management. As containerized applications become more complex, and handle increasingly sensitive workloads, implementing robust security controls at the application level becomes crucial for protecting workloads from potential threats, while maintaining operational agility. Through a comprehensive approach that addresses container vulnerabilities, runtime threats, and access management challenges, organizations can create a secure foundation for their EKS environments, while leveraging the full benefits of container orchestration.

Thus, let us examine these three critical components of application-level security, and their implementation strategies:

- **Container Security:** Container security forms the first line of defense, focusing on implementing secure container image management practices and vulnerability scanning. Organizations should utilize Amazon ECR with automated scanning enabled, implement strict image signing policies, and maintain a "`golden image`" repository of approved base images. Additionally, enforcing pod security standards through admission controllers helps ensure that containers run with appropriate security contexts, limiting capabilities, and preventing privilege escalation.
- **Runtime Security:** Runtime security in EKS environments focuses on protecting applications during execution through various defense mechanisms. This involves implementing Pod Security Policies or Pod Security Standards to enforce security configurations, utilizing runtime protection tools to detect and prevent anomalous behavior, and implementing proper resource quotas to prevent resource exhaustion attacks. Organizations should leverage AWS App Mesh or similar service mesh solutions to enforce mutual TLS between services, implement proper network policies for pod-to-pod communication, and utilize tools like AWS Distro for OpenTelemetry for runtime visibility and monitoring.
- **RBAC Implementation:** RBAC implementation in EKS provides fine-grained access control to Kubernetes resources, ensuring that the principle of least privilege is maintained throughout the application lifecycle. Organizations should create role definitions that precisely match job functions, implement service accounts for application workloads with minimal required permissions, and regularly audit RBAC configurations for potential security gaps. Integration with AWS IAM through IRSA (IAM Roles for Service Accounts) enables seamless and secure access to AWS services, while maintaining Kubernetes-native access controls. Regular reviews of RBAC policies, combined with comprehensive logging of access attempts through AWS CloudTrail, help maintain a strong security posture, while ensuring operational efficiency.

# Operational Level

Maintaining a robust security posture in Amazon EKS environments extends beyond initial configurations and deployments, requiring ongoing vigilance and proactive management at the operational level. As EKS clusters evolve and scale, organizations must implement consistent processes and tools to monitor, respond to, and mitigate potential security risks. Operational security in EKS encompasses a wide range of activities, from continuous monitoring and regular audits to incident response planning and systematic update management. By focusing on these operational aspects, organizations can ensure that their EKS environments remain secure, compliant, and resilient in the face of emerging threats, and changing business requirements.

The following core elements form the foundation of operational security in EKS environments:

- **Regular Audits:** Regular audits form the foundation of operational security, encompassing systematic reviews of cluster configurations, RBAC policies, and security controls. Organizations should leverage AWS Config and Security Hub to automate compliance checks, regularly review CloudTrail logs for suspicious activities, and conduct periodic assessments of security group configurations and network policies. These audits should also include vulnerability scanning of container images, reviewing service account permissions, and validating encryption configurations across the cluster.
- **Incident Response:** Incident response in EKS environments demands a well-defined strategy tailored to container-specific security challenges. This involves establishing clear procedures for detecting, investigating, and responding to security incidents across the container ecosystem. Organizations should implement automated alerting through CloudWatch for security events, maintain detailed runbooks for common security scenarios, and regularly test incident response procedures through security drills. Integration with tools like Guard Duty for threat detection and AWS Systems Manager for automated remediation helps ensure quick response times. Additionally, maintaining proper backup procedures and disaster recovery plans specific to containerized workloads ensures business continuity during security incidents.
- **Update Management:** Update management requires a systematic approach to maintaining the security and stability of EKS clusters and their workloads. This includes establishing processes for regular cluster version upgrades, worker node updates, and container image updates. Organizations should implement automated patch management using AWS Systems Manager, maintain staging environments for testing updates, and follow a controlled rollout process for applying changes. Version control for container images, implementing proper tagging strategies, and maintaining documentation of all system changes help ensure transparency and traceability. Regular testing of rollback procedures, and maintaining multiple environment parity helps minimize risk during updates, while ensuring operational reliability.

# Conclusion

Throughout this chapter, we have explored the crucial aspects of securing Amazon EKS environments, emphasizing the importance of a comprehensive security strategy that spans infrastructure, application, and operational levels. The complexity of containerized applications in EKS demands a multi-layered security approach that not only protects workloads, but also ensures compliance with regulatory requirements. From IRSA implementation to network security configurations, and from Pod Security Standards to secret management, each component plays a vital role in establishing a robust security posture.

The journey through EKS security has highlighted the significance of implementing proper access controls through IRSA, ensuring secure network architectures with appropriate VPC designs, and maintaining strong pod security through graduated enforcement profiles. Secret management with AWS Secrets Manager, coupled with comprehensive monitoring and compliance tools, provides the necessary foundation for protecting sensitive information, while maintaining operational efficiency. These elements work together to create a defense-in-depth strategy that addresses both current security requirements and emerging threats in container environments.

As organizations continue to adopt and scale their EKS deployments, maintaining security becomes an ongoing process rather than a one-time implementation. Regular security audits, continuous monitoring, and prompt incident response capabilities are essential for maintaining a strong security posture. The transition from Pod Security Policies to Pod Security Standards, the implementation of network policies for micro-segmentation, and the use of security groups and NACLs for multi-layered network security demonstrate the evolving nature of container security. Organizations must stay informed about new security features and best practices, while regularly reviewing and updating their security measures to address emerging threats effectively.

Thus, understanding and implementing these security concepts is vital for maintaining robust EKS environments. The integration of various AWS services for security, monitoring, and compliance provides organizations with the tools needed to build and maintain secure containerized applications. As we look to the future, the emphasis on automated security controls, continuous monitoring, and proactive threat detection will continue to grow, making it essential for organizations to adapt and enhance their security practices, while maintaining operational efficiency in their EKS deployments.

In the next chapter, we will delve into sophisticated deployment techniques that leverage this security groundwork, while ensuring reliability, scalability, and operational excellence. We shall also examine progressive delivery methods, canary deployments, blue-green deployments, and other advanced patterns that enable organizations to deploy applications confidently, while minimizing risk and maintaining high availability.

# Points to Remember

- IRSA provides fine-grained AWS service access control for pods through service account integration.
- Pod Security Standards offer three profiles (Privileged, Baseline, and Restricted) for graduated security enforcement.
- Network security requires proper VPC design with public/private subnet segregation.
- Secrets management should utilize AWS Secrets Manager with proper encryption and rotation policies.
- Regular security audits and compliance monitoring are essential for maintaining security posture.
- Container security begins with image scanning, and secure configuration management.
- RBAC implementation ensures proper access control at both Kubernetes and AWS levels.
- Operational security requires continuous monitoring, and incident response preparedness.
- Network policies should enforce micro-segmentation between workloads.
- Security groups and NACLs provide multi-layered network security.

# Multiple Choice Questions

1. What is the primary purpose of IAM Roles for Service Accounts (IRSA) in EKS?
    a. To manage cluster nodes
    b. To provide fine-grained AWS service access control for pods
    c. To configure network policies
    d. To scan container images
2. Which Pod Security Standard profile offers the most restrictive security controls?
    a. Privileged
    b. Baseline
    c. Restricted
    d. Standard

3. In EKS network design, where should worker nodes typically be placed?
   a. Public subnets
   b. Private subnets
   c. DMZ
   d. Internet Gateway
4. Which AWS service is recommended for managing secrets in EKS?
   a. AWS Secrets Manager
   b. AWS Systems Manager Parameter Store
   c. Amazon S3
   d. Amazon DynamoDB
5. Which tool can be used to automatically assess EKS clusters against CIS benchmarks?
   a. AWS Config
   b. Amazon Inspector
   c. kube-bench
   d. AWS Trusted Advisor
6. What is the purpose of a service mesh like AWS App Mesh in EKS security?
   a. To manage container images
   b. To enforce mutual TLS between services
   c. To configure IAM roles
   d. To patch worker nodes
7. Which AWS service provides threat detection capabilities specifically for EKS?
   a. AWS Shield
   b. Amazon Detective
   c. Amazon Guard Duty
   d. AWS WAF

8. What is the recommended approach for node hardening in EKS?
   a. Using default configurations
   b. Implementing read-only root file systems
   c. Disabling all security features
   d. Running nodes in public subnets
9. Which component is crucial for implementing fine-grained access control in Kubernetes?
   a. Security groups
   b. NACLs
   c. RBACs
   d. VPC endpoints
10. What is the key consideration when implementing secret rotation in EKS?
    a. Rotate secrets manually.
    b. Use long-term static credentials.
    c. Ensure that applications can handle credential updates gracefully.
    d. Store secrets in environment variables.

# Answers

1. b
2. c
3. b
4. a
5. c
6. b
7. c
8. b
9. c
10. c

# Key Terms

- **IAM Roles for Service Accounts (IRSA):** A feature that allows Kubernetes service accounts to assume IAM roles for accessing AWS services.
- **Pod Security Policy (PSP):** A cluster-level resource that controls security-sensitive aspects of pod specification.
- **Network Policy:** A specification of how groups of pods are allowed to communicate with each other, and other network endpoints.
- **VPC CNI:** The default networking plugin for EKS that enables native VPC networking for Kubernetes pods.
- **Secret Management:** The practice of securely storing, accessing, and rotating sensitive information like credentials and API keys.
- **Control Plane Logging:** The process of capturing and storing logs from the Kubernetes control plane components for auditing and troubleshooting.
- **RBAC (Role-Based Access Control):** A method of regulating access to computer or network resources, based on the roles of individual users.
- **CIS Benchmarks:** A set of best practices for securely configuring IT systems and software.
- **SOC 2 Compliance:** A voluntary compliance standard for service organizations that specifies how organizations should manage customer data.
- **Container Image Scanning:** The process of analyzing container images for known vulnerabilities and security issues.
- **Security Group:** A virtual firewall for controlling inbound and outbound traffic to AWS resources.
- **NACL (Network Access Control List):** An optional layer of security that acts as a firewall for controlling traffic in and out of subnets.
- **Guard Duty:** An AWS threat detection service that continuously monitors for malicious activity and unauthorized behavior.
- **App Mesh:** An AWS service mesh that provides application-level networking for services.
- **Least Privilege Principle:** The practice of limiting access rights for users to the bare minimum permissions they need to perform their work.

# CHAPTER 7
# Advanced Deployment Strategies

## Introduction

Modern software systems demand high agility, frequent updates, and zero-downtime releases. As application architectures become more distributed and containerized, the methods used to deploy these applications must evolve. Traditional deployment strategies—where entire applications are replaced at once—are increasingly inadequate for cloud-native workloads. Failures in such approaches can lead to service outages, user dissatisfaction, and business risks. Amazon Elastic Kubernetes Service (EKS), built on top of Kubernetes, supports a range of advanced deployment techniques that can reduce this risk, and increase delivery velocity, while maintaining operational control.

This chapter explores advanced deployment strategies that enable teams to release software safely, incrementally, and with rollback capabilities. Techniques such as **blue-green deployments**, **canary releases**, and **rolling updates** are designed to minimize impact, while changes are introduced in production environments. These models allow platform teams to validate functionality, monitor behavior, and dynamically control traffic during deployment. Each strategy provides a unique balance of safety, speed, and operational complexity, making it important to select the right approach, based on application requirements and business goals.

Alongside these strategies, the chapter introduces **GitOps**, an emerging standard for continuous delivery in Kubernetes environments. Using tools such as **ArgoCD**, GitOps workflows manage application state declaratively through version-controlled Git repositories. This approach promotes consistency, auditability, and automation across multiple environments. Combined with deployment automation, using CI/CD pipelines and tools like **Helm** and **GitHub Actions**, GitOps lays the groundwork for scalable, secure, and repeatable deployment processes in Amazon EKS.

Thus, by mastering these advanced deployment techniques, readers will gain the ability to operate resilient services, roll out updates with confidence, and recover from issues rapidly. Further, these practices are essential for organizations embracing DevOps, SRE, and cloud-native principles in production. So, whether supporting critical business services, or delivering frequent microservice updates, the deployment strategies discussed in this chapter equip platform engineers with the patterns and tooling needed to manage change effectively in Kubernetes environments.

# Structure

In this chapter, we will discuss the following topics:

- Blue-Green Deployment Patterns
- Canary Release Implementations
- Rolling Updates Strategies
- GitOps with ArgoCD
- Deployment Automation

# Blue-Green Deployment Patterns

Blue-green deployments are a release strategy designed to minimize downtime, and reduce risks during application updates. In this model, two nearly identical environments–referred to as "*blue*" (current production) and "*green*" (new version)–are maintained. At any given time, only one of these environments receives live production traffic. When a new application version is ready for deployment, it is deployed to the inactive (green) environment, tested, and then promoted by rerouting traffic to it. If issues arise, the deployment can be quickly rolled back by shifting the traffic back to the original (blue) environment.

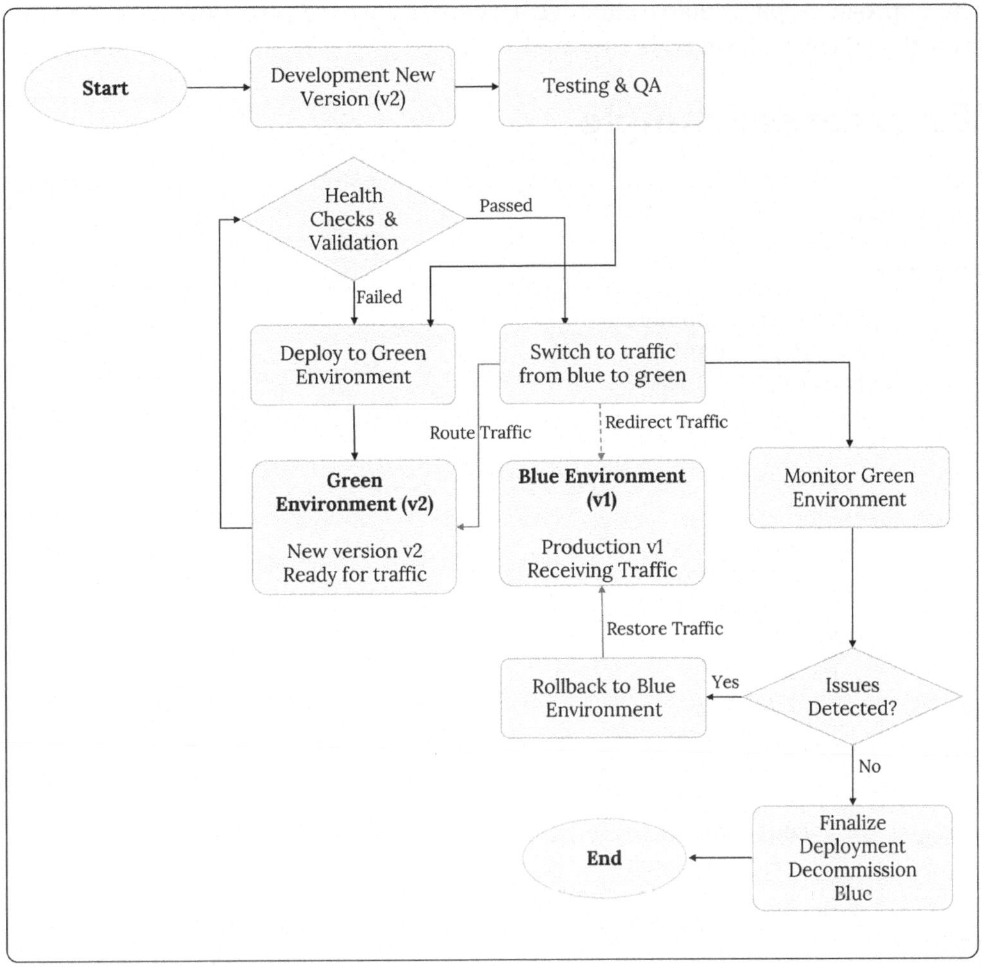


***Figure 7.1:*** *Reference Flowchart for Blue Green Deployment*

# Implementation in Amazon EKS

In Kubernetes on Amazon EKS, blue-green deployments can be implemented, using separate Deployments, Services, and ingress routing rules. This allows both versions of the application to exist simultaneously within the same cluster, while isolating the traffic routing between them.

A typical setup includes:

- Two separate **Deployment** resources (app-blue and app-green).
- A shared **Service** or **Ingress** controller (for example, AWS ALB or NGINX) for switching traffic.
- Optional automation through CI/CD or GitOps tools like ArgoCD.

This approach is particularly effective in scenarios where zero-downtime releases are critical, and rollback speed is essential.

## Kubernetes Example

Here is a simplified YAML snippet showing how blue and green deployments might be configured:

**Snippet 1**

```
apiVersion: apps/v1
kind: Deployment
metadata:
  name: app-blue
spec:
  replicas: 3
  selector:
    matchLabels:
      app: web
      version: blue
  template:
    metadata:
      labels:
        app: web
        version: blue
    spec:
      containers:
        - name: web
          image: my-app:v1
```

**Snippet 2**

```
apiVersion: apps/v1
kind: Deployment
metadata:
  name: app-green
spec:
  replicas: 3
  selector:
    matchLabels:
      app: web
      version: green
  template:
    metadata:
      labels:
        app: web
        version: green
    spec:
```

```
      containers:
        - name: web
          image: my-app:v2
```

A Corresponding Service can be used to switch traffic:

```
apiVersion: v1
kind: Service
metadata:
  name: web-service
spec:
  selector:
    app: web
    version: green  # Switch this to blue for rollback
  ports:
    - protocol: TCP
      port: 80
      targetPort: 8080
```

**Benefits**

- **Fast Rollback:** Switching traffic back to the blue version requires only a Service or Ingress update.
- **Zero Downtime:** The new version can be fully verified before it serves the production traffic.
- **Isolated Testing:** Green environment allows integration and end-to-end testing before exposure.

**Considerations**

- **Resource Overhead:** Maintaining two environments requires double the infrastructure during deployment.
- **Database Compatibility:**
  - Make **schema changes backward-compatible** so that both blue and green versions can function correctly during the transition.
  - **Stage database changes ahead of time**, such as adding new columns or tables without immediately removing the deprecated ones.
  - Use **feature flags or application logic** to activate new schema elements, only after switching environments.
  - Validate schema compatibility with migration tests in pre-production environments.
- **Stateful Services:** Additional complexity may arise when applying this strategy to applications that maintain session or persistent state.
- **Cost:** Blue-green deployments inherently require duplication of infrastructure—at least temporarily. This includes:

- Running two full environments in parallel (blue and green).
- Duplicating container images, pods, and associated resources.
- Potentially maintaining parallel databases or backups during migration.
- While this approach provides clear operational benefits– such as rollback, staging, and isolation–it increases **compute, storage, and networking costs** during deployment windows. To mitigate this:
- Keep green environments minimal, until validated (for instance, single replica).
- Use **Spot Instances** for non-production replicas.
- Schedule green environments to auto-scale down after testing or completion.
- Automate teardown of temporary infrastructure, post-deployment.

# Integrating with AWS Load Balancer Controller

When operating within Amazon EKS, many teams use the **AWS Load Balancer Controller** to manage ingress routing via Application Load Balancers (ALBs). This makes it easier to shift production traffic from one environment to another, without directly modifying core Kubernetes services. Blue-green traffic switching can be controlled using **Ingress annotations,** or by modifying the target group bindings dynamically.

For example, each version of the application (blue and green) can be associated with a different target group under the same ALB. A DNS CNAME or Route 53 entry can be updated to point to the target group representing the desired version. This pattern ensures that traffic redirection is handled at the edge, offering better latency, and minimizing client disruption.

# CI/CD Integration for Blue-Green Deployments

CI/CD tools such as **Jenkins**, **GitHub Actions**, or **ArgoCD** can automate the deployment, testing, and traffic switching process for blue-green deployments. This often includes:

- Deploying the green environment via Helm or kubectl.
- Running automated tests on the green deployment.
- Triggering a Service Selector or Ingress Update to route traffic to green.
- Notifying teams, and updating dashboards.

ArgoCD, in particular, is a strong fit due to its declarative model. Environments (blue and green) can be described as separate Application resources in Git, allowing for GitOps-based control and visibility.

## Monitoring and Health Validation

A critical component of blue-green deployment success is **pre- and post-switch validation**. Before shifting the traffic to the green environment, application health and business metrics must be validated. This can include the following:

- Liveness/readiness probes passing for all pods.
- Synthetic checks from monitoring systems (for example, Prometheus or CloudWatch Synthetics).
- Business KPIs such as API error rate, latency, or conversion rate remaining within thresholds.

Automating rollback, if post-deployment metrics degrade is a best practice. This can be managed through alerting rules tied to canary metrics, or error budgets (similar to SLO-based alerting).

## Blue-Green for Microservices

While blue-green deployment is commonly illustrated with monolithic applications, it is also applicable to **individual microservices**. In service-mesh-enabled clusters (for example, with AWS App Mesh or Istio), blue-green can be implemented at the request-routing level, instead of the ingress layer. This allows fine-grained control over service versioning, without impacting unrelated components.

For example, a user-facing API may route traffic to the new version of the recommendation engine (green) while still pointing to the current payment gateway (blue). This granularity enables progressive rollout across microservices with reduced system-wide risk.

## Summary and Best Practices

Blue-green deployments offer a robust and zero-downtime strategy for updating applications, particularly in production-critical environments. However, successful implementation requires careful orchestration, infrastructure planning, and validation processes. The following best practices ensure safe and maintainable blue-green rollouts in Amazon EKS environments.

- **Isolate environments using separate deployments and services:** Maintain clear separation between blue and green environments by deploying them as independent Deployment objects, each labeled with distinct version identifiers (for example, version: blue and version: green). Use Kubernetes Service resources to direct traffic to the active environment. This isolation enables independent validation of the new version, while ensuring that the production version remains untouched until promotion.

- **Use controlled traffic switching mechanisms:** Traffic should only be switched to the green environment after it has passed validation checks. In Kubernetes, this can be achieved by updating the Service Selector or leveraging Ingress Controllers such as AWS Load Balancer Controller or Istio for dynamic routing. On AWS, Application Load Balancer (ALB) target group weighting can be used to shift traffic in a staged manner, if required.
- **Pre-warm and validate the green environment before switching:** Ensure that the green environment is fully operational before routing production traffic. This includes confirming that all pods are in a ready state, database connections are active, and dependencies are functioning. Run automated smoke tests, API validations, or integration checks to confirm functional readiness. Validation should also include performance metrics such as latency, and error rate under simulated traffic.
- **Ensure backward compatibility of database schema changes:** When deploying new versions that involve database modifications, apply schema changes that are backward-compatible with the blue version. Avoid destructive operations like column drops during the deployment window. Migrate data or schema elements in advance if needed, and gate new functionality behind feature flags, until the environment is fully promoted.
- **Automate promotion, and rollback procedures:** Promotion from blue to green should be executed via declarative automation, not manual steps. Integrate promotion into CI/CD workflows or GitOps pipelines to reduce human error and improve repeatability. Similarly, rollback procedures should be predefined and tested—allowing teams to revert traffic to the blue environment quickly, if issues are detected.
- **Monitor application health during and after cutover:** Enable real-time observability using tools such as Prometheus, Grafana, or Amazon CloudWatch to monitor key indicators such as CPU/memory usage, request success rate, and application latency. Alerts should be configured to trigger rollback, if thresholds are exceeded, post-switch. Health checks should cover infrastructure metrics, and business KPIs alike.
- **Minimize green environment lifespan post-promotion:** Once the green version has been promoted and validated in production, clean up the blue environment to reclaim resources and reduce operational complexity. Retain logs or metrics for post-deployment analysis, but avoid maintaining dual environments longer than necessary, as this increases attack surface and cost.
- **Tag resources for cost tracking and auditing:** Use AWS and Kubernetes resource tagging to differentiate between blue and green deployments. This supports cost attribution, audit trails, and automation. Tags such as **`environment=green`**, **`deployment_version=v2`**, or **`owner=platform-team`**

can improve governance and simplify lifecycle management in multi-team environments.

# Canary Release Implementations

A canary release is a deployment strategy that gradually shifts traffic to a new version of an application, allowing teams to test changes with a subset of users in a production environment before performing a full rollout. The term originates from the practice of using canaries in coal mines to detect hazardous conditions early. Similarly, in software deployment, the canary version serves as an early warning system for performance regressions, errors, or unexpected behaviors.

This strategy reduces deployment risk by exposing only a small portion of users to changes at first, then incrementally increasing exposure as confidence builds. If an issue is detected, the rollout can be paused or rolled back, without affecting the majority of users, or impacting core business services.

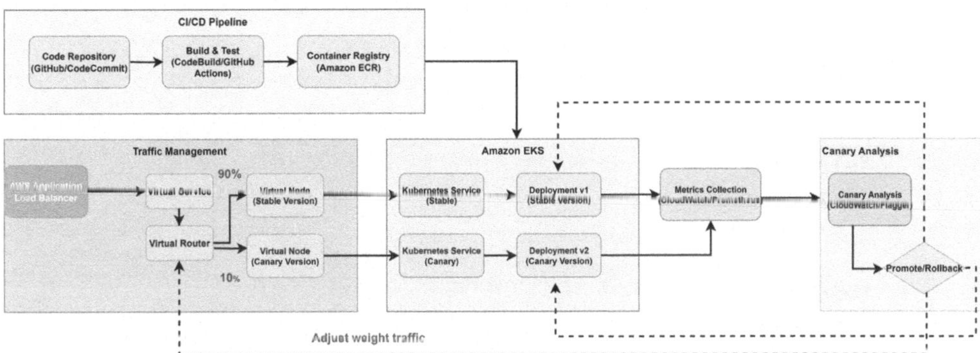


**Figure 7.2:** *Reference Flowchart for Canary Release Implementation*

## Benefits of Canary Releases

Canary deployments offer several key advantages in Amazon EKS environments:

- **Granular Control:** Traffic can be split in precise percentages between old and new versions.
- **Safe Rollout:** New versions can be tested against live production traffic with minimal impact radius.
- **Quick Rollback:** If an issue arises, traffic is reverted instantly to the stable version.
- **Observability Integration:** Canaries can be monitored using Prometheus, CloudWatch, or other tools to track metrics like latency, error rate, and request volume.

## Kubernetes-Based Canary Deployment

In Kubernetes, canary releases can be implemented in several ways:

- By using **multiple Deployments** (for example, v1 and v2) with varying replica counts and routing rules.
- Through **custom controllers** or service mesh features that support traffic splitting.
- With **Ingress or Gateway API** annotations such as in Istio, AWS App Mesh, or NGINX Ingress.

Here is a simplified example, using two Deployments, and modifying Traffic Routing via a Shared Service:

**Snippet 1**

```
apiVersion: apps/v1
kind: Deployment
metadata:
  name: web-v1
spec:
  replicas: 3
  selector:
    matchLabels:
      app: web
      version: v1
  template:
    metadata:
      labels:
        app: web
        version: v1
    spec:
      containers:
        - name: app
          image: my-app:v1
```

**Snippet 2**

```
apiVersion: apps/v1
kind: Deployment
metadata:
  name: web-v2
spec:
  replicas: 1
  selector:
    matchLabels:
      app: web
      version: v2
```

```
    template:
      metadata:
        labels:
          app: web
          version: v2
      spec:
        containers:
          - name: app
            image: my-app:v2
```

A corresponding service can be manually updated to control which version receives how much traffic, or automated via external tools.

# Traffic Splitting Techniques

A core requirement for canary deployments is the ability to route a configurable percentage of traffic to different versions of a service. In Kubernetes on Amazon EKS, this can be achieved, using service mesh technologies or ingress controllers that support weighted routing.

- **Istio** and **AWS App Mesh** allow declarative traffic splitting based on percentages, headers, or other routing rules.
- **NGINX Ingress Controller** supports weighted backends using annotations, although it is less dynamic than service meshes.
- **AWS Gateway API** (GA as of late 2023) also introduces richer traffic control natively.

Here is an example Istio VirtualService configuration to split the traffic between v1 and v2:

```
apiVersion: networking.istio.io/v1alpha3
kind: VirtualService
metadata:
  name: web
spec:
  hosts:
    - web.example.com
  http:
    - route:
        - destination:
            host: web
            subset: v1
          weight: 90
        - destination:
            host: web
            subset: v2
          weight: 10
```

This configuration routes 10% of traffic to the canary (v2) version, and 90% to the stable version.

# AWS-Specific Integration for Canary Deployments

Amazon EKS supports multiple native mechanisms for implementing canary deployments, using AWS-integrated traffic routing, including **App Mesh**, **Gateway API**, and the **AWS Load Balancer Controller**.

## App Mesh-Based Canary Releases

**AWS App Mesh** provides service mesh functionality with native support for traffic weighting, observability, and integration with CloudWatch and AWS X-Ray. Canary routing can be configured declaratively through App Mesh's VirtualRouter and VirtualService resources.

For example, two versions of a service can be registered as **App Mesh virtual nodes**, and a **VirtualRouter** can define how much traffic to send to each:

```
routes:
  - name: canary-route
    httpRoute:
      match:
        prefix: "/"
      action:
        weightedTargets:
          - virtualNode: web-v1
            weight: 90
          - virtualNode: web-v2
            weight: 10
```

This setup enables precise control over traffic distribution, without modifying Kubernetes services directly. Changes to traffic percentages can be automated or triggered through CI/CD pipelines.

## Gateway API (Next-Gen Kubernetes Networking)

The **Kubernetes Gateway API**, which AWS now supports via the AWS Gateway Controller, provides a more expressive and extensible framework for routing than traditional Ingress. The HTTPRoute resource supports traffic splitting between backends natively.

Example:

```
spec:
  rules:
    - backendRefs:
        - name: web-v1
          weight: 80
        - name: web-v2
          weight: 20
```

As the Gateway API matures, it is expected to replace Ingress for advanced use cases, and provides a vendor-neutral abstraction compatible with AWS Gateway Controller.

# AWS Load Balancer Controller and ALB-Weighted Target Groups

While not as dynamic as service meshes, **AWS Load Balancer Controller** supports weighted target groups, using **AWS ALB's native capabilities**. Canary-style deployments can be simulated by associating different Kubernetes services (each pointing to a different deployment) with separate target groups behind an ALB listener rule.

Traffic percentages are managed via ALB configuration, and updated via annotations or Infrastructure as Code.

## Metrics and Observability

Monitoring is necessary in canary rollouts. Observability tools must be tightly integrated to detect performance regressions, or functional errors quickly. Common metrics to monitor include:

- **Error rates (4xx/5xx)**
- **Latency (P95/P99 response times)**
- **Request volume**
- **Custom business KPIs (for example, cart abandonment and login failures)**

Tools such as **Prometheus**, **Amazon CloudWatch**, and **Datadog** can be used to observe both versions side-by-side. Alerting thresholds should be aggressive during the early phase of the rollout to trigger immediate rollback, if issues are detected.

It is also useful to employ **tracing tools** such as **AWS X-Ray**, **Jaeger**, or **OpenTelemetry** to trace requests through both service versions.

## Automation with Flagger and Argo Rollouts

To simplify canary workflows, tools such as **Flagger** and **Argo Rollouts** automate traffic shifting, metric analysis, and rollback:

- **Flagger** integrates with service meshes, or ingress controllers to progressively increase traffic to the canary version based on Prometheus metrics.
- **Argo Rollouts** is a Kubernetes controller that manages progressive delivery, using Kubernetes-native resources.

Flagger Example (with Prometheus and Istio):

```
apiVersion: flagger.app/v1beta1
kind: Canary
metadata:
  name: web
spec:
  targetRef:
    apiVersion: apps/v1
    kind: Deployment
    name: web
  service:
    port: 80
  analysis:
    interval: 1m
    threshold: 5
    metrics:
      - name: error-rate
        thresholdRange:
          max: 1
        interval: 30s
```

Flagger will automatically shift the traffic in increments, and halt if errors exceed the threshold, as well as rollback, if needed.

# Best Practices for Canary Releases

Implementing a successful canary release strategy requires more than just traffic splitting. It involves a combination of observability, automation, risk management, and disciplined rollback procedures. The following best practices help ensure that canary deployments are both effective and reliable in Amazon EKS environments.

- **Start small:** Begin by directing only a minimal percentage of user traffic—typically between 1% and 5%—to the canary version. This initial exposure allows teams to detect regressions, performance degradation, or unexpected behaviors in a low-risk environment. If no issues arise, traffic can be incrementally increased in predefined steps. Conservative traffic rollout reduces the likelihood of widespread impact during early validation.

- **Validate with real users:** To maximize the effectiveness of a canary deployment, direct a representative subset of real user traffic to the new version. This can be achieved using **header-based routing**, **IP-based segmentation**, or **geolocation filters** to target specific audiences. For example, internal teams or beta testers may be routed to the canary release, allowing for early feedback and real-world usage patterns, without affecting the general user base.
- **Automate rollback:** Rollbacks should not rely on manual intervention. Instead, integrate **automated rollback mechanisms** triggered by real-time observability signals—such as error rates, latency thresholds, or failed health checks. Tools like **Flagger**, **Argo Rollouts**, or custom Prometheus alert rules can pause rollouts, or revert to the previous version, if performance indicators fall outside acceptable boundaries. Automation reduces mean time to recovery, and enhances operational resilience.
- **Use feature flags:** By decoupling feature activation from deployment using **feature flag frameworks**, teams can release code to production, without immediately enabling the functionality. This allows for additional safeguards during a canary rollout. If a regression is tied to a specific feature, rather than the deployment mechanism itself, it can be disabled instantly, without rolling back the application version. Feature flags also support A/B testing, and gradual feature exposure strategies.
- **Avoid long-lived canaries:** A canary deployment is intended to be a temporary validation stage, not a permanent parallel production path. Maintaining long-lived canary versions increases infrastructure overhead, and complicates monitoring as well as troubleshooting. Once sufficient metrics confirm application stability, the canary should either be fully promoted to production or rolled back. Keeping the deployment lifecycle short ensures consistency, and avoids configuration drift or operational complexity.

# Rolling Update Strategies

Rolling updates are the default and most used deployment strategy in Kubernetes. This approach incrementally updates pods of a Deployment with the new version, replacing old pods gradually, while maintaining service availability. At any point during the rollout, a specified number of old and new pods coexist, allowing for continuous service, without downtime.

# Rolling Updates in Kubernetes

In a rolling update, the **Deployment Controller** updates pods in a controlled manner, based on two parameters:

- `maxUnavailable`: The maximum number of pods that can be unavailable, during the update.
- `maxSurge`: The maximum number of additional pods that can be scheduled above the desired number, during the update.

```
strategy:
  type: RollingUpdate
  rollingUpdate:
    maxUnavailable: 1
    maxSurge: 2
```

In this case, if the desired replica count is 4, up to 6 pods may be running at once (2 extra), and up to 1 pod may be temporarily unavailable.

**Benefits of Rolling Updates**

- **Zero Downtime:** Services remain available throughout the update cycle.
- **Simplicity:** Fully supported by Kubernetes with no extra tooling required.
- **Built-in Rollback:** Kubernetes tracks revision history, and allows rollbacks using kubectl rollout undo.

These advantages make rolling updates ideal for regular application updates, patching, and minor version upgrades.

# Observing and Controlling Rollouts

Monitoring a rolling update in real-time is critical to ensure that the new version is functioning as expected, and that the deployment strategy is not compromising availability. Kubernetes provides built-in tooling to observe and control rollout progress. Using the following commands, operators can track updates:

- `kubectl rollout status deployment <name>` – displays live progress of the update.
- `kubectl rollout history deployment <name>` – shows the history of past revisions.
- `kubectl rollout pause` and `kubectl rollout resume` – allow manual intervention to pause/resume an ongoing rollout, if anomalies are detected.

These tools are useful in environments where a hands-on deployment workflow is preferred, or in combination with observability platforms.

**Cloud-native Monitoring** solutions such as **Amazon CloudWatch**, **Prometheus**, and **Datadog** play a key role during rollouts. These tools can monitor pod health, latency metrics, and request error rates in real time. Alerts should be configured to notify teams of regressions in metrics such as:

- CPU/memory saturation
- Readiness probe failure rate
- HTTP 5xx response spikes
- High latency percentiles (P95/P99)

Additionally, **service mesh observability** (for example, with AWS App Mesh or Istio) can expose fine-grained metrics at the request level, which is helpful during progressive rollouts.

Using **dashboards and alerting thresholds**, teams can define success or rollback criteria tied to business KPIs–not just infrastructure metrics. For example, if a login success rate drops below 95% within 10 minutes of the rollout, automation should trigger rollback.

# Common Challenges

Although rolling updates are straightforward to configure, they do carry inherent risks, especially in complex or stateful workloads. The following are some common pitfalls and mitigation techniques:

- **Incompatible Application Versions:** Rolling updates assume that the new and old pods can coexist, without causing functional conflicts. If APIs, message formats, or shared data schemas are not backward-compatible, clients may fail during transition.

  **Mitigation:**

  - Use semantic versioning and design APIs for backward compatibility.
  - Decouple schema migration from application rollout.
  - Employ feature flags to activate changes after full rollout.

- **Slow Pod Initialization:** Long start-up times or delayed readiness probes can slow rollouts, or cause temporary unavailability, if Kubernetes marks too many pods as unavailable.

  **Mitigation:**

  - Use **initContainers** to handle preloading tasks.
  - Increase initialDelaySeconds in probes.
  - Adjust maxUnavailable to reduce concurrent pod unavailability.

- **Lack of Observability:** Without sufficient observability, detecting rollout failures becomes reactive, instead of proactive, often depending on user-reported issues.

  **Mitigation:**

  - Instrument applications with distributed tracing and metrics.
  - Use SLO-based alerting tied to real user experience.
  - Maintain dashboards to monitor both infrastructure, and application-level KPIs.

- **Rollout Stalls or Partial Failures:** If a rollout partially succeeds and stalls (for example, due to a misconfigured pod or quota limits), workloads can remain in an inconsistent state.

  **Mitigation:**

  - Review kubectl get events, and kubectl describe pod to identify blockers.
  - Pre-validate resource quotas and limits before deployment.
  - Define PodDisruptionBudgets to ensure minimum availability.

Rolling updates offer a reliable and Kubernetes-native way to deliver application changes incrementally with minimal disruption. However, as deployment frequency increases and infrastructure scales, managing rollouts manually becomes error-prone and operationally intensive. To address this, organizations are increasingly adopting **GitOps**—a declarative deployment approach that uses Git as the single source of truth for infrastructure and application state. Tools like **ArgoCD** enable automated, auditable, and version-controlled deployments directly from Git repositories, integrating seamlessly with Kubernetes, and supporting advanced deployment workflows such as progressive delivery, environment promotion, and rollback automation. The following section explores GitOps principles in detail, and provides a practical guide to implementing them with ArgoCD in Amazon EKS environments.

| Strategy | Zero Downtime | Risk Mitigation | Infra Overhead |
|---|---|---|---|
| Blue-Green | yes | Full | Higher ( 2 environments) |
| Canary Release | yes | Gradual | Moderate ( routing complexity) |
| Rolling Update | yes | Limited | Low |

***Table 7.1:*** *Comparison of Deployment Strategy*

# GitOps with ArgoCD

As infrastructure and application complexity increase, traditional deployment methods often struggle to maintain consistency, visibility, and repeatability across environments. GitOps addresses this challenge by treating Git as the single source of truth for declarative infrastructure and application configuration. In a GitOps workflow, changes are made via pull requests, approved by reviewers, and automatically synchronized to the target environment by a controller–ensuring that the live state of the cluster always matches the desired state defined in version control.

**ArgoCD**, a declarative GitOps operator for Kubernetes, enables continuous delivery by automatically syncing manifests from a Git repository to a Kubernetes cluster. It integrates seamlessly with Amazon EKS, and provides visibility, control, and rollback capabilities through a web UI, CLI, or API.

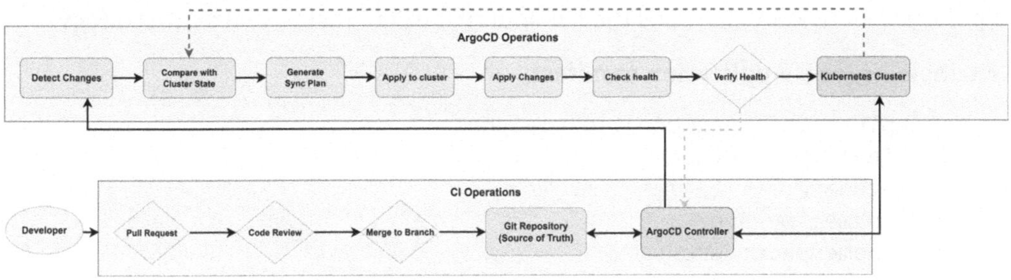


***Figure 7.3:*** *Reference Flowchart GitOps with ArgoCD*

# Benefits of GitOps with ArgoCD

Implementing GitOps with ArgoCD provides several operational benefits:

- **Declarative Deployments:** All application definitions, configurations, and policies are stored in Git, and applied in a predictable manner.
- **Auditability:** Every change is versioned, reviewed, and traceable, enabling strong governance and compliance alignment.
- **Automated Sync:** ArgoCD monitors Git repositories, and applies changes automatically or on approval, eliminating drift.
- **Self-healing:** If a resource is altered outside of Git (for example, via kubectl), ArgoCD can detect and revert unauthorized changes.
- **Environment Parity:** Staging, testing, and production environments can be replicated, using consistent Git-based configurations.

These features make ArgoCD a powerful tool for managing scalable deployments in Amazon EKS environments.

```
helm repo add argo https://argoproj.github.io/argo-helm
helm install argocd argo/argo-cd -n argocd --create-namespace
```

Once installed, the ArgoCD server can be exposed via a LoadBalancer, or port-forwarded locally. Login credentials can be retrieved from the argocd-initial-admin-secret secret.

```
kubectl -n argocd get secret argocd-initial-admin-secret -o
jsonpath="{.data.password}" | base64 -d
```

# Configuring Applications

ArgoCD deploys Kubernetes resources by linking them to Git repositories. An **Application** resource defines the Git source, target cluster, and sync strategy.

**Example ArgoCD Application manifest:**

```
apiVersion: argoproj.io/v1alpha1
kind: Application
metadata:
  name: my-app
  namespace: argocd
spec:
  project: default
  source:
    repoURL: https://github.com/my-org/my-repo
    targetRevision: main
    path: k8s/base
  destination:
    server: https://kubernetes.default.svc
    namespace: my-namespace
  syncPolicy:
    automated:
      prune: true
      selfHeal: true
```

This manifest ensures that changes in the k8s/base directory of the Git repository are automatically synced to the target namespace in your EKS cluster.

# Sync Policies and Deployment Strategies in ArgoCD

ArgoCD offers flexible sync policies that determine how and when changes in Git are applied to the Kubernetes cluster. These policies can be configured as **manual**, **automated**, or **scheduled**, depending on the desired level of control and automation.

- **Manual Sync:** Requires a user to manually initiate the deployment via the ArgoCD UI, CLI, or API. Useful in regulated environments where changes must go through an approval process.

- **Automated Sync:** ArgoCD watches the Git repository, and automatically applies any changes as soon as they are detected. Optional parameters include:
    - **`prune`:** Automatically deletes resources that are removed from the Git repository.
    - **`selfHeal`:** Detects out-of-band changes (for example, from kubectl), and reverts them to the Git-defined state.

    ```
    syncPolicy:
      automated:
        prune: true
        selfHeal: true
    ```
- **Hooks and Phases:** ArgoCD supports pre-sync, sync, and post-sync hooks, allowing for lifecycle automation such as database migrations or smoke tests, before fully applying changes.

## GitOps Environment Promotion

GitOps enables consistent deployment flows across environments such as **`dev`**, **`staging`**, and **`production`** through **branch-based** or **directory-based** promotion strategies:

- **Branch-Based:** Each environment ( for instance, dev, prod, and so on) corresponds to a separate Git branch. Merging code to a higher branch promotes the deployment.
    - **Pros:** Clear Git history per environment.
    - **Cons:** More complex branching strategies and merge conflicts.
- **Directory-Based:** Each environment is defined in a separate directory within the same branch (for example, /overlays/dev, /overlays/prod).
    - **Pros**: Simple structure, supports tools like Kustomize.
    - **Cons**: Harder to audit diff across environments.

This model encourages peer-reviewed pull requests, audit trails, and clear promotion workflows that align with DevOps best practices.

## Best Practices and Security Considerations

Implementing GitOps successfully in Amazon EKS environments requires more than synchronizing manifests from a Git repository. It involves adopting secure, scalable, and well-governed practices that enhance deployment reliability and organizational transparency. The following best practices ensure consistent, auditable, and resilient GitOps workflows with ArgoCD:

- **Use dedicated Git repositories, or scoped directories:** Structure your

Git repositories clearly by separating applications, environments, and configurations. For example, maintain different repositories or subfolders for dev, staging, and production. This reduces the risk of cross-environment contamination, and makes it easier to apply branch protections, and Role-based Access Control (RBAC). Clear separation also simplifies audit, and rollback processes.

- **Leverage Git branch protections, and access control:** Enable branch protection rules in your version control system to enforce pull request reviews, prevent direct pushes, and require signed commits. This helps maintain integrity in production-bound code, and ensures that every change is peer-reviewed and traceable. Integrating with tools such as GitHub, GitLab, or Bitbucket allows fine-grained permissions for different roles such as developers, reviewers, and platform engineers.
- **Restrict direct access to the Kubernetes cluster:** To enforce Git as the single source of truth, avoid direct changes to the EKS cluster, using kubectl or external tools. Any change made outside of Git undermines the GitOps model, and introduces configuration drift. In ArgoCD, enable the selfHeal option to automatically detect and revert unauthorized changes to maintain alignment, with the Git-defined desired state.
- **Implement progressive delivery and promotion workflows:** Use GitOps to model environment promotion workflows. For instance, changes can be deployed to the dev environment via merge to the dev branch, and promoted to staging and production via controlled pull requests and reviews. ArgoCD can monitor different branches or paths, enabling environment-specific deployment pipelines that are auditable and consistent.
- **Secure secrets and sensitive data outside Git:** Never store plaintext secrets in Git repositories. Instead, integrate ArgoCD with secret management solutions such as AWS Secrets Manager, HashiCorp Vault, or SOPS (Secrets Operations). This allows for secure, encrypted secret delivery at runtime, without exposing credentials or API keys in version control.
- **Audit with ArgoCD and Git commit history:** Enable logging in ArgoCD to track synchronization events, rollback actions, and user activities. Combined with Git commit history and pull request logs, this provides a full trace of "*who changed what, when, and why*"–a critical requirement for regulated industries, or teams operating under compliance frameworks such as SOC 2 or ISO 27001.
- **Use ApplicationSets for scalable multi-app management:** For managing hundreds of microservices or environment replicas, leverage ArgoCD's ApplicationSet controller. It enables dynamic generation of ArgoCD Application resources, based on Git metadata, directories, or template patterns–ideal for managing multi-tenant clusters or GitOps at scale.

- **Continuously monitor sync status and drift:** Set up alerts and dashboards to track the synchronization status of ArgoCD-managed applications. Alert when applications are out of sync, stuck, or failed to apply changes. Monitoring sync health ensures issues are identified proactively, before impacting the end users.

# Deployment Automation

As software delivery velocity increases, manual deployment processes can become a bottleneck, introducing delays, inconsistencies, and human errors. Deployment automation addresses this by introducing repeatable, scalable, and reliable workflows that push application changes from development to production with minimal manual intervention. In the context of Amazon EKS, deployment automation enables teams to ship new features faster, enforce governance policies, and maintain environment consistency across the application lifecycle.

Deployment automation can be achieved using CI/CD tools such as AWS CodePipeline, GitHub Actions, GitLab CI/CD, Jenkins, and Argo Workflows. Combined with declarative configurations, container registries ( for example, Amazon ECR), and GitOps principles, these tools orchestrate builds, tests, approvals, and cluster updates as part of a secure and streamlined pipeline.

# Components of an Automated EKS Deployment Pipeline

A typical deployment automation flow for Amazon EKS includes the following components:

- **Source Code Repository:** Stores application code and deployment manifests (for instance., GitHub, Bitbucket, CodeCommit, and so on).
- **CI/CD Engine:** Builds Docker images, runs unit/integration tests, and pushes to Amazon ECR.
- **Artifact Registry:** Amazon Elastic Container Registry (ECR) stores versioned application images.
- **Declarative Configs in Git:** Kubernetes YAMLs or Helm charts represent the desired cluster state.
- **CD Trigger  and Sync:** Changes in the Git repository trigger deployment to EKS, using ArgoCD, kubectl, or Helm.
- **Monitoring and Rollback Logic:** Metrics or alarms validate rollout success, and automate rollback, if thresholds are breached.

# Example: CI/CD Pipeline Flow

Here is a high-level deployment flow, using **GitHub Actions** and **ArgoCD** for GitOps automation.

```
on:
  push:
    branches:
      - main

jobs:
  deploy:
    runs-on: ubuntu-latest
    steps:
      - name: Checkout code
        uses: actions/checkout@v3

      - name: Build Docker image
        run: docker build -t my-app:${{ github.sha }} .

      - name: Push to Amazon ECR
        run: |
          aws ecr get-login-password | docker login --username
AWS --password-stdin <account>.dkr.ecr.region.amazonaws.com
          docker tag my-app:${{ github.sha }} <account>.dkr.ecr.
region.amazonaws.com/my-app:${{ github.sha }}
          docker push <account>.dkr.ecr.region.amazonaws.com/
my-app:${{ github.sha }}

      - name: Update manifest with new image
        run: |
          sed -i "s|image: .*|image: <ecr-repo-url>/my-app:${{
github.sha }}|" k8s/deployment.yaml
          git commit -am "Update image to ${{ github.sha }}"
          git push
```

This update to the Git repository then triggers ArgoCD to sync the new image version to the EKS cluster automatically.

# Helm-Based Automation

For teams managing Kubernetes manifests with Helm, deployment automation can be streamlined by templating configurations, and promoting them through Helm release pipelines.

Example Helm upgrade command (in a CI/CD step):

```
helm upgrade my-app ./charts/my-app \
  --namespace prod \
  --set image.tag=${IMAGE_TAG}
```

Helm values can be stored in separate environments (**`values-dev.yaml`**, **`values-prod.yaml`**) to allow safe testing and staged rollouts.

# Best Practices for Deployment Automation

Continuous Integration and Continuous Deployment (CI/CD) pipelines form the backbone of modern software delivery workflows. When integrated with Amazon EKS, CI/CD automation enhances consistency, reduces manual intervention, and enables rapid and reliable application rollouts. The following best practices help ensure secure, scalable, and maintainable CI/CD processes in Kubernetes environments.

- **Define pipelines as code for reproducibility:** Use declarative configurations (for example, YAML, JSON, or DSL) to define your CI/CD workflows. Tools such as GitHub Actions, GitLab CI/CD, Jenkins, and AWS CodePipeline support version-controlled pipeline definitions. This ensures that pipeline logic is trackable, testable, and portable across environments, promoting repeatability and auditability.
- **Integrate automated testing at every stage:** Every pipeline should include automated unit, integration, and optionally End-to-End (E2E) tests. These validations prevent regressions from reaching production, and help ensure application quality. Failures in any test stage should halt the pipeline immediately, maintaining high delivery standards. Tools such as JUnit, pytest, Postman, and Cypress can be integrated for comprehensive test coverage.
- **Use artifact versioning and tagging conventions:** Each build artifact, such as a Docker image, should be tagged with a unique identifier—typically using a commit SHA, build number, or semantic version. This enables traceability and rollback. Store artifacts in a centralized registry such as Amazon ECR, and reference these tags explicitly in Kubernetes manifests or Helm charts.
- **Decouple build and deployment stages:** Separate the image build process from the deployment process to increase modularity and flexibility. For example, build images in a CI pipeline, and trigger deployment only after successful test completion or manual approval. This separation allows for easier retries, audit logging, and environment-specific deployment logic.
- **Secure pipeline credentials and secrets:** Store secrets such as AWS credentials, tokens, and environment variables securely using native secret managers like AWS Secrets Manager, GitHub Actions Secrets, or Vault. Avoid hardcoding credentials, or embedding them in repository files. Rotate

credentials regularly, and use the least-privilege IAM roles scoped to pipeline requirements.

- **Use Helm or Kustomize for environment-specific overrides:** Instead of duplicating manifests across environments, use Helm charts or Kustomize overlays to manage configuration differences such as resource limits, replica counts, or image tags. This promotes consistency, while supporting flexibility across dev, staging, and production clusters.
- **Implement approvals and gated releases for sensitive environments:** Introduce manual approval steps for production deployments or high-impact changes. Use Slack, GitHub pull requests, or pipeline-native approvals (for example, in CodePipeline) to allow team leads or release managers to verify release readiness before proceeding.
- **Integrate observability into your deployment stages:** Emit metrics and logs for pipeline activity, using tools such as CloudWatch Logs, Prometheus, or OpenTelemetry. Track metrics like deployment duration, failure rate, and rollback frequency to assess pipeline efficiency. Dashboards and alerts help surface operational trends over time.
- **Rollback using Git or Helm history:** Enable automated rollback paths, using Helm's rollback feature or Git-based reversion workflows. Ensure that rollback logic is tested and documented. Rollback should be treated as a first-class action, not a last-resort recovery method.
- **Continuously improve pipeline performance and reliability:** Measure pipeline execution time, success rates, and deployment frequency. Optimize build caching, parallelize test suites, and archive flaky steps. CI/CD pipelines are living systems that benefit from regular tuning and modernization to meet the evolving application and team needs.

# Conclusion

In this chapter, we explored the principles and practices that enable safe, reliable, and scalable application delivery in Amazon EKS environments. Beginning with blue-green deployments, we learned how to isolate production and staging environments to achieve zero-downtime releases with rapid rollback capabilities. We then examined canary release strategies, which gradually expose changes to a subset of users, allowing teams to test new versions in real-time with measurable risk control. This section also included AWS-specific integrations such as App Mesh, Gateway API, and ALB-based traffic routing, reinforcing the practical relevance for EKS users.

We continued by detailing rolling update strategies, the native Kubernetes mechanism for incremental deployments. Through proper tuning of parameters such as maxSurge, maxUnavailable, and readiness probes, rolling updates can provide seamless upgrades with minimal service disruption. We also addressed common challenges such as version incompatibility and observability gaps, along with rollback mechanisms to maintain stability in high-stakes environments.

The chapter further introduced the GitOps model, using ArgoCD and highlighting the advantages of declarative configuration, automatic synchronization, and auditable workflows. GitOps helps ensure environment consistency, governance, and rapid recovery from configuration drift. Finally, we explored deployment automation techniques, using CI/CD tools, GitHub Actions, Helm, and ArgoCD to streamline build-test-release cycles across multiple environments.

These advanced strategies empower platform teams to increase delivery velocity, while maintaining operational reliability. When implemented effectively, they reduce release-related outages, accelerate feedback loops, and enable safer innovation. In the next chapter, we will shift our focus to observability and operational excellence, examining how to monitor, trace, and troubleshoot distributed workloads, running on Amazon EKS.

# Points to Remember

- Blue-green deployments provide isolated environments for staging and production, enabling zero-downtime rollouts, and fast rollback capabilities.
- Canary releases expose new versions to a small percentage of users first, allowing for controlled risk and data-driven promotion, or rollback decisions.
- Traffic splitting for canary releases can be implemented using Istio, AWS App Mesh, Gateway API, or ALB annotations on Amazon EKS.
- Rolling updates are natively supported in Kubernetes, and allow pods to be updated incrementally, using parameters like maxSurge and maxUnavailable.
- Observability is essential during rolling updates—readiness probes, error rates, and latency metrics should be actively monitored.
- ArgoCD enables GitOps-based deployment workflows, where Git acts as the source of truth and application changes are applied declaratively.
- GitOps strategies such as branch-based or directory-based promotions help maintain environment consistency, and facilitate code review workflows.
- Deployment automation using CI/CD tools like GitHub Actions, AWS CodePipeline, or Argo Workflows enhances release velocity, and reduces manual errors.
- Helm simplifies application parameterization and version control, supporting templated and repeatable deployments across environments.
- Secure secrets handling, rollback automation, and observability integration that are critical components of a production-grade deployment pipeline.

# Multiple Choice Questions

1. What is the primary benefit of a blue-green deployment strategy?
    a. Faster container image builds
    b. Direct updates to production pods
    c. Zero-downtime releases with quick rollback
    d. Automatically scales pod replicas
2. In a canary release, how is traffic typically managed?
    a. Redirected using kube-proxy
    b. Split incrementally between application versions
    c. Routed only through ingress
    d. Limited to internal pods via sidecar injection
3. Which of the following is used to control the number of new pods created during a rolling update?
    a. podAffinity
    b. restartPolicy
    c. maxSurge
    d. nodeSelector
4. What role does readinessProbe play in rolling updates?
    a. Deletes old pods
    b. Triggers a canary rollback
    c. Signals when a pod is ready to receive traffic
    d. Updates the deployment manifest
5. Which tool enables GitOps-style continuous delivery in Kubernetes?
    a. CloudFormation
    b. CodeDeploy
    c. ArgoCD
    d. Jenkins

6. In ArgoCD, what does the selfHeal option do?
    a. Detects pod health, using probes.
    b. Re-syncs to Git, if the cluster state drifts.
    c. Restarts the controller, if it crashes.
    d. Deletes old deployment history.
7. What deployment strategy gradually replaces old pods with new ones, while keeping the application running?
    a. Recreate strategy
    b. Blue-green deployment
    c. Rolling update
    d. Shadow rollout
8. Which AWS-native tool provides traffic shifting between virtual nodes for canary deployments?
    a. Amazon Route 53
    b. AWS App Mesh
    c. Amazon CloudTrail
    d. Amazon CodeGuru
9. What is a major risk when updating applications, without deployment automation?
    a. Higher EBS storage usage
    b. Over-provisioned subnets
    c. Inconsistent rollouts and human errors
    d. Excessive network ACL updates
10. Which feature of Helm helps in managing values across environments like dev and prod?
    a. Sidecar containers
    b. Parameterized volumes
    c. Value overrides
    d. StatefulSet templates

# Answers

1. c
2. b
3. c
4. c
5. c
6. b
7. c
8. b
9. c
10. c

# Key Terms

- **Blue-Green Deployment:** A release strategy that uses two identical environments (blue and green) to allow seamless traffic switching during application updates.
- **Canary Release:** A deployment technique where a new version is gradually introduced to a subset of users to test its performance before full rollout.
- **Rolling Update:** The default Kubernetes deployment strategy that incrementally updates pods, while maintaining application availability.
- **maxUnavailable:** A Kubernetes setting that defines how many pods can be taken offline, during a rolling update.
- **maxSurge:** A Kubernetes setting that specifies how many additional pods can be created temporarily, during a rolling update.
- **GitOps:** A deployment model that uses Git as the single source of truth for infrastructure, and application configurations.
- **ArgoCD:** A declarative, GitOps-based continuous delivery tool for Kubernetes that synchronizes cluster state with Git repositories.
- **Sync Policy:** In ArgoCD, the set of rules that govern how and when updates from Git are applied to a Kubernetes cluster.
- **Feature Flag:** A technique for enabling or disabling features at runtime, without changing application code, often used alongside canary or blue-green deployments.

- **CI/CD Pipeline:** A series of automated steps that build, test, and deploy code changes to production environments.
- **Helm:** A Kubernetes package manager that allows the definition, installation, and upgrade of applications, using templated YAML files.
- **Traffic Splitting:** A method of routing a percentage of requests to different service versions to support canary or progressive delivery.

# CHAPTER 8
# Observability and Monitoring

## Introduction

Modern containerized applications deployed on Amazon Elastic Kubernetes Service (EKS) demand comprehensive observability solutions to gain deep insights into system behavior and performance. This chapter presents an in-depth examination of implementing enterprise-grade observability through Amazon CloudWatch and AWS Distro for OpenTelemetry (ADOT), providing the foundation for understanding system state and behavior. We explore advanced distributed tracing methodologies utilizing AWS X-Ray with ADOT collectors, and sophisticated log aggregation techniques leveraging Amazon OpenSearch Service and CloudWatch Logs. The observability stack is enhanced with efficient log routing, using Fluent Bit for Container Insights and ADOT Collector, enabling real-time log processing, and detailed system analysis across AWS services.

Building upon these observability foundations, we explore robust monitoring solutions through AWS-managed services for Prometheus and Grafana, enabling proactive system oversight and incident response. Through systematic analysis and practical implementations, readers will acquire the expertise to develop custom metrics, establish effective alerting protocols, and create data-driven visualizations. This chapter delivers essential knowledge for implementing comprehensive monitoring frameworks that enable precise tracking of cluster health, application performance metrics, and end-user experience analytics. The methodologies and best practices presented herein are fundamental for organizations seeking to maintain high-availability services, and implement proactive incident response strategies in their EKS environments. By focusing on AWS-native services and AWS-optimized open-source tools, this comprehensive approach equips readers with the knowledge to architect a modern, scalable solution that leverages the full potential of the AWS ecosystem, ensuring precise monitoring in complex and distributed EKS deployments.

# Structure

In this chapter, we will discuss the following topics:

- AWS Observability and Monitoring Services
- Data Collection and Processing
- Log Management and Analysis
- Distributed Tracing
- Metrics Collection and Visualization
- Real-time Application Performance Monitoring

# AWS Observability and Monitoring Services

Observability and monitoring are crucial components in managing modern applications, particularly in complex and distributed environments like those built on Amazon EKS. Observability refers to the ability to understand the internal state of a system, based on its external outputs, encompassing metrics, logs, and traces. Monitoring, on the other hand, involves the continuous collection and analysis of these outputs to detect and respond to issues proactively.

The importance of robust observability and monitoring solutions cannot be overstated in today's fast-paced, cloud-native landscape. These tools enable teams to maintain high availability, optimize performance, troubleshoot issues quickly, and make data-driven decisions about scaling and resource allocation. They provide vital insights into user experience, help in capacity planning, and support compliance as well as security requirements.

A comprehensive observability and monitoring solution for EKS should possess the following key features:

- **Comprehensive data collection:** Ability to gather metrics, logs, and traces from all the components of the EKS cluster, including nodes, pods, containers, and applications.
- **Real-time processing:** Capability to ingest and analyze data in real-time, enabling rapid detection of anomalies and issues.
- **Scalability:** Ability to handle the high volume and velocity of data generated by large-scale EKS deployments, without performance degradation.
- **Correlation and context:** Tools to correlate data across different sources, and provide context for faster root cause analysis.

- **Customizability:** Flexibility to create custom metrics, dashboards, and alerts tailored to specific application needs.
- **Intelligent alerting:** Advanced alerting mechanisms that reduce noise, and focus on actionable insights.
- **Historical data retention:** Capacity to store and analyze historical data for trend analysis and capacity planning.
- **Integration capabilities:** Seamless integration with the existing DevOps tools and workflows.
- **Security and compliance:** Features to ensure data privacy, access control, and compliance with the relevant regulations.
- **Cost-effectiveness:** Efficient use of resources to provide comprehensive observability, without excessive operational costs.

By implementing a solution with these features, organizations can gain the visibility and control needed to effectively manage and optimize their EKS-based applications, ensuring reliability, performance, and a superior user experience.

*Figure* 8.1 represents an architecture for observability and monitoring, using Amazon Web Services (AWS) with an Amazon Elastic Kubernetes Service (EKS) cluster. It includes the following components:

- **Data Sources:** An EKS Cluster serves as the starting point for data collection.
- **Data Collection and Processing:** AWS Distro for OpenTelemetry and Fluent Bit are used to collect telemetry and log data from the EKS cluster.
- **Observability:** Amazon CloudWatch and AWS X-Ray, along with ADOT Collector, are used for monitoring and tracing applications running in the EKS cluster.
- **Logging:** CloudWatch Logs collects logs which are subsequently sent to Amazon OpenSearch Service for analysis and visualization.
- **Metrics and Monitoring:** Amazon Managed Service for Prometheus, Amazon Managed Grafana, and CloudWatch Container Insights enable metrics collection, visualization, and monitoring.

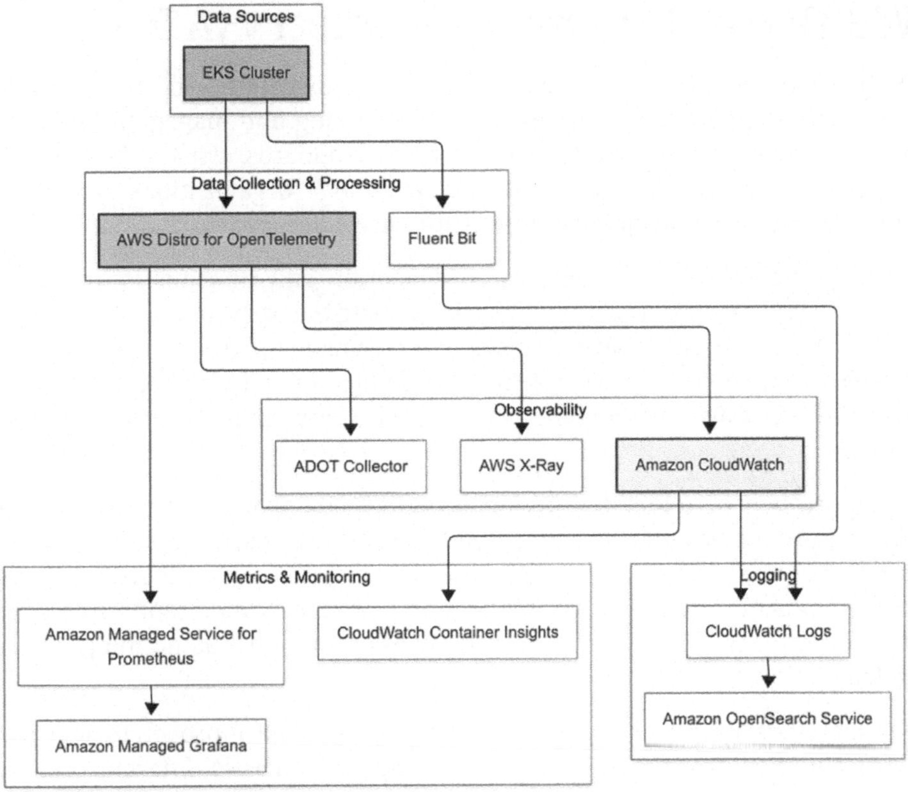


***Figure 8.1:*** *AWS Observability and Monitoring Architecture with EKS*

In the following sections, we will explore each component of the AWS Observability and Monitoring stack, understanding how these services work together to provide comprehensive visibility into your EKS environment.

# Data Collection and Processing

Modern containerized applications running on Amazon EKS generate vast amounts of telemetry data that needs to be efficiently collected, processed, and routed to observability backends. Two powerful tools stand at the forefront of this challenge: AWS Distro for OpenTelemetry (ADOT) and Fluent Bit. While ADOT excels at providing a comprehensive telemetry collection with native OpenTelemetry support and distributed tracing capabilities, Fluent Bit offers lightweight, efficient log processing and routing. Together, they form the backbone of data collection and processing in EKS environments. In the following section, we will explore how these complement each other, and how to implement them effectively in EKS clusters:

# AWS Distro for Open Telemetry (ADOT)

AWS Distro for OpenTelemetry (ADOT) is Amazon's distribution of the OpenTelemetry project, providing a unified framework for collecting and managing telemetry data across cloud applications. It adheres to open standards, while offering optimized performance for AWS environments, enabling organizations to implement comprehensive observability solutions, without vendor lock-in.

Telemetry encompasses the automated collection and transmission of monitoring data, including metrics, traces, and logs from distributed systems. This data provides crucial insights into application behavior, performance patterns, and system health. In modern cloud architectures, telemetry is fundamental for understanding complex distributed systems, maintaining service reliability, and ensuring optimal user experience.

The importance of telemetry lies in its ability to provide visibility into system operations. It enables teams to proactively identify issues, understand performance bottlenecks, track user experiences, and make data-driven decisions for system improvements. In cloud-native applications, where components are distributed and interconnected, telemetry becomes essential for maintaining operational excellence.

ADOT simplifies observability by providing a standardized approach to data collection and transmission. It offers consistent APIs and SDKs across different programming languages and frameworks, making it easier for developers to instrument their applications. The AWS optimization ensures efficient integration with AWS services, while maintaining compatibility with third-party observability platforms.

The architecture of ADOT consists of several key components such as:

- **Collectors:** The ADOT Collector is the core component that receives, processes, and exports telemetry data. It can be deployed as a sidecar, daemon, or standalone service.
- **Instrumentation Libraries:** Language-specific SDKs that developers use to instrument their applications, and generate telemetry data.
- **Processors:** Components that handle data modification, batching, and filtering before export.
- **Exporters:** Plugins that send data to various backends, including AWS services (CloudWatch, X-Ray, and so on) and third-party solutions.
- **Receivers:** Components that accept telemetry data from different sources and formats.

The Amazon Elastic Kubernetes Service (EKS) integrates seamlessly with AWS Distro for OpenTelemetry (ADOT) to provide comprehensive observability solutions for containerized applications. The key use cases include collecting and aggregating metrics, traces, and logs from microservices deployed on EKS clusters, enabling detailed performance monitoring and troubleshooting. ADOT on EKS allows teams to implement distributed tracing to track requests across service boundaries, monitor cluster and pod-level metrics, and gather application performance data that can be exported to various AWS services such as CloudWatch, X-Ray, and Amazon Managed Service for Prometheus. This integration is particularly valuable for organizations running complex microservices architectures, as it provides a standardized way to collect telemetry data, while maintaining compatibility with both AWS-native and third-party observability backends, making it easier to identify bottlenecks, debug issues, and optimize application performance in production environments.

As shown in *Figure* 8.2, ADOT in Amazon EKS is deployed through a multi-layered approach: At the management level, the ADOT Operator serves as the orchestrator, handling collector lifecycle and configurations across the cluster. Data collection takes place through two types of collectors: DaemonSet collectors that run on every node for node-level metrics, and Deployment collectors that serve as centralized aggregation points for cluster-wide telemetry. The actual telemetry data originates from application pods instrumented with OpenTelemetry SDKs, which emit metrics, traces, and logs. Additionally, control plane integration ensures monitoring of the core Kubernetes components. This comprehensive setup ensures thorough observability from individual node performance to overall cluster health, with data ultimately flowing to services such as CloudWatch and X-Ray for analysis.

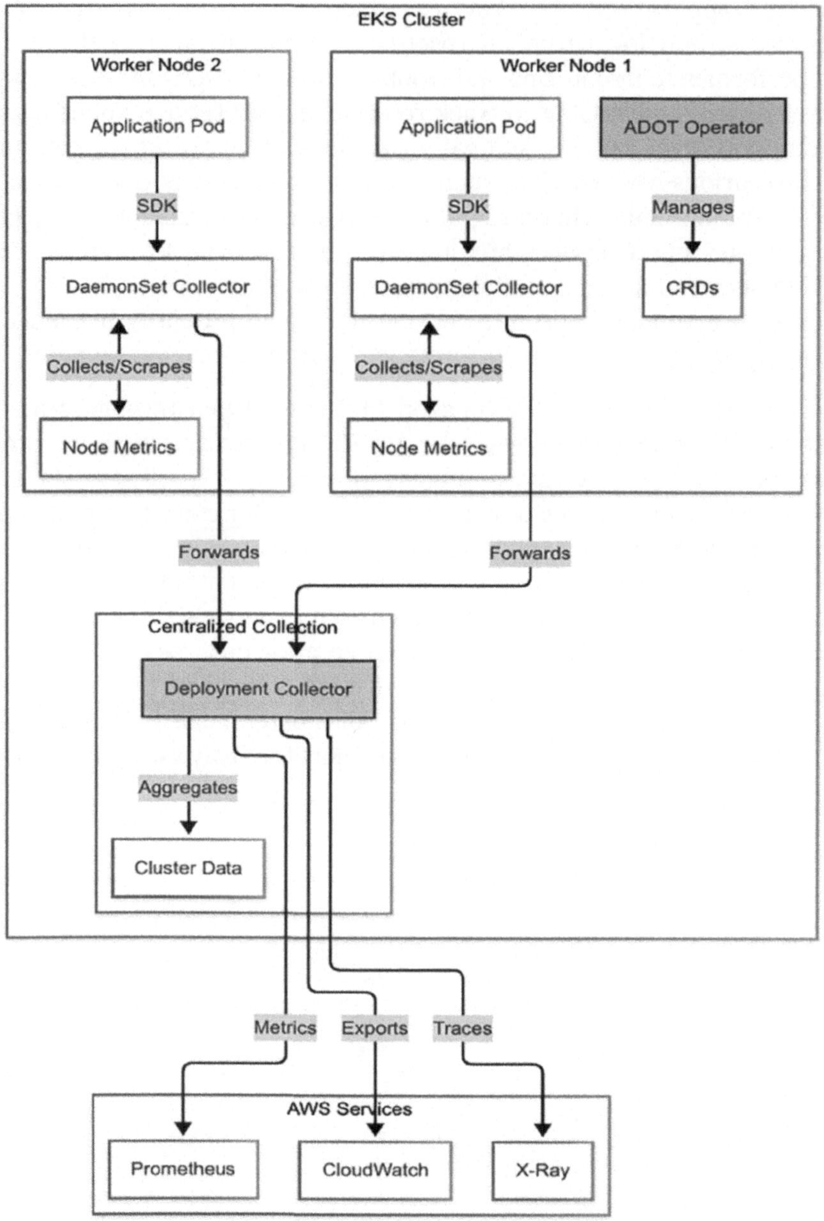


***Figure 8.2:*** *EKS Cluster with AWS Distro for Open Telemetry*

When implementing ADOT in EKS environments, several critical best practices should be followed to ensure optimal performance and reliability. For collector deployment, organizations should choose between DaemonSet (for node-level monitoring) or Deployment (for cluster-level monitoring), based on their specific workload requirements. Implementing appropriate sampling rates is crucial to balance data granularity with cost and performance impacts, especially in high-traffic environments. Teams should establish comprehensive alerting thresholds, and create intuitive dashboards that reflect Key Performance Indicators (KPIs) and Service Level Objectives (SLOs). Data retention policies should be carefully configured to maintain compliance, while managing storage costs effectively. Security best practices include implementing proper RBAC policies, using secure endpoints, and encrypting the sensitive data in transit and at rest. Regular monitoring of collector performance metrics helps prevent resource bottlenecks, and ensures efficient data collection. Lastly, maintaining the current versions of ADOT components is essential for accessing new features, security patches, and performance improvements, while following a structured update process to minimize potential disruptions to monitoring capabilities.

AWS Distro for OpenTelemetry represents a robust and scalable observability solution for EKS environments, providing unified telemetry data collection, and standardized instrumentation across cloud-native applications. Its integration with various AWS services and third-party tools, combined with proper implementation of best practices, enables organizations to build comprehensive observability pipelines that support both operational excellence and performance optimization goals.

# Fluent Bit

Fluent Bit is an open-source, lightweight log processor and forwarder designed specifically for cloud-native environments. It is written in C, making it highly efficient and resource-conscious, which is particularly important in containerized environments where resource optimization is crucial. As a Cloud Native Computing Foundation (CNCF) sub-project, it maintains strong community support and regular updates.

Fluent Bit is primarily used for log collection and forwarding, making it ideal for scenarios focused on log management. ADOT, on the other hand, is better suited for collecting metrics and traces, especially when implementing distributed tracing. While Fluent Bit excels in log processing, ADOT provides broader observability capabilities, including metrics and traces.

In an EKS environment, Fluent Bit operates as a DaemonSet, ensuring comprehensive log collection from every node in the cluster. Its architecture is specifically designed to handle the distributed nature of Kubernetes workloads, integrating seamlessly with EKS's container runtime and logging infrastructure, while maintaining minimal resource overhead.

When discussing logs in an EKS context, we are dealing with multiple layers of logging. Container logs encompass application container logs, init container logs, and sidecar container outputs. Kubernetes system logs include Kubelet, kube-proxy, and container runtime logs. Node-level logs contain system logs, journal logs, and host-level security information. Application-specific logs comprise web server logs, database logs, application runtime logs, and any custom application logging implemented within the containers.

Fluent Bit excels in EKS environments due to its native understanding of Kubernetes metadata and labels. It efficiently processes multi-line logs common in containerized applications, while handling dynamic pod creation and deletion. The ability to enrich logs with pod, namespace, and container information makes it invaluable for debugging and monitoring in Kubernetes environments.

Proper deployment configuration in EKS requires implementing DaemonSets with appropriate node tolerations and resource constraints. Organizations should configure resource requests and limits suitable for their EKS nodes, while implementing appropriate pod security contexts. Log processing should include filtering unnecessary system logs to optimize costs, configuring proper parsing for container runtime logs, and implementing effective log rotation and retention policies.

In modern EKS deployments, Fluent Bit handles the vital task of container log collection, processing, and real-time streaming, while enriching logs with Kubernetes metadata. ADOT complements this by managing application metrics collection, distributed tracing across microservices, and service mesh telemetry. This combination provides comprehensive observability coverage for EKS workloads.

# Log Management and Analysis

Log Management and Analysis is crucial for Elastic Kubernetes Service (EKS) applications as it provides visibility into application behavior, system performance, and security events. In a distributed Kubernetes environment, logs help diagnose issues, track user activities, monitor application health, and ensure that compliance requirements are met. Without proper log management, troubleshooting problems in containerized applications can become extremely challenging due to their ephemeral nature. and complex microservices architecture.

Before advancing further, please refer to *Figure* 8.3 to understand the AWS observability stack. This diagram outlines the key components of the stack and their relationship with AWS core services.

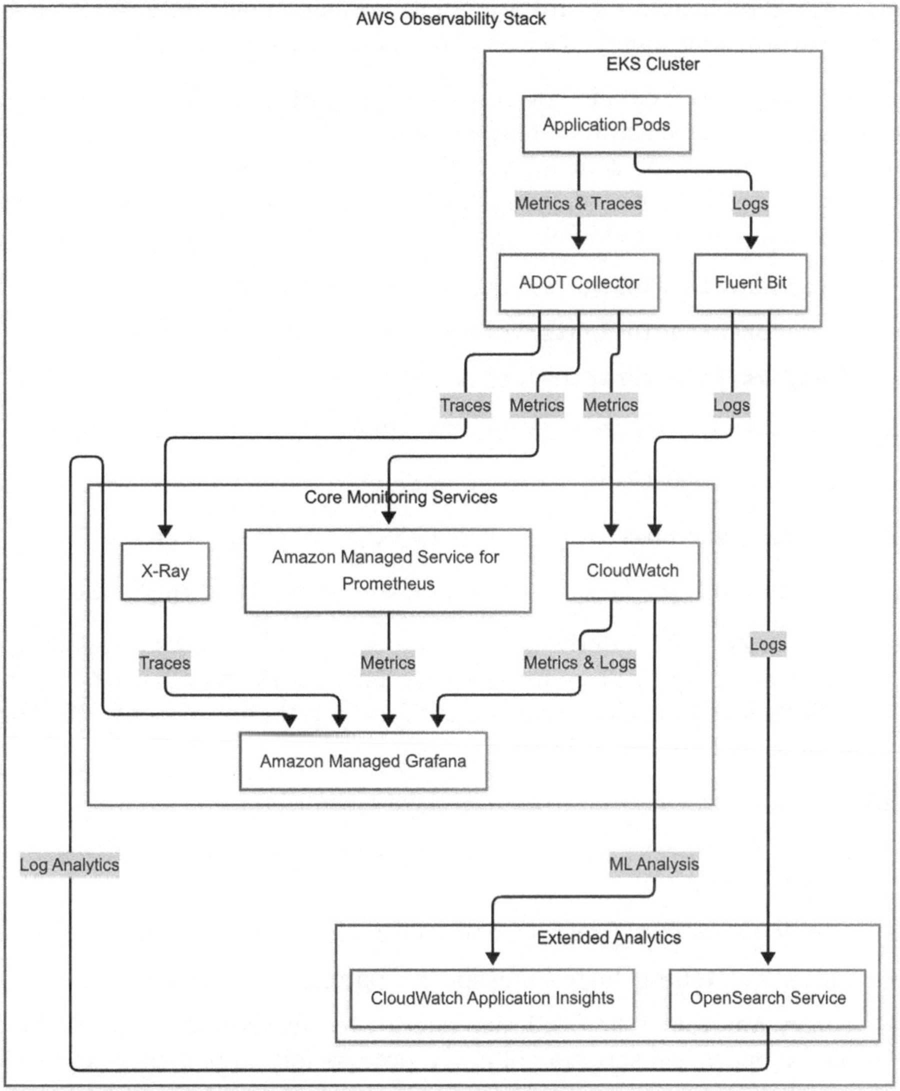


***Figure 8.3:*** *AWS Observability Stack*

Following are the AWS Services that work together for effective log management in EKS:

# Amazon CloudWatch Logs

CloudWatch Logs is a fully managed service that serves as a centralized logging solution for EKS clusters. It stores, monitors, and provides access to log files from various sources within your EKS environment, including container logs, application logs, and cluster control plane logs. In EKS, CloudWatch Logs become particularly important as they handle logs from multiple containers across different nodes and namespaces, providing a unified view of your entire cluster's operation.

CloudWatch Logs store data in Log Groups and Log Streams. For EKS, log groups are typically organized by cluster, namespace, and application components. Log streams within these groups represent individual container instances or pods. The data is stored with encryption at rest, using AWS KMS keys, and retention periods can be configured from one day to indefinitely. Common EKS-specific log groups include:

- `/aws/containerinsights/[cluster-name]/application`
- `/aws/containerinsights/[cluster-name]/host`
- `/aws/eks/[cluster-name]/cluster`

In EKS environments, logs are ingested through multiple methods such as:

1. **Container Logs:** Using Fluent Bit or Fluentd as DaemonSets on each node.
2. **Control Plane Logs:** Directly from EKS control plane when enabled.
3. **Application Logs:** Through application-level logging configurations.
4. **Node Logs:** From underlying EC2 instances, using CloudWatch Agent. The most common setup involves using Fluent Bit as a DaemonSet, which efficiently collects logs from all containers, and forwards them to CloudWatch Logs, with minimal resource overhead.

CloudWatch Logs processes data in several ways such as:

- **Real-time Processing:** Logs are processed as they arrive, using CloudWatch Logs Insights.
- **Metric Extraction:** Creating metrics from log data, using metric filters.
- **Pattern Matching:** Identifying specific patterns for alerting.
- **Query Analysis:** Using SQL-like queries to analyze the log data. The service also supports subscription filters to process logs in real-time, and send them to other AWS services like Lambda or Kinesis for further processing.

Production support teams gain significant advantages from CloudWatch Logs in their daily operations. The centralized logging system provides real-time visibility into application behavior, enabling quick identification and resolution of issues. Teams can perform comprehensive troubleshooting by correlating logs across different components of the EKS cluster, from container logs to control plane events. The ability to set up metric filters and alerts helps in proactive monitoring, allowing teams to address potential problems before they impact users. The search and analysis capabilities through CloudWatch Logs Insights enable teams to perform complex queries across massive amounts of log data, helping identify patterns and anomalies that might not be immediately apparent. Additionally, the integration with IAM ensures secure access control, while maintaining detailed audit trails for compliance requirements.

In real-world operations, CloudWatch Logs proves invaluable across various support scenarios. During incident response, teams can quickly trace error patterns by analyzing logs from multiple services simultaneously, significantly reducing Mean Time to Resolution (MTTR). For performance investigations, support teams can track application behavior over time, identifying bottlenecks or resource constraints that might affect user experience. When dealing with deployment issues, logs provide crucial information about container start up failures, configuration problems, or networking issues. In security incidents, the detailed log trail helps teams reconstruct events, and assess the impact. For capacity planning, historical log data helps teams understand usage patterns, and make informed decisions about scaling resources. The ability to correlate logs across microservices is particularly useful when troubleshooting complex and distributed issues that span multiple components of the EKS cluster.

Managing CloudWatch Logs effectively requires balancing comprehensive logging with cost efficiency. Teams should implement strategic log retention policies, keeping high-value logs longer, while setting shorter retention periods for verbose debug logs. Implementing log rotation, and configuring appropriate log levels helps manage storage costs while maintaining necessary visibility. Using CloudWatch Logs Insights queries efficiently is crucial - teams should focus on specific time ranges and use appropriate filters to reduce query costs and improve performance. Implementing log aggregation through tools like Fluent Bit helps optimize network usage, and reduce data transfer costs. Teams should regularly review and adjust logging strategies, using features such as metric filters to extract the key performance indicators, without storing excessive log data. Additionally, implementing log sampling for high-volume, low-priority events can significantly reduce costs, while maintaining representative data for analysis.

Whereas CloudWatch Logs provides robust logging capabilities, many organizations need more advanced search, visualization, and analytics capabilities. This is where Amazon OpenSearch Service (formerly Amazon Elasticsearch Service) comes into play, offering enhanced log analysis and visualization features that complement CloudWatch Logs.

# Amazon OpenSearch Service

Amazon OpenSearch Service is a fully managed service that enables you to perform interactive log analytics, real-time application monitoring, website search, and much more. In EKS environments, it serves as a powerful extension to basic logging capabilities, providing advanced search functionality, rich visualizations, and real-time analytics at scale. The service maintains compatibility with open-source

OpenSearch and Elasticsearch APIs, making it familiar to teams already using these technologies.

OpenSearch Service provides significant advantages for EKS log management. It offers powerful full-text search capabilities across container logs, making it easier to troubleshoot issues across microservices. The service enables real-time visualization and analysis of log data through OpenSearch Dashboards, providing immediate insights into application behavior. For EKS workloads, it offers scalability to handle high-volume container logs, and supports complex queries that help identify patterns in distributed systems. The integration with AWS security services ensures secure log storage and access control, while maintaining compliance **`requirements.OpenSearch`** architecture in EKS environments consists of several vital components working together to provide comprehensive log management. Data nodes form the backbone of the system, storing and processing log data while handling resource-intensive operations like indexing and search queries. Master nodes manage the cluster state, handling node membership and cluster-wide settings. Client nodes act as smart load balancers, routing requests and aggregating results. OpenSearch Dashboards serves as the primary visualization interface, providing customizable dashboards and real-time data exploration capabilities. The index management layer organizes logs efficiently, using features such as index lifecycle management and rollover policies. Security components include fine-grained access control, encryption mechanisms, and integration with AWS IAM, ensuring secure access to log data, while maintaining compliance requirements.

Log ingestion in OpenSearch follows several established patterns optimized for EKS environments. The primary method involves using Fluent Bit or Fluentd deployed as DaemonSets on each cluster node, efficiently collecting container logs and forwarding them to OpenSearch. These log shippers handle log parsing, transformation, and buffering, ensuring reliable delivery even during network issues. CloudWatch Logs integration provides another ingestion path, using Lambda functions or subscription filters to stream logs to OpenSearch. This pattern allows for centralized log collection and processing before forwarding to OpenSearch. Advanced configurations might include direct API ingestion for specific applications or custom log shipping solutions for specialized requirements. Each ingestion pattern includes retry mechanisms, back-pressure handling, and monitoring to ensure reliable log delivery.

OpenSearch provides multiple ways to access and analyze log data. OpenSearch Dashboards serves as the primary interface, offering real-time log viewing, powerful search capabilities, and customizable visualizations. Users can create specialized dashboards for different monitoring needs, from application performance to business metrics. The REST API enables programmatic access, supporting custom applications and automation workflows. Advanced features include alerting systems that monitor log patterns and trigger notifications, based on specific conditions. Machine learning capabilities can identify anomalies and trends automatically, while reporting tools generate scheduled summaries and analysis reports.

Various teams utilize OpenSearch differently, based on their specific needs. Production support teams rely on real-time log analysis for incident investigation and system health monitoring. They use predefined dashboards for quick access to critical metrics and error patterns. Development teams utilize detailed log analysis for debugging and performance optimization, often creating custom visualizations for specific application components. Security teams leverage OpenSearch for threat detection and compliance monitoring, using specialized dashboards and alerts for security events. Business analysts extract insights about system usage and trends, creating reports and forecasts based on log data patterns.

In production environments, OpenSearch proves invaluable across multiple scenarios. During incident management, teams use it to correlate errors across services, identify root causes, and verify resolution steps. Performance optimization involves analyzing latency patterns, resource utilization, and service dependencies. Security operations benefit from real-time threat detection and compliance monitoring capabilities. Business intelligence teams extract valuable insights about user behavior, service usage, and capacity requirements. The platform's flexibility allows teams to create specialized solutions for unique monitoring and analysis needs.

Effective cost management in OpenSearch requires a multi-faceted approach. Infrastructure optimization involves carefully selecting instance types and sizes, implementing hot-warm architectures, and using UltraWarm storage for older logs. Data lifecycle management includes setting appropriate retention periods, implementing index rollover policies, and configuring efficient snapshot strategies. Query optimization focuses on efficient index design, proper shard allocation, and caching strategies to reduce resource usage. Storage optimization involves compression techniques, selective logging practices, and automated cleanup policies for outdated indices.

Successful OpenSearch implementation follows established best practices. Architecture design should prioritize scalability and high availability, with proper consideration for disaster recovery. Security configuration must include comprehensive access controls, encryption at rest and in transit, and regular security audits. Monitoring and maintenance processes should cover cluster health, performance metrics, and capacity planning. Regular updates and optimizations ensure the system continues to meet evolving requirements. Documentation and training ensure that team members can effectively utilize the platform's capabilities.

Each of these aspects contributes to a robust and efficient logging infrastructure that supports the complex requirements of modern EKS applications, while maintaining cost-effectiveness and operational efficiency. Regular review and refinement of these components ensure that the system continues to meet the organizational needs as they evolve.

# Distributed Tracing

Distributed tracing is crucial in EKS environments because modern microservices architectures involve complex interactions between multiple services, making it challenging to understand the flow of requests, and identify performance bottlenecks. When an issue occurs in a distributed system, it can be extremely difficult to pinpoint the root cause without proper tracing. Distributed tracing provides end-to-end visibility by tracking requests as they flow through different services, helping teams understand service dependencies, latency issues, and error propagation patterns.

Refer to *Figure* 8.4 for visual representation of Distributed Tracing Workflows in microservices architectures for end-to-end visibility of requests as they traverse through various system components.

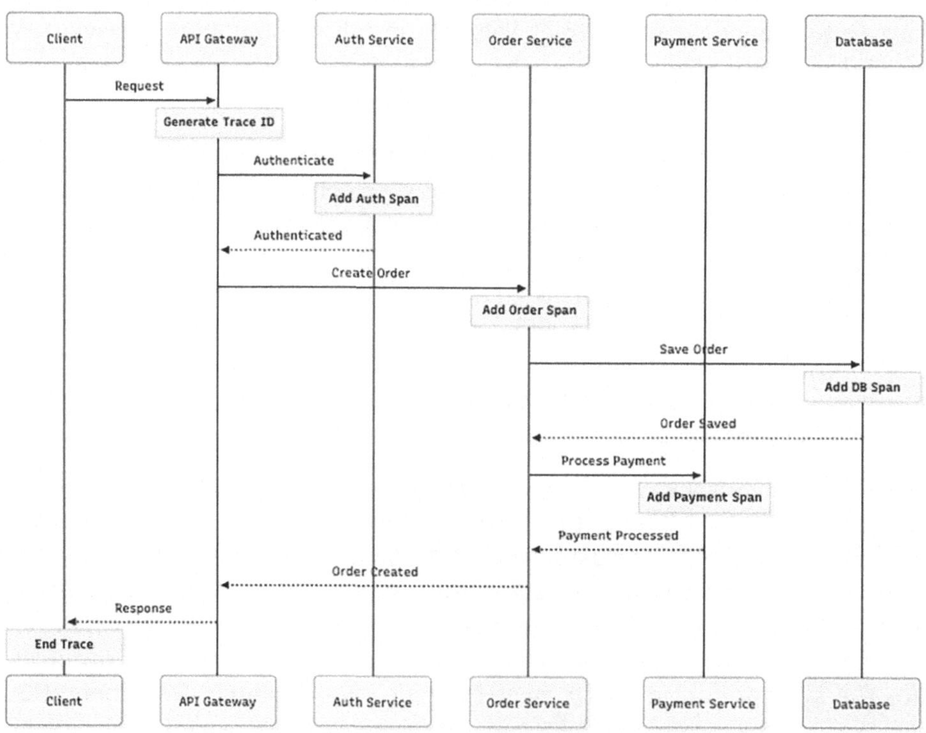


**Figure 8.4:** *Distributed Tracing Workflows*

Following are the AWS Services that work together for effective Distributed Tracking in EKS:

# AWS X-Ray

AWS X-Ray is a distributed tracing service that helps developers and support teams to analyze and debug production applications, particularly microservices architectures running on EKS. It collects the detailed information about requests that your application serves, providing a complete view of request paths, service dependencies, and latency distributions. In EKS environments, X-Ray provides visibility into both container-level and pod-level interactions, making it invaluable for understanding complex service meshes.

In EKS clusters, an X-Ray is typically deployed as a DaemonSet, ensuring that each node runs an X-Ray daemon. This daemon collects the trace data from your applications, and forwards it to the X-Ray service. Applications within EKS pods can be instrumented using the X-Ray SDK, which is available for multiple programming languages. The daemon automatically handles the buffering and transmission of trace data, reducing the overhead on your application containers.

Production support teams gain immediate visibility into complex distributed systems through X-Ray's comprehensive tracing capabilities. They can quickly identify bottlenecks, errors, and performance issues across the entire application stack. The ability to visualize service dependencies and request flows helps teams understand the impact of incidents, and make informed decisions during critical outages. Teams can track requests as they traverse through multiple microservices, making it easier to identify which service is causing delays or failures. This visibility significantly reduces the Mean Time to Resolution (MTTR), and helps prevent finger-pointing between different service teams. Additionally, historical trace data enables teams to perform trend analysis, and proactively identify potential issues before they impact the users.

Consider a scenario where users report slow checkout processes in an e-commerce application running on EKS. The support team can use X-Ray to trace the entire checkout flow, revealing that a third-party payment service is experiencing intermittent delays during peak hours. They can see exactly how long each service call takes, identify retry patterns, and determine if the issue affects specific regions or user segments. Another common scenario involves troubleshooting authentication failures. X-Ray traces might show that the authentication service is receiving malformed tokens from a specific microservice, allowing the team to quickly identify and fix the root cause. During deployment-related issues, teams can correlate service degradation with recent changes by comparing trace patterns before and after deployments, making rollback decisions more data-driven.

While X-Ray provides valuable insights, teams must carefully balance its implementation with cost and performance implications. The service charges, based on the number of traces recorded and stored, make sampling strategies crucial for cost management. High-traffic applications should implement intelligent sampling rules to capture representative data, without excessive costs. Additionally, teams should consider the performance overhead of trace instrumentation, typically keeping it below 1% of application response time. Storage duration of trace data should be optimized – while longer retention helps with historical analysis, it increases costs. Teams should regularly review their X-Ray usage patterns, and adjust the sampling rates as well as retention policies, based on actual needs and budget constraints. Further, it is recommended to start with conservative sampling rates, and gradually adjust based on the monitoring requirements and cost analysis.

# Metrics Collection and Visualization

Metrics collection and visualization are salient components in EKS environments as they provide quantifiable data about the health, performance, and resource utilization of containerized applications and cluster infrastructure. In dynamic environments where containers are constantly scaling and moving across nodes, having reliable metrics helps teams understand system behavior, predict potential issues, and make data-driven decisions. These metrics enable teams to establish baselines, identify anomalies, and ensure optimal resource allocation. Without proper metrics, teams would be flying blind in terms of understanding application performance, resource utilization patterns, and capacity planning needs.

Thus, following are the AWS Services that work together for effective Metrics Collection and Visualization in EKS:

## Amazon Managed Service for Prometheus

Amazon Managed Service for Prometheus (AMP) is a fully managed monitoring service that makes it easy to monitor containerized applications and infrastructure at scale. In EKS environments, it provides Prometheus-compatible APIs, while removing the operational complexity of managing Prometheus servers, storage, and high availability. AMP automatically scales the infrastructure needed to ingest, store, and query metrics, allowing teams to focus on monitoring rather than maintenance. The service seamlessly integrates with EKS clusters through the AWS Distro for OpenTelemetry (ADOT), or direct Prometheus server configuration.

AMP serves various roles within organizations running EKS workloads. Production support teams utilize AMP's ready-to-use dashboards and PromQL queries for real-time monitoring and troubleshooting. DevOps engineers leverage AMP's integration with AWS services to set up automated metric collection, and configure custom scrapers through ADOT collectors. SRE teams use AMP's powerful querying capabilities for SLO monitoring and capacity planning. Application developers benefit from language-specific client libraries to instrument their applications, and track custom metrics. Security teams appreciate AMP's integration with AWS IAM for fine-grained access control. Each persona accesses metrics through their preferred tools - whether direct PromQL queries, Grafana dashboards, or integrated CloudWatch views.

AMP proves invaluable in various EKS operational scenarios. During incident response, teams can quickly query historical metrics to understand anomaly patterns, using AMP's long-term storage capabilities. For performance optimization, teams analyze metrics like container CPU utilization, memory usage, and request latencies across services. During deployments, AMP helps compare performance metrics before and after changes, enabling quick rollback decisions if needed. Capacity planning becomes data-driven through AMP's ability to track resource utilization trends and predict scaling needs. Teams can also set up automated alerts based on metric thresholds, enabling proactive issue detection and resolution before users are impacted.

Production support teams gain significant advantages, using AMP in EKS environments. The service's managed nature eliminates the operational overhead of maintaining Prometheus servers, allowing teams to focus on monitoring rather than infrastructure. AMP's high availability and automatic scaling ensure reliable access to metrics during critical incidents. The service's integration with AWS security features provides secure access to metrics across team members. Support teams can leverage familiar Prometheus queries, while benefiting from AWS's managed infrastructure, making the transition to AMP straightforward. The ability to correlate metrics across multiple EKS clusters provides comprehensive visibility into distributed applications.

Effective AMP cost management in EKS environments requires strategic planning. Teams should implement metric filtering at the collection level to reduce ingestion volume, while maintaining essential visibility. Implementing appropriate scraping intervals helps balance monitoring granularity with costs. Using AWS tags for cost allocation enables teams to track and charge back metric expenses to specific applications or departments. Regular audits of metric usage patterns help identify opportunities for optimization, such as removing unused metrics or adjusting retention periods. Teams should also leverage AMP's integration with AWS Cost Explorer to monitor and forecast metric-related expenses.

Implementing AMP in EKS environments requires careful planning and execution. Teams should use AWS-provided tools like ADOT collectors for reliable metric collection and configure service discovery to automatically monitor new services. Implementation should include both infrastructure-level metrics and application-specific metrics through appropriate exporters and instrumentation. Teams should use AWS CloudFormation or Terraform to manage AMP workspace configurations and collection settings as code. Regular testing of metric collection, alerting, and dashboard configurations ensures reliability. Integration with the existing CI/CD pipelines helps maintain consistent monitoring across environment changes. Additionally, teams should implement proper IAM roles and security policies to control metric access, while enabling necessary cross-account, or cross-region monitoring capabilities.

These aspects together provide a comprehensive framework for leveraging Amazon Managed Service for Prometheus effectively in EKS environments, enabling teams to maintain robust monitoring, while benefiting from AWS's managed service capabilities.

While Amazon Managed Service for Prometheus excels at collecting and storing metrics from EKS environments, these metrics become truly valuable through effective visualization and analysis with Amazon Managed Grafana. The seamless integration between these services creates a comprehensive observability solution where AMP handles metric collection and storage, while AMG provides intuitive visualization and analysis capabilities. This combination is particularly powerful in EKS environments, where complex containerized applications require both robust metric collection and flexible visualization capabilities. Together, they provide a fully managed solution that removes operational overhead, while delivering enterprise-grade observability.

# Amazon Managed Grafana

Amazon Managed Grafana is a fully managed service that makes it easy to visualize and analyze operational data at scale. In EKS environments, it provides a powerful visualization platform for metrics, logs, and traces, without the operational overhead of managing Grafana servers. AMG seamlessly integrates with various AWS services, including Amazon Managed Service for Prometheus, CloudWatch, and X-Ray, providing a unified visualization layer for all observability data. The service handles scaling, updates, and high availability automatically, allowing teams to focus on creating effective dashboards, and deriving insights from their data.

Production support teams utilize AMG for real-time monitoring, incident investigation, and performance analysis through pre-built and custom dashboards. DevOps engineers leverage AMG to create comprehensive monitoring solutions, integrating multiple data sources and implementing automated dashboard provisioning. Application developers use AMG to visualize application-specific metrics and troubleshoot performance issues. SRE teams employ AMG for SLO monitoring and capacity planning through detailed visualization of trends and patterns. Each role benefits from AMG's ability to create role-specific views, while maintaining a centralized monitoring platform.

During incident response, teams use AMG to correlate data across different sources, helping quickly identify the root causes. A typical scenario involves viewing pod metrics alongside application logs and traces to understand service degradation. For capacity planning, teams create dashboards showing resource utilization trends and scaling patterns. Performance optimization involves analyzing latency distributions, error rates, and resource usage through specialized dashboards. During deployments, teams use AMG to compare before and after metrics, ensuring successful releases. The ability to share temporary dashboards during incident bridges, and create persistent views for post-mortems makes AMG invaluable for operational support.

AMG also provides significant advantages for production support teams in EKS environments. The unified view of metrics, logs, and traces enables faster troubleshooting, and reduced MTTR. Built-in authentication and role-based access control simplifies security management. Teams can create standardized dashboards for common scenarios, while allowing customization for specific needs. The ability to share dashboards and annotations improves collaboration during incidents. Integration with alerting systems helps teams stay proactive in identifying and addressing issues.

Effective cost management in AMG involves several key approaches. Teams should optimize dashboard refresh rates based on data update frequency and user needs. Implementing viewer roles instead of editor roles where appropriate helps manage license costs. Regular audits of dashboard usage help identify and remove unused dashboards. Teams should leverage dashboard templating to reduce the total number of dashboards needed. Implementing proper data source configuration helps minimize query costs from underlying services like Amazon Managed Service for Prometheus or CloudWatch.

Hence, successful implementation of Amazon Managed Grafana in EKS environments requires focus on certain key areas such as: Dashboard organization, data source integration, and user management. Dashboards should follow clear naming conventions with logical folder structures, moving from overview to detailed views, while utilizing templates for consistency. Data sources must be properly configured with optimized queries, appropriate authentication, and efficient caching strategies. User management should implement role-based access control with SSO integration and regular access reviews. Teams should adopt infrastructure as code for dashboard version control, establish regular review processes, and maintain comprehensive documentation. Integration with services like AMP and CloudWatch should be optimized for efficient metric collection. These practices together ensure a scalable, maintainable, and secure Grafana implementation that effectively serves various team needs, while maintaining operational excellence.

While Amazon Managed Grafana excels at visualizing metrics from various sources, CloudWatch Container Insights provides native and automated monitoring, specifically for EKS workloads. Container Insights automatically collects essential container-level metrics without manual configuration, and this data can be visualized through both native CloudWatch dashboards and AMG. This integration enables teams to leverage Container Insights' pre-built monitoring capabilities, while maintaining the flexibility to create custom visualizations in Grafana, creating a comprehensive EKS monitoring solution.

## CloudWatch Container Insights

CloudWatch Container Insights is a native AWS monitoring solution, specifically designed for containerized applications running on EKS. It automatically collects, aggregates, and summarizes metrics and logs from containerized applications and microservices. The service is crucial for EKS environments, as it provides out-of-the-box visibility into container performance, resource utilization, and application health, without requiring extensive configuration. Container Insights helps teams understand system behavior at both cluster and container levels, enabling proactive monitoring and faster troubleshooting of containerized applications. Container Insights eliminates the complexity of setting up monitoring infrastructure, offering immediate visibility through pre-built dashboards, and automated metric collection.

Container Insights provides multi-level monitoring capabilities crucial for EKS environments. At the cluster level, it tracks node count, pod status, and overall cluster capacity. Node-level metrics include CPU, memory, network, and disk utilization patterns. Pod-level monitoring covers resource usage, restart counts, and operational status. Service-level metrics track request counts, latency, and error rates. The service also collects container-specific metrics for detailed resource utilization analysis. All these metrics are automatically collected and presented through intuitive dashboards, enabling quick operational insights, and troubleshooting capabilities.

Production support teams rely on Container Insights for real-time monitoring and incident response, using pre-built dashboards to quickly identify issues. DevOps engineers utilize the service for capacity planning and infrastructure optimization, leveraging historical data for scaling decisions. Application developers access container-level metrics to debug performance issues, and validate application behavior. SRE teams use the service for SLO monitoring and reliability improvement initiatives. Each role benefits from Container Insights' automated collection and pre-built visualizations, while maintaining the ability to create custom views for specific needs.

In production environments, Container Insights proves invaluable across various scenarios. During incident response, teams can quickly identify resource constraints, or application issues by analyzing pod and container metrics. For capacity planning, historical data helps predict resource needs and optimize cluster sizing. Performance optimization involves analyzing CPU, memory, and network metrics to identify bottlenecks. During deployments, teams monitor container health metrics to ensure successful rollouts. The service's integration with CloudWatch Alarms enables proactive notification of potential issues, before they impact the users.

Further, Container Insights provide significant advantages for EKS operations teams. The automated metric collection eliminates the need for manual instrumentation, and reduces setup complexity. Pre-built dashboards enable immediate visibility into cluster health and performance. Integration with the existing AWS services simplifies the overall monitoring stack. The service's built-in alerting capabilities enable proactive issue detection and response. Historical data retention helps with trend analysis and capacity planning, while the unified view of metrics and logs streamlines troubleshooting processes.

Effective cost management in Container Insights involves several approaches. Teams should configure appropriate metric resolution based on monitoring needs, balancing granularity with cost. Implementing metric filters helps reduce data volume, while maintaining essential visibility. Log retention policies should be optimized, based on compliance and operational requirements. Regular reviews of metric usage help identify and remove unnecessary collections. Teams should also leverage CloudWatch's built-in cost allocation tags to track expenses across different applications and environments.

Thus, Container Insights works seamlessly with other AWS services, enhancing its value in EKS environments. Integration with CloudWatch Logs enables log analysis alongside metrics. Amazon Managed Grafana can visualize Container Insights metrics in custom dashboards. AWS X-Ray integration provides distributed tracing capabilities. Therefore, these integrations create a comprehensive monitoring solution that supports various operational needs, while maintaining simplicity and efficiency.

By effectively utilizing CloudWatch Container Insights, EKS support teams can maintain robust monitoring capabilities, while benefiting from AWS's managed service approach. Moreover, the combination of automated collection, pre-built dashboards, and comprehensive metrics makes it an essential tool for modern container operations and management.

*Table* 8.1 summarizes a structured view of cost optimization strategies across the AWS observability stack, helping organizations implement effective cost controls, while maintaining comprehensive monitoring coverage.

| **Service** | **Cost Management Strategy** |
|---|---|
| CloudWatch | Implement namespace-level filtering; Use dynamic sampling rates; Optimize log retention periods; Enable selective Container Insights |
| ADOT | Configure appropriate sampling rates; Filter unnecessary telemetry data; Optimize collector resources |
| Prometheus | Implement metric filtering; Adjust scraping intervals; Use efficient PromQL queries |
| Grafana | Optimize dashboard refresh rates; Use viewer roles where possible; Implement dashboard templates |

| | |
|---|---|
| X-Ray | Implement intelligent sampling; Optimize trace retention; Focus on critical paths |
| OpenSearch | Use hot-warm architecture; Implement index lifecycle policies; Optimize shard allocation |

**Table 8.1:** *Cost Management Strategy*

# Real-time Application Performance Monitoring

Real-time Application Performance Monitoring is critical for EKS applications, as it provides immediate visibility into application behavior, performance metrics, and user experience. In containerized environments where applications are distributed across multiple microservices, real-time APM helps teams quickly identify and respond to performance issues, bottlenecks, and failures, before they impact the end users. The dynamic nature of EKS workloads, with containers scaling and moving across nodes, makes real-time monitoring pivotal for maintaining application reliability and performance optimization.

Following are the AWS Services that work together for effective Real-time Application Performance Monitoring in EKS:

## Amazon CloudWatch

Amazon CloudWatch serves as a comprehensive monitoring and observability service that provides critical insights into EKS clusters and applications. In the EKS context, CloudWatch integrates deeply with container environments, collecting metrics, logs, and events from multiple layers - from the cluster level down to individual pods and containers. Through Container Insights, it automatically collects metrics like CPU utilization, memory usage, network traffic, and disk I/O for both the cluster infrastructure and containerized applications. This data is aggregated and presented in pre-built dashboards, making it easier to understand the overall health and performance of EKS workloads.

Production support teams rely heavily on CloudWatch for day-to-day operations. They typically start their day by reviewing CloudWatch dashboards for any anomalies or alerts that occurred during off-hours. During incident response, they use CloudWatch Logs Insights to perform real-time log analysis across multiple containers and applications, helping quickly identify root causes. The service's alarm feature is crucial for proactive monitoring - support teams set up alarms for various metrics such as pod restarts, node CPU utilization, or application-specific metrics. When troubleshooting performance issues, they utilize CloudWatch's metric math features to correlate different metrics and understand patterns.

In real-world scenarios, CloudWatch proves invaluable for various use cases. For instance, when an e-commerce application experiences sudden latency spikes, support teams can use CloudWatch to trace the issue across different microservices running in EKS. They might discover that increased database connections are causing the slowdown by correlating container metrics with RDS metrics. During high-traffic events such as sales promotions, teams use CloudWatch to monitor scaling activities, and ensure resources are properly allocated. The service also helps in capacity planning by providing historical data and trends.

When monitoring EKS environments with CloudWatch, costs can quickly escalate without proper management. Implement namespace-level filtering to collect metrics only from production-critical workloads rather than monitoring every namespace. Use dynamic sampling rates - higher frequency for critical microservices (like payment processing) and lower frequency for less critical ones. Consider using CloudWatch Agent with custom configurations to send only relevant container metrics instead of enabling all metrics. For log management, utilize Log Groups effectively by setting up log retention periods (for example, 30 days for general logs, 90 days for security logs). Implement log aggregation at the pod level before sending to CloudWatch to reduce ingestion volume. Use Container Insights selectively - enable it only for production namespaces while keeping it disabled for development and testing namespaces. Regularly review and clean up unused CloudWatch dashboards, metrics, and alarms to avoid unnecessary charges.

Amazon CloudWatch serves as a core monitoring and observability service for EKS environments, providing essential insights into container, pod, and cluster health through Container Insights. It enables production support teams to effectively monitor and troubleshoot EKS workloads through automated metrics collection, log aggregation, and customizable alerting mechanisms. The service's cost-effective monitoring strategies, including selective metric collection and intelligent log retention policies, help organizations optimize their monitoring expenses while maintaining comprehensive visibility. CloudWatch extends its capabilities through CloudWatch Application Insights, which adds machine learning-powered automated problem detection and correlation specifically for containerized applications in EKS. This intelligent monitoring automatically identifies potential issues across the application stack, from pod-level problems to infrastructure concerns, reducing mean time to resolution and operational overhead. Together, these capabilities create a robust monitoring solution that helps teams maintain reliable EKS environments, while balancing operational efficiency with cost optimization. The integration of traditional monitoring with intelligent insights makes CloudWatch an indispensable tool for modern containerized applications running on EKS.

# CloudWatch Application Insights

CloudWatch Application Insights is an intelligent monitoring and diagnostics service that enhances observability for EKS applications through automated problem detection and correlation. It uses machine learning to analyze patterns across containerized applications, automatically identifying potential issues and establishing relevant monitoring configurations. In EKS environments, it provides deeper visibility into application behavior, component relationships, and dependency mapping across microservices. The service automatically discovers application resources, monitors them for anomalies, and provides contextual insights that help quickly identify and resolve issues across the container ecosystem.

Production support teams leverage Application Insights to enhance their monitoring capabilities beyond basic metrics and logs. Teams benefit from automated problem detection that identifies issues such as memory leaks, pod crashes, or unusual application behavior patterns, before they become critical. The service's intelligent capabilities automatically identify potential problems, while providing contextual dashboards that consolidate relevant metrics and logs during incidents. The service's ability to correlate events across different components helps teams quickly understand the impact chain of incidents - for example, how a database performance issue affects specific microservices. Machine learning-based thresholds adapt to application behavior patterns, reducing false alarms, while ensuring critical issues are caught, particularly during high-stress scenarios like deployments or traffic spikes.

In practical applications, CloudWatch Application Insights proves particularly valuable in modern containerized environments. When managing microservices-based e-commerce platforms, it automatically detects increased latency in payment processing services and correlates it with database connection pool exhaustion in related services. During deployment windows, it identifies potential memory leaks or resource constraints before they impact production workloads. The service's intelligent anomaly detection helps support teams proactively address issues during high-traffic events or promotional periods by identifying unusual patterns in application behavior. In multi-tenant EKS clusters, it effectively identifies noisy neighbor issues affecting service performance, while during incident response, it automatically correlates pod crashes with underlying infrastructure issues or application dependencies, significantly reducing mean time to resolution.

In EKS environments, optimizing CloudWatch Application Insights requires a strategic approach while maintaining effective monitoring coverage. Start by implementing namespace-based filtering to focus monitoring on production-critical workloads rather than monitoring every service uniformly. Resource tagging should be utilized effectively to identify and monitor only business-critical pods and containers, reducing unnecessary data collection from development or testing workloads. Configure intelligent sampling rates where high-priority microservices receive comprehensive monitoring, while supporting services are monitored at lower frequencies. The service's built-in machine learning capabilities should be leveraged for anomaly detection instead of creating numerous custom metrics, which can increase costs. Regular review cycles are essential to identify and remove unused monitoring configurations, dashboards, and alerts that accumulate as applications evolve. Consider using automated component discovery selectively by defining specific criteria for monitored components, thereby preventing monitoring sprawl in large clusters.

The service enhances EKS operations through comprehensive integration capabilities and automated features. Automated issue detection and correlation across containerized applications significantly reduce manual analysis time. Contextual dashboards provide relevant metrics and logs during incidents, enabling faster response times. The integration with AWS Systems Manager enables automated remediation actions based on detected issues. Custom insight rules can be created to address specific application monitoring needs, while maintaining compatibility with existing monitoring tools. The service seamlessly integrates with CI/CD pipelines, allowing monitoring configurations to be managed as code, and automatically adjusted during deployments.

In conclusion, CloudWatch Application Insights transforms EKS monitoring by combining intelligent automation with machine learning-based analysis. Its automated problem detection and monitoring setup significantly reduces operational overhead, allowing teams to focus on resolution rather than configuration. The service's comprehensive approach to containerized application monitoring, from automated correlation to predictive insights, makes it a necessary tool for maintaining highly available and performant EKS environments, while optimizing operational efficiency.

# Conclusion

The comprehensive exploration of observability and monitoring in Amazon EKS environments demonstrates the critical importance of implementing robust monitoring solutions for modern containerized applications. Throughout this chapter, we have examined how AWS's integrated observability stack combines native services with managed open-source solutions to provide complete visibility into application and infrastructure health.

The integration of CloudWatch, X-Ray, and managed services for Prometheus and Grafana creates a powerful foundation for monitoring containerized applications. Organizations can leverage these tools to implement cost-effective, scalable monitoring solutions, while maintaining operational efficiency. The emphasis on automated collection, intelligent analysis, and integrated visualization capabilities ensures that teams can maintain high reliability, while minimizing manual overhead.

As containerized applications continue to evolve, the importance of robust observability solutions becomes increasingly critical. Organizations must stay updated with AWS's observability offerings, while balancing comprehensive monitoring with cost optimization. The practices and tools discussed in this chapter provide the foundation for successful EKS operations in modern cloud environments.

Upon completing this chapter, you should have gained a comprehensive understanding of AWS's observability stack for EKS and its integration patterns. This includes proficiency in implementing comprehensive logging solutions using CloudWatch Logs, Fluent Bit, and OpenSearch Service, as well as distributed tracing with AWS X-Ray and AWS Distro for OpenTelemetry. You should be comfortable setting up metrics collection and visualization using Amazon Managed Service for Prometheus and Grafana, and leveraging CloudWatch Container Insights for automated container-level monitoring. The chapter has also equipped you with knowledge on implementing intelligent monitoring through CloudWatch Application Insights and applying cost optimization strategies for observability in EKS environments. Additionally, you should be familiar with the best practices for log management and analysis in containerized applications, methods for implementing effective alerting and notification systems, and techniques for scaling observability solutions in tandem with application growth. This comprehensive skill set enables you to effectively monitor and manage complex EKS environments, ensuring optimal performance and reliability of your containerized applications.

These foundational concepts and practical implementations enable you to design and maintain effective observability solutions that support reliable, high-performing EKS applications, while optimizing operational efficiency and cost management.

In the next chapter, we will deep dive into EKS Storage and State Management, exploring advanced topics such as State Management, EKS Storage concepts, AWS Storage Options, Volume Management, and Security Considerations. This progression will ensure that readers are well prepared for real-world container storage challenges and troubleshooting.

# Points to Remember

- AWS observability stack combines CloudWatch, ADOT, Prometheus, and Grafana for comprehensive EKS monitoring.
- CloudWatch Container Insights provides automated collection of container-level metrics, and logs into EKS.
- AWS X-Ray enables distributed tracing across microservices in EKS environments.
- Fluent Bit serves as the primary log collector in EKS, deployed as a DaemonSet for efficient log processing.
- Amazon Managed Service for Prometheus eliminates the operational overhead of managing Prometheus servers.

- Amazon Managed Grafana provides visualization capabilities, without infrastructure management.
- CloudWatch Application Insights uses machine learning for automated problem detection.
- OpenSearch Service enables advanced log analytics and visualization capabilities.
- Effective cost management requires strategic implementation of sampling and retention policies.
- Integration between services enables correlation of metrics, logs, and traces for faster troubleshooting.

# Multiple Choice Questions

1. Which AWS service provides automated container-level metrics collection in EKS?
   a. AWS X-Ray
   b. CloudWatch Container Insights
   c. Amazon Managed Grafana
   d. OpenSearch Service
2. Which tool is commonly deployed as a DaemonSet for log collection in EKS?
   a. Prometheus
   b. Grafana
   c. Fluent Bit
   d. X-Ray
3. Which service provides distributed tracing capabilities in EKS?
   a. CloudWatch
   b. Prometheus
   c. AWS X-Ray
   d. Fluent Bit

4. Which AWS service uses machine learning for automated problem detection in EKS?

   a. CloudWatch Application Insights

   b. Amazon Managed Grafana

   c. AWS X-Ray

   d. OpenSearch Service

5. Which service provides visualization capabilities for metrics collected by Prometheus?

   a. CloudWatch

   b. X-Ray

   c. Amazon Managed Grafana

   d. Fluent Bit

6. Which AWS service enables advanced log analytics and visualization?

   a. CloudWatch

   b. OpenSearch Service

   c. X-Ray

   d. Prometheus

7. Which technology is used by AWS Distro for OpenTelemetry for data collection?

   a. Collectors

   b. Agents

   c. Scrapers

   d. Loggers

8. Which service is best suited for storing and analyzing historical metric data in EKS?

   a. X-Ray

   b. Amazon Managed Service for Prometheus

   c. Fluent Bit

   d. CloudWatch Logs

9. Which feature of CloudWatch Container Insights provides automated discovery of resources?
    a. Service Discovery
    b. Auto Detection
    c. Resource Mapping
    d. Dynamic Discovery
10. Which deployment method is recommended for X-Ray in EKS clusters?
    a. Sidecar
    b. DaemonSet
    c. StatefulSet
    d. Deployment

# Answers

1. b
2. c
3. c
4. a
5. c
6. b
7. a
8. b
9. a
10. b

# Key Terms

- **AWS Distro for OpenTelemetry (ADOT):** AWS's distribution of OpenTelemetry for collecting and managing telemetry data.
- **Container Insights:** CloudWatch feature for automated collection of container metrics and logs.

- **Distributed Tracing:** Method of tracking requests across multiple services in a distributed system.
- **Fluent Bit:** Lightweight log processor and forwarder optimized for containerized environments.
- **OpenSearch:** Managed service for log analytics and visualization (formerly Elasticsearch).
- **Prometheus:** Time-series database and monitoring system for metrics collection.
- **Grafana:** Visualization and analytics platform for metrics and logs.
- **X-Ray Traces:** Detailed request paths through distributed applications.
- **CloudWatch Application Insights:** ML-powered application monitoring service.
- **Metric Filter:** CloudWatch feature for extracting metrics from log data.
- **Log Group:** Logical grouping of log streams in CloudWatch.
- **Service Map:** Visual representation of service dependencies in X-Ray.
- **PromQL:** Query language used by Prometheus for data retrieval.
- **Collector:** Component in ADOT that receives and processes telemetry data.
- **Container Insights:** Automated monitoring solution for containerized applications.

# CHAPTER 9
# Storage and State Management

## Introduction

Storage and state management are critical challenges in containerized environments, particularly when deploying applications at scale on Amazon Elastic Kubernetes Service (EKS). This chapter explores the comprehensive framework for managing storage and state in EKS, providing architects and developers with the necessary knowledge to design and implement robust storage solutions.

In this chapter, we will examine the integration of EKS with AWS's storage services, including EBS, EFS, and FSx, as well as explore Kubernetes' native abstractions such as **`StorageClasses`**, **`PersistentVolumes`**, and **`PersistentVolumeClaims`**. The chapter also covers the crucial aspects such as performance optimization, security, high availability, and cost management, addressing the key considerations for production environments.

Through real-world scenarios and best practices, readers will gain a comprehensive understanding of effective storage and state management in EKS. This knowledge is vital for cloud architects, DevOps engineers, and developers working with containerized applications in AWS, as it directly impacts application reliability, performance, and operational efficiency in cloud-native environments.

## Structure

In this chapter, we will discuss the following topics in detail:

- State Management in Kubernetes
- EKS Storage Concepts
- AWS Storage Options for EKS
- Storage Classes in EKS
- Persistent Volume Management

- StatefulSet Applications
- Best Practices and Patterns
- Storage Monitoring and Troubleshooting
- Security Considerations
- Practical Examples and Use Cases

# State Management in Kubernetes

In the dynamic world of containerized applications, managing state effectively is one of the most crucial challenges, organizations face when adopting Kubernetes. While containers excel at running stateless workloads, many real-world applications require persistent data that survives container restarts, pod rescheduling, and cluster upgrades. This chapter explores the fundamental concepts of state management in Kubernetes, with particular focus on implementation within Amazon Elastic Kubernetes Service (EKS).

The architectural landscape of modern containerized applications in Kubernetes is fundamentally shaped by how applications handle state. Stateless applications, which treat each request as an independent transaction, operate like interchangeable parts in a machine - they can be created, destroyed, or replaced without impacting the system's functionality. In contrast, stateful applications maintain critical data across transactions, requiring careful consideration of data persistence, consistency, and identity. Understanding these differences is not just an academic exercise; it directly impacts how we design storage solutions, implement high availability, handle scaling, and manage deployments in Amazon EKS. As we dive deeper into these concepts, we shall explore how each type of application presents unique challenges and opportunities, ultimately influencing our choices in storage architecture and state management strategies.

## Stateless Applications

Stateless applications process each request independently, without relying on stored client session information, or persistent data between interactions. These applications are inherently more scalable and resilient in containerized environments because:

- Any instance can process any request.
- Instances can be created or destroyed without data loss concerns.
- Horizontal scaling is straightforward.
- They align naturally with container immutability principles.

Common examples of stateless applications include frontend web servers, content delivery services, and RESTful APIs that do not maintain client session data.

# Stateful Applications

Stateful applications, by contrast, maintain and rely on persistent data. They record the state of client interactions, and depend on this information to function correctly. Examples include:

- Databases (MySQL, PostgreSQL, and MongoDB)
- Message queues (Kafka, RabbitMQ)
- Caching layers (Redis, Memcached)
- File storage services and content management systems
- Applications with user session requirements

These applications present unique challenges in Kubernetes because they need:

- Persistent storage that survives pod lifecycle events
- Stable network identities
- Ordered deployment, scaling, and upgrades
- Data consistency guarantees
- Backup and recovery mechanisms

Kubernetes addresses these requirements primarily through StatefulSets and various storage abstractions, which we will explore throughout this chapter.

The ephemeral nature of containers creates the following significant challenges when managing stateful applications:

- **Storage Persistence:** Containers are designed to be immutable and disposable, with their file systems being ephemeral by default. When a container restarts, any data written to its file system is lost. For stateful applications, this fundamental characteristic requires special handling through persistent volumes.
- **Identity and Networking:** Stateful applications often require stable network identities. Database clusters, for instance, need to know exactly which node is the primary one, and which are replicas. In traditional environments, this is handled through fixed hostnames and IPs, but in Kubernetes, pods can be rescheduled to different nodes with different IPs.
- **Ordered Operations:** Many stateful applications have specific requirements for start-up, shutdown, and scaling operations. A database cluster might need its primary node to initialize before replicas can join, or it might require a specific decommissioning process when scaling down to ensure data integrity.
- **Data Consistency:** Ensuring data consistency when containers are being created, deleted, or moved between nodes is complex. Race conditions can

occur when multiple instances try to access the same data simultaneously, especially during scaling operations.

- **Backup and Recovery:** Implementing effective backup strategies for container-based applications requires careful planning. You need mechanisms to capture data at rest, transaction logs, and configuration information, all while minimizing impact on running applications.
- **Multi-AZ and Disaster Recovery:** For production workloads, data typically needs to be replicated across availability zones, or even regions. This requires sophisticated storage solutions that can handle the distributed data with proper consistency guarantees.

Storage management in Amazon EKS is a vital cornerstone of container orchestration that directly impacts application reliability, performance, and operational success. As organizations deploy both stateless and stateful workloads in Kubernetes, proper storage management becomes essential for ensuring data persistence across container restarts, maintaining application state, and meeting performance requirements of diverse workloads. It is not just about providing space for data–storage management in EKS addresses, this includes crucial concerns, including data reliability, scalability, cost optimization, security compliance, and high availability. Without proper storage management, organizations risk data loss, application downtime, performance bottlenecks, and increased operational costs. Furthermore, as applications scale and evolve, storage needs must adapt dynamically, making storage management an integral part of the broader container orchestration strategy. Thus, whether it is handling database workloads, maintaining compliance requirements, or ensuring business continuity, effective storage management in EKS is fundamental in building resilient, scalable, and production-ready containerized applications.

# EKS Storage Concepts

EKS Storage Concepts form the foundation of how Kubernetes manages persistent storage in containerized environments. Understanding these core concepts is necessary for effectively managing stateful applications, and their data requirements.

- **Storage Classes** serve as templates that define the characteristics and types of storage available in the cluster. They enable administrators to define different tiers of storage with varying performance, backup policies, and cost profiles. This abstraction allows for standardized storage provisioning across the cluster, while maintaining flexibility for different application needs.
- **PersistentVolumes (PVs)** represent the actual storage resources in the cluster. They abstract the underlying infrastructure details, and provide a standardized way to manage storage across different providers and types

– whether it is Amazon EBS volumes, EFS file systems, or other storage solutions. PVs exist independently of any pod, and have their own lifecycle.

- **PersistentVolumeClaims (PVCs)** act as storage requests made by applications, functioning as a bridge between pods that need storage, and the available Persistent Volumes. When a pod requests storage through a PVC, Kubernetes matches it with an appropriate PV based on the specified requirements and access modes. This abstraction allows developers to request storage, without needing to know the underlying storage infrastructure details.
- **Dynamic Volume Provisioning** further automates this process by automatically creating PVs when a PVC is submitted. This eliminates the need for cluster administrators to manually pre-provision storage resources, and enables a more scalable, self-service model for development teams. Thus, when combined with Storage Classes, dynamic provisioning provides a powerful way to automate storage management.
- **Storage Drivers and Container Storage Interface (CSI)** provide a standardized way for container orchestration systems like Kubernetes to expose arbitrary storage systems to their containerized workloads. This standardization allows storage vendors to develop plugins that work seamlessly across different container orchestration systems, while enabling EKS to support a wide range of storage solutions, without requiring changes to the core Kubernetes code.

Together, these concepts create a flexible and powerful storage management system that supports diverse application requirements, while maintaining simplicity and scalability in storage operations. Therefore, understanding how these components interact is the key to designing effective storage solutions in EKS.

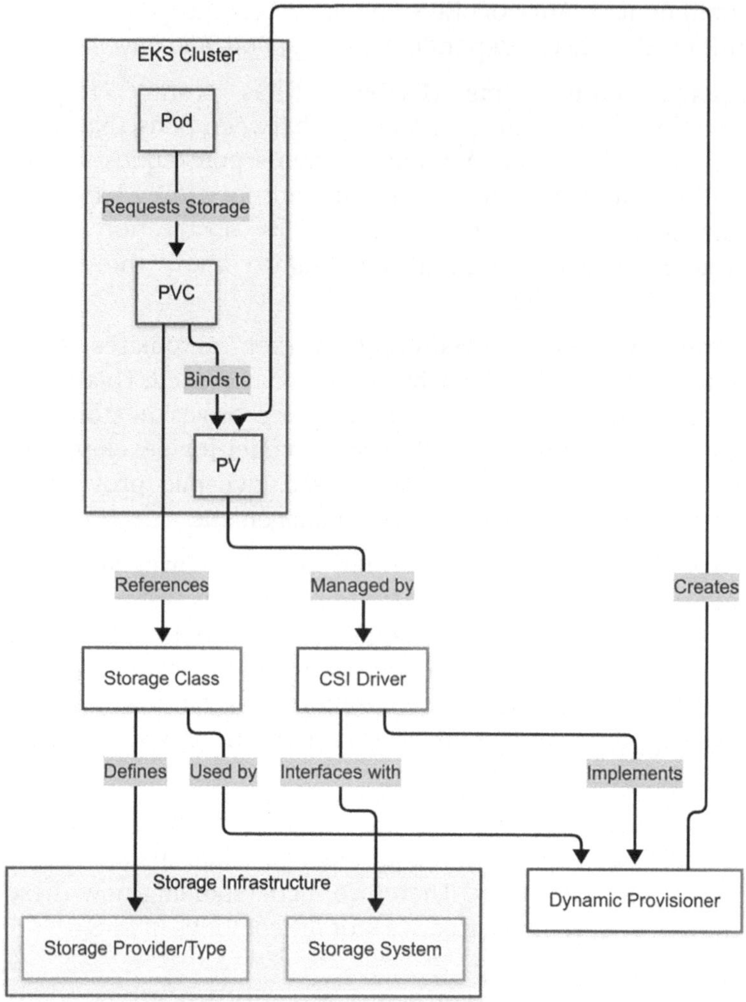


***Figure 9.1:*** *Flow of Storage Provisioning in EKS*

*Figure* 9.1 illustrates the complete storage workflow in Amazon EKS, showcasing how different components interact to provide persistent storage to applications. It begins with a Storage Class that defines the specifications and type of storage provider (like EBS or EFS) to be used. When a Pod needs persistent storage, it creates a storage request through a PersistentVolumeClaim (PVC), which references the appropriate Storage Class. The PVC then binds to a PersistentVolume (PV), which is automatically created by the Dynamic Provisioner, based on the Storage Class specifications. The Container Storage Interface (CSI) Driver implements the provisioning logic, and manages the PV, acting as a bridge between Kubernetes and the actual storage infrastructure. The CSI Driver interfaces with the underlying Storage System (such as Amazon Elastic Block Store or Amazon Elastic File System) to create and manage the actual storage volumes. This entire process is encapsulated within two main contexts:

The EKS Cluster (containing the Pod, PVC, and PV) and the Storage Infrastructure (containing the actual storage system and provider types), creating a seamless and the automated storage management system that abstracts the complexity of storage operations from the application developers.

When troubleshooting PV/PVC/CSI issues in EKS, it is crucial to understand common error scenarios, and have a structured approach to resolution. Frequently encountered problems include PVCs stuck in a pending state due to misconfigured StorageClasses, volume mount failures caused by CSI driver issues or inadequate permissions, and "`FailedAttachVolume`" events resulting from EBS volume limits or AZ mismatches. Performance issues often stem from incorrect storage type or IOPS configurations. To effectively troubleshoot, utilize kubectl describe commands for detailed resource information, examine CSI driver logs, and verify AWS resources using CLI commands. Review StorageClass configurations, monitor CloudWatch metrics for EBS volumes, and leverage AWS CloudTrail for API call auditing. Implement proper resource tagging, keep CSI drivers and EKS components updated, and use tools like kube-capacity for cluster resource analysis. Proactive monitoring with custom CloudWatch alarms for storage metrics can also help prevent issues. Thus, always adhere to AWS and Kubernetes best practices for storage management and security, when implementing solutions.

# AWS Storage Options for EKS

When deploying applications on Amazon Elastic Kubernetes Service (EKS), choosing the right storage solution is crucial for optimal performance, scalability, and cost-effectiveness. AWS provides several storage options that integrate seamlessly with EKS, each designed to meet different workload requirements and use cases. Hence, whether your applications demand high-performance block storage, shared file systems across multiple pods, or cost-effective object storage for large-scale data, understanding these storage solutions is vital for building resilient and efficient Kubernetes applications on AWS. Following are the primary storage solutions available for EKS workloads:

## Amazon Elastic Block Store (EBS)

From an EKS perspective, Amazon EBS provides block-level storage volumes that integrate directly with your Kubernetes pods as persistent volumes. As shown in *Figure* 9.1, the integration is managed through storage classes and the AWS EBS CSI (Container Storage Interface) driver that must be installed in your cluster to handle volume operations.

Thus, EKS automatically creates default storage classes for EBS, with gp2, typically serving as the default class. Other common options include gp3, io1, and sc1. You can define custom storage classes to specify volume types, IOPS, and other parameters. As an example shown below, a basic storage class configuration specifies the provisioner as ebs.csi.aws.com, and can include parameters for volume type and IOPS.

```
apiVersion: storage.k8s.io/v1
kind: StorageClass
metadata:
  name: ebs-sc
provisioner: ebs.csi.aws.com
parameters:
  type: gp3
  iops: "3000"
```

When implementing EBS storage in EKS, you start by creating a **PersistentVolumeClaim** (PVC) that references your desired storage class. Pods can then mount these volumes, using standard Kubernetes volume definitions. The EBS CSI driver handles the underlying volume lifecycle, including creation, attachment, mounting, unmounting, and deletion operations.

The following is an example of how to obtain a 4Gi EBS volume in an EKS environment:

First, you need to define a **PersistentVolumeClaim** (PVC) that requests a 4Gi EBS volume. Then, you create a Pod that uses this PVC. Here is how you would do this:

```
# PersistentVolumeClaim
apiVersion: v1
kind: PersistentVolumeClaim
metadata:
  name: ebs-claim
spec:
  accessModes:
    - ReadWriteOnce
  storageClassName: ebs-sc
  resources:
    requests:
      storage: 4Gi

# Pod using the PVC
apiVersion: v1
kind: Pod
metadata:
  name: app-pod
spec:
  containers:
    - name: app
      image: nginx
      volumeMounts:
        - name: storage
```

```
            mountPath: /data
      volumes:
        - name: storage
          persistentVolumeClaim:
            claimName: ebs-claim
```

This Pod definition creates a container, using the nginx image, and mounts the EBS volume at /data within the container. The volume references the PVC, we created earlier.

To apply these configurations:

1. Save the PVC definition to a file, for example, **`ebs-claim.yaml`.**

2. Save the Pod definition to a file, for example, **`pod-using-ebs.yaml`.**

3. Apply them to your EKS cluster:

```
kubectl apply -f ebs-claim.yaml
kubectl apply -f pod-using-ebs.yaml
```

When you create this Pod, EKS will automatically provision a 4Gi EBS volume, and attach it to the EC2 instance where the Pod is scheduled. The EBS CSI driver handles the details of creating and attaching the volume.

Remember, for this to work, you need to have the EBS CSI driver installed in your EKS cluster, and your nodes need the appropriate IAM permissions to work with EBS volumes.

EBS volumes have several important limitations in EKS. They can only be mounted to one pod at a time (**`ReadWriteOnce`** access mode), and must reside in the same Availability Zone as the node running the pod. In fact, it cannot be decreased in size, once created. These limitations significantly impact application architecture, and deployment strategies.

For optimal EBS usage in EKS, encrypt volumes at rest using KMS keys, implement proper IAM roles and policies, and use pod affinity rules for high-availability deployments. Monitor volume performance through CloudWatch metrics and Kubernetes events, and maintain regular backup strategies, using EBS snapshots.

EBS volumes in EKS are particularly well-suited for databases, content management systems, development environments, and applications requiring consistent I/O performance. They excel in scenarios where persistent block storage with predictable performance is needed.

Effective management of EBS volumes in EKS requires monitoring through CloudWatch metrics and Kubernetes events. The EBS CSI driver logs provide valuable troubleshooting information. Regular maintenance should include snapshot management, performance optimization, and capacity planning.

This storage solution serves as a fundamental building block for stateful applications in EKS, providing reliable, performant block storage when shared access is not required. Hence, understanding its capabilities and limitations is crucial for designing effective Kubernetes applications on AWS.

# Amazon Elastic File System (EFS)

EFS provides a managed NFS file system that enables shared storage access across multiple pods and nodes in your EKS cluster. Unlike EBS, EFS supports **ReadWriteMany** access mode, allowing multiple pods to simultaneously mount and access the same file system, even across different Availability Zones.

The AWS EFS CSI driver must be installed in your EKS cluster to enable EFS integration. This driver manages the mounting and lifecycle of EFS file systems. EFS access points can be used to create isolated application-specific entry points to your file system, each with its own identity, and root directory mapping.

The following example demonstrates creating a **StorageClass** for EFS, requesting storage through a **PersistentVolumeClaim**, and using it in a Pod – all configured to provision a shared 5Gi EFS volume mounted at **/shared-data** in the container.

```
# Storage Class for EFS
apiVersion: storage.k8s.io/v1
kind: StorageClass
metadata:
  name: efs-sc
provisioner: efs.csi.aws.com
parameters:
  provisioningMode: efs-ap
  fileSystemId: fs-xxxx
  directoryPerms: "700"

# PersistentVolumeClaim
apiVersion: v1
kind: PersistentVolumeClaim
metadata:
  name: efs-claim
spec:
  accessModes:
    - ReadWriteMany
  storageClassName: efs-sc
  resources:
    requests:
      storage: 5Gi

# Pod using EFS
apiVersion: v1
```

```
kind: Pod
metadata:
  name: app-using-efs
spec:
  containers:
    - name: app
      image: nginx
      volumeMounts:
        - name: efs-storage
          mountPath: /shared-data
  volumes:
    - name: efs-storage
      persistentVolumeClaim:
        claimName: efs-claim
```

EFS in EKS provides cross-AZ shared access with automatic scaling, requiring no pre-provisioning. It delivers consistent performance across mounted instances, while supporting AWS IAM for access control. The service includes built-in high availability, durability, and supports both encryption at rest, and in transit.

EFS excels in scenarios requiring shared access, such as content management systems, web serving environments, shared development environments, machine learning training data storage, container persistent storage, application logging, and media processing workflows.

EFS performance scales with file system size, utilizing a bursting model based on the file system's size. While it has higher latency compared to EBS, it offers flexible performance modes (General Purpose or Max I/O) and throughput modes (Bursting or Provisioned) to match the various workload requirements.

Security implementation includes encryption at rest, using KMS, IAM Roles for Service Accounts (IRSA), network security groups, access points with restricted paths, and TLS encryption for data in transit. These features ensure comprehensive protection for your shared data.

EFS requires specific network configurations, including enabled DNS hostnames in the VPC, mount targets in each subnet, and security groups allowing NFS traffic on port 2049. VPC endpoints can be configured for optimal routing.

In fact, EFS provides comprehensive monitoring through CloudWatch metrics, access logs for audit trails, lifecycle management policies, and integration with AWS Backup for data protection. These tools enable effective monitoring and management of your file system resources.

This shared storage solution proves invaluable for EKS workloads requiring concurrent access from multiple pods or nodes, and offering a scalable and managed file system that integrates seamlessly with Kubernetes persistent volume provisioning. The ability to share data across pods as well as nodes makes it especially suitable for collaborative workflows, and distributed applications.

# Amazon FSx for Lustre

Amazon FSx for Lustre provides a high-performance parallel file system that integrates with EKS, designed specifically for compute-intensive workloads, machine learning, and High Performance Computing (HPC) applications. It delivers fast processing speeds with sub-millisecond latencies and throughput up to hundreds of gigabytes per second.

Moreover, the AWS FSx CSI driver must be installed in your EKS cluster to enable FSx for Lustre integration. This driver manages the mounting and lifecycle of FSx file systems, handling the complexities of provisioning and attaching storage to your Kubernetes pods.

This example demonstrates creating a StorageClass for FSx for Lustre with **`SCRATCH_2`** deployment type and 1200 GB capacity, along with a Pod definition that mounts this FSx volume at **`/data`** path, using a **`PersistentVolumeClaim`** named **`fsx-claim`** for machine learning training workloads.

```
# StorageClass for FSx for Lustre
apiVersion: storage.k8s.io/v1
kind: StorageClass
metadata:
  name: fsx-sc
provisioner: fsx.csi.aws.com
parameters:
  subnetId: subnet-xxx
  securityGroupIds: sg-xxx
  deploymentType: SCRATCH_2
  automaticBackupRetentionDays: "1"
  storageCapacity: "1200"

# Usage in Pod
apiVersion: v1
kind: Pod
metadata:
  name: ml-training-pod
spec:
  containers:
    - name: training
      image: ml-training-image
      volumeMounts:
        - name: fsx-mount
          mountPath: /data
```

```
        volumes:
          - name: fsx-mount
            persistentVolumeClaim:
              claimName: fsx-claim
```

Amazon FSx for Lustre provides multiple deployment types: **SCRATCH_1** and **SCRATCH_2** for temporary workloads, and **PERSISTENT** for longer-term storage needs. **SCRATCH_2** offers better availability and data durability compared to **SCRATCH_1**, while **PERSISTENT** provides the highest level of reliability, and supports backups.

A unique feature of FSx for Lustre is its native integration with Amazon S3. Data can be automatically imported from S3 buckets, processed at high speeds using Lustre, and changes can be exported back to S3. This creates a seamless data pipeline for large-scale data processing workflows.

Amazon FSx for Lustre is particularly well-suited for machine learning training workloads, big data analytics, financial modeling, media transcoding, and electronic design automation. Its high throughput and low latency make it ideal for applications requiring fast processing of large datasets.

File system performance can be optimized by selecting appropriate storage capacity and deployment type. The throughput capacity scales with the file system size, and you can choose between SSD and HDD storage options based on your workload requirements.

Amazon FSx for Lustre requires specific network configurations, including subnet placement, security group settings, and proper VPC configuration. The file system must be accessible from your EKS nodes, and network latency can impact the overall performance.

Costs are based on storage capacity, throughput capacity, and deployment type. **SCRATCH** deployments are more cost-effective for temporary workloads, while PERSISTENT deployments are optimized for long-term storage needs with additional durability features.

CloudWatch metrics provide insights into file system performance, including throughput, IOPS, and latency. Regular monitoring helps ensure optimal performance, and identify potential issues before they impact workloads.

Amazon FSx for Lustre integrates with AWS IAM for access control, supports encryption at rest using AWS KMS, and can be configured with VPC security groups to control network access. Data in transit is automatically encrypted when using **PERSISTENT** deployment types.

This high-performance storage solution is ideal for EKS workloads requiring extreme performance and parallel access capabilities, particularly in scientific computing, machine learning, and other computation-intensive applications where storage speed directly impacts processing efficiency.

# Amazon S3 Integration

The integration between Amazon Elastic Kubernetes Service (EKS) and Simple Storage Service (S3) forms a critical component in modern cloud architecture. This combination enables containerized applications to effectively utilize scalable object storage, addressing key requirements for persistent data storage, backup management, and content delivery.

EKS, as a managed Kubernetes service, excels at container orchestration, while S3 provides virtually unlimited, highly durable storage. When properly integrated, these services create a robust foundation for applications requiring both computational power and reliable storage capabilities.

Understanding this integration is essential for architects and developers working with containerized applications, as it enables crucial functionalities such as application state management, log storage, backup systems, and efficient content delivery. The following sections will explore the practical aspects of implementing this integration, focusing on security, performance, and operational best practices.

The following matrix outlines the four primary integration methods between EKS and S3, highlighting their optimal use cases, advantages, limitations, and practical applications to guide architects and developers in selecting the most suitable approach for their specific needs.

| Integration Method | When to Use | Pros | Cons | Use Case Examples |
|---|---|---|---|---|
| **IRSA (IAM Roles for Service Accounts)** | • Need for fine-grained access control in Production environments | • Pod-level IAM permissions<br>• Better security<br>• Easy to audit<br>• Kubernetes native | • Requires OIDC provider setup<br>• Initial setup complexity | • Microservices requiring S3 access<br>• Production workloads<br>• Multi-tenant clusters |
| **AWS SDK in Pods** | • Simple applications<br>• Single-purpose pods<br>• Development environments | • Simple implementation<br>• Direct API access<br>• Flexible programming | • Less granular control<br>• Harder to manage at scale<br>• Credentials management overhead | • Basic file uploads<br>• Simple backup solutions<br>• Development/ testing |

| | | | | |
|---|---|---|---|---|
| **S3 CSI Driver** | • Need for file system-like access<br>• Legacy applications<br>• Direct mount requirements | • Familiar file system interface<br>• Standard Kubernetes volumes<br>• No code changes needed | • Performance overhead<br>• Limited S3 features<br>• Mount complexity | • Legacy applications<br>• Shared file access<br>• Read-heavy workloads |
| **S3 Bucket Operator** | • GitOps workflows<br>• Infrastructure as Code<br>• Automated bucket management | • Declarative management<br>• Version controlled<br>• Automated operations | • Additional resource overhead<br>• Learning curve<br>• Limited to bucket operations | • Dynamic bucket creation<br>• Environment replication<br>• Automated provisioning |

***Table 9.1:*** *Decision Matrix for EKS-S3 Integration Mechanisms*

The selection of an appropriate EKS-S3 integration mechanism hinges on following four critical dimensions:

- **Security Requirements:** Organizations with stringent security controls and compliance requirements should lean towards IRSA for its granular permissions and audit capabilities, while simpler applications with basic security needs may find the AWS SDK approach sufficient.
- **Scale Considerations:** Large-scale deployments with multiple clusters and applications benefit from IRSA's management capabilities, or the Bucket Operator's automation features, whereas smaller deployments can effectively utilize the straightforward AWS SDK integration.
- **Management Approach:** Teams embracing GitOps practices should consider the Bucket Operator for its declarative nature and version control benefits. Traditional operations teams might prefer IRSA or SDK approaches, while legacy application migrations often necessitate the CSI Driver's file system-like interface.
- **Application Architecture:** Modern cloud-native applications align well with IRSA's pod-level permissions model, legacy applications requiring direct file system access are better served by the CSI Driver, and simple applications can quickly implement the AWS SDK approach for basic S3 interactions.

# Storage Classes in EKS

Storage management in Amazon EKS represents a crucial aspect of container orchestration, where Storage Classes serve as the foundation for dynamic provisioning of persistent storage. These classes define different storage configurations and capabilities, enabling administrators and developers to efficiently manage storage resources across their Kubernetes workloads.

Storage Classes in EKS act as templates that define the properties of storage solutions available to applications. They abstract the underlying storage provider details, whether it is Amazon EBS, EFS, FSx, or other storage solutions, allowing applications to request storage resources without needing to understand the intricate details of the underlying infrastructure.

The significance of Storage Classes extends beyond simple storage provisioning. They enable organizations to implement tiered storage strategies, where different applications can consume storage resources, based on their specific performance, availability, and cost requirements. For instance, production workloads might utilize high-performance SSD-backed storage, while development environments could opt for more cost-effective alternatives.

Understanding Storage Classes becomes particularly important when designing highly available and cost-optimized applications in EKS. These classes provide the flexibility to define various storage parameters such as volume type, IOPS, encryption settings, and reclaim policies, all of which contribute to the overall effectiveness of the storage architecture.

In the following section, we will explore the different Storage Class options available in EKS, their configuration parameters, best practices for implementation, and common use cases that demonstrate their practical applications in real-world scenarios.

# Default Storage Classes

Default Storage Classes in Amazon EKS provide the foundational storage configuration for containerized applications when no specific storage requirements are specified. They serve as the automatic choice for PersistentVolumeClaims (PVCs) that do not explicitly request a particular storage class, ensuring that applications have access to storage resources without detailed configuration.

In EKS, the default storage class typically points to Amazon EBS (Elastic Block Store), with gp2, historically being the default choice, though gp3 is now recommended for better performance and cost optimization. This default configuration enables teams to quickly deploy applications without immediate storage decisions, while maintaining a reasonable baseline for performance and cost.

The default storage class is distinguished by a specific annotation (`storageclass.kubernetes.io/is-default-class: "true"`) in its configuration, and it is crucial to maintain only one default storage class per cluster to avoid confusion and potential conflicts. When applications create PVCs without specifying a storage class, this default configuration automatically provisions the storage resources, streamlining the deployment process, while ensuring consistent storage behavior across the cluster. This mechanism can be modified or reconfigured, based on specific cluster requirements, providing flexibility, while maintaining operational simplicity.

To view your cluster's default storage class:

```
kubectl get storageclass | grep "(default)"
```

# Custom Storage Class

Custom Storage Classes in Amazon EKS enable organizations to define specialized storage configurations that match their specific application requirements, moving beyond the limitations of default storage options. These custom configurations allow fine-grained control over storage parameters, performance characteristics, and cost optimization strategies.

By creating custom storage classes, administrators can define various storage profiles tailored to different workload needs. So, whether it is high-performance storage for databases, cost-optimized storage for development environments, or specialized configurations for specific applications, custom storage classes provide the flexibility to meet diverse requirements within the same cluster.

Custom storage classes offer comprehensive customization options through their configuration parameters. Administrators can specify the storage type selection such as gp2 or gp3, define performance parameters including IOPS and throughput settings, implement specific encryption requirements and key management strategies, configure volume binding modes for controlled provisioning, set appropriate reclaim policies for resource management, and implement cost allocation tagging for billing purposes. This rich set of configuration options ensures that storage resources precisely align with application needs, while maintaining operational efficiency and cost control.

Thus, to implement a custom storage class:

```
kubectl apply -f custom-storage-class.yaml
```

This flexibility in storage configuration ensures that applications can access storage resources that precisely match their performance, security, and cost requirements, while maintaining consistent management practices across the cluster.

The following is an example of a High-Performance Storage Class:

```
apiVersion: storage.k8s.io/v1
kind: StorageClass
metadata:
  name: high-performance
  labels:
    environment: production
    tier: premium
provisioner: ebs.csi.aws.com
```

```
parameters:
  type: gp3
  iops: "16000"
  throughput: "1000"
  encrypted: "true"
  kmsKeyId: "arn:aws:kms:region:account:key/key-id"  # Optional:
For encryption
volumeBindingMode: WaitForFirstConsumer
reclaimPolicy: Retain
allowVolumeExpansion: true
```

Once a Storage Class is created, it can be referenced in a **PersistentVolumeClaim** to request storage with specific characteristics. Here is how to utilize the above created **high-performance** storage class in a **PersistentVolumeClaim** configuration:

```
apiVersion: v1
kind: PersistentVolumeClaim
metadata:
  name: my-custom-pvc
spec:
  accessModes:
    - ReadWriteOnce
  storageClassName: high-performance
  resources:
    requests:
      storage: 100Gi
```

The **PersistentVolumeClaim** will automatically provision storage, based on the parameters defined in the referenced storage class, making it available for pod consumption.

# Reclaim Policies

Reclaim policies define the behavior of storage resources when their associated **PersistentVolumeClaims** (PVCs) are deleted, playing a crucial role in data lifecycle management and resource cleanup in Kubernetes clusters. These policies, configured within Storage Classes, offering three distinct behaviors: **'Retain'**, which preserves the volume and its data even after PVC deletion, requiring manual intervention for cleanup; **'Delete'**, which automatically removes the volume and its data when the PVC is deleted; and 'Recycle' (now deprecated), which attempts to clean the volume for reuse. The choice of reclaim policy significantly impacts data persistence and storage cost management – **'Retain'** is typically used for production workloads where data protection is paramount, while **'Delete'** is often employed in development environments, or for temporary storage needs where automatic cleanup is beneficial. For example:

```
apiVersion: storage.k8s.io/v1
kind: StorageClass
metadata:
  name: production-storage
provisioner: ebs.csi.aws.com
parameters:
  type: gp3
reclaimPolicy: Retain # Protects against accidental data loss
```

This policy configuration requires careful consideration based on the application's data persistence requirements, backup strategies, and compliance needs, as it directly affects both data safety and storage cost management in the cluster.

# Persistent Volume Management

Persistent Volume Management in Amazon EKS provides a robust framework for handling stateful data in containerized applications. This system abstracts the complexities of underlying storage infrastructure, while offering consistent and reliable data persistence across pod lifecycles and container restarts.

At its core, the persistent volume subsystem operates through three key components: PersistentVolumes (PVs) which represent the physical storage resources, PersistentVolumeClaims (PVCs) that act as storage requests from applications, and Storage Classes that define the types of storage available. This abstraction allows developers to focus on application requirements, while infrastructure teams maintain control over storage provisioning and management.

The system supports dynamic provisioning, where storage resources are automatically created, based on PVC requests as well as static provisioning for cases requiring pre-allocated storage resources. With integration to various AWS storage services such as EBS, EFS, and FSx, it provides flexibility in choosing the right storage solution for specific use cases.

To implement storage management:

```
# Example PVC requesting storage
apiVersion: v1
kind: PersistentVolumeClaim
metadata:
  name: data-volume
spec:
  storageClassName: gp3
  accessModes:
    - ReadWriteOnce
```

```
    resources:
      requests:
        storage: 20Gi
```

The lifecycle of PVs in EKS follows a well-defined path from provisioning through decommissioning. Manual PV provisioning involves explicit creation of storage resources by administrators, offering precise control over storage configurations and resource allocation, while dynamic provisioning automates this process through **StorageClasses**, enabling on-demand resource creation, based on PVC requests. These provisioning methods can be implemented, based on specific organizational needs and operational requirements.

Volume expansion and resizing capabilities allow for flexible storage management, enabling organizations to adapt to the changing application demands. This feature, when enabled through **StorageClass** configuration (**allowVolumeExpansion: true**), permits online volume expansion without application downtime, though the process requires careful monitoring and capacity planning. For example:

```
# StorageClass with volume expansion enabled
apiVersion: storage.k8s.io/v1
kind: StorageClass
metadata:
  name: expandable-storage
provisioner: ebs.csi.aws.com
allowVolumeExpansion: true
parameters:
  type: gp3

# PVC with increased storage request
apiVersion: v1
kind: PersistentVolumeClaim
metadata:
  name: expandable-pvc
spec:
  storageClassName: expandable-storage
  resources:
    requests:
      storage: 20Gi # Can be increased when needed
```

Backup and restore strategies form a critical component of data protection, typically implemented through various approaches such as EBS snapshots, AWS Backup integration, or third-party solutions like Velero. These strategies should align with business continuity requirements, and include regular testing of restore procedures. Organizations often implement a combination of methods:

```
# Example VolumeSnapshot
apiVersion: snapshot.storage.k8s.io/v1
kind: VolumeSnapshot
```

```
metadata:
  name: ebs-volume-snapshot
spec:
  volumeSnapshotClassName: csi-aws-vsc
  source:
    persistentVolumeClaimName: expandable-pvc
```

This comprehensive approach to PV lifecycle management ensures data persistence, scalability, and protection, while maintaining operational efficiency in Kubernetes environments.

# `StatefulSet` Applications

StatefulSets in Amazon EKS provide a robust framework for managing stateful applications, ensuring stable network identities and persistent storage for each pod. Unlike their stateless counterparts, StatefulSets maintain a unique, persistent identifier for each pod, enabling predictable naming, storage, and networking characteristics. These identifiers persist across pod rescheduling, making StatefulSets ideal for applications, requiring stable network identities and persistent storage.

Volume claim templates form an integral part of **`StatefulSet`** configurations, automatically creating persistent volume claims for each pod instance. This automation ensures that each pod receives its dedicated storage, maintaining data persistence across pod lifecycles. The template-based approach simplifies storage management, while maintaining consistency across all pod instances.

```
apiVersion: apps/v1
kind: StatefulSet
metadata:
  name: database-cluster
spec:
  serviceName: "database"
  replicas: 3
  volumeClaimTemplates:
  - metadata:
      name: data-volume
    spec:
      accessModes: [ "ReadWriteOnce" ]
      storageClassName: "high-performance"
      resources:
        requests:
          storage: 100Gi
```

Storage capacity planning requires careful consideration of application growth patterns, performance requirements, and cost constraints. Organizations should implement monitoring solutions to track storage utilization trends, and establish thresholds for capacity expansion. Regular capacity reviews ensure adequate storage resources, while preventing over-provisioning.

Performance optimization in stateful applications involves selecting appropriate storage classes, configuring optimal IOPS, throughput values, and implementing proper caching strategies. Regular performance monitoring and tuning ensure applications maintain the desired performance levels, while efficiently utilizing resources.

```
apiVersion: storage.k8s.io/v1
kind: StorageClass
metadata:
  name: high-performance
provisioner: ebs.csi.aws.com
parameters:
  type: gp3
  iops: "16000"
  throughput: "1000"
```

High availability considerations extend beyond basic replication. Proper pod anti-affinity rules ensure distribution across availability zones, while carefully configured update strategies minimize downtime during updates. Thus, storage replication and backup strategies play crucial roles in maintaining data availability.

```
spec:
  affinity:
    podAntiAffinity:
      requiredDuringSchedulingIgnoredDuringExecution:
      - labelSelector:
          matchExpressions:
          - key: app
            operator: In
            values:
            - database
        topologyKey: "topology.kubernetes.io/zone"
```

Backup and disaster recovery strategies should include regular snapshots, cross-region replication when necessary, and well-documented recovery procedures. Testing these procedures regularly ensures their effectiveness when needed. Implementation often combines AWS-native solutions with Kubernetes-specific tools.

```
apiVersion: snapshot.storage.k8s.io/v1
kind: VolumeSnapshotClass
metadata:
  name: ebs-snapshot-class
driver: ebs.csi.aws.com
deletionPolicy: Retain
```

Therefore, cost optimization requires balancing performance requirements with resource utilization. Implementing appropriate storage classes for different workloads, utilizing volume scaling features judiciously, and regularly reviewing storage usage patterns help maintain cost-effective operations. Organizations should consider implementing tagging strategies for better cost allocation and monitoring.

Database deployments represent a primary use case for StatefulSets, requiring careful consideration of storage performance, backup strategies, and scaling procedures. Message queues and other stateful services similarly benefit from **StatefulSet** capabilities, though each requires specific configuration adjustments for optimal performance.

```
apiVersion: apps/v1
kind: StatefulSet
metadata:
  name: postgresql
spec:
  serviceName: postgresql
  replicas: 3
  updateStrategy:
    type: RollingUpdate
  template:
    spec:
      containers:
      - name: postgresql
        image: postgres:latest
        volumeMounts:
        - name: data
          mountPath: /var/lib/postgresql/data
```

Scaling operations in StatefulSets follow ordered patterns, ensuring data consistency during scale-up or scale-down operations. This ordered scaling, combined with proper storage management, maintains application stability during capacity adjustments.

The successful implementation of stateful applications in EKS requires careful attention to these various aspects, from basic configuration through operational management and optimization. Regular review and adjustment of these patterns ensure continued effectiveness as application requirements evolve.

# Storage Monitoring and Troubleshooting

Effective storage monitoring in Amazon EKS involves leveraging both AWS and Kubernetes native tools to track critical metrics. Utilize CloudWatch to monitor EBS-specific metrics such as **VolumeReadOps**, **VolumeWriteOps**, **VolumeQueueLength**, and **VolumeThroughputPercentage**. Implement the Kubernetes Metrics Server to gather pod-level storage metrics, including ephemeral-storage usage. For comprehensive monitoring, deploy the Prometheus Operator with custom **ServiceMonitors** to scrape CSI driver metrics, exposing insights into volume provisioning latencies and operation success rates.

Common storage issues in EKS often stem from misconfigured **StorageClasses**, inadequate IOPS allocation, or zone mismatches between **PersistentVolumes** and nodes. Watch for "**FailedMount**" events in pod descriptions which may indicate issues with volume attachment or CSI driver failures. "**VolumeBindingFailed**" events often point to problems with dynamic provisioning, or storage quota limits. Performance degradation can occur when gp2 volumes hit their burst balance limits, or when using gp3 volumes without proper IOPS and throughput configurations.

For debugging, utilize kubectl commands like **kubectl describe pv <pv-name>** and **kubectl describe pvc <pvc-name>** to inspect volume states and events. Examine CSI driver logs, using **kubectl logs -n kube-system -l app=ebs-csi-controller** for provisioning issues. Use AWS CLI commands such as **aws ec2 describe-volumes** to verify EBS volume states and attachments. For network-related storage problems, employ tools like iperf3 to test throughput between nodes and volumes, especially in multi-AZ clusters.

Implement proactive storage capacity management by setting up CloudWatch alarms on the EBS **VolumeUsedBytes** metric. Create Kubernetes custom metrics using Prometheus Adapter, and allowing for **HorizontalPodAutoscaler** configurations, based on storage utilization. Leverage Kubernetes Events to trigger alerts on PersistentVolumeClaim failures, or when volumes enter a "**Pending**" state for extended periods. For more granular control, use AWS EventBridge to create rules that respond to EBS volume state changes, or CSI driver events.

Enhance your monitoring strategy by implementing custom Prometheus exporters to expose metrics such as storage provisioning times, volume attachment latencies, and CSI operation success rates. Use PromQL queries to create advanced alerting rules such as detecting patterns of increased I/O wait times across nodes that might indicate storage subsystem issues. Integrate EKS logging with AWS CloudTrail to track API calls related to storage operations, aiding in troubleshooting and audit processes.

For cost optimization, employ Kubernetes etcd-based garbage collection to clean up the unused **PersistentVolumes**, and create automated Lambda functions triggered by CloudWatch Events to detect and manage orphaned EBS volumes. Regularly audit your **StorageClasses** to ensure that they align with the current AWS EBS offerings and pricing models, adjusting for optimal performance and cost-efficiency as needed.

# Security Considerations

Security in Amazon Elastic Kubernetes Service (EKS) requires a comprehensive approach that addresses multiple layers of the container orchestration stack, from the infrastructure level to application workloads. As organizations increasingly adopt containerized applications and microservices architectures, the security considerations become more complex, requiring a deep understanding of both Kubernetes native security controls and AWS security services.

EKS security architecture builds upon AWS's shared responsibility model, where AWS manages the security of the control plane, while customers are responsible for securing worker nodes, workloads, and data. This distributed responsibility necessitates a well-planned security strategy that encompasses infrastructure security, data protection, access management, and network security. With the dynamic nature of containerized environments, traditional security approaches must be adapted to address the unique challenges of container orchestration such as ephemeral workloads, dynamic scaling, and multi-tenant environments.

The following sections detail the critical security considerations and best practices for protecting EKS clusters and their data, focusing on the key areas that organizations must address to maintain a robust security posture.

# Storage Encryption

Implement encryption at rest for all persistent volumes in EKS using AWS Key Management Service (KMS). Enable EBS encryption by default in your AWS account to ensure that all dynamically provisioned volumes are encrypted. For EKS-managed node groups, use launch templates with encrypted EBS volumes. When using Amazon EFS, enable encryption in transit and at rest. For secrets management, utilize AWS Secrets Manager or HashiCorp Vault, integrating them with your EKS cluster using the External Secrets Operator. Implement envelope encryption for sensitive data stored in etcd, using a custom encryption provider and KMS.

# Access Control and IAM Integration

Leverage AWS IAM Roles for Service Accounts (IRSA) to grant fine-grained permissions to pods without managing long-lived AWS credentials. Implement least privilege principles by creating separate IAM roles for different EKS components (for example, cluster autoscaler, external-dns, and cluster-autoscaler). Use Kubernetes RBAC in conjunction with AWS IAM, mapping IAM entities to Kubernetes ClusterRoles and Roles. Implement Pod Security Standards (PSS) to enforce security contexts, and limit pod privileges. For multi-tenant clusters, use Kubernetes namespaces in combination with Network Policies and `ResourceQuotas` to isolate workloads.

## Network Policies

Implement the AWS VPC CNI plugin with security groups for pods to apply granular network controls at the pod level. Use Kubernetes Network Policies to define ingress and egress rules between pods, enforcing micro-segmentation within the cluster. Implement Calico or Cilium for advanced network policy features such as egress gateway and DNS-based policies. For east-west traffic control, consider service mesh solutions like AWS App Mesh or Istio, which provide mTLS encryption and fine-grained traffic management.

## Security Best Practices

Regularly update EKS to the latest supported version, and apply security patches promptly. Use EKS-optimized AMIs for worker nodes, and keep them updated. Implement AWS GuardDuty for EKS to detect malicious activities and security threats. Enable control plane logging, and ship logs to a centralized SIEM solution. Use AWS Security Hub and Amazon Inspector to continuously assess your EKS environment against security best practices and compliance standards.

Implement image scanning in your CI/CD pipeline using tools like Amazon ECR image scanning or Trivy. Use admission controllers such as OPA Gatekeeper or Kyverno to enforce security policies at the cluster level. Implement pod disruption budgets to ensure high availability during node updates or failures. Use AWS PrivateLink to establish private connectivity between your VPC and EKS API server, reducing exposure to the public internet.

For data in transit, enforce TLS 1.2 or higher for all communications. Use AWS Certificate Manager (ACM) for managing and deploying TLS certificates to your ingress controllers. Implement AWS WAF in front of your Application Load Balancers to protect against the common web exploits.

Regularly conduct security audits, and penetration testing on your EKS clusters. Use tools like kube-bench to check your cluster against CIS Kubernetes Benchmark standards. Implement a comprehensive incident response plan that includes procedures for handling potential container escapes, or unauthorized access to the cluster.

Thus, by implementing these security measures, you can significantly enhance the security posture of your EKS clusters, and protect the sensitive data from unauthorized access or breaches. Remember that security is an ongoing process, requiring continuous monitoring, updating, and improvement to stay ahead of evolving threats in the Kubernetes ecosystem.

# Advanced Topics

The management of storage in Amazon EKS requires careful consideration of availability, performance, scalability, and cost optimization. As organizations deploy increasingly complex workloads on EKS, from stateful applications to data-intensive microservices, the demand for sophisticated storage solutions has grown significantly. Hence, understanding and implementing the right storage architecture is crucial for maintaining application performance, ensuring data durability, and managing operational costs effectively.

Modern EKS deployments must accommodate diverse storage requirements, ranging from high-performance block storage for databases to distributed file systems for shared access across multiple pods and nodes. Amazon EKS integrates seamlessly with various AWS storage services, including Amazon EBS, EFS, and FSx for NetApp ONTAP, each serving different use cases and workload requirements. Additionally, the platform's support for the Container Storage Interface (CSI) specification opens up possibilities for custom storage solutions and third-party integrations.

This section explores the comprehensive approach to storage configuration in EKS, focusing on multi-availability zone deployments, quota management, and custom storage solutions that enable organizations to build resilient and efficient container-based applications.

# Multi-AZ Storage Configurations

Amazon EKS supports robust multi-AZ storage configurations to ensure high availability and data durability. For block storage, use EBS volumes with topology-aware volume scheduling. This approach leverages the **`'WaitForFirstConsumer'`** volume binding mode in **`StorageClasses`**, ensuring pods are scheduled in the same AZ as their volumes, reducing cross-AZ latency. For shared file storage, Amazon EFS provides native multi-AZ capabilities, offering a single mount target that is accessible across all AZs in a region. This is particularly useful for stateful applications requiring shared access to data.

Amazon FSx for NetApp ONTAP (FSxN) offers another powerful option for multi-AZ configurations. FSxN provides a fully managed NetApp ONTAP file system that supports multi-AZ deployment for high availability. It offers advanced features such as instant snapshots, clones, and replication, making it ideal for enterprise workloads in EKS. Use the NetApp Trident CSI driver to integrate FSxN with your EKS cluster, allowing for dynamic provisioning of persistent volumes with ONTAP's enterprise-grade capabilities. *Figure* 9.2 illustrates the comprehensive multi-AZ storage configuration.

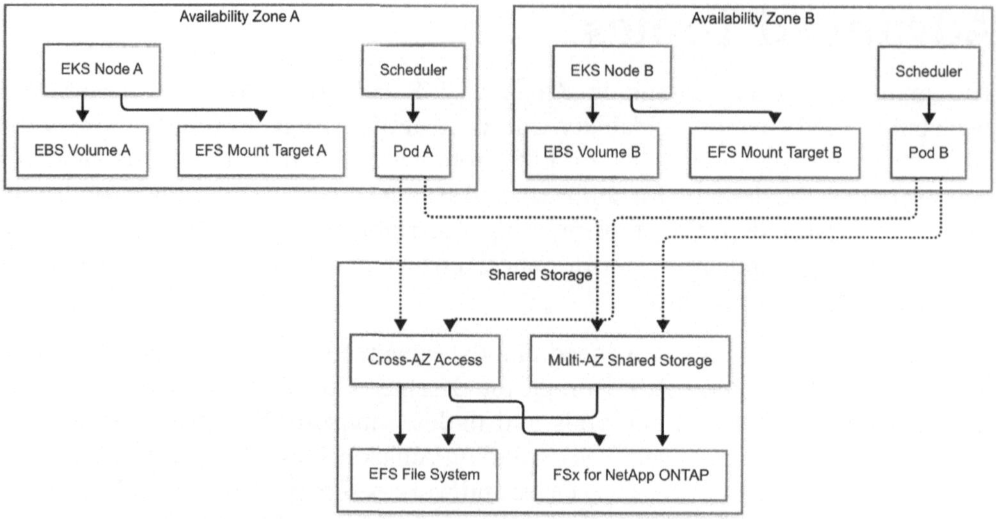


***Figure 9.2:*** *Multi-AZ Storage Configuration*

# Storage Quotas and Limits

Implement **ResourceQuotas** at the namespace level to control **PersistentVolume** claims and storage consumption. Set both storage capacity limits (for example, **requests.storage**) and object count restrictions (for example, **persistentvolumeclaims**) to prevent any single namespace from monopolizing cluster resources. Use **LimitRanges** to enforce default storage requests and limits for pods within namespaces. This ensures that even if developers do not specify resource requirements, pods will have sensible defaults.

Be aware of AWS-specific limits, such as the maximum number of EBS volumes that can be attached to an EC2 instance (typically 40 for nitro-based instances). For EFS, consider throughput limits and lifecycle management policies to optimize cost and performance. With FSxN, monitor and adjust the provisioned throughput capacity to meet your application's needs, while managing costs.

# Custom Storage Solutions

EKS supports the Container Storage Interface (CSI) specification, enabling integration with a wide range of storage providers. Beyond native AWS offerings, consider third-party solutions like Pure Storage, Portworx, or Robin.io for advanced data management features.

For FSxN, utilize the Trident CSI driver to create custom **StorageClasses** that leverage ONTAP's capabilities. For instance, create separate classes for high-performance SSD storage, cost-effective HDD storage, or classes that automatically enable features such as compression and deduplication.

Implement custom storage classes with specific parameters for different workload requirements. For instance, create an 'io1-high-iops' class for databases, specifying high IOPS and throughput values, or a 'st1-throughput-optimized' class for big data applications requiring high throughput.

For extreme performance requirements, consider using local storage provisioners like the Kubernetes Local Volume Static Provisioner. Manage these through custom operators, and use node affinity as well as pod affinity rules to ensure proper data locality and high availability.

Leverage Kubernetes Storage Objects such as **`VolumeSnapshots`** and **`VolumeSnapshotClasses`** for consistent backup and restore capabilities. Thus, with FSxN, you can create instantaneous snapshots and clones, enabling rapid deployment of test environments, or facilitating quick rollbacks.

Implement storage autoscaling solutions, either through custom operators, or by leveraging cloud-native services. For EFS, use EFS Intelligent-Tiering to automatically move infrequently accessed files to lower-cost storage tiers. With FSxN, take advantage of its built-in storage efficiency features, and consider implementing automated storage tier management, based on access patterns.

Finally, consider implementing a storage monitoring and analytics solution, such as Prometheus with custom exporters, to gain deep insights into storage usage patterns, performance metrics, and capacity trends across your EKS cluster. This data can inform decisions about storage class configurations, quota adjustments, and capacity planning.

Hence, by carefully designing your storage architecture with these advanced configurations and custom solutions, you can create a highly available, performant, and cost-effective storage infrastructure for your EKS workloads.

# Conclusion

Storage and state management in Amazon EKS represent critical components for building resilient, scalable, and performant containerized applications. This chapter has explored the comprehensive landscape of storage solutions available in EKS, from fundamental concepts to advanced implementations. The integration of various AWS storage services such as EBS, EFS, and FSx, combined with Kubernetes native storage abstractions, provides a robust framework for handling diverse application requirements.

The successful implementation of storage solutions in EKS requires careful consideration of multiple factors, including performance requirements, availability needs, security considerations, and cost optimization. Organizations must balance these factors, while designing their storage architecture, implementing appropriate monitoring solutions, and maintaining security best practices.

As containerized applications continue to evolve, the importance of effective storage management becomes increasingly crucial. Thus, understanding and implementing the concepts covered in this chapter will enable organizations to build and maintain robust storage solutions that meet their current needs, while providing flexibility for future growth.

The next chapter will explore on designing and implementing high availability and disaster recovery strategies in Amazon EKS.

# Points to Remember

- Storage Classes serve as templates for dynamic provisioning of persistent storage.
- EKS supports multiple storage options, including EBS, EFS, and FSx.
- StatefulSets provide ordered deployment and scaling for stateful applications.
- PersistentVolumes (PVs) and PersistentVolumeClaims (PVCs) abstract storage management.
- Security considerations must include encryption, access control, and network policies.
- Storage monitoring is vital for maintaining performance and availability.
- Multi-AZ configurations enhance reliability and availability.
- Resource quotas help manage storage allocation and prevent resource exhaustion.
- Custom storage solutions can be implemented using CSI drivers.
- Regular backup, and disaster recovery planning are essential.

# Multiple Choice Questions

1. Which AWS storage service provides shared file system access across multiple EKS pods?

   a. Amazon EBS

   b. Amazon EFS

   c. Amazon S3

   d. Amazon FSx

2. Which Kubernetes resource is used to define storage characteristics and provisioning parameters?
    a. `PersistentVolume`
    b. `StorageClass`
    c. `VolumeMount`
    d. `ConfigMap`
3. Which security feature is recommended for protecting data at rest in EKS storage?
    a. Network Policies
    b. KMS Encryption
    c. RBAC
    d. Security Groups
4. Which component manages the lifecycle of persistent volumes in EKS?
    a. Kubelet
    b. CSI Driver
    c. kube-scheduler
    d. etcd
5. Which storage access mode allows multiple pods to read and write to the same volume?
    a. `ReadOnlyMany`
    b. `ReadWriteOnce`
    c. `ReadWriteMany`
    d. `ReadOnlyOnce`
6. What is the primary purpose of StorageClass in EKS?
    a. To provide backup storage
    b. To define storage provisioning parameters
    c. To manage network policies
    d. To configure pod security

7. Which AWS service is recommended for cross-AZ shared file storage in EKS?
   a. Amazon EBS
   b. Amazon S3
   c. Amazon EFS
   d. AWS Backup
8. Which feature enables automatic creation of storage resources, based on PVC requests?
   a. Static Provisioning
   b. Dynamic Provisioning
   c. Manual Provisioning
   d. Automated Scaling
9. Which Kubernetes resource is used to maintain stable network identities for pods?
   a. Deployment
   b. ReplicaSet
   c. StatefulSet
   d. DaemonSet
10. Which tool is commonly used for monitoring storage metrics in EKS?
    a. kubectl
    b. CloudWatch
    c. kubeadm
    d. eksctl

# Answers

1. b
2. b
3. b
4. b
5. c

6. b
7. c
8. b
9. c
10. b

# Key Terms

- **Container Storage Interface (CSI):** Standard interface for container orchestration platforms to interact with storage providers
- **`PersistentVolume` (PV):** Kubernetes resource representing physical storage
- **`PersistentVolumeClaim` (PVC):** Storage request by a pod
- **StorageClass:** Template for dynamic storage provisioning
- **StatefulSet:** Kubernetes controller for managing stateful applications
- **Volume Snapshot:** Point-in-time copy of a persistent volume
- **Storage Provisioner:** Component responsible for creating storage resources
- **Access Modes:** Defines how storage can be mounted by pods
- **Reclaim Policy:** Defines what happens to storage when PVC is deleted
- **Storage Quota:** Limit on storage resources within a namespace
- **Multi-AZ Storage:** Storage configuration spanning multiple availability zones
- **CSI Driver:** Implementation of the Container Storage Interface
- **Volume Binding Mode:** Controls when volume binding and dynamic provisioning occur
- **Storage Encryption:** Protection of data at rest, using encryption mechanisms
- **IAM Roles for Service Accounts (IRSA):** AWS IAM integration with Kubernetes service accounts

# CHAPTER 10
# High Availability and Disaster Recovery

## Introduction

Ensuring service continuity and system resilience is a foundational objective in any production-grade cloud architecture. In Amazon EKS, High Availability (HA) and Disaster Recovery (DR) strategies are crucial for maintaining operational stability, meeting uptime requirements, and reducing the risk of business disruption. Kubernetes workloads are inherently dynamic and distributed, making it essential to implement designs that minimize single points of failure and support recovery from a variety of failure scenarios—ranging from infrastructure outages to accidental misconfigurations.

Amazon EKS offers the flexibility and scalability needed to architect for high availability across multiple Availability Zones (AZs) within a region. With the ability to distribute control plane and worker node resources across AZs, EKS enables zone-resilient workloads that continue to operate even during localized infrastructure failures. At the same time, implementing a robust backup solution ensures that critical cluster configurations and persistent data can be restored rapidly in the event of data loss, corruption, or human errors.

Disaster recovery in the context of EKS extends beyond Multi-AZ resilience. In mission-critical environments, preparing for full-region outages requires a cross-region failover architecture that can restore application functionality in a secondary AWS Region. Such architectures typically involve replicated storage, stateless application deployment strategies, DNS-based failover, and well-defined runbooks. These mechanisms not only support regulatory compliance and operational mandates, but also enhance customer trust by ensuring consistent service availability. This chapter provides comprehensive guidance on designing and implementing high availability and disaster recovery strategies in Amazon EKS. Through best practices, architectural patterns, and practical examples, readers will learn how to build resilient Kubernetes environments that align with enterprise requirements for availability, durability, and operational excellence.

# Structure

This chapter is organized into the following sections to provide a structured approach to high availability and disaster recovery in Amazon EKS:

- Multi-AZ Deployment Strategies
- Backup Implementation
- Cross-Region Failover Setup
- Business Continuity Planning
- Recovery Testing

# Multi-AZ Deployment Strategies

Designing for high availability in Amazon Elastic Kubernetes Service (EKS) begins with deploying workloads across multiple Availability Zones (AZs) within a region. Multi-AZ deployments help ensure that applications remain accessible even if one or more zones experience outages or degraded performance. Amazon EKS supports Multi-AZ architectures natively, allowing control plane components and worker nodes to span multiple AZs to achieve fault tolerance, operational resilience, and improved resource distribution.

# Application Layer Considerations

The application layer is one of the most critical aspects to consider when designing a highly available architecture on Amazon EKS. Unlike infrastructure components, which can often be made fault-tolerant by design, application-level resiliency depends on how workloads are architected, deployed, and monitored. High availability at the application layer begins with designing stateless workloads where possible, allowing for seamless replication and scaling across multiple Availability Zones. For stateful applications, careful handling of data persistence, session management, and storage access is necessary to prevent data loss or service interruptions during AZ failures.

In addition to architectural decisions, developers must ensure that applications can handle restarts, be re-scheduled on different nodes or zones, and recover gracefully from dependency failures. Leveraging Kubernetes-native constructs such as Deployments, StatefulSets, and DaemonSets allows workloads to benefit from automated orchestration and health management. Furthermore, resilience at this layer can be enhanced by building retry logic, graceful shutdown handling, and fallback mechanisms directly into the application code. These design considerations form the foundation for implementing more granular availability strategies such as pod distribution and disruption budgets.

- **Pod Distribution across AZs:** Utilize Kubernetes' topology spread constraints to evenly distribute pods across different AZs. This minimizes the impact of a zonal failure on application availability.

```
topologySpreadConstraints:
  - maxSkew: 1
    topologyKey: topology.kubernetes.io/zone
    whenUnsatisfiable: ScheduleAnyway
    labelSelector:
      matchLabels:
        app: my-app
```

- **Pod Disruption Budgets (PDBs):** Define PDBs to control the number of pods that can be taken down during voluntary disruptions, ensuring that a minimum number of pods remain available during maintenance or scaling events.

```
apiVersion: policy/v1
kind: PodDisruptionBudget
metadata:
  name: my-app-pdb
spec:
  minAvailable: 2
  selector:
    matchLabels:
      app: my-app
```

- **Health Checks and Readiness Probes:** Implement liveness and readiness probes to allow Kubernetes to detect and respond to application issues promptly, facilitating self-healing mechanisms.

# Control Plane Resilience

The control plane is the core of any Kubernetes cluster, responsible for managing the lifecycle, state, and orchestration of all workloads. In Amazon EKS, the control plane is fully managed by AWS, offering customers a reliable and highly available infrastructure out of the box. Despite being abstracted from user management, understanding the design and operational behavior of the control plane is necessary for building resilient systems. Control plane failures–such as API server unavailability, loss of etcd quorum, or scheduler issues–can prevent workload deployment, scaling, and monitoring actions, even if application pods remain operational.

By recognizing the critical role of the control plane, platform teams can align their architecture and operational practices with AWS's managed availability guarantees. This includes taking advantage of EKS's automatic distribution across Availability Zones, enabling control plane logs for visibility, and designing workloads that can gracefully tolerate temporary disruptions in control plane communication. A well-informed approach to control plane resilience not only helps reduce recovery times during outages but also reinforces the stability of the entire application stack running on the cluster.

- **Multi-AZ Deployment:** The control plane is automatically distributed across multiple AZs within a region, eliminating single points of failure.
- **Automated Scaling and Healing:** EKS monitors the health of control plane components, and automatically replaces unhealthy instances to maintain cluster stability.
- **Monitoring and Logging:** Enable control plane logging to capture audit, authenticator, controller manager, and scheduler logs. Integrate with Amazon CloudWatch for centralized monitoring and alerting.

# Data Plane Strategies

The data plane in Amazon EKS consists of the worker nodes that execute containerized workloads, and provide the compute, storage, and networking resources required by applications. Unlike the control plane, the data plane is user-managed, which means that achieving high availability and fault tolerance in this layer requires intentional planning and configuration. The distribution, provisioning, and scaling of nodes across multiple Availability Zones are central to ensuring that the failure of a single zone does not impact the overall workload availability. This responsibility extends to choosing the right mix of instance types, configuring appropriate networking, and implementing automation tools for efficient lifecycle management.

In resilient EKS environments, the data plane must be elastic, redundant, and observant. It should automatically respond to changes in demand, tolerate infrastructure interruptions, and maintain consistent application performance. This is achieved through a combination of strategies including managed node groups for simplified operations, Fargate profiles for serverless compute, and intelligent scaling engines like Cluster Autoscaler and Karpenter. Each of these components plays a role in balancing flexibility with reliability, enabling organizations to meet performance and uptime targets at scale. By designing a data plane that is both adaptive and geographically dispersed, platform teams can uphold the high availability expectations required for production-grade Kubernetes workloads.

- **Node Group Distribution:** Deploy worker nodes across multiple AZs by specifying subnets in different zones. This ensures that workloads can continue running, even if an AZ becomes unavailable.
- **Managed Node Groups:** Utilize EKS managed node groups to simplify the provisioning and lifecycle management of worker nodes. Managed node groups can span multiple AZs, and integrate with Cluster Autoscaler for dynamic scaling.

- **Fargate Profiles:** For workloads that benefit from serverless compute, EKS Fargate allows pods to run without managing the underlying EC2 instances. Fargate automatically distributes pods across AZs, and handles scaling.
- **Auto Scaling and Karpenter:** Implement Cluster Autoscaler or Karpenter to automatically adjust the number of nodes in response to workload demands. Karpenter offers more flexibility by launching nodes, based on pod requirements, and available capacity across AZs.

# Networking and Storage Considerations

Reliable networking and resilient storage are foundational to achieving high availability in Amazon EKS environments. In a Multi-AZ setup, these components should be architected to support seamless communication, fault tolerance, and consistent access to data, regardless of underlying infrastructure disruptions. Networking in Kubernetes spans service discovery, ingress routing, pod-to-pod communication, and traffic distribution across Availability Zones—all of which must function reliably even during partial outages. Similarly, storage solutions must be selected and configured, based on workload requirements, accounting for factors such as durability, access latency, AZ scope, and backup compatibility.

Designing a network architecture that spans multiple zones requires careful attention to subnet allocation, route table configuration, and service exposure patterns. The goal is to avoid bottlenecks, ensure low-latency communication, and eliminate single points of failure. On the storage side, a distinction should be made between block-level and file-level access, with technologies like Amazon EBS and EFS playing distinct roles in different availability scenarios. When implemented correctly, robust networking and storage strategies ensure that applications remain performant, and data remains accessible—even when certain parts of the infrastructure become impaired.

- **Load Balancing:** Deploy Network Load Balancers (NLBs) or Application Load Balancers (ALBs) with cross-zone load balancing enabled to distribute incoming traffic evenly across AZs.
- **Persistent Storage:** Use Amazon Elastic File System (EFS) for shared storage needs, as it provides multi-AZ availability. For block storage, consider Amazon FSx for NetApp ONTAP, which supports multi-AZ deployments. If you use Amazon EBS to provide Persistent Volumes, then you need to ensure that the pods and associated EBS volume are located in the same AZ.

# Monitoring and Observability

Monitoring and observability are vital components of a resilient Amazon EKS architecture, enabling early detection of failures, performance bottlenecks, and unexpected behaviors across the cluster. In high-availability environments, especially those spanning multiple Availability Zones, visibility into the health of applications, nodes, and underlying infrastructure becomes even more critical. Observability is not limited to metrics alone–it encompasses logs, traces, and events that together provide a holistic view of system behavior and dependencies. By proactively monitoring the control plane, data plane, and application workloads, operators can reduce Mean Time to Resolution (MTTR), improve incident response, and ensure Service-Level Objectives (SLOs) are consistently met. A well-instrumented EKS cluster allows teams to track the Key Performance Indicators (KPIs), validate scaling activities, and confirm that failover mechanisms operate as intended during disruptions.

- **Metrics Collection:** Integrate Prometheus and Grafana to collect and visualize metrics from applications and cluster components. Monitor the key indicators such as CPU utilization, memory usage, and pod health across AZs.
- **Logging:** Deploy Fluent Bit or Fluentd as DaemonSets to collect logs from all nodes, and forward them to centralized logging solutions such as Amazon CloudWatch Logs or Elasticsearch.
- **Distributed Tracing:** Implement tracing tools such as AWS X-Ray or Jaeger to gain insights into request flows, and identify bottlenecks within applications distributed across AZs.

Amazon EKS operates on a shared responsibility model for high availability and resilience. As shown in *Figure 10.1*, AWS manages the Control Plane's high availability by automatically distributing its components (API server, etcd, and scheduler) across three Availability Zones, handling updates, scaling, and recovery without user intervention. On the customer side, users are responsible for implementing resilience across their workloads and supporting infrastructure: This includes worker node distribution across AZs, auto-scaling configurations, application deployment strategies using PodDisruptionBudgets and health probes, storage resilience through appropriate EBS/EFS configurations, and backup procedures, along with network redundancy via load balancers, and comprehensive monitoring with recovery procedures. This clear delineation of responsibilities enables organizations to leverage AWS's expertise in managing the core Kubernetes infrastructure, while maintaining control over their application architecture and operational practices. Success in EKS high availability requires understanding and effectively managing this shared responsibility boundary, with regular testing of failover scenarios, and automated recovery procedures for user-managed components.

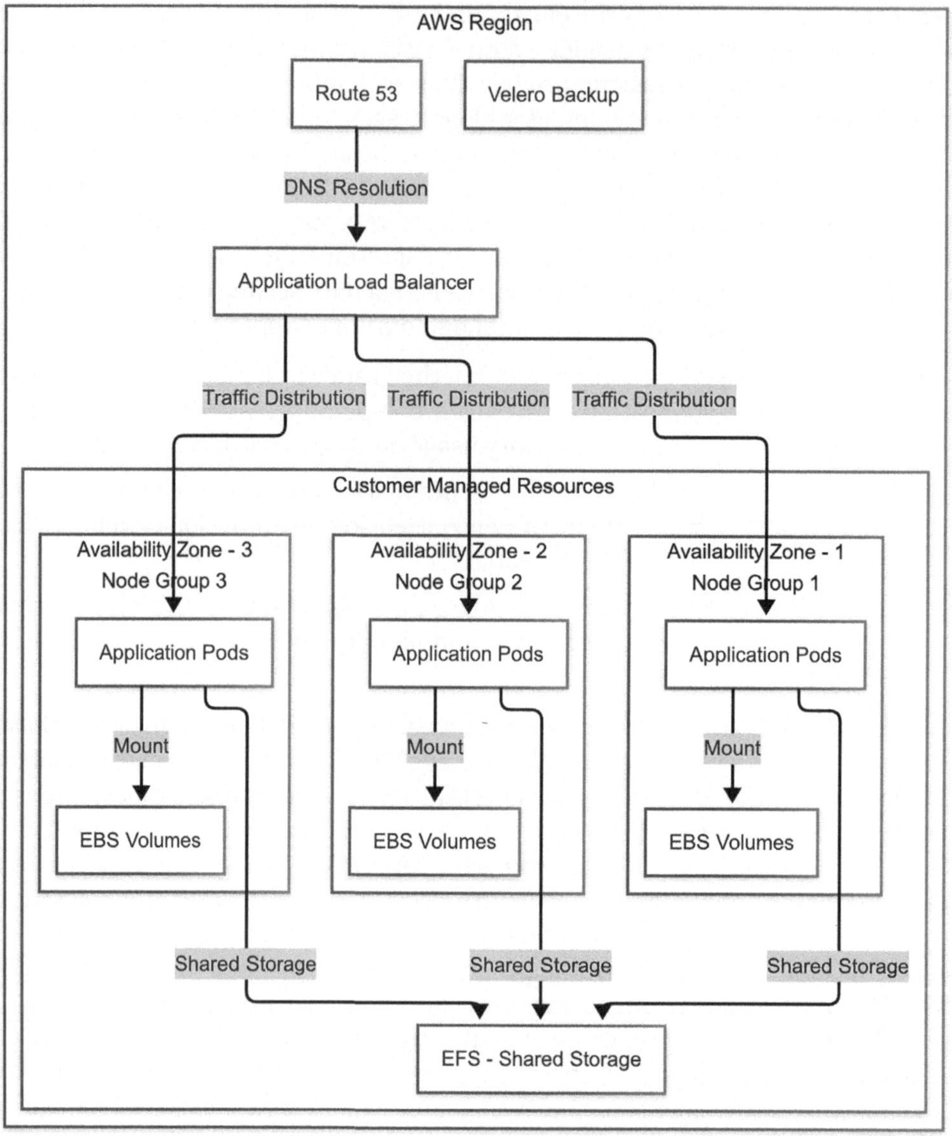


***Figure 10.1:*** *Reference Architecture of an EKS Implementation with Multi-AZ Deployment*

# Best Practices Summary

Bringing together the design principles discussed throughout the Multi-AZ Deployment Strategies section, it is necessary to align architectural decisions with well-established operational best practices. These best practices serve as guiding principles for implementing, maintaining, and validating high availability in Amazon EKS environments. They bridge the gap between theoretical reliability and real-world operational effectiveness, ensuring that system behavior is predictable under load and resilient under failure. Applying these practices consistently across infrastructure provisioning, workload placement, observability, and incident response allows platform teams to reduce risks, enhance stability, and maintain compliance with business continuity requirements. The following summary distills these recommendations into actionable guidance that can be applied across production-grade EKS clusters.

- **Distribute Resources:** Always deploy applications and worker nodes across multiple AZs to enhance fault tolerance.
- **Automate Scaling:** Leverage tools such as Cluster Autoscaler and Karpenter to automatically adjust resources, based on demand.
- **Monitor Proactively:** Set up comprehensive monitoring and alerting to detect and respond to issues promptly.
- **Test Resilience:** Regularly conduct failure injection tests to validate the system's ability to withstand AZ outages.

Thus, by adhering to these strategies and best practices, organizations can build robust, highly available EKS environments capable of maintaining service continuity in the face of infrastructure failures.

# Backup Implementation

A comprehensive backup strategy is a critical component of any High-Availability and Disaster Recovery (HA/DR) plan for Amazon EKS. In Kubernetes-based environments, data loss or corruption can result not only from infrastructure failures but also from human errors, misconfigurations, or malicious activities. Effective backup implementation ensures that both the cluster configuration and application state can be recovered in a timely and predictable manner, minimizing downtime and preserving business continuity. Backups should be automated, encrypted, and regularly tested as part of an ongoing reliability practice.

In Amazon EKS, backup requirements generally fall into two categories: Control plane and cluster configuration data, as well as workload-specific application data. Although the EKS control plane is managed by AWS, and does not require direct user backups, components such as Kubernetes manifests, custom resources, ConfigMaps, and secrets must be protected. Similarly, persistent volumes attached to pods– particularly for stateful workloads– should be included in the backup strategy to avoid data loss in the event of node failure or accidental deletion.

Several tools are available to facilitate backup and restore operations in EKS, including open-source solutions such as Velero. Velero is widely adopted for backing up Kubernetes objects and persistent volumes, offering support for scheduled backups, retention policies, and cross-cluster migration. AWS Backup can be used to back up AWS resources. Together, these tools form the foundation of a resilient backup implementation tailored to thc needs of containerized workloads.

# Using Velero for Kubernetes Backup

Velero is an open-source tool designed for backing up and restoring Kubernetes cluster resources and persistent volumes. In Amazon EKS environments, Velero enables platform teams to implement consistent, automated backup strategies that support disaster recovery, data migration, and cluster state preservation. It supports storing backups in Amazon S3, and taking volume snapshots using AWS native services like Amazon EBS. Additionally, Velero offers integration with Restic for backing up non-block volumes, such as those provisioned by Amazon EFS. As of the current AWS best practices, Velero can be installed using Helm, and configured securely with IAM Roles for Service Accounts (IRSA), removing the need to store static credentials in Kubernetes clusters. With features such as scheduled backups, restore testing, and cross-cluster portability, Velero is a robust and flexible choice for backup implementation in production-grade EKS clusters.

To install Velero in a secure and maintainable manner, Helm can be used for deployment alongside IAM Roles for Service Accounts (IRSA) to manage access. This approach enables fine-grained permissions for Velero operations, while eliminating the need to store static credentials within the cluster.

- **Helm for Installation:** Using Helm to install Velero provides a structured, scalable, and reproducible approach to deployment within Amazon EKS. Helm charts allow users to customize configurations through values files or inline parameters, enabling fine-grained control over backup storage locations, plugin versions, and runtime behavior. This method simplifies lifecycle management of Velero, including version upgrades and configuration changes, by treating the deployment as declarative infrastructure. Additionally, Helm-based installations integrate seamlessly with GitOps workflows, allowing platform teams to manage backup tooling as code and apply consistent deployments across multiple environments. Leveraging Helm enhances automation and maintainability, especially in dynamic, multi-cluster EKS landscapes.

```
helm repo add vmware-tanzu https://vmware-tanzu.github.io/helm-
charts
helm repo update

helm install velero vmware-tanzu/velero \
  --namespace velero \
  --create-namespace \
  --set credentials.useSecret=true \
  --set-file credentials.secretContents.cloud=./credentials-velero \
  --set configuration.provider=aws \
```

```
  --set configuration.backupStorageLocation.name=default \
  --set configuration.backupStorageLocation.bucket
=<YOUR_BUCKET_NAME> \
  --set configuration.backupStorageLocation.config.region
=<AWS_REGION> \
  --set configuration.volumeSnapshotLocation.name=default \
  --set configuration.volumeSnapshotLocation.config.region
=<AWS_REGION>
```

Replace **<YOUR_BUCKET_NAME>** and **<AWS_REGION>** with your specific S3 bucket name and AWS region.

- **Leverage IAM Roles for Service Accounts (IRSA):** IAM Roles for Service Accounts (IRSA) is the best practice for granting Kubernetes workloads secure, scoped access to AWS resources, without embedding the static credentials. In the context of Velero, IRSA enables the Velero server, and its associated pods to access S3 buckets, create volume snapshots, and interact with other AWS APIs, using a dedicated IAM role tied to a Kubernetes service account. This approach improves security posture by adhering to the principle of least privilege, and simplifying credential rotation, auditing, and access management. Hence, by leveraging IRSA, administrators can tightly control Velero's AWS permissions, while avoiding the operational complexity and risks associated with long-lived credentials, or shared IAM users.

The steps include:

1. Create an IAM OIDC provider for your EKS cluster.
2. Create an IAM role with a trust policy for the OIDC provider, and attach the necessary permissions.
3. Annotate the Velero service account with the IAM role, ARN.

This method enhances security by avoiding hardcoded credentials, and follows the AWS best practices.

- **Utilize Velero's Restic Integration for Non-EBS Volumes:** Velero's Restic integration extends backup capabilities to include persistent volumes that are not backed by Amazon EBS, such as Amazon EFS or other CSI-compatible storage classes. This is especially useful in environments where file-level backups are required, or where block-level snapshotting is not supported. Restic performs file system-level backups directly from the pod's volume mount, enabling granular data protection across a broader range of workloads. To use this integration, users must install Velero with the Restic feature enabled and annotate the appropriate pods or volumes for inclusion. While Restic introduces some operational overhead compared to native EBS snapshots, it provides a flexible and reliable solution for backing up non-standard volumes. Incorporating Restic into the backup strategy ensures that all application data, regardless of the underlying storage technology, can be protected and restored as part of a unified disaster recovery process. To enable this:

1. Install Velero with the **--use-restic** flag.
2. Ensure that the necessary annotations are added to the pods or volumes, you wish to back up with Restic.

This integration allows for comprehensive backups of all volume types in your EKS cluster.

- **Implement Scheduled Backups:** Implementing scheduled backups is essential to ensure consistent protection of critical workloads and configuration data, within Amazon EKS clusters. By automating backup operations, teams can eliminate the risk of human oversight and maintain regular restore points that align with organizational Recovery Point Objectives (RPOs). Velero supports native scheduling through Kubernetes Custom Resource Definitions (CRDs), enabling fine-grained control over backup frequency, scope, and retention policies. Administrators can define schedules to back up specific namespaces, resource types, or the entire cluster, with configurable Time-to-Live (TTL) durations for storage lifecycle management. Integrating scheduled backups into operational workflows not only simplifies compliance with business continuity requirements but also provides a foundation for predictable, repeatable disaster recovery processes. Here is an example of a schedule that backs up the production namespace every 6 hours.

```
apiVersion: velero.io/v1
kind: Schedule
metadata:
  name: production-backup
  namespace: velero
spec:
  schedule: "0 */6 * * *"
  template:
    includedNamespaces:
    - production
    ttl: 240h0m0s
```

This configuration ensures regular backups, and retention of backup data for 10 days.

- **Test Restores Regularly:** Regularly testing restore procedures is a critical component of any effective backup strategy. Backups are only valuable, if they can be reliably restored, and failure to validate them can lead to unexpected data loss or extended downtime during recovery scenarios. In Amazon EKS environments, periodic restore testing ensures that both Kubernetes objects, and persistent volume data can be accurately recovered and redeployed. These tests help verify the integrity of backup artifacts, expose configuration drifts or missing dependencies, and validate access permissions required during the restore process. Organizations should document and automate restore tests as part of their standard Disaster Recovery (DR) drills, incorporating them into CI/CD pipelines or scheduled operational checks. This practice reinforces operational confidence, and ensures readiness in the event of an actual disruption. Use the following command to restore from a specific backup:

```
velero restore create --from-backup <BACKUP_NAME>
```

Replace **<BACKUP_NAME>** with the name of the backup, you wish to restore.

# Cross-Region Failover Setup

Cross-region failover is a salient component of a robust disaster recovery strategy for production-grade Amazon EKS workloads. While Multi-AZ deployments provide high availability within a single AWS Region, they do not protect against region-wide outages caused by natural disasters, network partitioning, or large-scale service disruptions. Cross-region architectures are designed to minimize downtime and data loss by maintaining an operational standby environment in an alternate region, ready to take over in the event of a primary region failure.

Designing for regional failover introduces additional complexity compared to intra-region high availability. It requires a coordinated strategy that encompasses workload replication, state synchronization, DNS-based routing, infrastructure-as-code consistency, and automation for failover execution. In Kubernetes, this means not only replicating application manifests but also ensuring that persistent storage, IAM roles, secrets, and configuration policies are consistently deployed and maintained across regions.

Amazon EKS does not natively support multi-region clusters, so cross-region failover must be implemented through external orchestration and tooling. Typical strategies include maintaining an active/passive or active/active setup using infrastructure-as-code platforms such as Terraform, CI/CD pipelines, GitOps tools (for example, Argo CD), and shared storage solutions such as Amazon EFS with replication enabled. When paired with Route 53 failover policies and robust monitoring, this approach can achieve Rapid Recovery Time Objectives (RTOs), and ensure that critical services are quickly restored in an alternate region.

| Feature / Consideration | Multi-AZ Deployment | Cross-Region DR |
|---|---|---|
| **Scope** | Across Availability Zones in a single region | Across two or more AWS regions |
| **Purpose** | Protect against AZ-level failure | Protect against full region-level failure |
| **Latency** | Low (sub-millisecond) | Higher (inter-region distance) |

| **Data Replication** | Automatic within region (EBS, EFS) | Requires custom replication (e.g., EFS, S3 sync) |
|---|---|---|
| **Failover Mechanism** | Often automatic via load balancers or DNS | Manual or automated using Route 53 + GitOps |
| **Cost Impact** | Lower (shared infra, single control plane) | Higher (duplicate clusters, storage, infra) |
| **Implementation Complexity** | Low to medium | High (coordination, replication, automation) |
| **Ideal Use Case** | Standard availability targets (99.9%–99.99%) | Mission-critical systems requiring full resilience |
| **Example AWS Tools** | EKS, ASG, ALB/NLB, EFS | EFS Replication, Route 53, Velero, GitOps |

***Table 10.1:*** *Comparing Multi-AZ Deployments and Cross-Region Disaster Recovery*

Multi-AZ deployments are typically the first step toward high availability in EKS, and are well-suited for most production workloads.

Cross-region DR should be considered when regulatory requirements, customer SLAs, or business criticality demand protection against full regional failures.

Thus, organizations can combine both the strategies to build a resilient architecture such as: Multi-AZ for uptime, and cross-region DR for recovery assurance.

# Architecture Strategy and Key Components

Implementing cross-region failover in Amazon EKS requires a well-defined architecture that balances operational complexity, cost, and recovery objectives. At a high level, the architecture typically involves provisioning a secondary EKS cluster in a different AWS Region, and maintaining configuration as well as state synchronization between the primary and secondary environments. The goal is to create a standby environment that can either passively receive traffic during failure or remain partially active, depending on the selected failover model.

The cross-region failover architecture for Amazon EKS as shown in *Figure 10.2* implements a robust disaster recovery strategy by maintaining synchronized clusters across two AWS regions (for example, us-east-1 as primary and us-west-2 as secondary). Each region hosts a fully functional EKS cluster with its AWS-managed control plane, and multi-AZ worker nodes deployment. Route 53 sits at the global layer, providing intelligent DNS routing with health checks to facilitate automated failover between regions. Configuration consistency is maintained through a GitOps approach, where ArgoCD in each region continuously synchronizes with a central Git repository, ensuring identical application deployments and configurations. Data resilience is achieved through cross-region replication of both EFS (for shared storage) and S3 buckets, while Velero handles Kubernetes-specific backup and restore capabilities. Load balancers in each region manage traffic distribution across their respective multi-AZ worker nodes. This architecture ensures business continuity with minimal data loss (RPO) and quick recovery time (RTO) during regional failures, while the GitOps approach minimizes configuration drift, and enables rapid, consistent deployments across both regions.

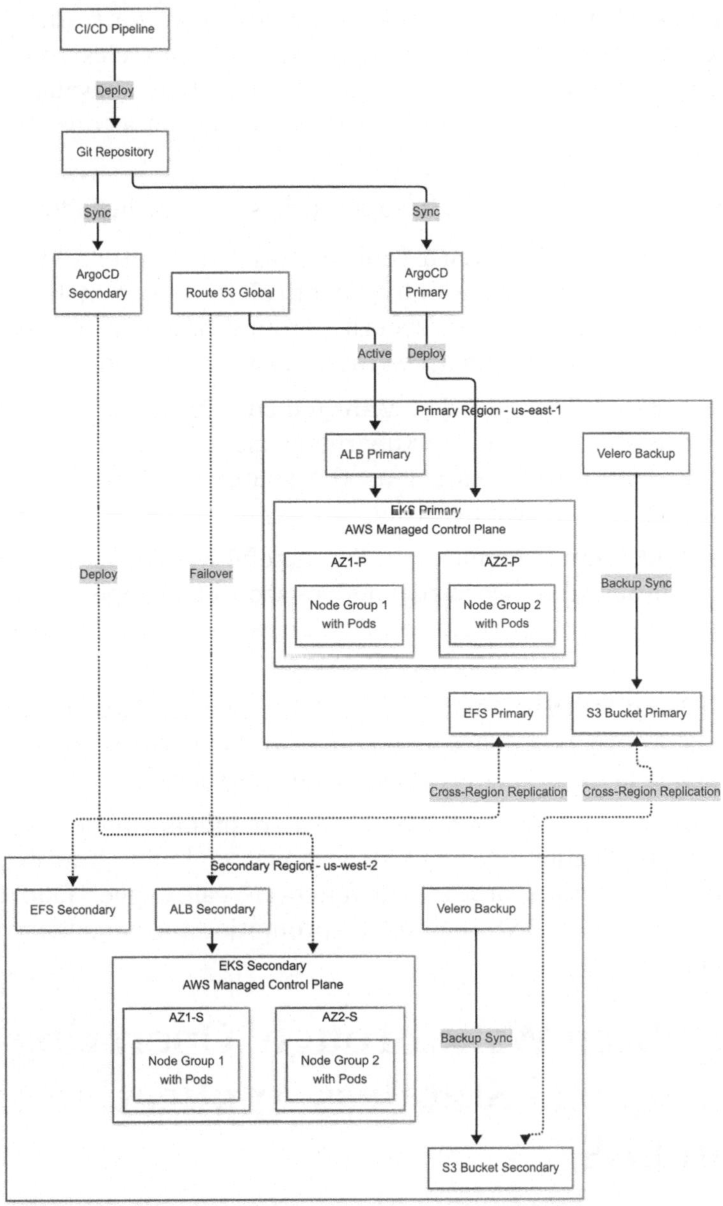


**Figure 10.2:** *Reference Architecture for a Cross-region Failover Setup*

There are two common approaches to cross-region failover:

- **Active/Passive Model:** In this model, the primary region handles all application traffic, while the secondary region remains idle but ready. Infrastructure and application manifests are synchronized regularly, and traffic is redirected to the secondary region, only in the event of a failure. This approach is cost-effective, but may result in a longer recovery time.
- **Active/Active Model:** Both regions handle production traffic simultaneously, typically using global load balancers and stateless microservices to distribute the workload. This model offers higher availability and faster recovery, but requires more efforts to manage data consistency and traffic routing.

The key architectural components to support these models include:

- **Infrastructure as Code (IaC):** Tools such as Terraform or AWS CloudFormation are necessary for provisioning identical resources in both regions. This includes VPCs, IAM roles, security groups, and EKS clusters. IaC ensures configuration parity, and accelerates cluster provisioning during failover.
- **GitOps-Based Configuration Management:** Tools such as Argo CD or Flux can be used to synchronize Kubernetes manifests and configurations across regions. Git repositories act as the source of truth, enabling automated reconciliation and drift detection.
- **Persistent Storage Replication:** For stateful workloads, shared storage must be synchronized between regions. Amazon EFS supports replication across regions, and S3 cross-region replication can be enabled for object storage use cases.
- **DNS-Based Failover:** Amazon Route 53 can be configured with health checks and failover routing policies to redirect traffic to the secondary region, when endpoints in the primary region become unreachable.
- **Monitoring and Automation:** Proactive monitoring of workload health, storage replication status, and regional endpoint availability is crucial. Automation scripts or Lambda functions can trigger failover operations, such as updating DNS records, or promoting the secondary cluster to the primary status.

# Step-by-Step Walkthrough: Operating a Multi-Regional Stateless Application Using Amazon EKS

Operating a stateless application across multiple AWS regions, using Amazon EKS requires a coordinated deployment strategy that emphasizes consistency, automation, and resilience. This walkthrough provides a practical, step-by-step guide to implementing a multi-regional architecture that enables seamless failover and high availability, without depending on stateful dependencies. By leveraging tools such as GitOps, AWS Load Balancer Controller, Amazon Route 53, and centralized observability, platform teams can build and operate parallel EKS environments capable of serving the global traffic. This approach ensures service continuity during regional outages, while also supporting latency-sensitive workloads through geographical distribution. The following sections outline the necessary configurations and code examples to help readers implement this architecture in a secure, maintainable, and scalable manner.

- **Deploy Amazon EKS Clusters in Multiple Regions:** Begin by provisioning two identical Amazon EKS clusters–one in each target region (for Instance, **`us-east-1`** and **`us-west-2`**). Use tools such as AWS CloudFormation, Terraform, or eksctl to ensure infrastructure consistency across both clusters, including node group types, networking configurations, and Kubernetes versions.
- **Use GitOps for Continuous Delivery:** Implement GitOps with a tool such as Argo CD or Flux to manage application deployment and configuration. Create a Git repository that serves as the single source of truth for your Kubernetes manifests and Helm charts. Configure each regional cluster to automatically sync with the Git repository, ensuring deployments remain consistent and reproducible across both environments.

**Code Example: Argo CD GitOps Application**

```
apiVersion: argoproj.io/v1alpha1
kind: Application
metadata:
  name: webapp-us-east
  namespace: argocd
spec:
  destination:
    namespace: default
    server: https://kubernetes.default.svc
  source:
    repoURL: https://github.com/example-org/webapp-config
    targetRevision: main
    path: overlays/us-east
  project: default
  syncPolicy:
    automated:
      prune: true
      selfHeal: true
```

- **Configure Service Exposure via ALBs:** Install the AWS Load Balancer Controller in each EKS cluster to provision Application Load Balancers (ALBs) for HTTP/S traffic management. Define Kubernetes Ingress resources with appropriate annotations for load balancer configuration. This setup enables public access to services hosted in each region, while Route 53 will control regional routing behavior.

**Code Example: Kubernetes Ingress with AWS Load Balancer Controller**

```
apiVersion: networking.k8s.io/v1
kind: Ingress
metadata:
  name: webapp-ingress
  annotations:
    alb.ingress.kubernetes.io/scheme: internet-facing
    alb.ingress.kubernetes.io/target-type: ip
    alb.ingress.kubernetes.io/healthcheck-path: /
    alb.ingress.kubernetes.io/healthcheck-port: traffic-port
    alb.ingress.kubernetes.io/healthcheck-protocol: HTTP
spec:
  rules:
    - host: webapp.example.com
      http:
        paths:
          - path: /
            pathType: Prefix
            backend:
              service:
                name: webapp-service
                port:
                  number: 80
```

- **Set Up Amazon Route 53 for Global DNS Failover:** Create Route 53 public hosted zone, and define DNS records for your application domain. Use a failover routing policy with health checks that monitor each region's ALB endpoint. When the primary region becomes unavailable, Route 53 automatically redirects traffic to the healthy regional endpoint (the secondary EKS cluster).

**Code Example: Route 53 Failover Routing Policy (Terraform)**

```
resource "aws_route53_record" "webapp_failover" {
  zone_id = var.zone_id
  name    = "webapp.example.com"
  type    = "A"
  set_identifier = "us-east"
  failover        = "PRIMARY"
  ttl             = 60
  records         = [aws_lb.east.dns_name]
  health_check_id = aws_route53_health_check.alb_us_east.id
}
```

```
resource "aws_route53_record" "webapp_failover_backup" {
  zone_id = var.zone_id
  name    = "webapp.example.com"
  type    = "A"
  set_identifier = "us-west"
  failover       = "SECONDARY"
  ttl            = 60
  records        = [aws_lb.west.dns_name]
  health_check_id = aws_route53_health_check.alb_us_west.id
}
```

```
Code Example: Route 53 Health Check (Terraform)
resource "aws_route53_health_check" "alb_us_east" {
  fqdn              = aws_lb.east.dns_name
  port              = 80
  type              = "HTTP"
  resource_path     = "/"
  failure_threshold = 3
  request_interval = 30
}
```

- **Centralize Configuration Management with Parameter Store or Secrets Manager:** To avoid duplication and drift in secrets or environment variables, store sensitive application configuration in a central system such as AWS Systems Manager Parameter Store or AWS Secrets Manager. Use Kubernetes external secrets solutions (for example, External Secrets Operator) to sync these securely into each cluster at runtime.
- **Set Up Centralized Observability:** Configure observability tooling across both clusters. Use:
    1. Amazon CloudWatch Container Insights for metrics,
    2. Fluent Bit or CloudWatch Logs for logs, and
    3. AWS X-Ray for distributed tracing.

  Ensure each region's observability data is centralized and tagged appropriately to distinguish between environments.
- **Automate and Validate the Failover:** Integrate AWS Health Checks, Route 53, and optionally Lambda functions to automate regional failover. Continuously test failover behavior by simulating failures ( for example, disabling the ALB in the primary region) and verifying that Route 53 redirects users to the healthy region, without manual intervention.
- **Operate and Maintain Region Independence:** Although your application is stateless, ensure that all supporting components (configurations, ingress, observability, DNS, and so on) are replicated and monitored independently

in each region. Design services so that neither region relies on synchronous communication with the other to avoid cross-region latency and coupling.

| Attribute | Multi-AZ Deployment | Cross-Region Disaster Recovery |
|---|---|---|
| **Scope** | Within a single AWS Region | Across two or more AWS Regions |
| **Latency** | Low (same-region communication) | Higher (inter-region network latency) |
| **Failover Type** | Automatic, zonal failover | Manual or automated failover with replication |
| **Cost** | Lower (shared resources) | Higher (duplicate infrastructure & data transfer) |
| **Implementation Time** | Faster and simpler | Requires extensive planning and infrastructure |
| **Use Case Fit** | Protection from AZ outages | Protection from full-region outages or disasters |
| **Storage Considerations** | EBS, EFS (same region) | Replicated storage (for example, EFS Replication) |
| **Example Tools** | ASG, NLB, PDBs, EKS Managed Node Groups | EFS replication, Route 53 failover, GitOps sync |

***Table 10.2:** Multi-AZ vs. Cross-Region DR: Summary and Trade-offs*

- Multi-AZ is sufficient for most high availability needs, and is simpler to configure.
- Cross-region DR protects against more severe failures (for example, region-wide outages) but costs more, and adds complexity.
- **Use Multi-AZ as a first step**, and evolve to cross-region DR, based on **business criticality** and **compliance** needs.
- Combine both where needed: Multi-AZ for HA, and cross-region setup for long-term resilience.

# Business Continuity Planning

Business Continuity Planning (BCP) is the process of ensuring that critical business operations can continue during and after a disruptive incident. In the context of Amazon EKS, BCP extends beyond infrastructure automation and technical failover to include organizational preparedness, workload prioritization, communication protocols, as well as recovery playbooks. While Multi-AZ and cross-region architectures address infrastructure resilience, business continuity ensures that services meet the Recovery Time Objectives (RTOs) and the Recovery Point Objectives (RPOs) as defined by business stakeholders. It aligns technical resilience with operational risk management, regulatory compliance, and customer expectations.

In Kubernetes environments, BCP encompasses identifying essential workloads, defining tiered recovery strategies, simulating operational outages, and maintaining clear runbooks for recovery execution. It also requires coordination between engineering, operations, and leadership teams to ensure that responses are not only technically effective but also timely and well-communicated. A sound BCP framework for Amazon EKS enables organizations to respond rapidly to service disruptions, maintain customer confidence, and minimize financial and reputational impacts. The following sections outline the key practices and frameworks for integrating BCP into your EKS operational model.

# Defining RTO and RPO

Recovery Time Objective (RTO) and Recovery Point Objective (RPO) are vital parameters that define the acceptable thresholds for downtime and data loss during a service disruption. These metrics guide the design of disaster recovery solutions, and directly influence the architecture, tooling, and operational procedures used in high-availability environments such as Amazon EKS.

RTO refers to the maximum amount of time a service can remain unavailable, before it causes unacceptable impact to the business. For example, an e-commerce checkout system may have an RTO of 5 minutes, requiring rapid failover and automation to ensure continuity. In contrast, a reporting dashboard may tolerate longer recovery times. RPO represents the maximum tolerable period in which data might be lost due to an incident. This metric is primarily influenced by the frequency of backups or replication. A low RPO (for example, under 5 minutes) demands continuous data synchronization, whereas a higher RPO ( for Instance, 4 hours) may suffice for less critical workloads backed by daily snapshots.

In Amazon EKS, RTO can be reduced through infrastructure automation, GitOps-based application deployment, and cross-region failover mechanisms. RPO can be optimized by configuring scheduled or continuous backups, using tools like Velero, EFS replication, or AWS Backup. These values should be defined collaboratively with business stakeholders to ensure that technical safeguards align with business expectations and regulatory requirements.

Establishing RTO and RPO early in the design phase helps determine appropriate trade-offs between cost, complexity, and availability, and lays the foundation for tiered service recovery planning as well as compliance audits.

# Workload Prioritization and Classification

Not all workloads are equal in terms of criticality. Classifying workloads into tiers, based on business impact allows teams to prioritize recovery efforts, and resource allocation during a disruption.

For example:

- **Tier 1**: Mission-critical applications that must be recovered immediately (for example, payment services).
- **Tier 2**: Important services that can tolerate limited downtime (for example, internal dashboards).
- **Tier 3**: Standard or batch workloads that can be restored later (for example, analytics jobs).

This classification should be reviewed periodically, and embedded into deployment workflows, ensuring that essential services are backed by appropriate SLAs and HA configurations, within the EKS architecture.

| Workload Tier | Recovery Time Objective (RTO) | Recovery Point Objective (RPO) | Examples |
|---|---|---|---|
| Tier 1 – Critical | ≤ 15 minutes | ≤ 5 minutes | Payment APIs, transactional systems |
| Tier 2 – Important | ≤ 1 hour | ≤ 15 minutes | Internal dashboards, partner APIs |
| Tier 3 – Standard | ≤ 4 hours | ≤ 1 hour | Reporting systems, batch workloads |
| Tier 4 – Non-Critical | ≤ 24 hours | ≤ 12 hours | Dev/test environments, archives |

**Table 10.3:** *Example RTO/RPO Targets by Workload Tier*

| Tier | Description | Recommended DR Strategy | Storage Type |
|---|---|---|---|
| 1 | Always-on, customer-facing | Active-active or warm standby | Replicated EFS, S3 |
| 2 | Business-impacting, tolerates delay | Active-passive, automated failover | EBS Snapshots, EFS |
| 3 | Operational workloads | Backup-restore | S3, slower restore OK |
| 4 | Low priority | Archive, manual restore | Glacier, S3 IA |

**Table 10.4:** *Workload Classification and DR Strategy*

## Creating and Maintaining Runbooks

A well-documented runbook is necessary for consistent and rapid incident response. Runbooks should contain step-by-step instructions for triggering failover, restoring backups, scaling alternate clusters, and verifying application health.

For Kubernetes and EKS, sample runbook components might include:

- Promoting a standby region to the primary by updating Route 53 records.
- Re-running Argo CD sync in the backup cluster.
- Restoring persistent volumes, using Velero.
- Notifying stakeholders via Slack or PagerDuty.

Runbooks should be version-controlled, regularly tested through simulation exercises, and stored in a location accessible during outages.

## Stakeholder Communication and Roles

Effective BCP is as much about communication as it is about infrastructure. During a disruption, different teams–engineering, operations, compliance, and customer support–must act in a coordinated manner. Defining clear roles and escalation paths ahead of time prevents confusion and delays.

The recommended practices include:

- Maintaining an up-to-date contact list of responsible personnel.
- Creating templates for customer-facing status updates.
- Integrating incident response tools such as AWS Chatbot, or Incident Ticketing system.
- Holding post-mortems after each incident to improve response plans.

## Simulating Business Disruptions and Validating BCP

To ensure that business continuity plans are effective, organizations must simulate realistic failure scenarios, and practice coordinated response procedures. These drills–often referred to as Disaster Recovery (DR) simulations or BCP tests–help validate assumptions, identify operational gaps, and build team confidence. In Amazon EKS, these simulations might involve shutting down node groups, intentionally failing health checks to trigger DNS failover, or running fault injection tests, using tools such as AWS Fault Injection Simulator, Gremlin, or LitmusChaos.

The recommended testing practices include:

- Conducting both planned tabletop exercises, and unannounced live failover drills.
- Measuring the time taken to detect, escalate, and resolve incidents.
- Verifying that workloads meet RTO/RPO objectives as defined.
- Including cross-functional teams to simulate full business impact, and response coordination.

Simulations should be documented and followed up with retrospectives that lead to improved runbooks, updated tooling, and clarified responsibilities.

# Business Continuity Planning Checklist

Developing a resilient Business Continuity Plan (BCP) requires structured actions that align operational priorities with cloud-native capabilities. The following checklist serves as a practical guide for ensuring continuity in Amazon EKS environments:

- **Define RTO and RPO for All Workloads:** Establish recovery time and recovery point objectives for each application, or service based on its business criticality. Use these metrics to shape infrastructure design, and backup strategies.
- **Classify and Tier Workloads:** Group workloads into tiers (for example, mission-critical, important, and non-essential) to prioritize their recovery sequence, and allocate resources effectively during failover scenarios.
- **Develop and Maintain Runbooks:** Create detailed, version-controlled runbooks, outlining specific steps to take during service disruptions. Include procedures for failover, restore, scaling, and verification.
- **Automate Infrastructure and Recovery Workflows:** Use Infrastructure as Code (IaC) and GitOps pipelines to automate failover, DNS updates, and cluster provisioning. This minimizes human errors, and accelerates recovery.
- **Establish Clear Communication Protocols:** Define roles, escalation paths, and stakeholder responsibilities. Prepare templates for internal notifications, and external customer communication.
- **Perform Routine DR Drills and Scenario Testing:** Schedule regular disaster recovery simulations to validate BCP effectiveness. Test both manual and automated processes, including cross-region failovers.
- **Ensure Access to Tools and Documentation during Incidents:** Store backup credentials, diagnostics scripts, and runbooks in high-availability systems (for example, cross-region S3 buckets, AWS Systems Manager, and so on).

- **Audit and Continuously Improve:** Post-incident reviews should feed back into the BCP. Update strategies, based on test results, changing architecture, or lessons learned from real incidents.

This checklist ensures that business continuity planning moves beyond theory, and becomes an actionable, repeatable practice tailored for EKS workloads and AWS's shared responsibility model.

| Scenario | Symptoms/Indicators | Recommended Action/Resolution |
|---|---|---|
| **Node failure in one AZ** | Pods in that AZ go Pending or terminate | Verify Auto Scaling Group configuration, and ensure subnets span multiple AZs as well as sufficient capacity is available. |
| **EFS mount failure in DR region** | Pods with PVCs fail to mount volumes | Ensure EFS replication is complete, and security groups/NFS mount targets are correctly configured. |
| **Route 53 failover does not trigger** | DNS resolution points to unhealthy region | Verify Route 53 health checks and failover routing policies; test using dig or nslookup. |
| **Cluster Autoscaler not scaling properly** | Pods stuck in Pending with Insufficient resources | Check cluster autoscaler logs for errors, and verify IAM permissions as well as resource thresholds. |
| **Karpenter provisions incorrect instance types** | Unexpected EC2 costs or under-provisioned nodes | Update Karpenter Provisioner constraints, and use tighter node selectors as well as maxPrice settings. |
| **Velero restore missing resources** | Restored cluster lacks secrets or CRDs | Ensure backup including all namespaces and custom resources, and check Velero logs for filtered objects. |
| **GitOps drift not corrected automatically** | Live cluster differs from declared Git state | Verify ArgoCD's self-heal setting is enabled; check Application sync status and RBAC permissions. |
| **Network partition during chaos test** | Services become unreachable across AZs or regions | Review VPC route tables, NACLs, and ensure that multi-AZ NLB setup supports fault tolerance. |

***Table 10.5:*** *Troubleshooting HA and DR Scenarios*

# Recovery Testing

Recovery testing is the practice of validating that disaster recovery and high availability mechanisms perform as expected when failures occur. In Kubernetes environments such as Amazon EKS, this involves simulating infrastructure, application, or service layer failures, and measuring the system's ability to maintain or restore functionality within defined recovery objectives. While architecting for availability is essential, recovery testing ensures that theoretical designs hold up under real-world conditions and operational pressure.

A comprehensive recovery testing strategy confirms not only the technical correctness of backup and failover mechanisms but also the readiness of teams and processes to respond during incidents. This includes validating RTO and RPO compliance, ensuring the accuracy of runbooks, and identifying gaps in automation or observability. In the context of EKS, recovery testing encompasses scenarios such as cluster failover, pod rescheduling across AZs, restoration of stateful volumes, DNS redirection, and CI/CD redeployments. The following sections outline recovery testing techniques, tools, and the best practices to support resilient and verifiable Kubernetes operations on AWS.

# Testing Scenarios

Effective recovery testing begins by identifying and designing test cases that reflect realistic failure conditions. These scenarios should align with the defined RTO/RPO targets, and cover a wide range of potential disruptions. In Amazon EKS, typical recovery test cases include:

- **AZ Failure Simulation:** Force termination of nodes in a single Availability Zone to confirm pod rescheduling and service continuity.
- **Node Group Disruption:** Manually cordon and drain node groups, or simulate scaling failures to test application rebalancing.
- **Data Loss Recovery:** Delete sample application state, and attempt restoration from Velero or AWS Backup snapshots.
- **Cross-Region Failover:** Simulate a full-region outage by disabling cluster endpoints or DNS routes, and redirecting traffic via Route 53.

Each test should be documented with a defined objective, execution plan, success criteria, and rollback procedure. Recovery testing should be treated as an ongoing practice, integrated into release cycles and operational reviews.

# Chaos Engineering

Chaos engineering introduces controlled failure into the system to test resilience under stress. Unlike static recovery drills, chaos tests assess the dynamic behavior of services during unexpected degradation. Tools such as AWS Fault Injection Simulator, Gremlin, and LitmusChaos enable platform teams to simulate real-world failure modes like:

- Network latency between pods or services.
- Random container restarts or memory exhaustion.

- API throttling or rate limit breaches.
- Nodes or AZ shutdowns.

Thus, by executing chaos experiments in lower environments–or under strict production guardrails–organizations can uncover hidden interdependencies, improve observability coverage, and validate automated mitigation strategies. Chaos engineering complements recovery testing by ensuring that the system not only recovers but also remains stable under adverse conditions.

## Post-Recovery Validation

Following any recovery event or simulation, it is necessary to conduct a formal validation to confirm that systems have returned to a healthy and fully functional state. Post-recovery validation includes:

- **Application Health Checks:** Ensure that readiness and liveness probes pass across all restarted services.
- **Data Integrity Verification:** Validate that the restored data is consistent and complete.
- **Monitoring and Alerting Review:** Confirm that alerts were triggered and responded to as expected.
- **Runbook Audit:** Review the accuracy and completeness of procedures followed during the test.
- **Performance Baseline Comparison:** Assess whether service latency, throughput, or error rates have regressed post-recovery.

Additionally, post-mortems or incident reviews should be conducted after major recovery tests to identify the areas for improvement. These learnings should be incorporated into updated runbooks, refined alerting strategies, and improved automation.

## Recovery Testing Checklist

The following checklist provides a structured approach to validating recovery capabilities in Amazon EKS environments:

- **Define Clear Test Objectives:** Establish the purpose, scope, and expected outcomes for each recovery test scenario, aligned with your RTO and RPO targets.
- **Simulate Infrastructure Failures:** Test scenarios such as node group loss, AZ failure, and cluster endpoint inaccessibility to validate workload rescheduling and continuity.

- **Validate Backup and Restore Workflows:** Regularly restore from Velero or AWS Backup snapshots to confirm data recoverability, and persistent volume functionality.
- **Conduct Cross-Region Failover Drills:** Disable DNS routing or application endpoints in the primary region, and redirect traffic to the secondary region, using Route 53.
- **Leverage Chaos Engineering Tools:** Use AWS Fault Injection Simulator, Gremlin, or LitmusChaos to induce controlled disruptions, and assess system resilience.
- **Automate Test Execution Where Possible:** Integrate failure simulations and recovery validation into CI/CD pipelines, or use scripts to standardize test execution.
- **Monitor System Response and Alerting:** Ensure that observability tools detect and report failures accurately during tests, and that response procedures are followed.
- **Review and Update Runbooks:** After each test, audit the steps taken, and revise documentation to reflect any procedural gaps or lessons learned.
- **Perform Post-Recovery Validation:** Verify application health, data consistency, and system performance to confirm successful recovery.
- **Log Results and Continuously Improve:** Maintain a record of recovery tests, outcomes, and action items. Use this feedback loop to enhance tooling, training, and infrastructure resilience.

| **Scenario / Failure Type** | **Tool Used** | **Expected Behavior / Recovery Outcome** |
|---|---|---|
| Node Termination in One AZ | AWS FIS, LitmusChaos | Pods are rescheduled on healthy nodes in other AZs; HPA or Cluster Autoscaler may trigger new node provisioning. |
| Kubelet Crash on Select Nodes | LitmusChaos | Node becomes NotReady; pods are evicted and rescheduled by Kubernetes. |
| Delete Control Plane Endpoint (Simulated) | AWS FIS | Control plane remains available (managed by AWS); clients may retry transient errors. |
| Network Partition between Pods | LitmusChaos (Network Loss) | Service retries or timeouts occur; inter-zone traffic resumes once partition is lifted. |

| | | |
|---|---|---|
| EBS Volume Unavailable | Manual test / FIS script | Stateful pod fails or restarts; use EFS for higher resilience, if needed. |
| Region-Level Resource Blackhole (Failover Test) | Route 53 failover simulation | Traffic should route to standby region, if health checks fail in primary. |
| Crash Application Pod | kubectl delete pod | Deployment/ReplicaSet auto-restores missing pod; no data loss, if stateful volumes are managed. |

**Table 10.6:** *Chaos Testing Scenarios and Expected Behaviors*

# Conclusion

In this chapter, we explored the principles, architectures, and operational practices required to build highly available and disaster-resilient environments, using Amazon EKS. Starting with Multi-AZ deployment strategies, we examined how to distribute workloads, design for zone failure, and utilize tools like topology-aware scheduling and pod disruption budgets. We then extended the scope to cross-region failover, highlighting methods for replicating infrastructure, synchronizing application state, and using DNS routing to manage regional failover events.

We also covered backup implementation strategies, using tools such as Velero and AWS Backup, emphasizing the importance of securing both Kubernetes configurations and persistent data. Business continuity planning was introduced as a broader organizational discipline, involving RTO/RPO definitions, workload classification, incident response runbooks, and communication planning. Finally, recovery testing practices—such as chaos engineering, failover simulation, and post-recovery validation—were detailed to ensure that resilience strategies function as expected under real-world conditions.

Together, these topics provide a comprehensive framework for achieving operational excellence and continuity in cloud-native workloads on Amazon EKS. In the next chapter, we will shift our focus to **Application Resilience and Observability**, where we explore how service-level monitoring, distributed tracing, and fault-tolerant application design contribute to long-term platform stability.

# Points to Remember

- Multi-AZ deployments enhance fault tolerance by distributing EKS worker nodes and resources across multiple Availability Zones within a region. Use topology-aware scheduling and load balancing to ensure zone-resilient workloads.

- Amazon EKS control planes are automatically deployed across three Availability Zones by AWS, but worker node placement and subnet configuration must be explicitly managed by users for full high availability.
- Cross-region failover strategies require replicating infrastructure and application configurations in a secondary region, supported by DNS failover ( for example, Route 53), GitOps deployment patterns, and replicated storage.
- Backup solutions such as Velero and AWS Backup are essential for protecting Kubernetes configurations and persistent volume data. Integration with IAM Roles for Service Accounts (IRSA) improves security posture.
- Recovery Time Objective (RTO) and Recovery Point Objective (RPO) define the allowable limits for service downtime and data loss. These metrics should be defined per workload to shape the HA/DR strategies.
- Business continuity planning includes classifying workloads by criticality, maintaining incident runbooks, defining escalation paths, and conducting recovery simulations to ensure organizational readiness.
- Recovery testing validates the effectiveness of failover, backup, and restore mechanisms. This includes both planned drills and chaos engineering experiments, using tools such as AWS Fault Injection Simulator and Gremlin.
- Post-recovery validation is necessary to confirm that services are functioning correctly after disruption. Always verify application health, data consistency, and system performance after a recovery event.
- Documentation, automation, and continuous improvement are foundational to maintaining resilience. Regularly update runbooks, infrastructure templates, and operational practices, based on test results and incident learnings.

# Multiple Choice Questions

1. What is the primary purpose of a Multi-AZ deployment in Amazon EKS?
    a. Reduce storage costs
    b. Improve CI/CD performance
    c. Enhance availability and fault tolerance
    d. Speed up Kubernetes upgrades
2. Which AWS service is typically used to configure DNS-based failover between EKS clusters?
    a. CloudWatch
    b. Route 53

   c. App Mesh

   d. AWS Load Balancer Controller

3. Which tool enables backup and restore of Kubernetes resources in Amazon EKS?

   a. CloudTrail

   b. AWS Shield

   c. Velero

   d. Prometheus

4. What does RPO stand for in disaster recovery planning?

   a. Resource Provisioning Option

   b. Recovery Process Objective

   c. Recovery Point Objective

   d. Regional Protection Objective

5. Which storage option provides native support for cross-AZ availability in AWS?

   a. Amazon EBS

   b. Amazon EFS

   c. Amazon S3 Glacier

   d. Local NVMe

6. What type of testing intentionally introduces faults to assess system resilience?

   a. Unit Testing

   b. Load Testing

   c. Chaos Engineering

   d. Integration Testing

7. In a cross-region failover setup, which component is responsible for routing traffic to a healthy region?

   a. Ingress Controller

   b. EBS Snapshot Scheduler

   c. Route 53 Health Check
   d. IAM Role
8. What is the best practice for securing Velero's access to AWS resources?
   a. Use root user credentials.
   b. Store credentials in ConfigMaps.
   c. Configure IAM Roles for Service Accounts (IRSA).
   d. Manually enter credentials during backup.
9. Which Kubernetes object helps prevent service disruptions during voluntary node maintenance?
   a. Horizontal Pod Autoscaler
   b. Pod Disruption Budget
   c. NodeSelector
   d. Deployment
10. Why is recovery testing essential for EKS disaster recovery plans?
   a. It reduces cluster creation time.
   b. It ensures that observability integrations are working.
   c. It validates that failover, backup, and restore mechanisms are performing as expected.
   d. It enhances log retention.

# Answers

1. c
2. b
3. c
4. c
5. b
6. c
7. c
8. c

9. b
10. c

# Key Terms

- **Availability Zone (AZ):** A distinct physical location within an AWS Region, designed to isolate failure from other zones. It is used to build fault-tolerant applications.
- **Multi-AZ Deployment:** A high availability strategy that involves distributing infrastructure and workloads across multiple Availability Zones.
- **Recovery Time Objective (RTO):** The maximum acceptable duration of downtime for a service or system, following a disruption.
- **Recovery Point Objective (RPO):** The maximum acceptable amount of data loss measured in time, indicating how recent a backup must be for recovery.
- **Disaster Recovery (DR):** The set of processes and technologies used to restore services and data after a major failure or outage.
- **Cross-Region Failover:** A resilience technique where traffic or workloads are redirected from a primary AWS Region to a secondary one in case of regional disruption.
- **Pod Disruption Budget (PDB):** A Kubernetes policy that defines the minimum availability of pods during voluntary disruptions such as upgrades or node draining.
- **Velero:** An open-source tool used to back up and restore Kubernetes cluster resources as well as persistent volumes.
- **Route 53:** AWS's scalable DNS and routing service, often used to implement health-checked, DNS-based failover.
- **Chaos Engineering:** A discipline that introduces controlled failure into systems to test their resilience and response capabilities.
- **IAM Roles for Service Accounts (IRSA):** A secure way of granting AWS permissions to Kubernetes workloads by associating IAM roles with service accounts.
- **Fault Injection Simulator (FIS):** An AWS service that simulates faults in applications to improve resilience and reliability.
- **Business Continuity Plan (BCP):** A strategy outlining how a business will maintain operations and recover from disruptions.

# Chapter 11
# Cost Optimization and Resource Management

## Introduction

In today's cloud-native landscape, the difference between a successful Kubernetes deployment, and a budget nightmare often comes down to one critical factor: Cost optimization. As organizations increasingly migrate to Amazon EKS, many find themselves facing the classic cloud computing paradox – the very flexibility and scalability that makes Kubernetes attractive can also lead to spiraling costs, if not managed properly. A recent study by the Cloud Native Computing Foundation revealed that 68% of organizations reported higher-than-expected Kubernetes costs, with some experiencing cloud bills up to three times their initial estimates.

The art of optimizing EKS clusters is not just about cutting costs – it is about building a sustainable, efficient infrastructure that delivers the maximum value for every dollar spent. Hence, whether you are running a startup watching every penny, or managing enterprise-scale deployments, understanding how to balance cost optimization with performance is no longer optional – it is imperative.

In this chapter, we will dive deep into proven strategies, tools, and techniques that will help you master the economics of running EKS clusters. From leveraging spot instances to implementing sophisticated cost allocation strategies, you will learn how to transform your Kubernetes infrastructure from a cost center into a model of operational efficiency.

## Structure

In this chapter, we will discuss the following topics:

- Understanding EKS Cost Components
- Spot Instances Implementation

- Capacity Planning Strategies
- Resource Quotas Management
- AWS Cost Explorer Integration
- Budget Alerts and Monitoring

# Understanding EKS Cost Components

The true cost of running an Amazon Elastic Kubernetes Service (EKS) cluster extends far beyond the basic cluster management fee. Like an iceberg, the visible costs represent only a fraction of the total investment. Organizations frequently underestimate their EKS expenditure by focusing solely on worker node costs, only to be surprised by the cumulative impact of various interconnected components. A 2023 FinOps Foundation survey revealed that 73% of organizations exceeded their initial Kubernetes budget estimates primarily due to overlooking these auxiliary costs.

Let us break down the three major cost pillars of an EKS infrastructure, each contributing to total operational expenses in unique ways. This understanding will serve as the foundation for implementing effective cost optimization strategies and making informed architectural decisions.

# Control Plane Costs

While the base EKS control plane fee of $0.10 per hour ($72 per month) appears straightforward, it is often misunderstood as a fixed, predictable cost. In practice, control plane expenses vary significantly, based on architectural decisions and geographical deployment strategy. Organizations running multi-region deployments for high availability might find their control plane costs multiplying - a single application deployed across three regions immediately triples this baseline cost to $216 per month.

- **EKS Cluster Management Fee:** The $0.10 per hour per cluster fee represents your entry point into the EKS ecosystem. This non-negotiable fee applies regardless of cluster size or workload intensity. Organizations implementing multiple clusters for development, staging, and production environments should factor in these cumulative base costs.
- **Control Plane Scaling Considerations:** The control plane's resource utilization patterns influence operational costs beyond the base fee. High-frequency API calls, numerous custom resources, and extensive use of controllers can necessitate additional control plane capacity. Organizations running large-scale applications may need to implement specific optimization measures to manage these demands effectively.

- **Regional Pricing Variations:** While the base control plane fee remains constant across most regions, associated costs such as data transfer and API calls vary by location. Deploying in regions like São Paulo or Sydney typically incurs higher costs compared to North American regions. Organizations must balance geographic presence requirements with these regional cost variations, when designing their global EKS infrastructure.

# Worker Node Costs

Worker nodes typically represent the largest portion of your EKS infrastructure costs, often accounting for 70%–80% of total cluster expenses. A 2024 cloud cost analysis revealed that organizations frequently overspend by 25%–35% on worker nodes due to suboptimal instance choices and sizing decisions. Understanding these costs is not just about knowing the price per hour – it is about making strategic decisions that balance performance, availability, and cost-effectiveness.

- **EC2 instance pricing** forms the core of your worker node costs, with rates varying significantly across instance types and regions. Standard on-demand pricing provides maximum flexibility but at premium rates, while Reserved Instances offer substantial discounts of up to 72% for committed usage. Spot Instances present the most aggressive cost-saving opportunity, with potential savings of up to 90% off on-demand prices, though they require careful application architecture to handle interruptions.
- **Storage costs** through EBS volumes add another dimension to worker node expenses. While the default gp3 volumes offer a good balance of performance and cost, organizations often overlook the cumulative impact of storage costs across their cluster. For example, a typical production cluster with 20 nodes, each provisioned with 100GB gp3 volumes, incurs approximately $200 monthly in storage costs alone.
- **Data transfer costs** complete the worker node cost picture, often becoming significant in multi-region or hybrid cloud architectures. Inter-AZ traffic within a region costs about $0.02 per GB, while cross-region transfer can reach $0.09 per GB. These costs can accumulate rapidly in distributed applications, particularly those handling large data volumes or running data-intensive microservices.

*Figure 11.1* provides a hierarchical view of EKS cost components, breaking them down into three main categories: Control Plane Costs, Worker Node Costs, and Additional Components. Each category is further divided into specific cost elements, with some key pricing details included. The color-coding and layout help to visually distinguish between different cost categories, and their relationships.

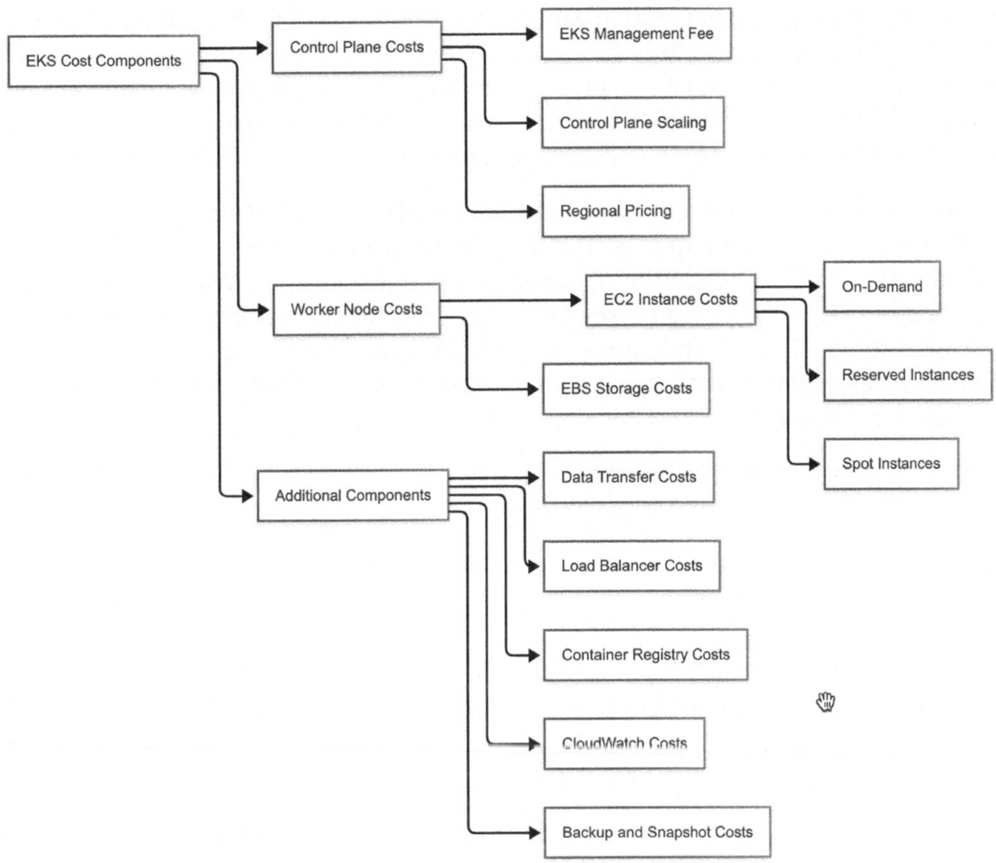


**Figure 11.1:** EKS Cost Components

# Additional Components

The hidden costs of EKS operations often lurk in these auxiliary components which can collectively add 15-30% to your monthly cloud bill. While organizations meticulously plan their node and control plane expenditures, these supplementary services frequently emerge as unexpected cost drivers. According to the recent FinOps surveys, these '*peripheral*' costs surprised 63% of organizations during their first year of EKS adoption.

Load balancer services, vital for routing external traffic to your applications, start at $16.20 per Application Load Balancer (ALB) monthly, with additional costs for each processed GB. A typical production environment running multiple microservices might require several ALBs, quickly accumulating to hundreds of dollars monthly in load balancing costs, alone. Network Load Balancers, while more expensive at $19.80 per month, become necessary for specific use cases like WebSocket applications or high-throughput scenarios.

Container registry costs through Amazon ECR compound with scale. While the first 500MB of storage monthly is free, subsequent storage costs $0.10 per GB-month, with data transfer charges applying for image pulls. Organizations maintaining numerous application versions and environments often find their ECR costs growing exponentially, particularly in CI/CD pipelines where frequent image updates occur.

CloudWatch monitoring represents another significant cost center, charging for both metric storage and API requests. The default monitoring configuration might cost $7-10 per node monthly, but comprehensive monitoring with custom metrics and detailed logging can multiply this figure several times. Additionally, backup and snapshot costs for persistent volumes, while often overlooked in initial planning, can add substantial overhead, especially in data-intensive applications where regular snapshots are crucial for disaster recovery.

```
# Example cost calculation
Monthly EKS Cluster Cost =
(Control Plane Hours × $0.10) +
  (Worker Node Instance Hours × Instance Price) +
  Storage Costs +
  Network Transfer Costs +
  Additional Service Costs
```

*Table* 11.1 provides a comprehensive overview of the various cost elements associated with running Amazon EKS, from the core management fees to the variable costs of worker nodes, and additional services.

| Component Type | Service | Base Cost | Variable Factors |
|---|---|---|---|
| **Control Plane** | | | |
| | EKS Management Fee | $0.10/hour per cluster | • Region • Number of clusters |
| **Worker Nodes** | | | |
| | EC2 On-Demand | Varies by instance type | • Instance size • Region • Usage hours |
| | EC2 Reserved Instance | Up to 72% off On-Demand | • Term length • Payment option • Instance type |
| | EC2 Spot Instance | Up to 90% off On-Demand | • Market demand • Instance type • Region |
| | EBS Storage | gp3: $0.08/GB-month | • Volume type • Size • IOPS |
| **Network** | | | |
| | Data Transfer (Inter-AZ) | $0.02/GB | • Traffic volume • Direction |

| | | | |
|---|---|---|---|
| | Data Transfer (Internet) | $0.09/GB | • Region • Volume |
| | Application Load Balancer | $16.20/ALB | • Number of ALBs • Processed GB |
| **Additional Services** | | | |
| | ECR | $0.10/GB-month | • Image size • Storage duration • Pull requests |
| | CloudWatch | $0.30/metric/month | • Number of metrics • Data retention • API calls |
| | Snapshots | $0.05/GB-month | • Volume size • Retention period |

***Table 11.1:*** *EKS Cost Components*

# Spot Instances Implementation

In the pursuit of EKS cost optimization, Spot Instances emerge as a game-changing strategy, offering potential savings of up to 90% compared to On-Demand pricing. However, this compelling cost advantage comes with specific operational considerations that demand careful implementation. The recent data from AWS shows that organizations successfully implementing Spot Instances in their EKS clusters achieve average savings of 65-75%, while maintaining production-grade reliability.

**For instance:** A typical EKS cluster running 20 t3.large instances on-demand costs approximately $1,400 monthly. The same cluster, properly configured with Spot Instances, could run for as little as $420 monthly – a dramatic reduction that could translate to over $11,000 in annual savings. Yet, according to a 2024 cloud usage report, only 38% of EKS users fully leverage Spot Instances, largely due to concerns about workload interruption, and implementation complexity.

In this section, we will demystify Spot Instance implementation, providing you with practical strategies and configurations that balance cost savings with operational stability. From understanding the fundamental pricing models to implementing robust interruption handling, you will learn how to transform Spot Instances from a cost-saving opportunity into a production-ready reality.

# Understanding Spot Instances

Spot Instances represent AWS's unused EC2 capacity, available at discounts of up to 90% off On-Demand prices. However, this dramatic cost reduction comes with a crucial caveat: AWS can reclaim these instances with just two minutes' notice, when capacity is needed elsewhere. Think of Spot Instances as a dynamic marketplace where cloud resources are traded, based on supply and demand, similar to commodity markets.

Pricing models for Spot Instances fluctuate, based on real-time supply and demand dynamics. For example, a t3.large instance that costs $0.0832 per hour on-demand might be available for as little as $0.0250 per hour as a Spot Instance. These prices vary by region, time of day, and instance type, creating opportunities for strategic instance selection. Organizations that master Spot pricing patterns often implement automated bidding strategies, switching between instance types and regions to maintain optimal pricing.

Interruption handling becomes critical when working with Spot Instances. The two-minute warning provided by AWS must be leveraged effectively to ensure application resilience. Modern Kubernetes applications should be designed to handle these interruptions gracefully, using techniques like pod disruption budgets and automated node draining. Data from AWS shows that well-architected Spot workloads achieve 99.99% availability despite instance interruptions.

Instance diversity strategy serves as your insurance policy against Spot interruptions. Rather than depending on a single instance type, successful implementations typically spread workloads across multiple instance families and sizes. For example, a production deployment might use a mix of t3.large, m5.large, and r5.large instances, each capable of running the target workload, but with different price-performance characteristics. This diversification reduces the impact of capacity shortages in any single instance pool.

# Spot Instance Configuration

Configuring Spot Instances in EKS requires a deliberate approach to node group setup that balances cost savings with operational reliability. The configuration below represents a battle-tested pattern that has helped organizations achieve up to 70% cost reduction, while maintaining production-grade stability. Using eksctl, we shall define a mixed-instance node group that leverages multiple instance types to maximize availability and optimize costs.

The following configuration demonstrates a production-ready Spot Instance setup that implements key best practices. Here, we are defining a node group that can scale from 2 to 10 nodes, using a diverse selection of instance types to protect against Spot interruptions. The instance types chosen (t3.large, t3a.large, and m5.large) offer similar performance characteristics, but tap into different capacity pools, significantly reducing the risk of simultaneous interruptions:

```
# Spot Instance configuration
apiVersion: eksctl.io/v1alpha5
kind: ClusterConfig
metadata:
  name: eks-spot-cluster
  region: us-west-2
```

```
nodeGroups:
  - name: spot-ng
    instanceType: mixed
    minSize: 2
    maxSize: 10
    spot: true
    instanceTypes: ["t3.large", "t3a.large", "m5.large"]
```

This configuration creates a robust foundation for Spot Instance usage, where the minSize ensures baseline capacity, while maxSize allows for demand-based scaling. The mixed instance strategy is particularly effective in regions such as us-west-2, which typically shows strong Spot availability patterns. Organizations using this configuration report achieving consistent 99.95% uptime, while maintaining significant cost savings.

# Handling Spot Interruptions

Graceful handling of Spot Instance interruptions is the cornerstone of reliable Spot-based deployments. Organizations that effectively implement interruption handling report 99.9% application availability despite using Spot Instances. The AWS Node Termination Handler (NTH) serves as your first line of defense, automating the process of gracefully draining nodes, when interruption notices arrive. Thus, by implementing this critical component, you can transform the inherent volatility of Spot Instances from a liability into a manageable operational pattern.

*Figure* 11.2 demonstrates the seamless interaction between AWS services, the Node Termination Handler, and the Kubernetes Control Plane to ensure minimal disruption during Spot Instance terminations.

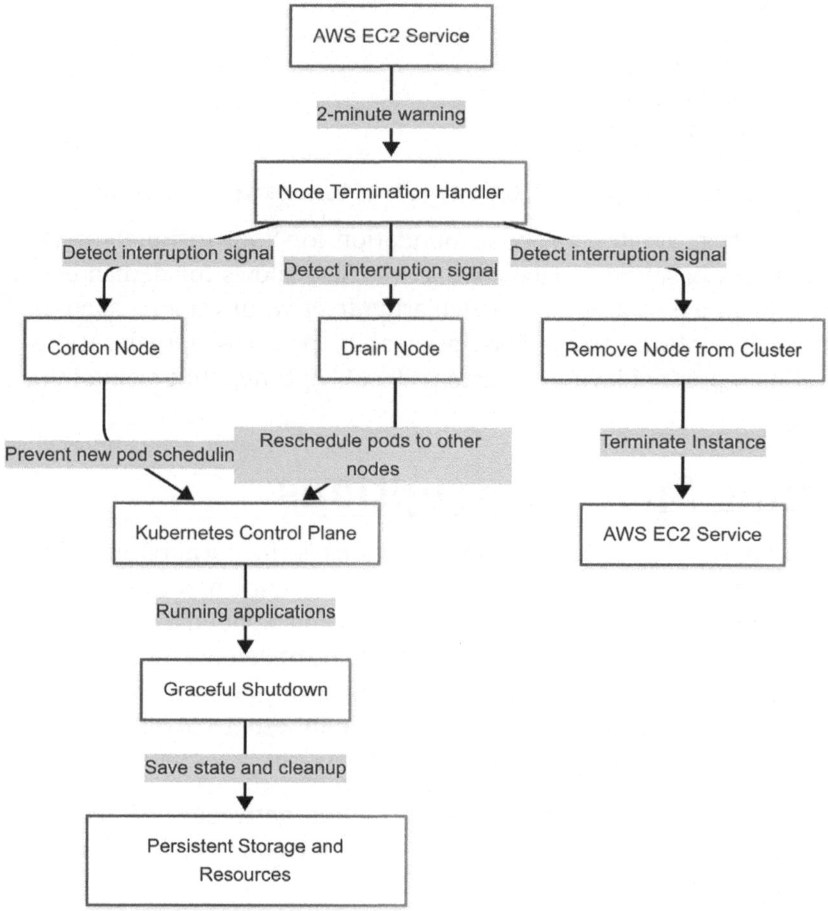


***Figure 11.2:*** *Spot Instance Interruption Handling*

The following DaemonSet Configuration deploys the AWS Node Termination Handler across your cluster, ensuring that every Spot Instance is monitored for interruption signals. This handler acts as an automated safety net, initiating pod evacuation procedures within the crucial two-minute warning window:

```
# Example Configuration
apiVersion: apps/v1
kind: DaemonSet
metadata:
  name: aws-node-termination-handler
  namespace: kube-system
spec:
  selector:
    matchLabels:
      app: aws-node-termination-handler
```

```
    template:
      metadata:
        labels:
          app: aws-node-termination-handler
      spec:
        containers:
        - name: aws-node-termination-handler
          image: amazon/aws-node-termination-handler:v1.13.3
```

The Node Termination Handler works by constantly monitoring the EC2 metadata service for interruption notices. When a notice is received, it automatically cordons and drains the affected node, ensuring that running applications are safely rescheduled, before the instance terminates. This automated process typically completes within 60-90 seconds, well within the two-minute warning period, minimizing the risk of application disruption.

# Best Practices for Spot Usage

Successfully leveraging Spot Instances requires a strategic blend of careful planning, and robust implementation. The most successful EKS deployments, using Spot Instances achieve cost savings of 60-90%, while maintaining production-grade reliability by following three core best practices.

Application suitability assessment serves as your crucial first step. Ideal Spot candidates include stateless applications, distributed systems, and batch processing workloads that can handle interruptions gracefully. When assessing applications, evaluate their state management requirements, recovery capabilities, and business impact tolerance. For instance, CI/CD pipelines, data processing jobs, and horizontally scaled web applications typically perform excellently on Spot Instances, while single-instance databases or applications with strict uptime requirements may not be suitable candidates.

Mixing instance types provides the vital resilience against interruptions. Implement a diverse instance strategy using 3–5 different instance types across multiple families. For example, combine **`t3.large`**, **`m5.large`**, and **`c5.large`** instances to create a robust instance pool. This diversity reduces the risk of simultaneous interruptions by spreading workloads across different capacity pools. Data shows that organizations using mixed instance types experience 65% fewer interruption-related incidents compared to those relying on a single instance type.

Implementing graceful shutdown procedures completes your Spot Strategy. Configure appropriate termination grace periods (minimum 120 seconds), implement readiness probes, and set up Pod Disruption Budgets (PDBs). Your applications should include shutdown hooks that handle interruption signals properly, ensuring critical operations complete, and the state is saved before instance termination. The Node Termination

Handler should work in concert with these application-level procedures to ensure smooth workload transitions during Spot interruptions.

# Capacity Planning Strategies

Effective capacity planning in EKS represents the delicate balance between over-provisioning that leads to unnecessary costs, and under-provisioning, which risks application performance. Recent cloud optimization studies reveal that organizations typically overspend by 30-45% due to ineffective capacity planning, while those implementing robust capacity strategies achieve 99.9% availability with 25-35% lower infrastructure costs.

**Consider this scenario:** A rapidly growing e-commerce platform initially provisioned their EKS cluster for 100,000 daily users, only to face performance degradation during a holiday season spike of 300,000 users. Conversely, another company over-provisioned their development environments by 200%, maintaining idle capacity that cost them an additional $150,000 annually. These real-world examples underscore the pivotal importance of precise capacity planning.

The key to successful EKS capacity planning lies in understanding the interplay between four critical dimensions: workload analysis, resource right-sizing, autoscaling configuration, and performance-cost trade-offs. Each dimension requires careful consideration and continuous refinement as your applications evolve and business demands change. In this section, we will explore how to master these dimensions to build a resilient, cost-effective, and high-performing Kubernetes infrastructure.

# Workload Analysis

Understanding historical usage patterns forms the cornerstone of effective EKS cluster planning and optimization. By analyzing past resource consumption trends across CPU, memory, network, and storage metrics, organizations can establish baseline requirements and identify recurring patterns in application behavior. This historical analysis should span multiple business cycles to capture seasonal variations and periodic spikes in demand, providing insights into both regular operational patterns and exceptional usage scenarios.

Peak load identification requires careful examination of resource utilization during high-demand periods, considering both expected peaks during normal business operations, and unexpected surges from special events or marketing campaigns. This analysis should account for the correlation between different resource types, as peak CPU usage might not coincide with peak memory or network utilization. Understanding these peak patterns helps in determining appropriate buffer capacities and scaling thresholds, ensuring the cluster can handle maximum loads, while maintaining performance and reliability.

Growth projections extend beyond historical patterns to incorporate business forecasts, planned feature releases, and market expansion plans. These projections should consider both organic growth in the existing workloads, and the addition of new applications or services to the cluster. Organizations need to factor in not just linear growth, but also step changes that might occur from new product launches, market expansion, or business acquisitions. This forward-looking analysis ensures that the cluster architecture can scale effectively to meet the future demands, while maintaining cost efficiency and performance objectives.

# Resource Right-Sizing

Effective resource right-sizing in EKS requires a systematic approach to aligning container resource allocations with actual application requirements. The resource management relies on precise specification of compute resources through requests and limits, forming the foundation of efficient container orchestration and workload optimization. The following pod specification demonstrates a well-balanced resource configuration that exemplifies the best practices in container resource allocation, where requests establish baseline guarantees and limits prevent resource overconsumption. This carefully crafted balance between minimal resource requirements and maximum allowable usage ensures optimal performance, while maintaining cluster efficiency.

```
# Example Resource right sizing
apiVersion: v1
kind: Pod
metadata:
  name: resource-optimized-pod
spec:
  containers:
  - name: app
    resources:
      requests:
        memory: "64Mi"
        cpu: "250m"
      limits:
        memory: "128Mi"
        cpu: "500m"
```

# Autoscaling Configuration

Effective scaling strategies in Amazon EKS require a multi-layered approach to resource management, combining pod-level scaling with cluster-wide capacity adjustments. The Horizontal Pod Autoscaler (HPA) represents the first line of defense in maintaining application performance under varying loads, automatically adjusting the number of pod replicas, based on observed metrics. When integrated with the

Cluster Autoscaler, this creates a comprehensive scaling solution that ensures both application responsiveness and infrastructure efficiency.

# Horizontal Pod Autoscaling (HPA)

HPA automatically scales the number of pods in response to observed metrics, primarily CPU and memory utilization. The configuration above sets a target CPU utilization of 70%, maintaining between 2 and 10 replicas to handle varying workloads. This mechanism ensures applications remain responsive while efficiently utilizing cluster resources. HPA can also work with custom metrics from Amazon CloudWatch or Prometheus, enabling scaling, based on application-specific indicators like queue length or request latency.

The following HPA configuration demonstrates a production-grade implementation that balances responsiveness with resource efficiency:

```
# HPA configuration
apiVersion: autoscaling/v2
kind: HorizontalPodAutoscaler
metadata:
  name: sample-app-hpa
spec:
  scaleTargetRef:
    apiVersion: apps/v1
    kind: Deployment
    name: sample-app
  minReplicas: 2
  maxReplicas: 10
  metrics:
  - type: Resource
    resource:
      name: cpu
      target:
        type: Utilization
        averageUtilization: 70
```

# Cluster Autoscaler Configuration

The Cluster Autoscaler complements the HPA by automatically adjusting the number of nodes in response to pod scheduling requirements. In EKS, this typically involves configuring Auto Scaling Groups with appropriate launch templates and scaling policies. The Cluster Autoscaler monitors for pods that cannot be scheduled due to insufficient resources, and triggers node scaling accordingly, while also identifying and removing underutilized nodes to optimize costs.

```
# Example Cluster Autoscaler deployment for EKS:
apiVersion: apps/v1
kind: Deployment
metadata:
  name: cluster-autoscaler
  namespace: kube-system
spec:
  replicas: 1
  selector:
    matchLabels:
      app: cluster-autoscaler
  template:
    metadata:
      labels:
        app: cluster-autoscaler
    spec:
      serviceAccountName: cluster-autoscaler
      containers:
      - name: cluster-autoscaler
        image: k8s.gcr.io/autoscaling/cluster-autoscaler:v1.23.0
        command:
        - ./cluster-autoscaler
        - --v=4
        - --stderrthreshold=info
        - --cloud-provider=aws
        - --skip-nodes-with-local-storage=false
        - --nodes=2:10:eks-nodegroup-name
        env:
        - name: AWS_REGION
          value: us-west-2
    resources:
          requests:
            cpu: 100m
            memory: 300Mi
          limits:
            cpu: 200m
            memory: 500Mi
```

## Custom Metrics-Based Scaling

Beyond standard resource metrics, EKS supports advanced scaling scenarios using custom metrics. Organizations can implement scaling decisions, based on business-specific metrics such as request rates, queue depths, or custom application metrics. This is achieved through the Kubernetes Metrics Server and custom metrics adapters, enabling sophisticated scaling behaviors that align directly with business requirements and application-specific performance indicators.

The following custom metrics pipeline establishes an end-to-end monitoring solution in EKS, where Prometheus Service Monitor automatically discovers and collects metrics from application endpoints, while the Prometheus Adapter translates these metrics for Kubernetes' autoscaling decisions. This integration, combined with properly configured application deployments exposing relevant metrics, enables scaling based on business-specific indicators, rather than just basic resource metrics.

```
# Custom Metrics Pipeline
apiVersion: monitoring.coreos.com/v1
kind: ServiceMonitor
metadata:
  name: sample-app-monitor
spec:
  selector:
    matchLabels:
      app: sample-app
  endpoints:
  - port: metrics
    interval: 15s
```

# Performance versus Cost Trade-offs

Optimizing EKS deployments requires carefully balancing performance requirements against infrastructure costs. This delicate equilibrium involves strategic decisions across compute resources, storage configurations, and networking options, where each choice impacts both application performance and operational expenses. Understanding these trade-offs enables organizations to design cost-effective architectures that meet performance objectives, while maintaining fiscal responsibility. *Table 11.2* serves as a decision-making framework, illustrating how different priorities in performance versus cost affect various aspects of EKS cluster configuration, from instance selection to monitoring strategies.

| Decision Factor | High Performance Priority | Cost Optimization Priority | Balanced Approach |
|---|---|---|---|
| **Instance Types** | On-demand, compute-optimized (c5, c6g), Dedicated instances, Latest generation | Spot instances, Burstable (t3, t4g), Right-sized instances | Mix of on-demand and spot, General purpose (m5, m6g), Reserved instances |
| **Node Groups** | Large node count, Homogeneous instances, Multi-AZ deployment | Minimum viable nodes, Mixed instance types, Single AZ with failover | Moderate node count, Mixed instance policy, Strategic Multi-AZ |

| **Storage** | Provisioned IOPS (io2), EFS Standard, Local instance storage | GP2/GP3 volumes, EFS One Zone, S3 with lifecycle | GP3 with custom IOPS, EFS Standard-IA, Balanced storage tiers |
|---|---|---|---|
| **Networking** | Enhanced networking, AWS Global Accelerator, Cross-zone load balancing | VPC endpoints, Regional resources, Single-zone balancing | Selective enhanced networking, Regional with CDN, Conditional cross-zone |
| **Scaling** | Aggressive horizontal scaling, Proactive node scaling, Large scaling buffer | Conservative scaling, Reactive node scaling, Minimal buffer | Moderate scaling rules, Balanced thresholds, Optimized buffer |
| **Monitoring** | Detailed monitoring, 1-minute intervals, Full tracing enabled | Basic monitoring, 5-minute intervals, Essential metrics only | Selected detailed metrics, Mixed intervals, Critical path tracing |
| **Typical Cost** | $$$$$ | $ | $$$ |
| **Best For** | Mission-critical apps, High-performance workloads, Real-time processing | Dev/test environments, Batch processing, Cost-sensitive workloads | Production apps, Standard business apps, Mixed workloads |

**Table 11.2:** *EKS Performance vs. Cost Trade-offs*

# Resource Quotas Management

Effective resource management in Amazon EKS requires a comprehensive approach to quota implementation, ensuring fair resource allocation, while maintaining operational efficiency across multiple workloads and teams. Through the strategic use of ResourceQuotas and LimitRanges, organizations can establish clear boundaries for resource consumption, prevent resource monopolization, and maintain predictable cluster performance.

This section explores the essential components of resource quota management, from basic compute resource limits to sophisticated multi-tenant configurations, providing practical examples and best practices for implementing these controls in production environments.

# Implementing Resource Quotas

ResourceQuotas serve as the primary mechanism for controlling resource consumption within Kubernetes namespaces, establishing hard limits on compute, storage, and object counts.

The following configuration demonstrates a production-grade implementation that defines CPU and memory constraints, ensuring predictable resource utilization, while preventing any single namespace from monopolizing cluster resources:

```
apiVersion: v1
kind: ResourceQuota
metadata:
  name: compute-resources
spec:
  hard:
    requests.cpu: "4"
    requests.memory: 4Gi
    limits.cpu: "8"
    limits.memory: 8Gi
```

This quota configuration sets reasonable bounds for a typical development namespace, where requested resources are set at half of the maximum limits, providing both guaranteed resources and burst capacity for peak workloads.

# LimitRange Configuration

LimitRange resources complement ResourceQuotas by enforcing default and boundary values at the container level, ensuring consistent resource specifications across all workloads within a namespace. The following configuration establishes sensible defaults for CPU and memory allocation, providing a balance between guaranteed resources and maximum constraints that helps prevent both under and over-provisioning:

```
apiVersion: v1
kind: LimitRange
metadata:
  name: default-limits
spec:
  limits:
  - default:
      cpu: 500m
      memory: 512Mi
    defaultRequest:
      cpu: 200m
      memory: 256Mi
    type: Container
```

This configuration sets default requests at 40% of limits, creating an efficient resource utilization profile, while maintaining headroom for workload variations.

# Quota Monitoring and Enforcement

Effective quota management in Amazon EKS extends beyond implementation to include comprehensive monitoring and enforcement strategies, ensuring ongoing compliance with established resource constraints, while maintaining operational efficiency. This critical aspect of cluster management combines namespace-level quotas, multi-tenant isolation, and robust monitoring mechanisms to create a well-governed environment.

```
# Example CloudWatch Alarm for Quota Usage
apiVersion: cloudwatch.aws.com/v1alpha1
kind: MetricAlarm
metadata:
  name: quota-threshold-alert
spec:
  metricName: ResourceQuotaUsage
  namespace: AWS/EKS
  dimensions:
    - name: ClusterName
      value: production-cluster
    - name: Namespace
      value: team-a
  threshold: 80
  evaluationPeriods: 3
  datapointsToAlarm: 2
  comparisonOperator: GreaterThanThreshold
  statistic: Average
  period: 300
```

A comprehensive quota management strategy requires well-defined namespace quotas aligned with team requirements, proper multi-tenant isolation through network policies, and RBAC configurations, as well as robust monitoring through CloudWatch metrics and automated alerts. Organizations should implement real-time usage tracking, proactive threshold alerting, and automated responses to potential violations, while monitoring resource utilization trends and quota consumption patterns across namespaces. Thus, by leveraging AWS native tools alongside Kubernetes metrics, teams can maintain visibility into resource usage, while ensuring compliance with organizational policies and budget constraints, creating a balanced and efficient operational environment.

# AWS Cost Explorer Integration

AWS Cost Explorer provides a comprehensive framework for analyzing EKS infrastructure costs through three key components. The foundation begins with proper Cost Explorer configuration, including detailed billing activation and strategic tag implementation for accurate cost tracking. Custom reporting capabilities extend this functionality through programmatic access, enabling automated cost analysis and reporting through AWS SDK integrations. Building upon this foundation, effective cost attribution strategies ensure accurate allocation of expenses to specific services, teams, and projects, creating a transparent model for resource utilization and optimization. Together, these components create a robust cost management system that enables organizations to make data-driven decisions about their EKS infrastructure spending.

# Setting Up Cost Analysis

The foundation of effective EKS cost management lies in proper configuration of AWS Cost Explorer, enabling organizations to gain granular visibility into their container infrastructure spending. This crucial setup phase encompasses three vital elements that form the basis for accurate cost analysis and attribution.

Proper configuration begins with enabling detailed billing to capture comprehensive cost data across all EKS components and associated AWS services. This is complemented by implementing a strategic tagging strategy that reflects organizational structure, application hierarchies, and business units. Cost allocation tags then bridge the gap between infrastructure resources and business context, enabling meaningful cost attribution and chargeback models. Together, these elements create a robust foundation for understanding and optimizing EKS infrastructure costs, providing the visibility needed for informed decision-making about resource allocation and utilization. Refer to *Figure* 11.3, for example, "*The chargeback model, Tag Hierarchy, and Cost Attribution*".

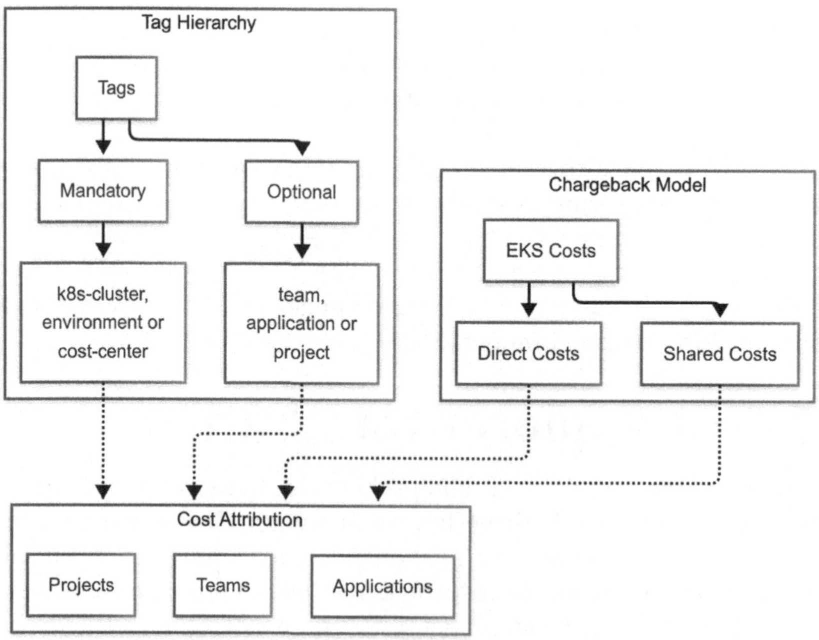


**Figure 11.3**: *Chargeback Model, Tag Hierarchy and Cost Attribution*

## Enabling Detailed Billing

Enabling detailed billing in AWS Cost Explorer provides granular visibility into EKS infrastructure costs through comprehensive usage data capture, and hourly level tracking. By activating Cost and Usage Reports (CUR) and detailed billing features, organizations gain access to specific metrics for each cluster component, from worker nodes to associated services, enabling effective cost analysis and optimization strategies.

To enable detailed billing for EKS cost analysis:

1. Navigate to the **AWS Billing and Cost Management Dashboard**, and access **Cost Explorer**.
2. Create a CUR with hourly granularity and resource ID inclusion, specifying an S3 bucket for report storage.
3. Activate relevant cost allocation tags, both AWS-generated and user-defined, to track EKS-specific resources.
4. Configure additional settings, including data refresh frequency and retention period.

Note that it may take up to 24 hours for tag activation and detailed billing data to appear in your reports. Please refer to AWS public documentation to enable and setup detailed billing reports.

## Tag Configuration

Effective tag configuration in AWS Cost Explorer forms a salient component of EKS cost management, enabling granular tracking and attribution of infrastructure expenses. By implementing a systematic tagging strategy, organizations can categorize resources across multiple dimensions such as environment (prod, dev, staging), team ownership, cost center, project, and application components. A well-structured tagging framework includes mandatory tags for essential categorization (for example, **'kubernetes:cluster'**, **'environment'**, **'team'**) and optional tags for specific use cases (for example, **'project-phase'**, **'compliance-level'**, **'backup-frequency'**). This hierarchical approach to tagging not only facilitates accurate cost allocation, but also enables detailed analysis of spending patterns, resource utilization, and optimization opportunities across the EKS infrastructure.

```
# Example Tag Structure:
Mandatory Tags:
- kubernetes:cluster: <cluster-name>
- environment: prod|dev|staging
- team: <team-name>
- cost-center: <cost-center-id>
```

```
Optional Tags:
- project: <project-name>
- application: <application-name>
- backup: yes|no
```

## Cost Allocation Tags

Cost allocation tags serve as the foundation for tracking and attributing EKS infrastructure expenses by combining AWS-generated and user-defined tags. Through strategic implementation of mandatory operational tags and business-specific identifiers, organizations can create detailed cost attribution models that enable accurate chargeback mechanisms and informed resource allocation decisions. This structured approach to cost tracking ensures transparency, while supporting optimization efforts across the EKS environment.

Setting up cost allocation tags in AWS requires a straightforward yet strategic approach through the AWS Management Console. Begin by navigating to AWS Cost Management, where you will access the Cost Allocation Tags section to configure both AWS-generated and user-defined tags. From there, select the User-Defined Tags option to view and manage custom tags specific to your organization's needs. Finally, activate relevant tags that align with your cost tracking requirements, keeping in mind that activation may take up to 24 hours to reflect in cost reports. This foundational setup enables detailed cost tracking and attribution across your EKS infrastructure.

# Creating Custom Reports

Custom cost reporting in Amazon EKS extends beyond standard AWS Cost Explorer capabilities by leveraging the AWS SDK to create tailored analysis solutions. Through programmatic access to cost and usage data, organizations can build sophisticated reporting mechanisms that provide deeper insights into their EKS infrastructure spending patterns.

The following Python implementation demonstrates a practical approach to retrieving cluster-specific cost data, enabling automated reporting and custom visualizations:

```
import boto3

def get_eks_costs():
    client = boto3.client('ce')

    response = client.get_cost_and_usage(
        TimePeriod={
            'Start': '2024-01-01',
            'End': '2024-01-31'
        },
```

```
            Granularity='MONTHLY',
            Metrics=['UnblendedCost'],
            GroupBy=[
                {'Type': 'TAG', 'Key': 'kubernetes:cluster'}
            ]
        )
        return response
```

This example showcases how to query specific time periods, apply granularity controls, and filter by Kubernetes cluster tags, providing a foundation for building comprehensive cost analysis solutions.

# Cost Attribution Models

Cost attribution in Amazon EKS requires a methodical, three-tiered approach to mapping infrastructure expenses across the organization. By combining detailed service-level analysis, precise organizational mapping, and fair cost distribution mechanisms, organizations can create a comprehensive framework for understanding and managing their container infrastructure investments. This multi-dimensional approach not only enables transparent cost allocation and informed decision-making, but also facilitates accountability and optimization across all operational levels, ensuring efficient resource utilization, while maintaining clear visibility into spending patterns throughout the container infrastructure landscape.

- **Service-Level Costing:** Service-level costing provides granular visibility into resource consumption by individual components within the EKS infrastructure. This approach tracks costs across various elements, including compute instances, storage volumes, load balancers, and network transfers, enabling detailed understanding of how different services contribute to overall infrastructure expenses. Thus, by implementing detailed service-level cost tracking, organizations can identify resource-intensive components, optimize service configurations, and make informed decisions about architectural improvements.
- **Team/Project Attribution:** Team and project attribution establishes clear ownership of infrastructure costs by mapping expenses to specific organizational units and initiatives. Through strategic tag implementation and resource organization, costs can be accurately allocated to development teams, business units, or specific projects. This granular attribution enables teams to understand their infrastructure spending patterns, maintain budget accountability, and identify opportunities for cost optimization, within their specific domains.
- **Chargeback Models:** Chargeback models provide the framework for fair and transparent cost distribution across different organizational units consuming EKS resources. These models can range from simple direct allocation, based

on resource consumption to more sophisticated approaches that consider shared resources, overhead costs, and varying service levels. Therefore, by implementing well-defined chargeback mechanisms, organizations can promote responsible resource utilization, enable accurate budgeting, and maintain equitable cost distribution, while supporting different business requirements and priorities.

# Budget Alerts and Monitoring

Effective cost control in Amazon EKS requires a proactive approach to budget monitoring and alert management. By implementing comprehensive monitoring solutions that combine AWS Budgets, CloudWatch Alarms, and Cost Anomaly Detection, organizations can maintain tight control over their infrastructure spending, while quickly identifying and responding to unexpected cost variations. This section explores the implementation of these critical monitoring components, from basic budget setup through sophisticated anomaly detection mechanisms.

Cost monitoring in EKS environments presents unique challenges due to the dynamic nature of containerized workloads, auto-scaling behaviors, and shared resource utilization. AWS Budgets provide the foundation for cost tracking through customizable thresholds and alerts, while CloudWatch Alarms enable real-time monitoring of specific metrics that impact costs. Cost Anomaly Detection adds an intelligent layer of monitoring by identifying unusual spending patterns, and potential cost optimization opportunities.

Through strategic configuration of budget thresholds, metric monitoring, and automated alerting systems, organizations can create a robust early warning system for potential cost overruns. This integrated approach to budget monitoring combines automated detection with structured response procedures, enabling teams to maintain fiscal responsibility, while ensuring optimal resource utilization across their EKS infrastructure.

# Budget Configuration

Implementing effective budget controls for EKS infrastructure requires a multi-tiered system that provides timely notifications as spending approaches predefined thresholds. Through strategic configuration of AWS Budgets, organizations can monitor and manage container-related expenses, maintaining proactive oversight of their infrastructure costs, and ensuring timely awareness of potential overruns.

AWS Budgets offers a programmatic approach via the AWS SDK, enabling organizations to create and manage sophisticated budget configurations. These configurations monitor expenses across various dimensions of container deployments, involving the setup of appropriate thresholds, monitoring periods, and notification channels. This ensures timely alerts when spending approaches or exceeds defined limits, allowing for proactive cost management and automated actions, when necessary.

*Figure 11.4* illustrates a typical budget alert setup, demonstrating how alerts are configured at various spending levels, and the corresponding actions triggered.

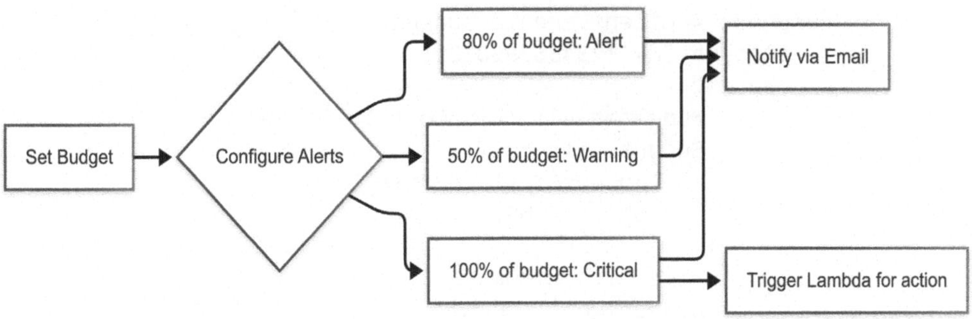


**Figure 11.4:** *Budget Management*

The following sections outline different approaches for AWS Budget setup:

# Console Setup

This section talks about configuring AWS Budgets through the AWS Management Console. Setting up budget controls in AWS begins with accessing the Billing dashboard, and selecting the "**`Budgets`**" section. Under the AWS Budgets menu, select "**`Create budget`**", and choose the "**`Cost budget`**" option for tracking EKS infrastructure spending. Next, define the monthly budget allocation and establish a tiered alert system with notifications at key thresholds – typically 50% for early awareness, 80% for proactive planning, and 90% for immediate action. Configure notification destinations by adding email recipients or SNS topics to ensure that relevant stakeholders receive timely alerts. Fine-tune the budget scope by implementing filters, based on specific tags, AWS services, or accounts, creating precise tracking mechanisms for EKS-related expenses. This systematic approach to budget configuration enables organizations to maintain granular control over their container infrastructure costs, while ensuring proactive notification of potential overruns.

# Programmatic Implementation

AWS Budgets can be programmatically configured using the AWS SDK, enabling automated creation and management of budget alerts through code. This approach allows organizations to implement consistent budget controls across multiple EKS clusters or AWS accounts, while maintaining version control and infrastructure as code principles.

The following Python implementation demonstrates how to create a monthly budget with customizable thresholds and notification settings:

```
def create_budget_alert(budget_amount, email):
    client = boto3.client('budgets')

    response = client.create_budget(
        AccountId='123456789012',
        Budget={
            'BudgetName': 'EKS-Monthly-Budget',
            'BudgetLimit': {
                'Amount': str(budget_amount),
                'Unit': 'USD'
            },
            'TimeUnit': 'MONTHLY',
            'BudgetType': 'COST'
        }
    )
```

This code example establishes a foundation for automated budget management, enabling scalable and reproducible cost control implementations across EKS environments.

# Monitoring Systems

Effective monitoring in Amazon EKS environments requires a multi-layered approach that combines infrastructure metrics, application performance data, and cost analytics to provide comprehensive operational visibility. Through the integration of AWS CloudWatch, Container Insights, and custom monitoring solutions, organizations can establish real-time oversight of their container infrastructure, while maintaining proactive alerting for potential issues. This monitoring framework enables immediate detection of performance anomalies and cost variations, while providing the analytical foundation for continuous optimization.

CloudWatch Alarms form a critical component of the EKS monitoring strategy by providing automated surveillance of key metrics and triggering notifications, when predefined thresholds are breached. Organizations can configure metrics ranging from basic infrastructure indicators such as CPU utilization and memory consumption to sophisticated custom metrics that reflect business-specific concerns. Alarm thresholds should be carefully calibrated to balance between early warning and alert fatigue, while notification configurations ensure that the right teams receive timely alerts through appropriate channels like SNS topics, email, or incident management systems.

In the upcoming sections, we will discuss more on setting up metrics for effective EKS monitoring, configuring appropriate alarm thresholds for different scenarios, and implementing notification systems for timely alerts.

## Setting up Metrics

CloudWatch metrics provide the foundation for monitoring EKS cluster health and performance through systematic collection and analysis of operational data. Organizations can leverage both built-in EKS metrics and custom metrics to create a comprehensive monitoring solution that addresses infrastructure, application, and business requirements.

```
# Example CloudWatch Metric Configuration
Resources:
  EKSCPUUtilizationMetric:
    Type: AWS::CloudWatch::Metric
    Properties:
      MetricName: CPUUtilization
      Namespace: AWS/EKS
      Dimensions:
        - Name: ClusterName
          Value: production-cluster
        - Name: NodeGroup
          Value: worker-nodes
      Period: 300
      Statistic: Average
      Unit: Percent

# Custom Container Metric
  ApplicationMetric:
    Type: AWS::CloudWatch::Metric
    Properties:
      MetricName: RequestLatency
      Namespace: Custom/EKS
      Dimensions:
        - Name: ServiceName
          Value: api-service
      Period: 60
      Statistic: Average
      Unit: Milliseconds
```

These metric configurations enable monitoring of both system-level performance indicators and application-specific metrics, providing the data foundation for effective alarming and automation in EKS environments.

## Alarm Thresholds

Setting appropriate alarm thresholds in CloudWatch requires careful consideration of workload patterns, business requirements, and operational capacity. Through strategic threshold configuration, organizations can establish an effective early warning system that balances between proactive alerting and alert fatigue, ensuring timely response to potential issues in their EKS environment.

```
# Example CloudWatch Alarm Threshold Configurations
Resources:
  CPUUtilizationAlarm:
    Type: AWS::CloudWatch::Alarm
    Properties:
      AlarmName: EKS-CPU-Utilization-High
      AlarmDescription: CPU utilization exceeds threshold
      MetricName: CPUUtilization
      Namespace: AWS/EKS
      Dimensions:
        - Name: ClusterName
          Value: production-cluster
      Threshold: 80           # Triggers when CPU usage exceeds 80%
      Period: 300             # Evaluation period of 5 minutes
      EvaluationPeriods: 2    # Number of periods to evaluate
      DatapointsToAlarm: 2.   # Must breach threshold twice to alarm
      ComparisonOperator: GreaterThanThreshold
      TreatMissingData: notBreaching
      Statistic: Average

  MemoryUtilizationAlarm:
    Type: AWS::CloudWatch::Alarm
    Properties:
      AlarmName: EKS-Memory-Usage-High
      Threshold: 85           # Triggers when CPU usage exceeds 80%
      EvaluationPeriods: 3    # Evaluate over 3 periods
      DatapointsToAlarm: 2    Must breach threshold twice to alarm
      ComparisonOperator: GreaterThanThreshold
```

The common threshold patterns include:

- **Warning Level**: 70% utilization - Early notification for capacity planning
- **Critical Level**: 85% utilization - Immediate action required
- **Emergency Level**: 95% utilization - Potential service impact

This multi-tiered approach to threshold configuration enables graduated responses to emerging issues, while maintaining operational stability. The configuration examples demonstrate how to set up alarms with appropriate evaluation periods and breach thresholds, ensuring reliable detection of genuine issues, while minimizing false alarms.

## Notification Configuration

CloudWatch alarm notifications form the vital link between issue detection and operational response in EKS environments. So, by implementing a structured notification strategy that leverages Amazon SNS topics and integrates with various communication channels, organizations can ensure that the right teams receive timely alerts with appropriate context for effective incident response.

The following is an example of CloudWatch alarm notification. This configuration demonstrates:

- SNS topic creation for alert aggregation
- Alarm integration with SNS
- Email subscription for notifications
- Alert and recovery notifications

```
# Example CloudWatch Alarm Notification Configuration
Resources:
  EKSAlertTopic:
    Type: AWS::SNS::Topic
    Properties:
      TopicName: eks-alerts
      DisplayName: EKS Alerts

  CPUUtilizationAlarm:
    Type: AWS::CloudWatch::Alarm
    Properties:
      AlarmName: EKS-CPU-High
      AlarmDescription: CPU utilization exceeded threshold
      AlarmActions:
        - !Ref EKSAlertTopic
      OKActions:
        - !Ref EKSAlertTopic
      MetricName: CPUUtilization
      Namespace: AWS/EKS
      Threshold: 80
      Period: 300
      EvaluationPeriods: 2
      ComparisonOperator: GreaterThanThreshold
      TreatMissingData: notBreaching

  EmailSubscription:
    Type: AWS::SNS::Subscription
```

```
      Properties:
        Protocol: email
        TopicArn: !Ref EKSAlertTopic
        Endpoint: ops-team@example.com
```

This configuration establishes a complete notification pipeline where an SNS topic (**EKSAlertTopic**) serves as the central notification hub, receiving alerts from a CloudWatch alarm monitoring CPU utilization (**CPUUtilizationAlarm**). When CPU usage exceeds 80% for two consecutive 5-minute periods, the alarm triggers notifications through the SNS topic, which then forwards these alerts to subscribed email endpoints (**ops-team@example.com**). The setup includes both alarm and recovery notifications, ensuring that the teams are informed, when issues both arise and resolve.

# Cost Anomaly Detection

AWS Cost Anomaly Detection leverages machine learning to identify unusual spending patterns and potential cost inefficiencies in EKS environments. By analyzing historical spending patterns, and establishing baseline behaviors, this service helps organizations proactively identify and respond to unexpected cost variations, before they significantly impact budgets.

The system begins with configuring anomaly detection rules tailored to EKS workload patterns, setting appropriate sensitivity thresholds, and defining notification preferences. When anomalies are detected, automated response procedures trigger alerts through predefined channels, enabling rapid investigation and mitigation. The Root Cause Analysis is facilitated through detailed cost attribution data, and integration with CloudWatch metrics, allowing teams to quickly identify the sources of unexpected spending, whether from misconfigured resources, unexpected scaling events, or changes in usage patterns. This comprehensive approach to cost monitoring ensures organizations maintain financial control, while optimizing their EKS infrastructure investments.

## Setting up Anomaly Detection

AWS Cost Anomaly Detection enables organizations to implement automated monitoring of EKS spending patterns through machine learning-based analysis. This service helps to identify unexpected cost variations by establishing normal spending baselines, and detecting deviations that could indicate inefficiencies or issues in your EKS infrastructure.

```
# Example Cost Anomaly Detector Configuration
Resources:
  EKSCostDetector:
    Type: AWS::CE::AnomalyDetector
    Properties:
```

```
Name: eks-cost-anomalies
MonitorType: DIMENSIONAL
MonitorDimension: SERVICE
MonitorSpecification:
  Dimensions:
    - Name: Service
      Value: AmazonEKS
  Tags:
    - Key: Environment
      Values:
        - Production
ThresholdExpression:
  Threshold: 100  # Detect variations above $100
AlertSubscriptions:
  - Type: EMAIL
    Address: finance-team@example.com
  - Type: SNS
    TopicArn: !Ref AnomalyAlertTopic
ReportFrequency: DAILY
```

This configuration creates a specialized detector focused on monitoring EKS service costs, identifying spending variations above $100 from the established baseline. The detector monitors specifically the Amazon EKS service in the Production environment through dimensional filtering, sending alerts through both email notifications to the finance team, and an SNS topic when anomalies are detected. Reports are generated daily to ensure regular monitoring and timely detection of cost irregularities.

This enables proactive identification of cost anomalies, while maintaining flexibility in notification and response mechanisms.

# Response Procedures

Establishing structured response procedures for cost anomalies ensures consistent and effective handling of unexpected spending patterns in EKS environments. These procedures combine automated responses with human intervention to quickly identify, assess, and remediate cost-related issues, before they significantly impact budgets.

The following is an example of Response Workflow Configuration. The AWS Step Functions state machine implements a tiered response system for cost anomalies, automatically evaluating the severity based on the anomaly amount and triggering appropriate notifications. When an anomaly is detected, the workflow evaluates its magnitude such as: Amounts exceeding $1000 trigger high-priority alerts to both on-call and finance teams through urgent channels, while anomalies between $500–$1000 generate standard notifications to the platform team. This automated response ensures that cost anomalies receive appropriate attention and response based on their severity, streamlining the incident management process.

```
# Example Response Workflow Configuration
Resources:
  AnomalyResponseWorkflow:
    Type: AWS::StepFunctions::StateMachine
    Properties:
      Definition:
        StartAt: EvaluateAnomalyLevel
        States:
          EvaluateAnomalyLevel:
            Type: Choice
            Choices:
              - Variable: "$.anomalyAmount"
                NumericGreaterThan: 1000
                Next: HighPriorityResponse
              - Variable: "$.anomalyAmount"
                NumericGreaterThan: 500
                Next: MediumPriorityResponse
            Default: LowPriorityResponse

          HighPriorityResponse:
            Type: Task
            Resource: !GetAtt NotifyTeam.Arn
            Parameters:
              Channel: "urgent"
              Message: "Critical cost anomaly detected"
              Recipients: ["oncall-team", "finance-team"]

          MediumPriorityResponse:
            Type: Task
            Resource: !GetAtt NotifyTeam.Arn
            Parameters:
              Channel: "standard"
              Message: "Significant cost variation detected"
              Recipients: ["platform-team"]
```

Response Levels:

- **High Priority:** Immediate action required (>$1000)
- **Medium Priority:** Investigation needed ($500-$1000)
- **Low Priority:** Monitoring and analysis (<$500)

This automated workflow ensures appropriate escalation and response, based on the severity of detected cost anomalies.

## Root Cause Analysis

Root cause analysis in EKS environments combines four key dimensions: Resource utilization analysis examining infrastructure metrics, configuration change review tracking system modifications, and workload pattern analysis evaluating application behaviors, and cost impact assessment quantifying financial implications. This comprehensive analysis framework enables organizations to identify and address the root causes of cost anomalies effectively.

The investigation process follows a structured approach starting with thorough data collection across all dimensions. Teams then conduct pattern analysis to correlate events, and identify causal relationships, followed by impact assessment to quantify effects and prioritize actions. The process concludes with remediation planning that addresses both immediate fixes and long-term preventive measures, ensuring comprehensive resolution of cost anomalies in EKS environments.

# Conclusion

This chapter has provided a comprehensive overview of Amazon EKS cost management and optimization strategies, beginning with fundamental cost components, and advancing through practical implementation methods. The discussion encompassed vital elements from control plane operations and worker node management to the strategic use of Spot Instances for cost reduction. Through detailed exploration of capacity planning, resource quotas, and AWS Cost Explorer integration, the chapter established a framework for effective cost control, while maintaining optimal performance. The implementation of proactive monitoring systems and automated alerts ensures that organizations can manage their EKS environments efficiently, while preventing unexpected cost escalations.

After completing this chapter, you should have now been familiar with several key concepts in EKS cost management. Understanding the multi-faceted nature of EKS costs enables effective optimization strategies, while Spot Instance implementation requires careful planning but offers significant cost savings. Capacity planning and resource quotas form the foundation of cost control, and integration with AWS cost management tools enables data-driven decision making. Proactive monitoring and anomaly detection prevent unexpected cost escalations. This comprehensive approach to EKS cost management provides organizations with the tools and strategies needed to maintain efficient, cost-effective container infrastructure, while ensuring optimal performance and reliability.

# Points to Remember

- EKS cost components encompass three primary areas: Control plane charges for managing the Kubernetes control plane, worker node costs for compute resources, and additional service fees for features such as load balancing and storage.

- Capacity planning requires continuous analysis of historical usage patterns, peak load identification, and growth projections to ensure efficient resource allocation, while maintaining performance requirements.
- Resource quotas and LimitRange configurations provide essential controls for managing resource consumption across namespaces, preventing overconsumption, while ensuring fair resource distribution among teams.
- Spot Instance implementation can significantly reduce compute costs by leveraging unused AWS capacity, but requires proper configuration and handling of interruptions through tools like Node Termination Handler.
- AWS Cost Explorer integration enables detailed cost analysis through customizable reports and dashboards, providing visibility into spending patterns, and enabling data-driven optimization decisions.
- Budget alerts and monitoring systems form a critical component of cost management, combining CloudWatch metrics, custom thresholds, and automated notifications for proactive cost control.
- Cost anomaly detection leverages machine learning to identify unusual spending patterns, enabling quick response to unexpected cost increases through automated alerts and structured investigation procedures.
- Performance versus cost trade-offs require careful consideration of instance types, scaling policies, and storage configurations to balance operational requirements with budget constraints.
- Multi-tenant environments benefit from namespace-level budget management, implementing quota controls and chargeback models to maintain cost accountability across different teams and projects.
- Regular monitoring and optimization of EKS infrastructure costs require a combination of automated tools, well-defined processes, and continuous analysis of resource utilization patterns to maintain cost efficiency.

# Multiple Choice Questions

1. Which AWS service is primarily used for detailed cost analysis of EKS clusters?
    a. CloudWatch
    b. Cost Explorer
    c. Systems Manager
    d. CloudTrail

2. What is the primary benefit of using Spot Instances in EKS?
    a. Improved performance
    b. Enhanced security
    c. Cost savings
    d. Better availability
3. Resource Quotas in EKS operate at which level?
    a. Pod level
    b. Node level
    c. Namespace level
    d. Cluster level
4. Which metric is NOT typically monitored for cost anomaly detection?
    a. CPU utilization
    b. Network traffic
    c. DNS queries
    d. Storage usage
5. What is the recommended first step in capacity planning?
    a. Implementing auto-scaling
    b. Analyzing historical usage
    c. Setting up alerts
    d. Configuring quotas
6. CloudWatch Alarms in EKS should be configured to trigger based on:
    a. Single data point
    b. Multiple evaluation periods
    c. Random checks
    d. Manual verification
7. Which feature enables automatic distribution of EKS costs across teams?
    a. Cost allocation tags

    b. Resource quotas
    c. LimitRange
    d. Pod security policies

8. What is the primary purpose of LimitRange in EKS?
    a. Network control
    b. Storage management
    c. Default resource limits
    d. Access control

9. Cost anomaly detection in AWS uses which technology?
    a. Blockchain
    b. Machine learning
    c. Manual review
    d. Fixed thresholds

10. Which tool is considered to be the best for implementing pod-level resource constraints?
    a. Resource Quotas
    b. LimitRange
    c. Cost Explorer
    d. Budget Alerts

# Answers

1. b
2. c
3. c
4. c
5. b
6. b
7. a
8. c

9. b
10. b

# Key Terms

- **Cost Explorer:** AWS service for analyzing and visualizing cost distribution across resources, enabling detailed financial tracking and reporting of EKS infrastructure.
- **Resource Quotas:** Control mechanism limiting total resource consumption within Kubernetes namespaces to prevent overutilization, and manage costs effectively.
- **Spot Instances:** Cost-effective compute option, using spare AWS capacity at reduced prices, providing significant savings for interruptible workloads.
- **Budget Alerts:** Automated notification system monitoring spending patterns and alerting, when costs approach or exceed defined thresholds.
- **Cost Anomaly Detection:** Machine learning-based system identifying unusual spending patterns and potential cost inefficiencies in EKS environments.
- **LimitRange:** Kubernetes resource defining default compute constraints and limits at the container level within namespaces.
- **CloudWatch Alarms:** Monitoring service triggering notifications, based on metric thresholds for cost and performance management.
- **Capacity Planning:** Strategic process analyzing historical usage, and forecasting future resource requirements for optimal cost efficiency.
- **Cost Allocation Tags:** Metadata labels enabling detailed cost tracking and attribution across different organizational units and projects.
- **Chargeback Models:** Frameworks for distributing EKS infrastructure costs, based on actual resource consumption by different teams or projects.

# CHAPTER 12
# Performance Tuning and Scaling

## Introduction

In today's cloud-native landscape, running applications on Amazon Elastic Kubernetes Service (EKS) is just the beginning. The real challenge lies in ensuring these applications perform optimally, while efficiently managing resources and costs. As organizations adopt containerized architectures, they must understand and implement various scaling mechanisms, each serving different use cases and requirements.

This chapter explores comprehensive strategies for optimizing application performance, implementing effective scaling mechanisms, and maintaining efficient resource utilization in EKS environments. We delve into various scaling approaches, including Horizontal Pod Autoscaling (HPA), Vertical Pod Autoscaling (VPA), and cluster-level scaling through Cluster Autoscaler and Karpenter. Understanding these mechanisms and their integration is crucial for developing robust scaling strategies.

Resource management is the key focus, covering proper configuration of resource requests and limits, node optimization, and instance type selection. We examine effective monitoring and alerting strategies, along with network performance tuning, to ensure optimal communication between components.

This chapter addresses performance analysis through monitoring setup with Prometheus and Grafana, benchmarking methodologies, and load testing techniques. These practices help identify and resolve performance bottlenecks efficiently. Cost optimization strategies are integrated throughout, demonstrating how to balance performance requirements, with resource utilization and leverage AWS-specific features for cost management.

Thus, by the end of the chapter, readers will have a comprehensive understanding of how to implement effective performance tuning and scaling strategies in their EKS environments, ensuring their deployments can handle modern application demands, while maintaining efficiency and cost-effectiveness.

# Structure

In this chapter, we will discuss the following topics:

- Understanding Performance Optimization and Scaling
- Understanding Kubernetes Scaling Mechanisms
- Horizontal Pod Autoscaling
- Vertical Pod Autoscaling
- Cluster Autoscaling
- Resource Optimization
- Performance Benchmarking in EKS
- Load Testing for EKS

# Understanding Performance Optimization and Scaling

Deploying applications on Amazon Elastic Kubernetes Service (EKS) represents only the first step in modern cloud-native operations. The more complex challenge comes from maximizing application performance, while maintaining resource efficiency and cost control. With organizations rapidly expanding their container-based workloads, implementing effective performance optimization and automated scaling strategies has become essential for sustainable operations.

Performance optimization in EKS goes far beyond simply keeping applications running. It directly impacts several crucial aspects of your operations, such as:

- **Cost Efficiency:** Properly optimized EKS clusters ensure that you are not over-provisioning resources, and helping to maintain optimal cloud spending. Without proper optimization, organizations often find themselves paying for unused capacity, or struggling with unexpected cost spikes.
- **User Experience:** In production environments, application performance directly correlates with user satisfaction. Slow response times or service interruptions can lead to lost business opportunities and damaged reputation. Optimized EKS clusters help maintain consistent performance under varying loads.
- **Resource Utilization:** Modern applications face dynamic workload patterns. During peak hours, your applications might need significantly more resources than during off-hours. Hence, effective performance optimization ensures resources are available when needed, while avoiding waste during lower-demand periods.

- **Operational Reliability:** Well-optimized clusters are more reliable and easier to maintain. They are less likely to experience unexpected outages, and can better handle sudden traffic spikes, or resource demands.

Kubernetes provides several scaling strategies, each serving different use cases and requirements:

- **Horizontal Scaling:** This is a dynamic scaling strategy that fundamentally involves automatically adding or removing pod replicas to match current demand patterns. When workload increases, the system spawns new pods to distribute the load; when demand decreases, it removes excess pods to conserve resources. This approach is particularly well-suited for stateless applications, such as web servers, API gateways, and frontend services, where each instance can operate independently without maintaining local state. One of the key advantages of horizontal scaling is its inherent ability to provide enhanced fault tolerance through redundancy – by running multiple copies of the same application, the system remains operational even if individual pods fail, with traffic automatically redistributing to healthy instances. This scaling method aligns perfectly with microservices architectures, where each service can scale independently based on its specific requirements, enabling precise resource allocation and efficient handling of varying workloads. For instance, in an e-commerce platform, the product catalog service might need more replicas during a sale event, while the checkout service scales based on actual transaction volume.
- **Vertical Scaling:** This represents a fundamental capacity management strategy that focuses on adjusting resource allocations (CPU and memory) for the existing pods, rather than changing the number of pod instances. At its core, this approach involves modifying the computational power and memory capacity allocated to running pods, similar to upgrading or downgrading the specifications of a virtual machine. This method proves particularly valuable for stateful applications like databases, where data consistency and state maintenance are critical and splitting workloads across multiple instances might be complex or undesirable. Thus, by fine-tuning resource allocations at the pod level, vertical scaling enables precise optimization of resource usage, ensuring applications have exactly what they need to perform efficiently without waste. The strategy often proves less disruptive than horizontal scaling in certain scenarios, especially for applications that maintain session states or require persistent connections, as it does not involve the complexity of redistributing workloads across multiple instances. For example, when a database needs more processing power, simply increasing its CPU allocation might be more straightforward than implementing database sharding across multiple pods.

- **Cluster Scaling:** This operates at the infrastructure level, focusing on the dynamic management of underlying EC2 instances within an EKS cluster to meet changing workload demands. Unlike pod-level scaling strategies, cluster scaling takes a broader approach by automatically adjusting the total number of worker nodes in response to the cluster's overall resource requirements. This scaling mechanism continuously monitors cluster-wide metrics and workload patterns, adding nodes when resources are constrained or when pods remain unscheduled due to insufficient capacity, and removing nodes during periods of lower demand when existing workloads can be consolidated onto fewer instances. This intelligent resource management directly translates to infrastructure cost optimization, as organizations only pay for the compute resources they actually need at any given time. The system maintains a careful balance between ensuring adequate capacity for both scheduled workloads, and the unexpected demand spikes, while preventing over-provisioning. For instance, during peak business hours, the cluster might automatically expand to accommodate increased traffic, while scaling down during off-hours to minimize costs, all while maintaining enough headroom to handle sudden workload increases or planned deployments. This automated approach to infrastructure scaling ensures optimal resource utilization, while maintaining application performance and reliability across varying workload conditions.

After exploring the fundamental aspects of performance optimization and scaling strategies, in the next section, let us dive deeper into how Kubernetes implements these scaling mechanisms. Therefore, understanding these core concepts is crucial for effectively managing your EKS clusters, and ensuring optimal resource utilization.

# Understanding Kubernetes Scaling Mechanisms

Kubernetes provides a sophisticated and flexible scaling framework that operates at multiple levels within your cluster. Each scaling mechanism serves a specific purpose, working either independently or in concert to maintain application performance and resource efficiency. The interplay between these different scaling types forms the foundation of Kubernetes' adaptive resource management system.

The scaling architecture in Kubernetes can be visualized as a layered approach, starting from individual pod resources up to the cluster infrastructure level. Each layer has its own set of metrics, triggers, and control mechanisms that administrators can configure to achieve their desired outcomes.

In modern cloud-native applications, effective scaling is crucial for maintaining performance while optimizing resource utilization. Kubernetes offers a comprehensive scaling framework that operates at multiple levels, each serving different operational needs and use cases. Thus, understanding these mechanisms is necessary for building resilient and efficient EKS deployments.

Kubernetes supports three primary scaling mechanisms, each addressing different aspects of application and infrastructure management. **Horizontal Pod Autoscaling (HPA)** manages the number of pod replicas, **Vertical Pod Autoscaling (VPA)** handles resource allocation adjustments, and **Cluster Autoscaling** manages the underlying node infrastructure. These mechanisms can work independently or in combination to provide comprehensive scaling solutions.

Effective scaling decisions rely on accurate and relevant metrics. Kubernetes provides various built-in metrics through its metrics server, including CPU utilization, memory usage, and custom metrics support. These indicators help determine when and how to scale resources. For example, CPU-based scaling might trigger when utilization exceeds 70%, while custom metrics might track application-specific indicators like request latency or queue length.

Making informed scaling decisions requires careful consideration of multiple factors. This includes setting appropriate thresholds, understanding application behavior under different loads, and balancing responsiveness with stability. Best practices focus on avoiding oscillation, ensuring proper resource requests and limits, and implementing gradual scaling policies to prevent system instability.

In the following sections, we will explore each of these aspects in detail, providing practical examples and implementation guidelines for EKS environments. Understanding these fundamentals will enable you to design and implement effective scaling strategies that align with your application requirements and business objectives.

# Horizontal Pod Autoscaling

Horizontal Pod Autoscaling is crucial for EKS applications as it automatically adjusts the number of pod replicas based on observed metrics such as CPU utilization or custom metrics. This dynamic scaling ensures optimal resource utilization and maintains application performance during varying workload conditions. Without HPA, applications might either waste resources during low-traffic periods or suffer performance degradation during traffic spikes. HPA helps achieve the perfect balance between cost efficiency and performance by matching resource allocation to actual demand in real-time.

# HPA Architecture and Components

HPA Architecture and Components represents a sophisticated orchestration system within Kubernetes that automatically adjusts the number of pod replicas based on observed metrics and defined thresholds. This dynamic scaling mechanism is essential for modern cloud-native applications, particularly in environments with variable workload patterns.

The architecture is designed with a clear separation of concerns, combining control systems, metrics collection, and scaling logic into a cohesive system. At its foundation, HPA integrates seamlessly with Kubernetes' core functionality, while providing extensibility for custom requirements. The system operates through a continuous feedback loop, where metrics are collected, analyzed, and acted upon to maintain optimal application performance and resource utilization.

Understanding the HPA architecture and its components is crucial for DevOps engineers and platform administrators, as it forms the backbone of automatic scaling decisions in Kubernetes environments. The system's modular design allows for both simple CPU/memory-based scaling scenarios and complex, custom-metric-driven scaling strategies, making it adaptable to diverse application requirements and organizational needs.

However, before diving into the individual components and their interactions, it is important to note that HPA's architecture follows key principles of cloud-native design: It is declarative, self-healing, and operates autonomously once configured. *Figure* 12.1 shows the key components and their roles in enabling automated scaling, within Kubernetes clusters.

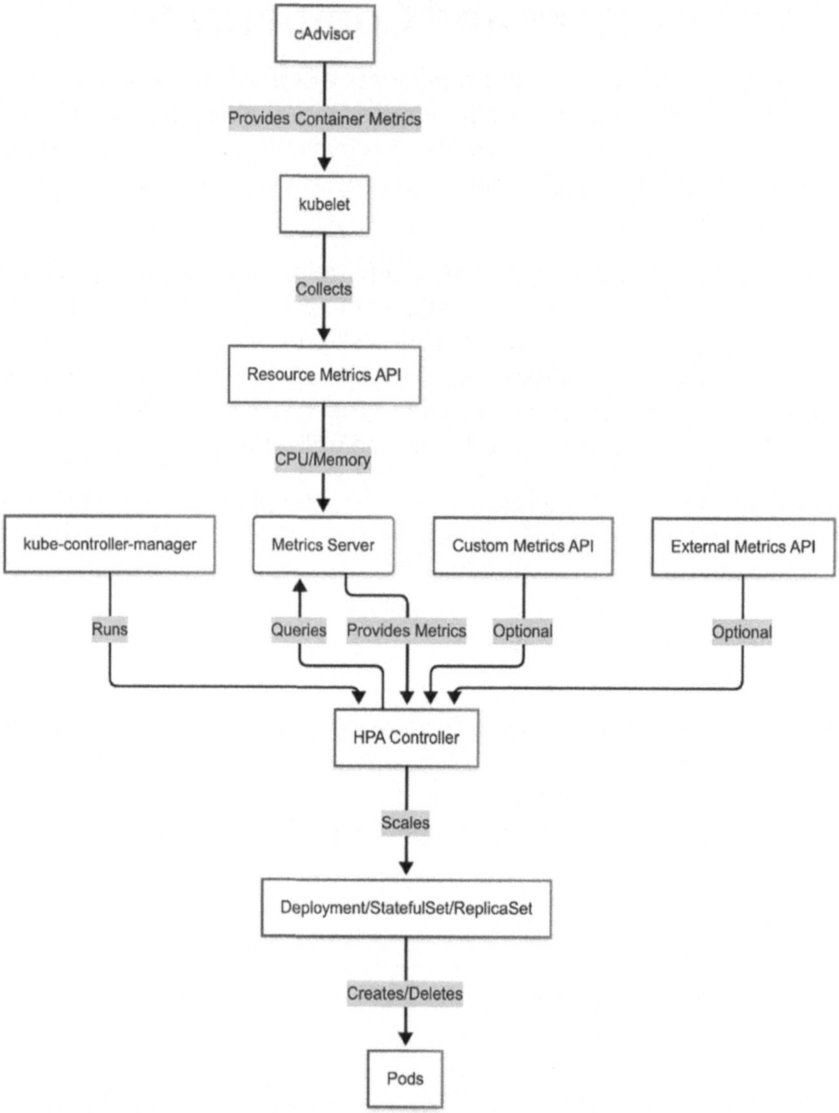


**Figure 12.1:** *Components and Interface of Horizontal Pod Autoscaler*

- **Metrics Server Setup:** The Metrics Server is a crucial component for Horizontal Pod Autoscaling in EKS. It serves as a cluster-wide aggregator of resource usage data, which HPA relies on for making scaling decisions. Setting up the Metrics Server in EKS typically involves deploying it using kubectl apply commands or through Helm. The process includes applying the **`metrics-server`** deployment YAML, ensuring proper RBAC permissions are in place, and validating that the **`metrics-server`** pods are running correctly. Common configuration steps involve setting appropriate flags such as **`--kubelet-`**

**`preferred-address-types`** and **`--kubelet-insecure-tls`**, as well as defining resource requests and limits for the metrics-server itself. After deployment, it is necessary to verify that the metrics-server is correctly reporting metrics, which can be done using kubectl top nodes and kubectl top pods commands. Proper setup of the Metrics Server is fundamental to the effective functioning of HPA in an EKS environment.

- **Custom Metrics Configuration:** Implementing custom metrics for HPA in EKS requires additional setup beyond the basic Metrics Server. This typically involves deploying a Prometheus stack, along with the Prometheus Adapter for Kubernetes metrics or APIs. The adapter plays a crucial role in translating Prometheus metrics into a format that HPA can understand and use for scaling decisions. Configuring custom metrics involves defining specific metric rules in the adapter's configuration, setting up **`ServiceMonitors`** for efficient metric collection, and ensuring that proper RBAC permissions are in place. A key aspect of this process is mapping application-specific metrics to Kubernetes custom metrics API endpoints through the adapter configuration. This setup allows for more sophisticated and application-specific scaling decisions, enabling HPA to respond to a wider range of scenarios beyond just CPU and memory usage.
- **Basic HPA Configuration:** The fundamental configuration of Horizontal Pod Autoscaling in EKS involves creating an HPA resource that specifies key parameters for scaling. This includes defining the target resource (typically a Deployment), setting minimum and maximum replica counts, and specifying target metrics for scaling decisions. A basic HPA configuration would typically include the API version, kind (**`HorizontalPodAutoscaler`**), metadata, and a spec section. Within the spec, you would define the **`scaleTargetRef`** to point to the resource being scaled, set **`minReplicas`** and **`maxReplicas`** to establish scaling boundaries, and specify metrics such as CPU utilization targets. This basic setup forms the foundation for autoscaling in EKS, allowing for automatic adjustment of pod counts, based on observed resource utilization or custom metrics.
- **Advanced HPA Settings:** Advanced HPA configurations in EKS offer more nuanced control over scaling behaviors. These settings include features like scaling policies, stabilization windows, and the ability to use multiple metrics for scaling decisions. You can define different scaling behaviors for scale-up and scale-down events, set cool down periods to prevent rapid fluctuations in pod counts, and implement sophisticated scaling rules based on various metrics. Advanced features allow for percentage-based scaling or fixed-number pod adjustments, setting of stabilization windows to smooth out scaling actions, and the use of multiple metrics including custom application metrics for more informed scaling decisions. These advanced settings also

enable fine-tuning of scale-up and scale-down behaviors separately, and consideration of cross-zone scaling dynamics in multi-zone clusters. Properly configured advanced settings can lead to more stable and efficient autoscaling in complex EKS environments.

- **CPU-Based Scaling:** CPU-based scaling is the most common implementation of HPA in EKS environments. This method works by continuously monitoring the CPU utilization of pods against their defined CPU requests. When implementing CPU-based scaling, it is crucial to set appropriate CPU requests and limits for your pods, as these values directly influence scaling decisions. Understanding the relationship between CPU requests and scaling thresholds is key to effective autoscaling. Considerations should be given to the impact of burst workloads on scaling decisions and the potential for CPU throttling events. Generally, setting the target CPU utilization between 50% and 80% provides a good balance between resource efficiency and headroom for traffic spikes. Regular monitoring and adjustment of these settings, based on observed application behavior is essential for maintaining optimal performance and resource utilization.
- **Memory-Based Scaling:** Memory-based scaling in EKS requires careful consideration due to the non-compressible nature of memory resources. Unlike CPU, which can be overcommitted to some extent, memory usage directly impacts application performance and stability. When implementing memory-based scaling, it is crucial to set appropriate memory requests and limits for your pods. Understanding your application's memory usage patterns is vital, as is considering scenarios involving potential memory leaks. Proper memory monitoring should be implemented to detect anomalies quickly. Due to memory's non-compressible nature, it is generally advisable to set conservative scaling thresholds for memory-based autoscaling. This approach helps prevent situations where pods are terminated due to memory pressure, before new pods can be scheduled, and become ready to handle traffic.
- **Custom Metrics Scaling:** Custom metrics scaling in EKS allows for more sophisticated and application-specific scaling decisions. This approach involves using metrics beyond standard CPU and memory usage, enabling autoscaling, based on business-specific indicators. Implementing custom metrics scaling typically requires setting up Prometheus for metric collection and configuring the Prometheus Adapter to expose these metrics to the Kubernetes API. In the HPA configuration, you would define these custom metrics, specifying the metric name and target values for scaling decisions. For example, you might scale, based on the number of HTTP requests per second, queue length, or any other application-specific metrics. Real-world considerations for custom metrics scaling include monitoring the latency between metric collection and scaling actions, handling potential metric collection failures, and implementing

fallback mechanisms. It is also important to balance multiple metrics for scaling decisions, and understand their impact on both application performance and infrastructure costs. Custom metrics scaling offers great flexibility, but requires careful design and ongoing optimization to be effective.

Horizontal Pod Autoscaling in Amazon EKS enables dynamic workload scaling by balancing performance with resource efficiency. Successful implementation requires careful configuration of metrics and scaling behaviors, while considering integration with other AWS services. Starting with basic resource-based scaling and progressing to more complex metrics, organizations must regularly fine-tune parameters, based on actual workload patterns.

The synergy between HPA and EKS's managed platform provides a robust foundation for scalable, cost-effective applications in AWS. Success depends on continuous monitoring and optimization, ensuring that applications remain responsive and efficient as they scale within the AWS ecosystem. This adaptive approach maximizes the benefits of Kubernetes autoscaling, while maintaining operational efficiency in cloud infrastructure.

# Vertical Pod Autoscaling

Vertical Pod Autoscaling is crucial in EKS environments as it automatically adjusts CPU and memory resource requests as well as limits for pods, based on their actual usage patterns. This is particularly important for applications where horizontal scaling is not optimal or possible, such as stateful applications or those with licensing constraints. VPA helps optimize resource utilization by ensuring pods have the right amount of resources allocated, preventing both underutilization and resource starvation, which is crucial for maintaining application performance and cost efficiency in AWS environments.

# VPA Architecture and Components

The VPA architecture consists of three main components working together in EKS. The VPA Recommender continuously analyses pod resource utilization, and generates optimization recommendations. The VPA Updater applies these recommendations by either updating running pods (with the auto mode), or only affecting new pods (with the initial mode). The VPA Admission Controller modifies new pod requests to include the suggested resource limits and requests. These components work alongside the Metrics Server, which provides the historical resource usage data necessary for making informed scaling decisions. VPA also includes a History Storage component that maintains a record of resource recommendations and usage patterns. *Figure 12.2* illustrates the main components and interactions with VPC architecture in Amazon EKS.

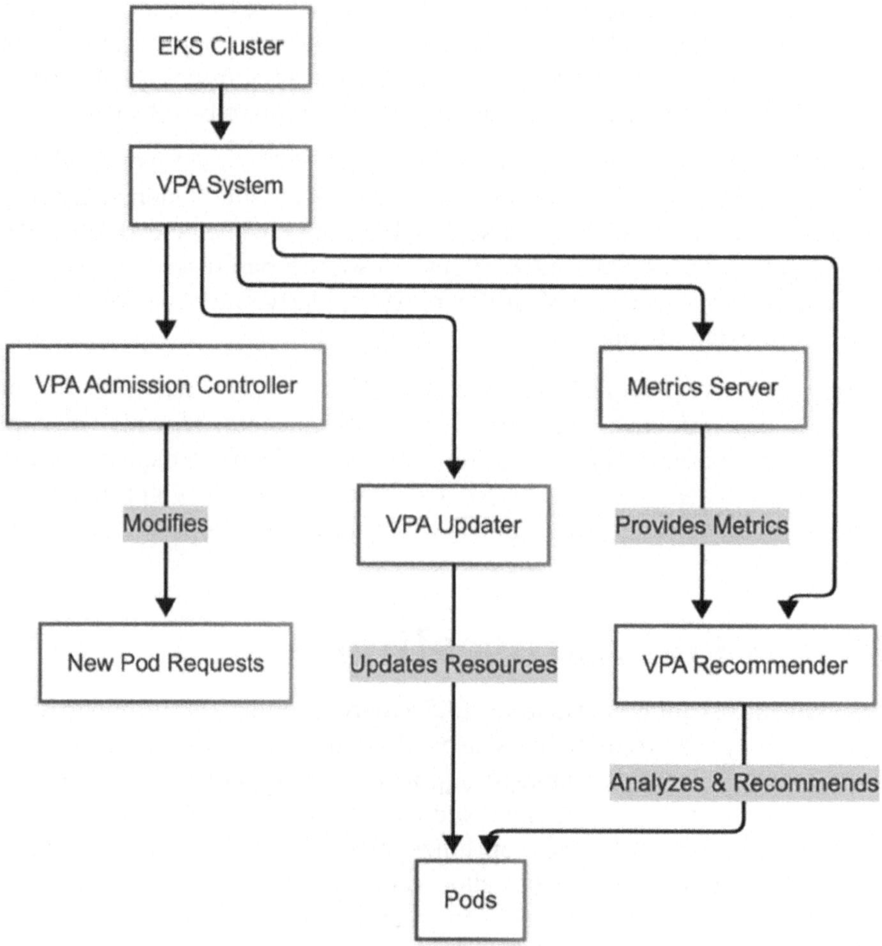


***Figure 12.2:*** *Vertical Pod Autoscaling (VPA) in EKS*

- **VPA Recommender:** The VPA Recommender serves as the analytical brain of the Vertical Pod Autoscaling system in EKS. It continuously monitors and analyzes resource utilization patterns of pods, using sophisticated machine learning algorithms. The Recommender processes historical and real-time data about CPU and memory usage, generating optimized recommendations for resource requests and limits. It considers various factors including usage trends, spikes in resource consumption, and application behavior patterns to make intelligent scaling decisions. The Recommender also implements safety mechanisms to prevent extreme recommendations that could potentially destabilize applications.
- **VPA Updater:** The VPA Updater is responsible for implementing the recommendations provided by the Recommender component. Operating in either "**`Auto`**" or "**`Initial`**" mode, it manages the actual resource adjustment

process. In "**Auto**" mode, it can evict and restart pods with new resource settings, ensuring they align with the latest recommendations. In "**Initial**" mode, it only affects new pods, making it safer for production environments where pod disruption should be minimized. The Updater includes mechanisms to prevent thrashing and ensures smooth transitions during resource adjustments.

- **VPA Admission Controller:** The Admission Controller acts as a gatekeeper for pod creation requests in the EKS cluster. It intercepts pod creation requests, and modifies them to include the VPA's recommended resource requests and limits before they are admitted to the cluster. This component ensures that new pods start with optimized resource allocations, based on the Recommender's analysis. The Admission Controller also validates that the modifications comply with any defined constraints and cluster policies.

# VPA Implementation

Implementing Vertical Pod Autoscaling (VPA) in Amazon EKS follows a structured approach, beginning with essential prerequisites and initial setup.

## Prerequisites and Initial Setup

Ensure your EKS cluster is running, and has the metrics-server installed and operational. Install the required Custom Resource Definitions (CRDs) for VPA. This involves applying the VPA CRDs to your cluster, using kubectl. Next, deploy the VPA components including the Recommender, Updater, and Admission Controller using the official manifests or Helm charts. Verify the installation by checking that all VPA pods are running in the designated namespace:

```
# Install VPA CRDs and components
kubectl apply -f https://raw.githubusercontent.com/kubernetes/au-
toscaler/master/vertical-pod-autoscaler/deploy/vpa-v1-crd.yaml

kubectl apply -f https://raw.githubusercontent.com/kubernetes/au-
toscaler/master/vertical-pod-autoscaler/deploy/vpa-rbac.yaml
kubectl apply -f https://raw.githubusercontent.com/kubernetes/au-
toscaler/master/vertical-pod-autoscaler/deploy/vpa-v1-components.
yaml
```

## Basic VPA Configuration Phase

Start by creating a VPA resource for your target deployment in "Off" mode, which allows for observation of recommendations without implementing actual changes. This conservative approach enables monitoring of VPA's suggestions and validation of its behavior, before making any resource adjustments. The configuration should include appropriate minimum and maximum resource boundaries to ensure safe operation, within your cluster's constraints.

```
apiVersion: autoscaling.k8s.io/v1
kind: VerticalPodAutoscaler
metadata:
  name: my-app-vpa
spec:
  targetRef:
    apiVersion: "apps/v1"
    kind: Deployment
    name: my-app
  updatePolicy:
    updateMode: "Off"
  resourcePolicy:
    containerPolicies:
      - containerName: '*'
        minAllowed:
          cpu: "100m"
          memory: "50Mi"
        maxAllowed:
          cpu: "1"
          memory: "500Mi"
```

## Production Implementation

This phase involves gradually updating the VPA configuration to "Initial" mode for new pods, and then potentially to "Auto" mode for non-critical workloads. The production configuration should include carefully considered resource limits, safety margins, and specific policies for different container types. Implementation should be accompanied by comprehensive monitoring through AWS CloudWatch or similar tools to track resource usage patterns and VPA's effectiveness.

# Best Practices for VPA Implementation

VPA should be configured thoughtfully in EKS environments, starting with the "Off" mode to observe recommendations before enabling automatic updates. It is recommended to use VPA in conjunction with HPA, but not on the same metrics – for example, using VPA for memory and HPA for CPU. Critical pods should use the "**`Initial`**" mode, rather than "**`Auto`**" mode to prevent disruptions from pod restarts. Regular monitoring of VPA recommendations and actual resource usage helps in fine-tuning the configuration. Thus, it is important to set appropriate min/max resource boundaries to prevent excessive scaling, and maintain predictable resource allocation.

```
apiVersion: autoscaling.k8s.io/v1
kind: VerticalPodAutoscaler
metadata:
  name: my-app-vpa
spec:
  targetRef:
    apiVersion: "apps/v1"
    kind: Deployment
    name: my-app
  updatePolicy:
    updateMode: "Auto"
  resourcePolicy:
    containerPolicies:
      - containerName: '*'
        controlledResources: ["cpu", "memory"]
        minAllowed:
          cpu: "200m"
          memory: "100Mi"
        maxAllowed:
          cpu: "2"
          memory: "1Gi"
```

# Maintenance and Optimization

Establish regular review processes for VPA performance and recommendations, implement proper monitoring and alerting for resource changes, and maintain documentation for troubleshooting procedures. Integration with other AWS services and coordination with HPA should be configured as needed. Hence, regular assessment of VPA's impact on application performance and cost optimization ensures continued effectiveness of the autoscaling strategy.

```
# Example of VPA with detailed configuration
apiVersion: autoscaling.k8s.io/v1
kind: VerticalPodAutoscaler
metadata:
  name: my-app-vpa
  annotations:
    vpa-update-policy: "maintenance-window-only"
spec:
  targetRef:
    apiVersion: "apps/v1"
    kind: Deployment
    name: my-app
  updatePolicy:
    updateMode: "Auto"
  resourcePolicy:
    containerPolicies:
```

```
      - containerName: '*'
        mode: "Auto"
        minAllowed:
          cpu: "200m"
          memory: "100Mi"
        maxAllowed:
          cpu: "2"
          memory: "1Gi"
        controlledResources: ["cpu", "memory"]
```

**VPA Limitations**

Despite its benefits, VPA in EKS comes with several important limitations that need careful consideration. A significant constraint is the requirement for pod restarts when implementing resource changes in "**Auto**" mode, which can cause service disruptions. VPA shows incompatibility, when used alongside Horizontal Pod Autoscaler on the same metrics, limiting flexibility in scaling strategies. The system's focus on CPU and memory means other resource types such as network or storage I/O are not addressed in the scaling decisions. There can be notable delays between workload changes and VPA's recommendations, which might not suit environments requiring rapid adaptation. So, the interaction with Cluster Autoscaler needs careful management to prevent unexpected cluster growth and associated costs.

# Integration of HPA and VPA

Integrating VPA with HPA in Amazon EKS requires a strategic approach to leverage the strengths of both mechanisms. The key is to separate their responsibilities: typically, VPA manages memory scaling, while HPA handles CPU-based or custom metric scaling. This separation prevents conflicts and optimizes resource utilization.

Implementation involves creating distinct VPA and HPA resources for the same deployment. VPA is configured to focus on memory metrics, with its update Policy set to either "**Auto**" or "**Initial**". Concurrently, HPA is set up to monitor CPU utilization or other performance metrics.

**For example:**

**VPA Configuration (memory-focused):**

```
apiVersion: autoscaling.k8s.io/v1
kind: VerticalPodAutoscaler
metadata:
  name: my-app-vpa
spec:
  targetRef:
    apiVersion: "apps/v1"
    kind: Deployment
    name: my-app
```

```
    updatePolicy:
      updateMode: "Auto"
    resourcePolicy:
      containerPolicies:
        - containerName: '*'
          controlledResources: ["memory"]
          minAllowed:
            memory: "100Mi"
          maxAllowed:
            memory: "1Gi"
```

**HPA Configuration (CPU-focused):**

```
apiVersion: autoscaling/v2beta1
kind: HorizontalPodAutoscaler
metadata:
  name: my-app-hpa
spec:
  scaleTargetRef:
    apiVersion: apps/v1
    kind: Deployment
    name: my-app
  minReplicas: 2
  maxReplicas: 10
  metrics:
  - type: Resource
    resource:
      name: cpu
      targetAverageUtilization: 50
```

Close monitoring of the interaction between VPA and HPA is crucial, as VPA's resource adjustments can impact HPA's scaling decisions. A staged rollout approach is recommended, starting with non-critical workloads. Regular tuning and observation ensure that both the autoscalers work effectively together. The following *Figure 12.3* provides a visual representation of the best practices and potential pitfalls to consider, when integrating Horizontal Pod Autoscaling (HPA) and Vertical Pod Autoscaling (VPA) in an EKS environment.

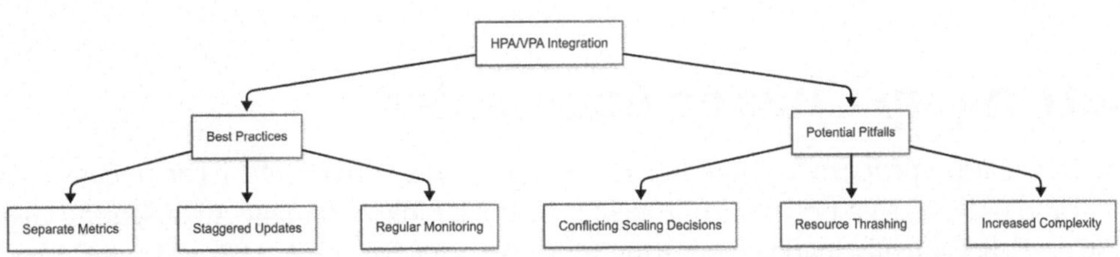


***Figure 12.3:*** *HPA/VPA Integration: Best Practices and Potential Pitfalls*

This integration provides a comprehensive autoscaling solution in EKS, optimizing both pod-level resources and overall application scaling. However, it also introduces complexity, requiring well-trained operations teams, and robust monitoring practices. When properly implemented, this approach leads to improved resource utilization, cost efficiency, and application performance in EKS environments.

# Cluster Autoscaling

Cluster Autoscaling is a critical component for managing EKS infrastructure efficiently by automatically adjusting the number of nodes in response to resource demands. When pods cannot be scheduled due to insufficient cluster capacity, the Cluster Autoscaler automatically provisions new nodes, and when nodes are underutilized, it scales them down to optimize costs. This automation is necessary for handling varying workload demands, ensuring applications have the resources they need, while maintaining cost efficiency in AWS environments. The Cluster Autoscaler works seamlessly with other AWS services, and integrates with EKS's managed node groups and Fargate profiles, providing flexibility in scaling strategies.

Implement effective node group design by using a mix of On-Demand and Spot instances to balance reliability with cost savings. Configure appropriate minimum and maximum node counts to prevent over-provisioning. Use node termination handlers to gracefully handle Spot instance interruptions. Regular monitoring of scaling patterns helps identify opportunities for optimization. Consider using Savings Plans or Reserved Instances for predictable workloads. Implement proper tagging for cost allocation and tracking. Monitor and adjust scaling thresholds, based on actual usage patterns to prevent unnecessary scaling events.

In addition to that, Coordinate Cluster Autoscaling with pod-level autoscaling (HPA and VPA) ensure efficient resource utilization. Consider the interaction between different scaling mechanisms to prevent conflicts. Implement proper readiness and liveness probes to ensure proper scheduling decisions. Use pod disruption budgets to protect critical workloads during scaling events. Consider the impact of cluster scaling on application deployment strategies. Implement proper monitoring and alerting for both infrastructure as well as application metrics to ensure comprehensive scaling oversight.

# Setting up Cluster Autoscaler

The installation process for Cluster Autoscaler begins with creating the necessary IAM roles and policies that grant the autoscaler permissions to manage Auto Scaling Groups (ASGs). This typically involves creating an IAM role with the **`AutoScalingFullAccess`** policy, along with specific permissions for EC2 instance management. The Cluster Autoscaler is then deployed using Helm, or by applying YAML manifests directly to the cluster. When using Helm, the process involves adding the autoscaler repository and installing it with cluster-specific values. The installation must include proper configuration of the cluster name, AWS region, and node group identifiers to ensure that the autoscaler can correctly identify and manage the cluster's resources.

The basic configuration of Cluster Autoscaler requires several key components. First, configure the autoscaler deployment with the correct AWS region and cluster name in its command-line arguments. Essential parameters include setting appropriate minimum and maximum node counts for each Auto Scaling Group, typically defined in the ASG configuration. The following is an example configuration:

```
apiVersion: apps/v1
kind: Deployment
metadata:
  name: cluster-autoscaler
  namespace: kube-system
spec:
  template:
    spec:
      containers:
      - command:
        - ./cluster-autoscaler
        - --cloud-provider=aws
        - --namespace=kube-system
        - --node-group-auto-discovery=asg:tag=k8s.io/cluster-
autoscaler/enabled,k8s.io/cluster-autoscaler/<cluster-name>
        - --scale-down-delay-after-add=10m
        - --balance-similar-node-groups=true
        - --skip-nodes-with-system-pods=true
```

This configuration should include all the  vital settings such as scan intervals (how often the autoscaler checks for scaling needs), scale-down delay (typically 10 minutes to prevent thrashing), and node group discovery tags. Additionally, set up proper resource requests and limits for the Cluster Autoscaler pods themselves to ensure reliable operation. The basic setup should also include configuring CloudWatch metrics and alarms for monitoring scaling activities.

After installation and basic configuration, validate the setup by monitoring the Cluster Autoscaler logs and testing scaling scenarios. Verify that the autoscaler can successfully add nodes, when pods are pending due to insufficient resources, and remove the nodes, when the utilization is low. Set up proper monitoring through CloudWatch or other monitoring tools to track scaling activities, and ensure the autoscaler is functioning as expected. This validation phase is crucial for ensuring the autoscaler can effectively manage your cluster's capacity, while maintaining cost efficiency and performance requirements.

Advanced configurations in Amazon EKS Cluster Autoscaler centers around sophisticated node group management and scaling policies that leverage AWS-specific features.

**Node Group Management** in EKS utilizes AWS Auto Scaling Groups (ASGs) with managed node groups, allowing for efficient handling of diverse workload requirements. A production EKS cluster typically implements multiple node groups, each configured with specific EC2 instance types tailored to different workloads. For example, compute-intensive applications might use a node group with C-type instances, while data processing workloads utilize R-type instances. EKS managed node groups can be configured with AWS features such as mixed-instance policies to combine On-Demand and Spot instances, reducing costs, while maintaining reliability. The configuration includes AWS-specific features such as EKS tags for auto-discovery, capacity rebalancing for Spot instances, and integration with AWS Node Termination Handler for graceful pod evacuation. Example configurations in EKS often include:

```
eksctl create cluster --name=eks-cluster \
--managed \
--node-type=m5.large \
--nodes-min=2 \
--nodes-max=10 \
--node-volume-size=50 \
--node-labels="workload=general" \
--asg-access
```

**Scaling Policies** in EKS context leverage AWS Auto Scaling Group policies and CloudWatch metrics for more refined control. These policies are configured to work with EKS-specific constraints and AWS service limits, ensuring smooth scaling operations. The configuration includes EKS-specific settings such as launch templates, custom CloudWatch metrics, and AWS Auto Scaling Group parameters. Scaling decisions can be influenced by AWS-specific metrics like EC2 capacity availability and Spot instance interruption notices. Advanced configurations often integrate with AWS services like CloudWatch for monitoring, EventBridge for automation, and AWS Systems Manager for parameter management. A typical scaling policy configuration in EKS might include:

```
apiVersion: apps/v1
kind: Deployment
metadata:
  name: cluster-autoscaler
spec:
  template:
    spec:
      containers:
      - command:
```

```
        - ./cluster-autoscaler
        - --cloud-provider=aws
        - --aws-region=region-name
        - --node-group-auto-discovery=asg:tag=k8s.io/cluster-au-
toscaler/enabled
        - --scale-down-delay-after-add=10m
        - --balance-similar-node-groups=true
        - --expander=least-waste
```

These EKS-specific configurations enable organizations to fully leverage AWS capabilities, while maintaining efficient cluster operations. Regular monitoring through AWS CloudWatch and cost analysis via AWS Cost Explorer help optimize these configurations for both performance and cost-effectiveness in the AWS environment.

The best practices for EKS Cluster Autoscaling begin with proper AWS infrastructure setup and configuration. Implement multi-AZ deployments using managed node groups with appropriate instance diversity, combining On-Demand and Spot instances for cost optimization. Configure proper IAM roles with least-privilege access and implement comprehensive AWS tagging strategies for resource management. Set up CloudWatch monitoring dashboards specifically for autoscaling metrics, including custom metrics for application-specific scaling needs. Essential configurations include setting appropriate pod disruption budgets, implementing proper node draining procedures through AWS Node Termination Handler, and configuring scaling thresholds, based on historical workload patterns analyzed through CloudWatch Insights.

Troubleshooting in EKS Cluster Autoscaling requires a systematic approach focusing on AWS-specific components and Kubernetes integration points. Common issues often stem from AWS service quotas, IAM permission misconfigurations, or networking constraints within VPC settings. When investigating scaling issues, start by examining CloudWatch logs for autoscaler events and AWS API calls. Use kubectl and AWS CLI commands to gather diagnostic information:

```
# Check autoscaler logs
kubectl -n kube-system logs -f deployment/cluster-autoscaler

# Verify node group status
aws eks describe-nodegroup --cluster-name <cluster>
--nodegroup-name <nodegroup>

# Monitor scaling events
aws cloudwatch get-metric-statistics --metric-name GroupDesired-
Capacity --namespace AWS/AutoScaling
```

Implement proactive monitoring by setting up CloudWatch alarms for critical metrics such as failed scaling activities, EC2 instance launch failures, and pod scheduling issues. When scaling problems occur, systematically check for resource quotas, node selector/affinity rules, and AWS service limits. Regular maintenance should include reviewing and updating scaling configurations, based on CloudWatch metrics and Cost Explorer data, ensuring optimal performance and cost efficiency.

# Karpenter

This represents a next-generation Kubernetes cluster autoscaler designed specifically for AWS workloads, offering significant improvements over the traditional Cluster Autoscaler. Unlike the traditional Cluster Autoscaler that works with predefined Auto Scaling Groups, Karpenter directly provisions EC2 instances based on pod requirements, providing faster and more efficient scaling. It integrates deeply with AWS services, utilizing EC2 Fleet and Spot Instance integration for optimal instance selection and cost management. Karpenter makes real-time decisions about instance types, sizes, and purchase options (On-Demand/Spot) based on actual workload requirements, rather than being constrained by predetermined node groups.

Setting up Karpenter in EKS involves creating appropriate IAM roles and provisioners that define scaling behaviors. A typical Karpenter configuration includes:

```
apiVersion: karpenter.sh/v1alpha5
kind: Provisioner
metadata:
  name: default
spec:
  requirements:
    - key: "node.kubernetes.io/instance-type"
      operator: In
      values: ["m5.large", "m5.2xlarge", "c5.large", "r5.large"]
  limits:
    resources:
      cpu: "1000"
      memory: 1000Gi
  providerRef:
    name: default
  ttlSecondsAfterEmpty: 30
```

Karpenter excels in scaling scenarios requiring fast response times and diverse instance types. It significantly reduces scaling latency compared to traditional Cluster Autoscaler, often provisioning nodes in under a minute. The solution automatically bins workloads to appropriate instance types, optimizes instance selection for cost efficiency, and rapidly deprovisions unused capacity. This results in better resource utilization, and potentially significant cost savings, especially in dynamic environments with varying workload patterns. Additionally, Karpenter's integration with AWS features such as Spot Instances and capacity-optimized allocation strategies provides enhanced cost optimization capabilities, while maintaining workload reliability.

Amazon EKS provides two robust autoscaling solutions: The traditional Cluster Autoscaler and Karpenter. The Cluster Autoscaler, with its mature architecture and reliance on Auto Scaling Groups, offers predictable scaling behavior, and remains a solid choice for standard workload requirements. Karpenter, designed specifically for AWS, provides faster scaling, intelligent instance selection, and simplified operations through direct EC2 integration, making it particularly effective for dynamic workloads and cost optimization.

The choice between these solutions depends on specific needs: Organizations valuing stability and familiar AWS constructs might prefer Cluster Autoscaler, while those prioritizing efficiency and reduced operational overhead might choose Karpenter. Some organizations effectively utilize both solutions for different workload types. While Cluster Autoscaler continues to serve reliably, Karpenter's AWS-native approach represents the evolution of cluster autoscaling in EKS, offering enhanced capabilities for modern cloud-native applications.

Organizations should evaluate both options, based on their specific requirements, considering workload patterns, operational complexity, cost optimization needs, and team expertise to ensure optimal cluster performance and cost efficiency.

# Resource Optimization

Resource optimization in EKS is crucial for maintaining efficient operations, while controlling cloud costs. It involves carefully balancing compute resources, memory allocation, and storage utilization across containers and nodes. Proper resource optimization ensures that applications have the resources they need to perform optimally, while preventing over-provisioning that leads to unnecessary costs. In EKS environments, this becomes particularly important due to the direct correlation between resource usage and AWS billing, where inefficient resource allocation can significantly impact operational costs.

Common scenarios where resource optimization proves critical include microservices architectures where hundreds of containers run simultaneously, each requiring precise resource allocation. Machine learning workloads benefit from optimized GPU and memory resources, ensuring expensive compute resources are fully utilized. E-commerce applications need optimization during varying traffic patterns, ensuring that resources scale efficiently during peak times and scale down during quiet periods. Development and testing environments benefit from optimization to reduce costs during non-business hours. Batch processing jobs require optimization to ensure efficient resource usage during processing windows, while releasing resources when idle.

Utilize AWS cost optimization features such as Spot Instances that are appropriate for non-critical workloads. Implement proper tagging strategies for cost allocation and tracking. Use AWS Savings Plans or Reserved Instances for predictable workloads. Regularly review and adjust resource allocations, based on actual usage patterns. Leverage AWS Compute Optimizer for EC2 instance recommendations. Use AWS Systems Manager for configuration management, and implement AWS Budgets for cost control as well as alerting. Also, utilize AWS Organizations for multi-account resource optimization strategies.

# Resource Requests and Limits

Resource Requests and Limits in Amazon EKS represent critical configurations that directly impact application performance, cluster efficiency, and cost optimization. These settings define the minimum guaranteed resources (requests) and maximum allowable resources (limits) for containers running in EKS pods. In AWS environments, proper configuration of these parameters is particularly pivotal as they influence pod scheduling, node utilization, and ultimately, the AWS infrastructure costs. Understanding how to calculate and implement these settings effectively ensures optimal resource utilization across your EKS cluster, while maintaining application performance and controlling costs.

Calculation strategies involve analyzing workload patterns through AWS CloudWatch metrics, Container Insights, and Kubernetes monitoring tools to determine appropriate resource values. These calculations must consider the specific characteristics of AWS instance types, pod density goals, and cost implications. Implementation guidelines focus on translating these calculations into practical Kubernetes configurations, while adhering to AWS best practices for resource management. Both aspects require careful consideration of AWS-specific features, such as instance type capabilities, auto-scaling behaviors, and cost optimization opportunities, to create an efficient and cost-effective EKS environment.

## Resource Requests and Limits in Amazon EKS

Calculation strategies for resource requests and limits in EKS require a data-driven approach combined with practical application monitoring. Start by analyzing historical resource usage patterns through CloudWatch Container Insights or Prometheus metrics to establish the baseline requirements. CPU requests should typically be set at the P50 (median) usage level, while limits can be set at P90 or P95, allowing for traffic spikes. Memory requests should be set based on P90 usage patterns since memory is non-compressible and critical for application stability. The calculation process should consider peak usage patterns, daily/weekly trends, and specific application behavior under load. Tools like AWS CloudWatch Container Insights provide valuable metrics for these calculations:

```
# Example resource calculation based on metrics
CPU Request = P50 of historical CPU usage
CPU Limit = P90 of historical CPU usage
Memory Request = P90 of historical memory usage
Memory Limit = P90 + 20% safety margin
```

# Implementation Guidelines and Best Practices

Resource implementation in EKS follows Kubernetes best practices, while considering AWS-specific considerations. Start with conservative resource settings and adjust based on monitoring data. Implement resources in your deployment manifests with clear requests and limits:

```
# Example implementation with requests and limits
apiVersion: apps/v1
kind: Deployment
metadata:
  name: app-deployment
spec:
  template:
    spec:
      containers:
      - name: app
        resources:
          requests:
            cpu: "250m"      # 0.25 vCPU
            memory: "512Mi"  # 512 MiB
          limits:
            cpu: "500m"      # 0.5 vCPU
            memory: "1Gi"    # 1 GiB
```

# Node Optimization

Node Configuration Optimization in Amazon EKS involves strategic decisions about infrastructure components that directly impact cluster performance, scalability, and cost-effectiveness. This optimization process focuses on selecting appropriate EC2 instance types, and implementing effective node group strategies that align with specific workload requirements, while leveraging AWS's diverse instance offerings. Proper node configuration is crucial for maintaining optimal resource utilization, ensuring cost efficiency, and supporting various application workload patterns across your EKS cluster.

## Instance Type Selection in EKS

The selection of EC2 instance types for EKS nodes requires careful consideration of workload characteristics and business requirements. General-purpose instances (t3/t4g, m5/m6g families) serve as excellent baseline choices for diverse workloads, while compute-optimized instances (c5/c6g) support CPU-intensive applications, and memory-optimized instances (r5/r6g) handle data-intensive workloads. Consider AWS Graviton processors for improved price-performance ratios, especially for ARM-compatible workloads. Instance selection should account for pod density, resource requirements, and network performance needs. For instance, if your applications require high pod density, choose instances with sufficient ENI capacity and IP addresses. The following is an example implementation:

```
apiVersion: eksctl.io/v1alpha5
kind: ClusterConfig
metadata:
  name: production-eks
spec:
  nodeGroups:
    - name: general-workload
      instanceTypes: ["m6g.xlarge", "m6i.xlarge"]
      desiredCapacity: 3
      minSize: 2
      maxSize: 10
    - name: compute-intensive
      instanceTypes: ["c6g.2xlarge", "c6i.2xlarge"]
      desiredCapacity: 2
      labels: {workload-type: compute}
```

## Node Group Strategies in EKS

Node group strategies involve organizing nodes to optimize resource utilization, cost, and operational efficiency. Implement multiple node groups to separate different workload types and requirements. Use EKS managed node groups for simplified operations and automatic node updates. Combine On-Demand and Spot instances strategically – use On-Demand for critical workloads and Spot instances for fault-tolerant applications to optimize costs. Consider implementing node groups across multiple Availability Zones for high availability. Example configuration:

```
apiVersion: eksctl.io/v1alpha5
kind: ClusterConfig
metadata:
  name: production-eks
spec:
  managedNodeGroups:
    - name: critical-workload
```

```
      instanceTypes: ["m6i.xlarge"]
      desiredCapacity: 3
      minSize: 2
      maxSize: 5
      availabilityZones: ["us-west-2a", "us-west-2b"]
      labels: {workload: critical}
    - name: spot-workload
      instanceTypes: ["m6g.xlarge", "m6i.xlarge", "m5.xlarge"]
      desiredCapacity: 2
      spotInstancePools: 3
      labels: {workload: spot}
      taints:
        - key: spotInstance
          value: "true"
          effect: PreferNoSchedule
```

# Network Performance Tuning

Network performance optimization in EKS is crucial for maintaining efficient container communications, ensuring security, and maximizing throughput across the cluster. The configuration of the Container Network Interface (CNI) and implementation of network policies directly impacts application performance, security posture, and overall cluster efficiency. Proper network tuning becomes increasingly important as clusters grow and application communication patterns become more complex.

Network performance issues in EKS commonly manifest in several key scenarios. High latency between services often stems from improper CNI configuration, particularly around MTU settings, or overly restrictive network policies that impede efficient communication. Pod-to-pod communication problems frequently arise from misconfigured network policies, kube-proxy issues, or DNS resolution failures within the cluster. Organizations commonly encounter insufficient IP addresses for pods, requiring adjustments to **`WARM_IP_TARGET`** and **`MINIMUM_IP_TARGET`** settings in CNI configuration or enabling prefix delegation for higher pod density. Intermittent connection drops may occur due to EC2 instance network performance issues, DNS timeouts, or improperly configured TCP keep alive settings. External connectivity slowdowns often result from suboptimal NAT gateway configurations, VPC networking bottlenecks, or AWS service endpoint issues. These scenarios particularly impact high-traffic microservices architectures, data-intensive applications, and globally distributed systems.

*Figure* 12.4 shows the main components of network performance tuning and integration with AWS services. The dotted lines show the relationship between EKS networking components and their corresponding AWS services, demonstrating how network performance tuning spans both Kubernetes and AWS-specific optimizations.

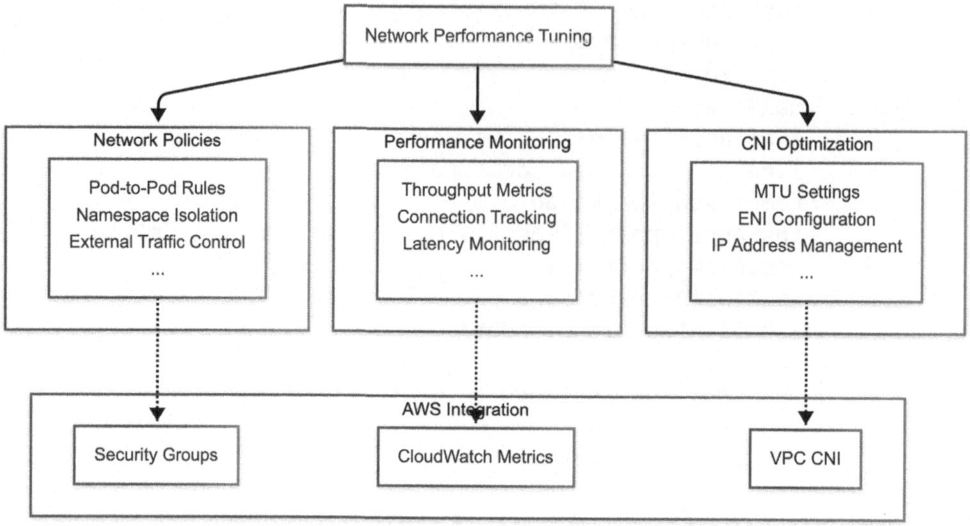


***Figure 12.4:*** *Network Performance Components*

# CNI Optimization

Amazon EKS's AWS VPC CNI plugin requires specific optimization to achieve optimal performance. The configuration involves tuning parameters such as IP address management, ENI configurations, and prefix delegation to maximize pod density and network performance. The key optimization areas include configuring appropriate **WARM_IP_TARGET** and **MINIMUM_IP_TARGET** values to ensure efficient IP address pre-allocation, enabling prefix delegation for increased pod density, and optimizing MTU settings for better throughput. Please refer the following implementation example:

```
apiVersion: v1
kind: ConfigMap
metadata:
  name: amazon-vpc-cni
  namespace: kube-system
data:
  WARM_IP_TARGET: "5"
  MINIMUM_IP_TARGET: "2"
  ENABLE_PREFIX_DELEGATION: "true"
  ENABLE_POD_ENI: "true"
  MTU: "9001"
```

# Network Policies

Network policies in EKS provide crucial security controls by defining how pods communicate with each other and external resources. Implementation should follow a zero-trust approach, starting with restrictive policies, and selectively allowing required communications. Example of a basic network policy:

```
apiVersion: networking.k8s.io/v1
kind: NetworkPolicy
metadata:
  name: restrict-traffic
spec:
  podSelector:
    matchLabels:
      app: backend
  policyTypes:
  - Ingress
  - Egress
  ingress:
  - from:
    - podSelector:
        matchLabels:
          app: frontend
    ports:
    - protocol: TCP
      port: 8080
  egress:
  - to:
    - namespaceSelector:
        matchLabels:
          purpose: monitoring
    ports:
    - protocol: TCP
      port: 9090
```

Resource optimization in Amazon EKS encompasses three critical pillars: resource management through requests and limits, node configuration optimization, and network performance tuning. These components work together to create an efficient and cost-effective Kubernetes environment. Resource requests and limits provide the foundation for container-level resource allocation, while node configuration optimization ensures efficient infrastructure utilization through strategic instance type selection and node group management. Network performance tuning, including CNI optimization and network policies, completes the picture by ensuring secure and efficient communication.

Successful EKS resource optimization requires continuous monitoring and adjustment, based on actual usage patterns, along with strategic infrastructure decisions that balance performance requirements with cost efficiency. Regular evaluation using AWS CloudWatch metrics and cost analysis tools helps maintain optimal resource utilization while supporting business objectives. As EKS environments evolve, this iterative approach to resource optimization ensures clusters remain efficient, cost-effective, and performant, enabling organizations to maximize the benefits of their containerized applications in AWS.

## Troubleshooting

Resolving network performance issues requires a systematic approach beginning with comprehensive diagnostics. Start by collecting baseline metrics, using kubectl commands for resource usage and CloudWatch metrics for network throughput and packet loss. Network policy debugging should include detailed policy analysis using kubectl describe network policy and temporary policy disablement to isolate issues. CNI troubleshooting involves examining CNI logs, verifying ENI and IP address assignments, and reviewing CNI metrics through the metrics endpoint. Performance testing should utilize tools like iperf3 for network throughput testing and implement distributed tracing with AWS X-Ray to identify latency issues. AWS-specific checks should include reviewing VPC Flow Logs, consulting AWS Trusted Advisor for networking recommendations, and analyzing the AWS Personal Health Dashboard for potential AWS networking issues. Advanced diagnostics may require using tcpdump or Wireshark for detailed packet analysis, implementing eBPF-based tools for kernel-level network insights, and leveraging AWS Network Insights for VPC-level network path analysis. This systematic approach ensures thorough investigation and resolution of network performance issues in EKS environments.

# Performance Benchmarking in EKS

Performance benchmarking in EKS is vital for establishing baseline performance metrics, identifying potential bottlenecks, and ensuring optimal resource utilization across containerized applications. It provides valuable insights into how applications behave under various load conditions, helping organizations make informed decisions about resource allocation, scaling strategies, and infrastructure investments. In the context of EKS, benchmarking is particularly important due to the complex interplay between Kubernetes components, AWS infrastructure, and application workloads. It helps in fine-tuning cluster configurations, optimizing costs, and maintaining consistent application performance as workloads evolve.

Common scenarios for performance benchmarking in EKS include evaluating different instance types for node groups, assessing the impact of auto-scaling policies, and comparing various CNI configurations. Benchmarking is essential when migrating applications to EKS, helping to right-size resources and validate performance expectations. It's also crucial for capacity planning, allowing organizations to predict resource needs for future growth. Performance benchmarks are valuable for comparing different deployment strategies, such as evaluating the performance impact of using Fargate versus EC2 instances for specific workloads.

Effective performance benchmarking in Amazon EKS requires a structured approach that combines appropriate tools, frameworks, and comprehensive metrics collection. This methodical process is crucial for accurately assessing and optimizing the performance of containerized applications within the EKS environment. By implementing robust benchmarking methodologies, organizations can gain valuable insights into their cluster's behavior under various conditions, identify performance bottlenecks, and make data-driven decisions to enhance overall system efficiency.

The selection of appropriate benchmarking tools and frameworks is fundamental to obtaining reliable and actionable performance data in EKS. Popular tools include open-source solutions such as k6, Apache JMeter, and Gatling for load testing, and Prometheus with Grafana for metrics visualization. EKS-specific tools such as kube-bench for Kubernetes security benchmarking and Helm for deploying consistent test environments are also valuable. For example, a basic k6 load test script for an EKS-hosted application might look like:

```
import http from 'k6/http';
import { check, sleep } from 'k6';

export let options = {
  stages: [
    { duration: '2m', target: 100 }, // Ramp up to 100 users
    { duration: '5m', target: 100 }, // Stay at 100 users for 5
minutes
    { duration: '2m', target: 0 },   // Ramp down to 0 users
  ],
};

export default function() {
  let res = http.get('http://my-eks-service.default.svc.cluster.
local');
  check(res, { 'status was 200': (r) => r.status == 200 });
  sleep(1);
}
```

# Metrics Collection

Effective metrics collection is crucial for comprehensive performance analysis in EKS. Key areas to focus on include cluster-level metrics such as CPU utilization, memory usage, and network throughput; pod-level metrics including resource consumption, start-up times, and scaling behavior; application-specific metrics like response times, error rates, and throughput, as well as infrastructure metrics covering EC2 instance performance and EBS volume IOPS.

Implement a multi-layered approach to metrics collection. Combine Prometheus for detailed in-cluster metrics with CloudWatch Container Insights for AWS-specific data. Use custom exporters for application-specific metrics not covered by standard tools. Implement proper tagging and labeling strategies to correlate metrics across different layers of the stack. For comprehensive analysis, integrate metrics from various sources, including CloudWatch Container Insights for EKS-specific metrics, Prometheus ServiceMonitors for application-level metrics, AWS X-Ray for tracing and latency analysis, and VPC Flow Logs for network performance data.

# Setting up Monitoring

Effective monitoring is vital for maintaining and optimizing EKS cluster performance and reliability. The combination of Prometheus for metrics collection and Grafana for visualization provides a comprehensive monitoring solution that integrates well with EKS's architecture. This setup enables organizations to track cluster health, application performance, and resource utilization, while providing actionable insights for optimization and troubleshooting.

## Prometheus Configuration

Prometheus configuration in EKS involves setting up the Prometheus operator and configuring appropriate ServiceMonitors to collect metrics from various cluster components. The setup typically begins with deploying Prometheus, using Helm charts, configured specifically for EKS environments. A typical Prometheus configuration includes service discovery for auto-detection of pods and services, retention policies for metrics data, and appropriate resource allocation.

```
# Example prometheus Configuration
apiVersion: monitoring.coreos.com/v1
kind: Prometheus
metadata:
  name: prometheus
  namespace: monitoring
spec:
  serviceAccountName: prometheus
  serviceMonitorSelector:
    matchLabels:
      release: prometheus
  resources:
    requests:
      memory: "512Mi"
      cpu: "500m"
    limits:
      memory: "2Gi"
      cpu: "1000m"
```

```
  storage:
    volumeClaimTemplate:
      spec:
        storageClassName: gp2
        resources:
          requests:
            storage: 50Gi
  additionalScrapeConfigs:
    - job_name: 'eks-pods'
      kubernetes_sd_configs:
        - role: pod
      relabel_configs:
        - source_labels: [__meta_kubernetes_pod_annotation_pro-
metheus_io_scrape]
          action: keep
          regex: true
```

# Grafana Dashboards

Grafana implementation in EKS focuses on creating comprehensive dashboards that visualize key metrics from both Prometheus and AWS CloudWatch. Configure Grafana with appropriate data sources, and create dashboards that provide insights into cluster performance, application metrics, and resource utilization.

```
# Example configuration for different aspects of the EKS cluster
apiVersion: integreatly.org/v1alpha1
kind: GrafanaDashboard
metadata:
  name: eks-cluster-monitoring
  namespace: monitoring
spec:
  json: |
    {
      "dashboard": {
        "id": null,
        "title": "EKS Cluster Overview",
        "panels": [
          {
            "title": "Node CPU Usage",
            "type": "graph",
            "datasource": "Prometheus",
            "targets": [
              {
                "expr": "sum(rate(container_cpu_usage_seconds_to-
tal{container!=\"\"}[5m])) by (node)"
              }
            ]
```

```
            },
            {
              "title": "Memory Usage",
              "type": "graph",
              "datasource": "Prometheus",
              "targets": [
                {
                  "expr": "sum(container_memory_usage_bytes) by
(node)"
                }
              ]
            }
          ]
        }
      }
```

To conclude, these monitoring components work together to provide comprehensive visibility into your EKS environment. Regular maintenance includes updating Prometheus and Grafana configurations, refining alert thresholds, and adjusting dashboard layouts, based on operational needs. The integration with AWS-specific features such as CloudWatch Container Insights enhances the monitoring capability, providing a complete view of both Kubernetes and AWS resources. This setup enables proactive management of cluster health and performance, supporting both day-to-day operations, and long-term capacity planning.

# Analysis and Optimization

Effective analysis and optimization in EKS environments require a systematic approach to identifying performance bottlenecks, and implementing targeted improvements. This process involves analyzing metrics across multiple layers of the stack, from container-level performance to cluster-wide resource utilization, and implementing strategic optimizations that enhance the overall system efficiency. Understanding the interplay between EKS components, AWS infrastructure, and application workloads is crucial for making informed optimization decisions.

## Performance Bottleneck Identification

Identifying performance bottlenecks in EKS requires comprehensive analysis of metrics collected through CloudWatch, Prometheus, and other monitoring tools. Start by examining key performance indicators such as CPU utilization, memory usage, network throughput, and API server response times. Use AWS X-Ray for tracing request paths, and identifying latency issues across microservices. Common bottlenecks often emerge in resource constraints, network configuration, or scaling limitations. For example, analyzing pod start-up latency might reveal issues with image pull times, or resource constraints:

```
apiVersion: v1
kind: Pod
metadata:
  name: performance-analysis
  annotations:
    prometheus.io/scrape: "true"
    prometheus.io/port: "9090"
spec:
  containers:
  - name: analysis-container
    image: performance-tools:latest
    resources:
      requests:
        memory: "256Mi"
        cpu: "250m"
      limits:
        memory: "512Mi"
        cpu: "500m"
```

CloudWatch Insights queries can help identify specific bottlenecks:

```
fields @timestamp, @message
| filter kubernetes.container_name like /app.*/
| stats avg(duration) as avg_duration,
        max(duration) as max_duration,
        count(*) as request_count
| sort avg_duration desc
```

# Optimization Strategies

Once bottlenecks are identified, implement targeted optimization strategies that address specific performance issues, while considering the broader impact on the EKS cluster. This might involve adjusting resource allocations, optimizing container images, or refining auto-scaling configurations. Implement changes systematically, starting with non-production environments to validate improvements.

Optimization strategies should consider both immediate performance improvements, and long-term scalability. This includes fine-tuning node group configurations, implementing efficient service mesh patterns, and optimizing network policies. Regular performance testing validates the effectiveness of implemented optimizations. The following is an example of optimization configuration:

```
apiVersion: autoscaling/v2
kind: HorizontalPodAutoscaler
metadata:
  name: optimized-scaling
spec:
  scaleTargetRef:
```

```
    apiVersion: apps/v1
    kind: Deployment
    name: target-deployment
  minReplicas: 2
  maxReplicas: 10
  metrics:
  - type: Resource
    resource:
      name: cpu
      target:
        type: Utilization
        averageUtilization: 65
  behavior:
    scaleDown:
      stabilizationWindowSeconds: 300
    scaleUp:
      stabilizationWindowSeconds: 60
```

# Load Testing for EKS

In the dynamic world of containerized applications running on Amazon EKS, understanding how your systems perform under pressure is not just a best practice–it is a critical necessity. Load testing serves as your window into application behavior under various conditions, helping to ensure that your services remain resilient and responsive, regardless of the user demands.

As organizations increasingly deploy mission-critical applications on EKS, the ability to accurately simulate real-world usage patterns, and stress test your infrastructure becomes paramount. Load testing helps answer crucial questions such as: Will your applications scale effectively during peak traffic? How does your system handle sudden spikes in user activity? Are your auto-scaling configurations optimized for your workload patterns?

Modern load testing in EKS environments goes beyond simple stress testing. It encompasses a comprehensive approach that includes selecting appropriate testing tools, implementing various testing strategies, and analyzing results to optimize performance. Hence, whether you are using popular tools such as k6 for its developer-friendly approach or JMeter for its extensive testing capabilities, the goal remains the same, that is to ensure your EKS applications deliver consistent performance under any condition.

In this section, we will explore the essential components of effective load testing in EKS environments. We shall also examine different testing tools and their specific strengths, dive into various testing strategies from gradual load increases to spike testing, and discuss how to analyze and act on testing results. By understanding and implementing these practices, you will definitely be better equipped to maintain high-performing, reliable applications in your EKS clusters.

# Load Testing Tools

The selection of appropriate load testing tools plays a pivotal role in effectively evaluating EKS application performance. Modern load testing tools must not only generate realistic user traffic, but also integrate seamlessly with Kubernetes environments, while providing detailed insights into the system behavior.

Therefore, let us explore two powerful load testing tools that are particularly well-suited for EKS environments. Each brings unique strengths to performance testing containerized applications.

## K6 for Load Testing

K6 stands out in the load testing landscape through its innovative approach to performance testing, combining developer-friendly scripting with powerful cloud-native capabilities. At its core, K6 brings together modern software development practices with robust performance testing features, making it particularly well-suited for organizations running applications on EKS. The tool's architecture reflects a deep understanding of contemporary DevOps practices and cloud-native requirements, providing features that align perfectly with the demands of modern application testing.

The true strength of K6 lies in its ability to seamlessly integrate with existing development workflows, while providing enterprise-grade load testing capabilities. Its lightweight, efficient architecture coupled with extensive protocol support makes it an ideal choice for testing complex, distributed systems running on EKS. The tool's approach to resource utilization and test execution reflects a deep understanding of cloud environments, allowing organizations to conduct comprehensive performance testing without the overhead traditionally associated with enterprise load testing tools. Thus, whether used in local development environments or as part of automated CI/CD pipelines, K6 provides the flexibility and power needed to ensure application performance at scale.

K6 maintains a remarkably low memory footprint, while efficiently handling concurrent executions. It supports a wide range of protocols including HTTP/HTTPS, WebSocket, and gRPC, making it versatile for different application types. The tool's efficient resource utilization makes it ideal for large-scale load testing in cloud environments.

Modern development workflows benefit from K6's straightforward CI/CD integration capabilities. The tool can be easily incorporated into the existing pipelines, with support for major CI/CD platforms. Test results can trigger pipeline decisions, enabling automated performance testing as part of the deployment process.

```
# This configuration shows how K6 can be integrated into a CI/CD
pipeline
# to automate performance testing during deployments
performance:
  image: loadimpact/k6
  script: k6 run ./tests/performance.js
```

K6 also provides sophisticated testing capabilities, including scenario-based testing, modular test composition, and data-driven testing approaches. Its comprehensive result analysis features enable real-time metrics visualization and performance regression detection, helping teams identify and address performance issues quickly.

The following example K6 test script sets up a load test against an EKS service with four distinct stages of traffic (ramp-up, steady state, peak load, and scale down), while making HTTP GET requests and validating both the response status and performance thresholds. The script uses virtual users to simulate real-world traffic patterns, with built-in checks for response status (200) and response time (<500ms), making it ideal for testing EKS service resilience and performance under different load conditions.

```
// Example K6 test script for EKS service
import http from 'k6/http';
import { check, sleep } from 'k6';

// Load test configuration
export const options = {
    stages: [
        { duration: '3m', target: 50 },     // Ramp-up phase
        { duration: '5m', target: 50 },     // Steady state
        { duration: '2m', target: 100 },    // Peak load
        { duration: '1m', target: 0 },      // Scale down
    ],
};
// Test Execution Logic
export default function() {
    const response = http.get('http://your-eks-service/api/end-
point');

    check(response, {
        'is status 200': (r) => r.status === 200,
        'response time < 500ms': (r) => r.timings.duration < 500
    });

    sleep(1);
}
```

# JMeter for Kubernetes

JMeter provides a comprehensive testing platform with its rich GUI and extensive plugin ecosystem. When deployed in EKS, it can be configured as distributed testing nodes for large-scale load generation.

```
<!-- Example JMeter test plan configuration -->
<?xml version="1.0" encoding="UTF-8"?>
<jmeterTestPlan version="1.2" properties="5.0">
  <hashTree>
    <ThreadGroup guiclass="ThreadGroupGui" testclass="ThreadGroup">
      <elementProp name="ThreadGroup.main_controller">
        <stringProp name="LoopController.loops">100</stringProp>
        <stringProp name="ThreadGroup.num_threads">50</stringProp>
        <stringProp name="ThreadGroup.ramp_time">300</stringProp>
      </elementProp>
      <!-- HTTP Sampler Configuration -->
      <HTTPSamplerProxy>
        <stringProp name="HTTPSampler.domain">your-eks-service</
stringProp>
        <stringProp name="HTTPSampler.port">80</stringProp>
        <stringProp name="HTTPSampler.protocol">http</stringProp>
      </HTTPSamplerProxy>
    </ThreadGroup>
  </hashTree>
</jmeterTestPlan>
```

The above XML code shows a basic test plan structure where the Thread Group configuration specifies 50 concurrent users (threads) executing 100 test iterations, with a gradual ramp-up time of 300 seconds. The HTTP Sampler section defines the target EKS service properties, including domain, port (80), and protocol (http). When deployed in EKS, this configuration allows JMeter pods to distribute the testing load across multiple nodes, effectively simulating large-scale user traffic. The test parameters can be adjusted based on specific performance testing requirements, making it flexible for various load testing scenarios. This setup particularly benefits from Kubernetes' inherent scalability, allowing testers to dynamically adjust the testing capacity as needed.

JMeter for EKS offers several key features and advantages that make it an excellent choice for large-scale performance testing. It seamlessly integrates with Kubernetes, allowing for distributed load generation across multiple pods, which can be easily scaled up or down based on testing requirements. This scalability enables the simulation of massive user loads, closely mimicking real-world traffic patterns. JMeter's rich GUI and extensive plugin ecosystem provide a user-friendly interface for test creation and result analysis, while its compatibility with EKS allows for efficient resource utilization and cost management in the cloud environment. The distributed architecture ensures better test reliability and accuracy, as it can generate load from multiple geographic locations. Additionally, JMeter's open-source nature and strong community support make it a flexible and continuously improving tool for DevOps teams working in Kubernetes environments.

Thus, both JMeter and K6 can be efficiently deployed in Amazon EKS using Kubernetes manifests, as shown in the following code for orchestrated test execution. K6, being cloud-native and designed with containerization in mind, integrates seamlessly with Kubernetes environments, allowing for distributed load testing through simple pod deployments. JMeter, though more traditional, can also be effectively containerized and orchestrated in EKS using custom Docker images and Kubernetes configurations.

```
# Example Kubernetes manifest for test execution
apiVersion: batch/v1
kind: Job
metadata:
  name: load-test
spec:
  template:
    spec:
      containers:
      - name: k6-test
        image: loadimpact/k6
        args: ["run", "/scripts/test.js"]
        volumeMounts:
        - name: test-scripts
          mountPath: /scripts
      volumes:
      - name: test-scripts
        configMap:
          name: test-scripts
      restartPolicy: Never
```

Load testing in Amazon Elastic Kubernetes Service (EKS) is a critical practice for ensuring the reliability, scalability, and performance of applications deployed in containerized environments. As organizations increasingly adopt Kubernetes for orchestrating their containerized workloads, it becomes essential to validate that these systems can handle expected and unexpected traffic patterns effectively. EKS, being a managed Kubernetes service, provides a robust platform for deploying and scaling applications, but it also requires thorough testing to optimize its performance under various load conditions. By implementing strategic load testing approaches in EKS, teams can identify bottlenecks, verify auto-scaling capabilities, and ensure that their applications maintain high performance and availability even under extreme stress. This process not only helps in fine-tuning the application and infrastructure configurations but also provides valuable insights into capacity planning and cost optimization in cloud-native environments. Following are the key testing strategies for EKS Load Testing:

1. **Gradual Load Testing:** Start with a baseline load and gradually increase it to understand system behavior. This helps identify performance bottlenecks and scaling thresholds by incrementally adding load until system performance degrades.
2. **Spike Testing:** Simulate sudden bursts of traffic to test auto-scaling capabilities of EKS clusters. This verifies how well the system handles unexpected traffic spikes and recovers from high-load situations.
3. **Endurance Testing:** Run sustained load tests over extended periods (hours or days) to identify memory leaks, resource exhaustion, or performance degradation over time. This helps verify system stability under continuous load.
4. **Geographic Distribution:** Deploy load generators across multiple AWS regions to simulate realistic user patterns and test latency across different locations. This provides insights into global performance characteristics.
5. **Resource Monitoring:** Continuously monitor cluster metrics, pod scaling, node utilization, and application performance during tests. This helps correlate system behavior with load patterns and identify bottlenecks.
6. **Fault Injection:** Introduce deliberate failures (pod termination, node failures) during load tests to verify system resilience and recovery mechanisms. This ensures the system maintains performance during infrastructure issues.

These strategies should be implemented as part of a comprehensive testing plan, with clear objectives and success criteria for each test scenario.

Thus, establishing robust load testing practices requires a systematic approach that begins with proper test environment setup, and extends through test execution to results documentation. Tests should be conducted in environments that closely mirror production configurations, including all dependent services and integrations. Regular testing schedules should be maintained, with particular emphasis on testing before major releases or infrastructure changes. Documentation of test conditions, results, and optimization efforts ensures knowledge retention, and enables continuous improvement of both testing processes and application performance.

# Conclusion

In this chapter, we covered a comprehensive range of topics related to performance tuning and scaling in Amazon EKS. We began by exploring Kubernetes scaling mechanisms, including Horizontal Pod Autoscaling, Vertical Pod Autoscaling, and

Cluster Autoscaling. The chapter also delved into resource optimization techniques, focusing on efficient management of CPU, memory, and storage resources. We examined node configuration optimization strategies, including instance type selection and node group management, as well as network performance tuning, covering CNI optimization and implementation of network policies. The discussion extended to performance benchmarking methodologies and tools specific to EKS environments, along with setting up and configuring monitoring solutions like Prometheus and Grafana for comprehensive cluster and application monitoring. We explored load testing strategies and tools, including the use of K6 and JMeter for EKS environments, and introduced advanced scaling solutions such as Karpenter, offering the next-generation autoscaling capabilities for AWS workloads. Throughout the chapter, we emphasized on the best practices for implementing and managing these various scaling and optimization techniques in production EKS clusters, including analysis of performance bottlenecks and strategies for ongoing optimization and maintenance. This comprehensive overview will certainly equip readers with the knowledge to effectively manage and scale their containerized applications in AWS environments.

# Points to Remember

- Different scaling mechanisms (HPA, VPA, Cluster Autoscaler) serve different purposes, and can be used together effectively.
- Resource requests and limits are fundamental to proper pod scheduling and resource utilization.
- Node configuration optimization directly impacts cluster efficiency and cost.
- Network performance tuning is crucial for maintaining efficient container communications.
- Proper monitoring setup with Prometheus and Grafana is essential for optimization.
- Regular performance benchmarking helps identify potential bottlenecks early.
- Integration between various AWS services enhances scaling capabilities.
- Cost optimization requires careful balance of resource allocation and utilization.
- Load testing is crucial for validating scaling configurations.
- Karpenter provides the ideal next-generation scaling capabilities, specifically for AWS workloads.

# Multiple Choice Questions

1. What is the primary purpose of Horizontal Pod Autoscaling (HPA) in EKS?
    a. To adjust pod resource limits
    b. To automatically scale the number of pod replicas based on metrics
    c. To scale the cluster nodes
    d. To modify container images
2. Which component is vital for HPA to function in EKS?
    a. CloudWatch
    b. Prometheus
    c. Metrics Server
    d. Grafana
3. What is the main advantage of Karpenter over traditional Cluster Autoscaler?
    a. Lower cost
    b. Direct EC2 instance provisioning without node group constraints
    c. Better security
    d. Faster pod scheduling
4. When implementing VPA, which mode is recommended for critical production workloads?
    a. Auto mode
    b. Initial mode
    c. Off mode
    d. Recreate mode
5. What is the recommended target CPU utilization range for HPA in most cases?
    a. 20–40%
    b. 50–80%
    c. 90–100%
    d. 10–30%

6. Which AWS service is commonly used for monitoring EKS cluster metrics?

    a. CloudWatch Container Insights

    b. AWS Config

    c. AWS Systems Manager

    d. AWS Inspector

7. What is the primary purpose of resource requests in EKS?

    a. To limit maximum resource usage

    b. To guarantee minimum resource allocation

    c. To set billing thresholds

    d. To configure auto-scaling

8. Which scaling mechanism is the most appropriate for stateful applications?

    a. Horizontal Pod Autoscaling

    b. Vertical Pod Autoscaling

    c. Cluster Autoscaling

    d. Manual Scaling

9. What is the default metrics collection interval for the Cluster Autoscaler?

    a. 10 seconds

    b. 15 seconds

    c. 30 seconds

    d. 60 seconds

10. Which tool is best suited for conducting load tests in EKS with JavaScript-based scripts?

    a. JMeter

    b. K6

    c. Apache Bench

    d. Gatling

# Answers

1. b
2. c
3. b
4. b
5. b
6. a
7. b
8. b
9. b
10. b

# Key Terms

- **Horizontal Pod Autoscaling (HPA)**: An automated mechanism that adjusts the number of pod replicas based on observed metrics such as CPU utilization or custom metrics.
- **Vertical Pod Autoscaling (VPA)**: A system that automatically adjusts the CPU and memory resource requests/limits for pods based on their usage patterns.
- **Cluster Autoscaler**: A component that automatically adjusts the size of the Kubernetes cluster by adding or removing nodes based on resource demands.
- **Karpenter**: A flexible, high-performance Kubernetes cluster autoscaler that provisions nodes directly in response to workload demands.
- **Resource Requests**: The minimum amount of compute resources (CPU/memory) that a container needs to be scheduled.
- **Resource Limits**: The maximum amount of compute resources that a container is allowed to use.
- **Node Groups**: A collection of EC2 instances with similar configurations managed as a single unit in EKS.
- **Metrics Server**: A cluster-wide aggregator of resource usage data that collects CPU and memory metrics from nodes and pods.
- **CloudWatch Container Insights**: An AWS monitoring solution that collects, aggregates, and summarizes metrics and logs from containerized applications.

- **Prometheus**: An open-source monitoring and alerting toolkit designed for reliability and scalability in cloud environments.
- **Grafana**: A multi-platform analytics and interactive visualization web application for metrics monitoring.
- **Load Testing**: The process of simulating expected application usage to evaluate performance and identify bottlenecks.
- **Performance Benchmarking**: The process of measuring and comparing system performance against established standards or previous results.
- **Container Network Interface (CNI)**: A specification and set of libraries for configuring network interfaces in Linux containers.
- **Network Policies**: Kubernetes resources that specify how groups of pods are allowed to communicate with each other and other network endpoints.

# Index

## N

## R



## S

## W